Settlement, Economy, and Cultural Change at the End of the European Iron Age

Excavations at Kelheim in Bavaria, 1987–1991

by

Peter S. Wells

with special reports by

Carl Blair, Pam J. Crabtree, Michael N. Geselowitz, Hansjörg Küster, Susan Malin-Boyce, Matthew L. Murray, Bernhard Overbeck, and Frederick Suppe

INTERNATIONAL MONOGRAPHS
IN PREHISTORY

Archaeological Series 6

© 1993 by International Monographs in Prehistory
All rights reserved

Printed in the United States of America
All rights reserved

ISBN 1-879621-12-6 (Paperback)
ISBN 1-879621-13-4 (Hard Cover)

Library of Congress Cataloging-in-Publication Data

Wells, Peter S.
　　Settlement, economy, and cultural change at the end of the European Iron Age : excavations at Kelheim in Bavaria, 1987–1991 / by Peter S. Wells ; with special reports by Carl Blair ... [et al.].
　　　　p.　cm. — (Archaeological series ; 6)
　　Includes bibliographical references.
　　ISBN 1-879621-13-4 (hard cover : alk. paper). — ISBN 1-879621-12-6 (pbk. : alk. paper)
　　1. La Tène period—Germany—Kelheim. 2. Excavations (Archaeology)—Germany—Kelheim. 3. Kelheim (Germany)—Antiquities. 4. Germany—Antiquities. 5. Material Culture—Germany—Kelheim.　I. Title.　II. Series: Archaeological series (Ann Arbor, Mich.) ; 6.
DD901.K38W45 1993
936.3—dc20　　　　　　　　　　　　　　　　　　　　　　　　　　　　　　　　　　93-46319
　　CIP

This book is printed on acid-free paper. ∞

International Monographs in Prehistory
P.O. Box 1266
Ann Arbor, Michigan　48106-1266
U.S.A.

Tel. (313) 761-9068

Table of Contents

Preface v

Acknowledgments vii

The Project and its Context
    1. The Project and its Context 1
    2. The Setting—Kelheim in its Environment 7
    3. Research History at Late Iron Age Kelheim 11

The University of Minnesota Excavations, 1987–1991
    4. The Course of Excavation 14
    5. Results of Excavations 19
    6. The Archaeological Material Recovered 38

Analysis
    7. Chronology of the Oppidum Occupation 54
    8. The Carbonized Plant Remains, by Hansjörg Küster 57
    9. Vertebrate Faunal Remains from Kelheim, by Pam J. Crabtree 61
    10. Iron Production at Kelheim, by Carl Blair 66
    11. Labor Specialization in Late Iron Age Temperate Europe: The Evidence
        from the Kelheim Iron, by Michael N. Geselowitz 77
    12. Paste Groups as a Unit of Analysis: Preliminary Report on the Ceramics
        from the 1987 Excavations on the Mitterfeld, by Susan Malin-Boyce 83
    13. The Four Celtic Coins, by Bernhard Overbeck and Peter S. Wells 89
    14. Trade at Kelheim 93
    15. The Landscape Survey, 1990–1991, by Matthew L. Murray 96

Interpretation
    16. Material Culture and Settlement: Site Structure, Economic Behavior,
        and Communication 135
    17. Material Expression of Ritual and Cult 145
    18. The Oppida and Cultural Change in Late Iron Age Europe 149

Continuity at Kelheim
    19. Continuity of Religious Tradition at Kelheim and the Foundation of
        Weltenburg Abbey, by Frederick Suppe 156

    20. Conclusion 162

References Cited 163

The Authors 181

Preface

This volume presents preliminary results of three seasons of excavation at the Late Iron Age oppidum settlement of Kelheim, including analytical studies of materials recovered and interpretation of the significance of the findings. Research on the materials presented here is ongoing, and more detailed reports will follow at a later date.

The volume is divided into four main sections. The first, titled "The Project and its Context," explains the reasons for our investigations at Kelheim, the questions we addressed, the character of the landscape, and the history of archaeological research there.

The second, "The University of Minnesota Excavations, 1987–1991," describes the techniques of excavation used and the progress over the three field seasons, and presents the results of the excavations, regarding both settlement features and artifact distribution, as well as an overview of the character of the material recovered. Many illustrations are included here, especially in Chapter 6, in order to show the range of pottery, metal, and other objects from the site.

The third section, "Analysis," includes special studies of several categories of materials, as well as discussion of the chronology of the occupation and presentation of the results of the landscape survey around the Late Iron Age settlement.

The final section, "Interpretation," attempts to address some major questions about late prehistoric Europe from the perspective of our excavation and analytical results at Kelheim. I divide this section into three chapters. The first focuses on the character of the settlement, the nature of the economic activities carried out by its inhabitants, and the ways in which they manipulated material culture to communicate social and political information to members of their own community and to others. The second considers evidence for ritual activity at Kelheim, as a part of the cultural life of the community. The third addresses the question of change, using our preliminary results from Kelheim to examine larger questions of why the oppida developed around 130–120 B.C. and why they disappeared.

In the fifth section, "Continuity at Kelheim," Frederick Suppe presents his investigations into ritual behavior in the Kelheim region and uses this theme to argue for strong continuity of tradition from prehistoric times into the Middle Ages.

Acknowledgments

Archaeological field research is usually a complex enterprise that depends upon the support, participation, and cooperation of a large number of people and institutions. In the course of our excavations and museum work at Kelheim, we have benefited from the productive efforts of many participants and the support of several institutions.

Bernd Engelhardt, Director of the Landshut office of the Bayerisches Landesamt für Denkmalpflege, kindly granted us permission to carry out our research at Kelheim and provided wise counsel and logistical support when they were needed. Ingrid Burger-Segl, Director of the Archäologisches Museum in Kelheim, permitted us to use the excellent facilities of that museum for processing and storing our finds and our equipment. Michael M. Rind, County Archaeologist for Kreis Kelheim, gave valuable logistic assistance to the project and offered his expert knowledge of the archaeology of the Kelheim area. I especially thank these three individuals for their constant support and excellent advice.

Financing for the research was provided by several institutions. The National Science Foundation supported, through grant number BNS900416402, the excavations in 1990 and 1991, as well as the processing and study of the results. The Research Explorations program of the University of Minnesota coordinated the participation of many excellent volunteers in both the excavation and museum aspects of the research during the 1987, 1989, 1990, 1991, and 1992 field seasons. Susan Henderson, coordinator of the REX program, and Helen Penrose, program assistant, were very helpful. Earthwatch and the Center for Field Research of Watertown, Massachusetts, provided research support and volunteers during the 1987 field season. The Graduate School, the Office of International Education, the Center for Ancient Studies, and the Department of Anthropology, all of the University of Minnesota, also contributed to the success of the research.

In Kelheim, the farmers who work the fields on the Mitterfeld and the owners of the land generously allowed us to excavate. I thank Georg Appel, Xaver Frischeisen, Franz Kleiner, and Josef Pletl for their friendly cooperation. The Hoechst Corporation generously provided the research team with accomodation during the first field season.

Student and volunteer participants in the excavations and in the museum research were Joyce Albers, Barbara Anderson, Vernice Anderson, Bettina Arnold, Carl Blair, Benjamin Bleske, Candida Briggs, Barbara Brown, Christina Conlee, Nathaniel Dickey, Gary Ditschler, Daniel Dowling, Sean Dunham, William Fitts, Louis Gottwalt, Gloria Greis, Lev Grossman, Carol Haines-Donahue, Janice Hauff, Ingrid Heim, Victoria Helgeson, Homer Hruby, Jiyul Kim, Elise Kuutti, Keven Larson, Paul Lehman, Sara Light, Susan Malin-Boyce, Trude Mallory, Wendy Marino, George Martin, Colin Matchett, Matthew Murray, Luella Nystrom, Kenneth Olson, Shirley Olsen, Ann O'Grady-Schneider, Vincent Osier, Regina Overholt, Erick Parker, Karina D'Allesandro Parker, David Peterson, Margie Pollack, John Pollack, Stephen Potthoff, Francis Prussner, Vanessa Rousseau, Candy Schnepf, Glenn Smoot, Jennifer Trimble, Dorothy Uhler, Rebecca Vance, Jennifer Wahlsten, Karen Walker, Philip Wesemann, Nancy Wicker, Gertraud Wickizer, Patricia Willging, Michelle Wirth, Valerie Woelfel, and Susan Wunderlich.

Minnesota teachers who participated in 1991 and 1992 through the Research Explorations for Teachers program at the University of Minnesota were Raymond Arsenault, Jill Brand, Margaret Brimijoin, Alan Hargreaves, Mary Hill, Charlene Jassim, Ervin Kuutti, Sally Legrand, Constance Letts, Barbara Mauk, Nancy Milkes, Dorothy Perkins, and Betty Wammer.

My wife Joan and my sons Christopher and Nicholas helped with many aspects of planning and carrying out the fieldwork and provided their usual strong moral support.

Jutta Kluge generously gave me a copy of her doctoral dissertation, which includes a comprehensive overview of Late Iron Age materials recovered at Kelheim prior to 1987. Christian Etzel kindly sent his master's thesis concerning the excavations by the Landesamt für Denkmalpflege on the Mitterfeld in 1987 and on the top of the Michelsberg in 1988.

Jan Bouzek (Prague), Miloš Čižmář (Brno), Thomas Fischer (Munich), Hans-Eckart Joachim (Bonn) and Matthias Leicht (Erlangen) provided helpful advice in the course of my study of the settlement features and the materials that we recovered.

Chapter 1
The Project and its Context

The Oppida of Late Iron Age Temperate Europe

During the latter part of the second and the final century before Christ, a new kind of settlement appeared throughout temperate Europe between the Alps and the North European Plain, from central France in the west to Slovakia in the east (Figure 1.1). These differed from earlier settlements in size, in the imposing walls around them, and in the dense habitation and manufacturing debris recovered on many of them. While both regional and individual variations between oppidum settlements are apparent, significant similarities exist among the different oppida, particularly as regards the wall structures. Depending upon the strictness of the criteria used, researchers identify between 30 and 150 sites in temperate Europe as oppida. As early as 1914, Déchelette called attention to the strong similarities in the objects recovered at the then-known sites across Europe, and his demonstration of this uniformity played an important part in thinking and research about the oppida throughout the first half of the 20th century.

These settlements are called oppida because Julius Caesar used that term in reference to the strongholds he encountered in the course of the wars he waged in Gaul between 58 and 51 B.C. Caesar provides our only substantial historical

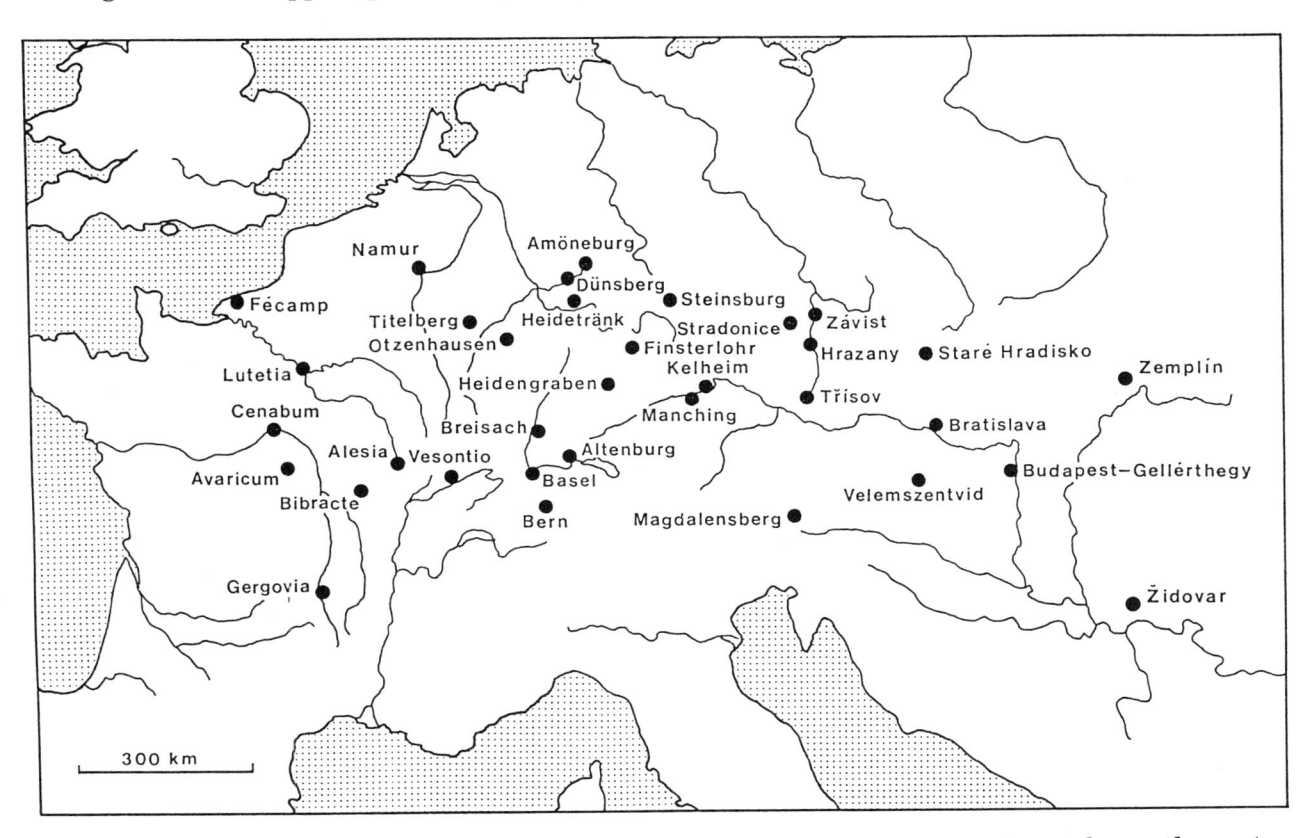

Figure 1.1. Map showing locations of some of the principal oppida. Kelheim is situated near the center of the distribution of these sites.

commentary on these sites, and he tells us about the political, economic, social, and religious role of the oppidum settlements (Dehn 1951). Except for Caesar's accounts of the sites in Gaul during this late period, we are left exclusively with the archaeological evidence to understand these settlements. Caesar's commentary about the oppida in Gaul can probably not be applied except with great care to regions east of the Rhine. By the middle of the final century B.C. when Caesar was in Gaul, that part of Europe had been exceptionally heavily influenced by Rome. Roman armies had been active in the south of Gaul since around 200 B.C., and with the establishment of the province of Gallia Narbonensis around 120 B.C., Rome became ever more intensively involved in political and economic developments there (Rivet 1988). Gaul as a whole was considerably more "Romanized" than other parts of temperate Europe (Nash 1978, Roymans 1990). Thus the large communities in Gaul may have been quite different from those east of the Rhine.

The late period at which Caesar observed the Gallic sites was different in many respects from the first 70 or 80 years during which oppida existed, as we shall see. And Caesar as a general had his particular biases in observing and commenting on the oppida in Gaul—his understanding of the sites and their role in Gallic life was influenced by his role there, and he may have consciously introduced a particular slant to affect his reading audience (Roymans 1990 provides a good recent commentary on such texts).

The oppida are important for our understanding of the end of the Iron Age in Europe and indeed for our understanding of the development of European civilization subsequently. They were the largest and most complex settlements of the indigenous peoples of temperate Europe before the Roman conquest and the changes that accompanied it. Many of them were centers of manufacturing and commerce on a scale considerably larger than any earlier sites. The evidence currently available indicates that they played dominant roles in the cultural landscape of Late Iron Age Europe. Thus in order to understand the period as a whole, we must have a better understanding of these sites. According to Caesar in his commentaries on Gaul, many were political and religious focal points as well as economic centers. They represent a development toward urbanism and societal complexity unlike any other in prehistoric temperate Europe.

Anthropological archaeologists and historians of early Europe pose the question whether the oppida can be classified as "towns" or "cities" (Goudineau and Kruta 1980, Wells 1984, Audouze and Buchsenschutz 1989) and, of course, it depends upon what we mean by those terms. If, as in many discussions, the critical factors for recognition of urbanism are large population size and presence of substantial numbers of persons who were not primarily food producers, then many of the oppida can be considered urban. Population estimates are very difficult to make for the oppida, but communities in the range of 3000-5000 persons are likely for some of the sites, and perhaps a higher figure would be reasonable for the most densely inhabited large sites, such as Manching (discussion in Wells 1984, 164-166). Manufacturing activities on many of the oppida suggest the existence of fulltime specialists, especially in iron production and tool manufacture, and perhaps in other crafts as well (Jacobi 1974).

For broad anthropological consideration of the urbanization process, the oppida of Late Iron Age Europe offer a valuable case. Standard overviews of urbanization in a worldwide perspective often focus on the Near East, Mesoamerica, and South America, and neglect the case of temperate Europe as "secondary," because it was in contact with other, already urban societies in the Mediterranean region. But especially with the current emphasis on understanding internal dynamics of culture change, rather than explaining change principally as the result of contact and interaction, the oppida present a special case for development of theory. Oppida were established quite quickly over much of temperate Europe, and recent research in Europe provides fine chronological control of the material that demonstrates the change processes. Since the oppida emerged at a time when written records were being produced by Greek and Roman writers, we have the benefit of historical information about the wider context during the changes. Ongoing research at oppidum settlements, as well as at other, smaller settlements throughout temperate Europe is generating a rich and well-documented data base for the refinement of models for the process of change. In coming years, the case of the oppida of temperate Europe has the potential to offer uniquely detailed information for the development of theory in the formation of urban centers and urban society.

As recent chronological investigations show, the oppida were first established sometime around 130-120 B.C. Many other significant changes are apparent in the archaeological record at this time, and study of them contributes to our overall understanding of the oppida and of the Late Iron Age context. The dominant burial practice changed at this time, from inhumation with elaborate grave goods (Bujna 1982, Waldhauser 1987) to cremation with few or no goods. (In limited regions, especially along the Main River and west of the Middle Rhine, substantial grave goods continued to be placed in the cremation burials.) A new kind of structure for ritual activity was built throughout the countryside of Late Iron Age Europe, the rectangular *Viereckschanzen*, representing a new medium for communication and ritual at the time of the oppida. And a new emphasis on hoarding activity accompanied the establishment and growth of the oppida, including two main categories of hoards, iron tool and implement hoards (Rybová and Motyková 1983) and hoards of gold coins and rings (Furger-Gunti 1982).

Archaeological Research at the Oppida

The walls of many oppida are still imposing structures in the landscapes of temperate Europe (Figure 1.2), and they were important in stimulating early research on these sites. The rich settlement deposits also brought early attention, as farmers and builders found settlement debris indicative of intensive habitation on many sites.

The oppida have been objects of study since the beginnings of systematic archaeology in Europe (Collis 1984a provides a good discussion of the history of research on these sites). Major investigations were carried out in the middle of the 19th century in France, under the direction of Napoleon III. At Bibracte near Autun, Bulliot and Déchelette conducted extensive excavations over several decades. By the early 20th century, archaeologists were comparing sites across the whole of temperate Europe and finding remarkable similarities in topographical situations, wall structures, and objects recovered at them (Pič 1906, Déchelette 1914, Werner 1939). Caesar's commentaries played an important role in the interpretation of the archaeological finds.

Shortly after the Second World War, large-scale research began at many of the oppida, including Manching in southern Germany, Staré Hradisko in Moravia, Hrazany and Závist in Bohemia, and the Magdalensberg in Austria. Smaller-scale excavations were carried out at many sites throughout Europe. Attention shifted from the walls surrounding the settlements—the object of much of the earlier research—to the settlements themselves. New questions focused on the internal structure of the oppidum settlements, on evidence for manufacturing and trade, and on the chronology of occupation. Yet because of the very large size of these sites, compared to others of prehistoric Europe, it has been difficult to obtain comprehensive pictures of the settlements inside the walls. At Manching, for example, the most extensively excavated oppidum in Europe and a model for well-organized and well-funded research, the over 80,000 square meters of the site that have been excavated constitute a very small portion of the 380-hectare site. As the excavations of the late 1960s, 1970s, and 1980s at Manching show (Schubert 1972; Maier 1985, 1986), different parts of the settlement varied considerably in density of habitation remains and in activities that took place on them. Unfortunately, detailed plans of excavated settlement areas have been published for only a small number of oppida (particularly those cited above), and hence it is not possible to make general studies of internal structure and organization of many of the sites. Numerical data on quantities of artifactual materials, such as pottery, metalworking debris, tools, and bronze and glass ornaments recovered on different parts of the settlements are rare in the published literature, and this lack hinders systematic comparison of settlement structures at the different oppida. The material presented here from Kelheim is intended to contribute this kind of information in the hope that other researchers will find it useful for comparison with sites they are investigating.

Changing Views of the Oppida

Caesar's descriptions of the oppida of Gaul suggest urban centers with many of the features that Romans associated with city life in the Mediterranean world (Dehn 1951). Researchers working east of the Rhine often viewed the results of investigations at oppidum sites there in terms of urban patterns (Werner 1939). The excavation results from the first campaigns at Manching, conducted between 1955 and 1961, that focused on the central part of the site (Krämer 1958, 1962), contributed to this model of the oppida as large prehistoric cities.

Subsequent excavation work at Manching and elsewhere has shown that the situation was more complex. Excavations conducted at Manching in the late 1960s, 1970s, and 1980s on parts of the site south and north of the center show that those locations were not densely occupied, and the remains on them show a different character from those in the central part of the site. Investigations at Staré Hradisko have not yielded any clear center, but instead a quite uniform pattern of cultural remains over an extensive area (Meduna 1970a; Čižmář 1989a). Similarly, research at Závist has produced evidence for dispersed settlement units within the enclosing wall (Motyková, Drda, Rybová 1990).

The Oppida and the End of European Prehistory

The oppida are important for a general understanding of the Late Iron Age in temperate Europe and as a case in the process of urbanization (see above), and also as the principal settlement type at the time when detailed written accounts first become available that deal with regions north of Mediterranean Europe. Thus in a sense they are both a phenomenon of prehistoric Europe, in that the peoples of temperate Europe were not writing their own histories, and of early historic Europe, insofar as Caesar described the oppida of Gaul in some detail and other authors related events that were contemporaneous with the oppida and that affected them directly. Rome was expanding its military and political power and its economic influence in Gaul during the time that the oppida were flourishing, and considerable historical evidence relates to those developments (Nash 1978). The Cimbri and the Teutoni, thought to have come from northern continental Europe, are first mentioned for the year 113 B.C. and are described in textual sources as moving across much of temperate Europe. The Suebi, the Helvetii, and the Boii are among other groups named in the historical sources who migrated during this period. Thus Greek and Roman historical sources portray this as a time of considerable disturbance in much of temperate Europe, involving complex interactions among peoples we know as Celts, Germans, and Romans. Questions surrounding the Roman con-

Figure 1.2. Photograph showing the wall at the oppidum of Altenburg on the upper Rhine River in southwest Germany, looking south-southwest. The interior of the oppidum was to the left, the exterior to the right.

quest and the oppida are complex. For Gaul, Caesar's commentaries provide a perspective on those interactions, but for regions east of the Rhine the relationship is not as clear. Whereas earlier studies suggested that the oppida were abandoned following the Roman conquest (e.g. Krämer 1962), the newer dating evidence suggests that they were given up well before the Roman arrival in their landscapes. Hence the relgionship between the Roman conquest and the oppida needs to be redefined in the light of this new evidence.

The University of Minnesota Kelheim Research, 1987–1991

The oppida of temperate Europe pose many important and exciting questions about late Celtic civilization, the process of economic intensification and urbanization in the Late Iron Age, and the changes that accompanied the expansion of Rome beyond the Alps. In terms of the amount of land enclosed by the walls, Kelheim is one of the largest of the oppida, and it is situated near the center of the distribution of the sites (Figure 1.1). All indications from earlier finds at Kelheim (see Chapter 3) suggested that Kelheim was a typical oppidum, in some respects at least. The first excavation campaigns at Kelheim conducted by the University of Minnesota have been aimed at addressing a limited set of questions at this important site, the answers to which should provide a better understanding of the character of these settlements and of their role in the cultural landscape of the Late Iron Age.

Our research topics revolve around three principal themes—the organization of the settlement, the range and scale of economic activities that were carried out on the site, and the role that the oppidum played in its cultural landscape. The questions that guided the design and the execution of the research can be summarized as follows:

1. What does the distribution of settlement features and of portable cultural material tell about the spatial organization of the Late Iron Age settlement?

2. What economic activities are represented on the site, and what can the spatial arrangement of the evidence indicate about the organization of those activities?

3. Was the whole settlement planned at the outset, or did it grow as an agglomeration of small habitation units?

4. What interactions are evident between the community at the oppidum and other communities?

The Approach and Contribution of this Project

The principal task involved in collecting information to address these questions was to investigate how space within the oppidum settlement was used and to collect all possible materials from explored surfaces that could bear on the research questions. The first issue was to determine whether the enclosed area at Kelheim was densely built up, like a medieval city crowded within its walls; whether there was a built-up core in the center, and open farmland around it; or whether the settlement comprised distinct built-up areas, like discrete hamlets.

The principal challenge of the Kelheim research was to design a research strategy that would enable us to collect information about the extent, density, and character of the settlement, as well as to recover the relevant portable materials, with limited time and resources. The project needed to be conducted in the context of summer excavation seasons within an American academic schedule, and fieldwork assistance was provided by students and volunteers from the United States, not teams of hired local workers.

The solution I designed was one of excavating a series of trenches on different portions of the Mitterfeld (Figure 5.1), using consistent techniques of excavation, recovery, and recording throughout. In the recovery and processing of portable artifacts, emphasis was placed on quantification as a means of obtaining information about distributions. Artifactual materials were counted and weighed, by recovery-unit, to enable us to compare quantities, as well as character, of pottery, daub, iron implements, iron-working debris, animal bones, and other categories of materials on different parts of the site.

The results of this three-year campaign of excavation (1987, 1990, 1991) and two seasons of museum research (1989, 1992) have been successful in providing an indication of the character of the settlement on different parts of the Mitterfeld in the Late Iron Age. The results permit ready comparison with results of much more extensive and longer-term excavations at other oppidum sites, such as Manching, Hrazany, Závist, and Staré Hradisko, and allow us to understand the position of Kelheim in the context of the Late Iron Age oppida as a whole. The numerical data that we have collected provide a unique set of information about densities of distributions of different categories of artifactual materials on the settlement, yielding a new perspective on settlement organization at an oppidum site. The special studies included in this volume offer an unusually rich and detailed source of information about the oppidum at Kelheim, its economy, and its relation to the Late Iron Age landscape.

# Chapter 2
# The Setting—Kelheim in its Environment

Location

Kelheim is situated near the center of the European continent, in the southern German state of Bavaria (Bayern), at the northern edge of the administrative district of Lower Bavaria (Niederbayern). It is located at the confluence of the Altmühl River into the Danube River (Figure 2.1; see also Figure 15.1).

Topography and Geology

Topographically and geologically, Kelheim is situated at the boundaries of three different regions (Figure 15.1). It is on the northern edge of the Alpine Foreland. The rocks of this landscape were formed from sedimentary deposits of sands and gravels in a sea that existed in the geosyncline north of the Alps at the time of the crustal folding that formed them. These deposits were pushed upward at the close of the Tertiary Period and now form the sandstones and limestones characteristic of the Alpine Foreland. As the land has risen, streams have cut through the sediments to form the hills and valleys of the modern landscape.

The part of the Alpine Foreland just south of Kelheim is called the Tertiary Hills. It extends from the Danube in the north to the Munich Plain in the south, and from the Lech River in the west to Passau in the east. This landscape comprises low hills with gentle slopes and shallow valleys created by the streams. The bedrock is bedded horizontally, and stones near the surface are generally soft. The brown earth soils are fertile and easily worked, and the region has long been of major agricultural importance.

Modern surface features result largely from changes during the Pleistocene glaciations. The Tertiary Hill region was not covered by glaciers, but sands and gravels carried by the rivers of meltwater during warmer phases deposited thick layers of sediment over the region. These deposits form the terraces of sand and gravel that now lie above the rivers. Deposits of wind-blown loess are also well represented in the Kelheim region, though much of the loess that once existed in the area has probably been eroded. Important deposits still exist in many places around modern Kelheim (Rutte 1981a, 29).

West and north of Kelheim is the Franconian Jura, comprised of rocks of Triassic and Jurassic age. This formation accounts for the thick deposits of limestone around Kelheim, through which both the Danube and Altmühl Valleys are cut.

The valley of the Danube River at Kelheim forms the boundary between northern and southern Bavaria. All of the Bavarian rivers that originate in the Alps flow into the Danube, and these streams carried the melt waters and sediments from all of the phases of the Pleistocene glaciations. The broad Danube Valley and, in places such as just east of the modern city of Kelheim, the flat Danube plain, formed as the result of such downwashings into the Danube River.

Between Weltenburg and Kelheim, the Danube has over the millennia cut through the limestone of the Jura and created a deep and spectacular gorge. Over a course of five kilometers, the river flows between 70-meter-high limestone walls. At Kelheim, the gorge ends, and the valley broadens into a flat floodplain.

The Michelsberg hill just west of modern Kelheim, and the hills to the north, across the Altmühl, and south, across the Danube, are formed by massive limestone 270–300 m thick. Deposits of clay made up of water-laid sediments from lakes, rivers, and swamps overlie much of the limestone. Some portions of the hills, including the northwest corner of the oppidum site, are also covered with loess and loess-clay, probably deposited during the Würm Glaciation.

The broad valley of the Altmühl River, now largely transformed by the construction of the Rhein-Main-Donau Canal, was originally the valley of the Danube, which shifted its bed into the present course some 300,000-200,000 years ago.

Chapter 2 - Wells

The Altmühl Valley sediments consist of fluvial deposits of gravels, sands, and clays washed down by the Altmühl and by water runoff from the hills on either side of the valley.

(The foregoing discussion of geology is based on Dickinson 1953, Elkins 1968, Gerndt 1976, Rutte 1981a and 1981b.)

Settlement History

Occasional finds of handaxes in the region of Kelheim suggest human activity as early as 100,000 years ago (Engelhardt 1987, 23) and settlement remains in cave sites of the Altmühl Valley date from around 80,000 years ago on. Numerous Middle

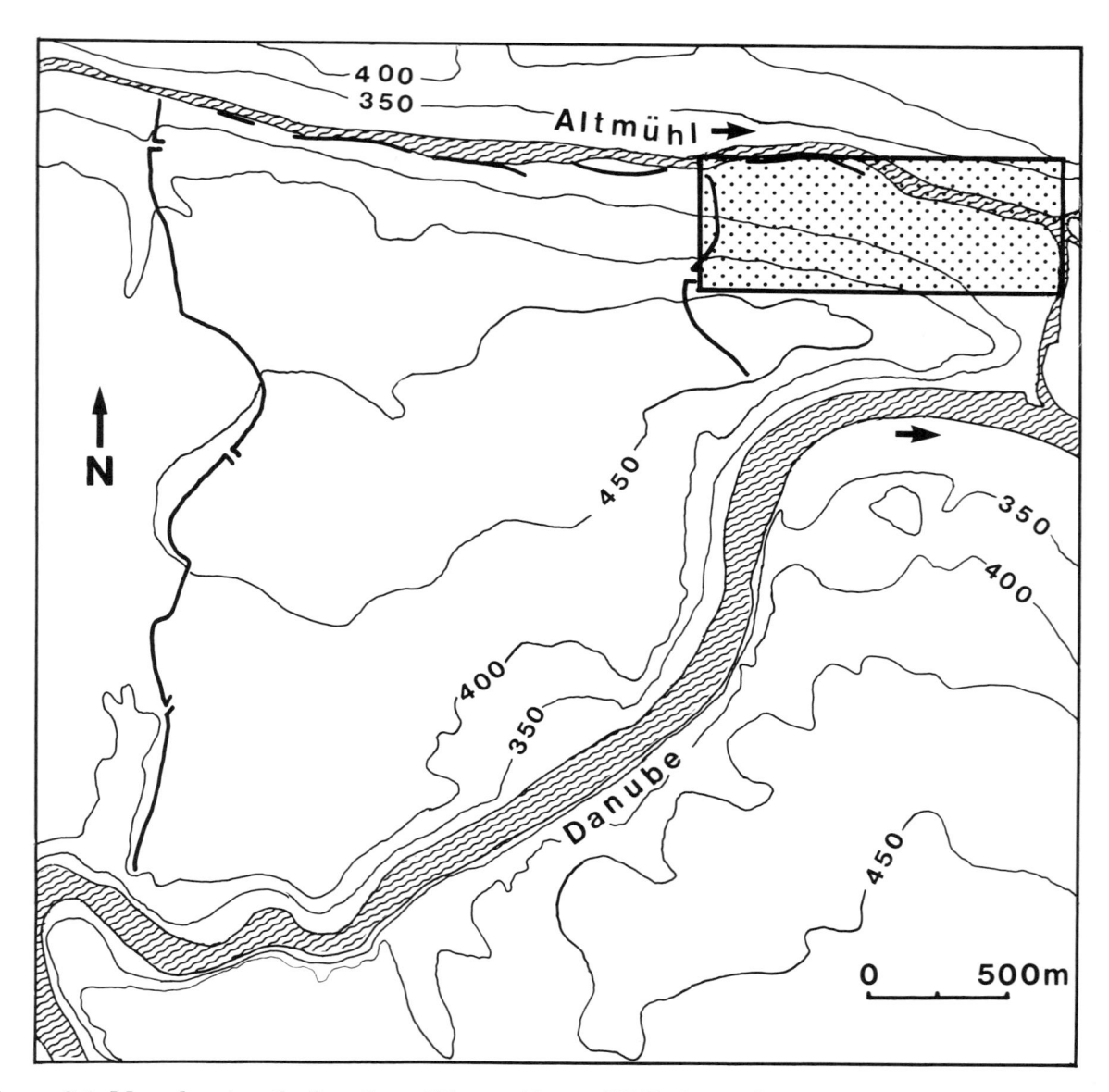

Figure 2.1. Map showing the location of the oppidum of Kelheim at the confluence of the Altmühl and Danube Rivers. The heavy black lines mark the courses of the fortification walls of the Late Iron Age settlement, one forming the western boundary (with three in-turned gates), another along the southern bank of the Altmühl River, and the third separating the eastern third of the site from the rest (this wall has one in-turned gate). The contour lines are labeled in meters above sea level. The shaded rectangle in the upper right shows the location of the map in Figure 4.1. The valley land inside this shaded rectangle and south of the Altmühl River is known as the Mitterfeld; this is the location of the densest settlement remains of the Late Iron Age occupation known from the site.

Palaeolithic rock shelter sites, among them the Schulerloch, the Klausen Caves, and the Sesselfelsgrotte, have been investigated in the limestone cliffs between Kelheim and Neuessing, about six km up the Altmühl Valley. Upper Palaeolithic and Mesolithic settlement activity is well represented at many of the same sites (Burger 1984a, 10-18).

Neolithic settlement remains have been identified at a number of locations around Kelheim, and a complete Early Neolithic village has been excavated at Hienheim, just six km up the Danube from the Kelheim oppidum (Modderman 1977). Evidence for extensive flint-mining during the Neolithic has been recovered at several sites near Kelheim, including Arnhofen (Engelhardt and Binsteiner 1988) and Lengfeld (Rind 1991a).

The Early Bronze Age is represented by settlement remains on the Frauenberg just south of the Late Iron Age oppidum and on the Mitterfeld at Kelheim, and Bronze Age graves have been found abundantly both in and around Kelheim (Hochstetter 1980). The Late Bronze Age Urnfield Period is exceptionally well represented, with one of the largest cemeteries known in Europe from that time situated in what is now part of the city of Kelheim, excavated in the early part of this century (Müller-Karpe 1952). Remains of Late Bronze Age houses were found nearby. Other settlement and cemetery remains of the period are documented from both within and around Kelheim.

Cemetery and settlement remains of both the Early and the Late Iron Age are abundant in the Kelheim region (Engelhardt 1987 and Rind 1988 and 1989 provide overviews of recent discoveries).

During the Roman Period, an important Roman military camp was constructed at Eining, on the east bank of the Danube six km southwest of the oppidum (Fischer and Spindler 1984). At Hienheim, on the west Danube shore, was the eastern terminus of the *limes* wall that marked the boundary of the Roman territory between the Rhine and the Danube. A small Late Roman fortress has been excavated on the Frauenberg, on the south shore of the Danube just across the river from the southwestern corner of the oppidum (Spindler 1981a, 1985). Roman settlement remains and cemeteries are known from the south bank of the Danube at Kelheim, but the Roman armies did not cross the Danube, and thus Kelheim itself was never incorporated into the Roman Empire.

The early medieval period is well represented at Kelheim (Engelhardt 1980). Germanic-style pottery and metal objects have been found on both sides of the Danube, and Reihengräber cemeteries of the Baiuvari, the Germanic group ancestral to the Bavarians, appear at Kelheim in the sixth century. Like early medieval graves of most of central and western Europe in this period, men's burials are characterized by iron weaponry, women's by sets of personal ornaments. Signs of conversion to Christianity in the region become numerous around 600 A.D., around the time of the establishment of the monastery at Weltenburg (see Chapter 19). Small early churches and crosses of iron and gold make their appearance at about this time as well.

The name "Cheleheim" first appears in written sources between the years 865 and 885, and archaeological remains attest to settlement at Kelheim during that period. Kelheim's modern character is shaped by the medieval walled city, dating from the 12th and 13th centuries, when Kelheim was the residence of the Wittelsbach dukes of Bavaria (Withold 1974, Ettelt 1983).

Modern Kelheim

Three of the four city gates from the medieval wall, and their towers, survive today, as do portions of the wall, lending the core of modern Kelheim a medieval flavor. The city has a population of around 15,000 and serves as the principal town in the northern part of Lower Bavaria. Kelheim is a *Kreisstadt*, or county seat. It remains an important agricultural center and is today the site of several modern factories. The natural beauty of the Altmühl and Danube Valleys contributes to a local tourist trade of considerable importance.

As of 1992, Kelheim is the southern terminus of the Rhein-Main-Donau Canal, a canal that has been constructed to link the Main River with the Danube, allowing ships to pass from the North Sea and the Rhine River system, to the Danube and ultimately to the Black Sea. The southernmost part of the canal runs through the valley of the Altmühl River, and the final stretch of the canal was completed in the summer of 1992, after a period of construction lasting 30 years.

The Late Iron Age Settlement at Kelheim

The Late Iron Age settlement is situated on a triangular limestone plateau at the confluence of the Altmühl River into the Danube, and in the valley of the Altmühl, just west of the medieval and modern town of Kelheim. The valleys of the Altmühl and Danube here are deep and steep-sided; there

Chapter 2 - Wells

is little flat land along the Danube River west of the town, only in the Altmühl Valley is there land suitable for human habitation and farming. A large wall constructed during the Late Iron Age along the western edge of the site forms its western boundary, while the joining rivers form the northern, eastern, and southern perimeters (Figure 2.1). The western wall is about 3300 m long and still stands to a height of about five m. The boundaries enclose roughly 600 ha of land, including a large hilltop portion comprising about 90% of the total area of the site, and a long, narrow strip of valley land along the Altmühl River.

The hilltop part of the site is for the most part wooded today, and it is administered by the Forest Office of the State of Bavaria. At the easternmost point of the plateau, overlooking the confluence of the rivers and the city of Kelheim, stands a large monument built of Kelheim limestone known as the Befreiungshalle. This monument was constructed, under the orders of King Ludwig I of Bavaria, between 1842 and 1863 as a memorial to battles fought against Napoleon in the years 1813-1815. The structure is 60 m high and 49 m wide, and it dominates the eastern end of the hilltop. In the course of its construction, the easternmost end of the plateau was apparently scraped clean of soil, thereby obliterating any traces of earlier settlement activity on the hilltop there (see Chapter 3). A plan dating from 1837 shows a wall across the end of the plateau where the monument now stands (Engelhardt 1982, 6-7 fig. 1). Aside from this end of the plateau where the monument is situated, along with the nearby parking lot and souvenir stands to accomodate visitors, the rest of the Michelsberg hilltop seems quite undisturbed. The Late Iron Age walls are very well preserved, and thousands of iron-mining pits and slag heaps are readily apparent on the surface in the forest. Despite regular observation and some systematic searching by archaeologists, no indication of substantial Iron Age settlement activity has been identified on the Michelsberg.

The settlement of Late Iron Age Kelheim was in the valley of the Altmühl River, on its south bank between the river and the Michelsberg. The distance along the Altmühl Valley from the outer wall to the confluence of the Altmühl into the Danube just west of the medieval walled city of Kelheim is about 3.5 km. The valley land south of the Altmühl River is not more than 200 m wide and in most places is considerably narrower. Along this narrow strip of valley land, modern farmers have found objects deriving from the Late Iron Age settlement. The easternmost 600 m of the valley is now occupied by houses, but the 1837 map shows the Mitterfeld still empty of buildings (Engelhardt 1982, 6-7 fig. 1). When cellar holes are dug for the construction of new houses, Late Iron Age settlement materials are regularly encountered.

West of the built-up portion of the Mitterfeld, the valley land is primarily agricultural, bearing in recent years crops of wheat, barley, rapeseed, maize, and strawberries.

Chapter 3
Research History at Late Iron Age Kelheim

Earliest Information

As at many oppidum settlements with massive surviving walls, in the case of Kelheim, people living in and around the town must have been always conscious of the great wall system that extended from the Altmühl River in the north across the valley and over the Michelsberg to the Danube, and the short, inner wall that also connected the Altmühl with the Danube. The first definite information we have about discovery of sub-surface archaeological remains of the Late Iron Age occupation dates from 1861, when construction of houses began on the parcel of land along the Altmühl Valley just west of the town of Kelheim (much of the following discussion is based on Kluge 1987, 3-6 and Etzel 1990, 5-7). To judge from later materials recovered in the course of construction in this area, it is likely that rich deposits were disturbed without much notice, but some special items received attention. In 1863, a bronze jug, a large iron lance point, and perhaps an iron sword, were recovered during the digging of a foundation for a house (Krämer 1985, 137, pl. 70). An iron shield boss and a graphite-clay vessel were also found in 1863 in the same general area, apparently in the course of construction work. It is not clear whether these five objects were collected together or not; Werner's (1954, 1978) and Krämer's interpretations of the scanty surviving records is that they were from two distinct finds. They may have been grave goods in cremation burials.

Beginning of Organized Research and Collecting

In 1894 several members of the local historical association of Kelheim became active in following up information about archaeological finds in and around Kelheim, for example in the context of gravel digging and farming. Finds were excavated or purchased, sometimes restored, and carefully recorded in an inventory book. In some cases drawings and photographs of important objects were included. Some early systematic excavation also took place on a substantial scale, for example the important Late Bronze Age cemetery of some 260 graves investigated between 1907 and 1936 (Müller-Karpe 1952).

Since 1908, Paul Reinecke was employed by the General Conservatory of Art Works and Antiquities of Bavaria, and in 1911 he was appointed especially for Upper and Lower Bavaria, the Upper Palatinate (Oberpfalz), and Bavarian Swabia. He worked closely with the historical association and processed important finds from the region (Reinecke 1911). In an important paper of 1924, Reinecke suggested that the place named Alkimoennis by the Greek geographer Ptolemy, who was writing around A.D. 150-180 in Alexandria, was the Late Iron Age settlement of Kelheim (for recent discussion of this identification see Nierhaus 1981, 1983). In a later study, Reinecke (1935) published the earthworks and iron-working remains at Kelheim and in the vicinity and suggested that Kelheim had been a major site of iron-production in the Late Iron Age. This article was highly influential. From the appearance of this paper on, Kelheim has been regarded in the literature as a major center of iron production.

In 1939 Heinz Behaghel (1940) excavated one Late Iron Age and three early medieval iron-smelting furnaces on the Michelsberg, just north of the cliffs at the edge of the Danube Gorge, in the part of the forest called Stadtlerholz. Behaghel (1952) also published a hoard of iron tools that was found on the Mitterfeld. Behaghel was killed in the Second World War, and his excavation records have not been recovered.

In 1960, Klaus Schwarz directed excavation of several slag piles and iron-mining pits on the Michelsberg (Schwarz, Tillmann, and Treibs 1966). One large pit, 18 m long and 7 m deep, could be dated to the Late Iron Age on the basis of radiocarbon determinations.

Chapter 3 - Wells

Rescue Excavations Since 1960

In connection with the construction of the Rhein-Main-Donau Canal, major movement of earth has taken place in the lower Altmühl Valley. The bed of the Altmühl River was shifted, new banks were built up, and a system of locks was installed. Since 1960, several campaigns of rescue archaeology have been carried out to investigate parcels of land in the valley prior to canal construction. In addition, salvage excavations have been conducted on several house lots on Mitterfeldstrasse, as the modern settlement expands west of the town of Kelheim.

Between 1964 and 1972, Fritz-Rudolf Herrmann (1969, 1973, 1975) directed rescue excavations at both the outer wall and the inner wall in the Altmühl Valley, and opened three long, narrow trenches across the valley, perpendicular to the river, between the Altmühl and the Michelsberg. Two trenches were inside the inner wall system, one was outside (Herrmann 1975, 299 fig. 1). These excavations were conducted in order to study features of the Late Iron Age settlement at locations that would be disturbed by the construction of the canal and its locks. Herrmann ascertained that the walls were built up of earth, with facings of dry stone masonry and with vertical posts about 1.5 m apart made of tree trunks 40-60 cm thick—the technique known from earlier research as the "Kelheim type" wall structure. Herrmann's two trenches across the Mitterfeld east of the inner wall revealed a continuous cultural layer along the valley lands, and uncovered the remains of three houses on the upper slope of the valley. Pottery and other materials recovered were similar to those from Manching, indicating occupation in the same period.

Between 1976 and 1988 the Bayerisches Landesamt für Denkmalpflege, under the local leadership of Bernd Engelhardt, conducted 24 separate excavations between Kelheim and Berching to the west along the route of the new canal (Rind 1988, 18-20). Among them were several large-scale rescue investigations on the site of the Late Iron Age settlement.

When construction began in 1976 on the new lock situated at the western end of the Mitterfeld, workers started to remove a long mound of earth along the Altmühl that was thought to be a modern protection against flooding. They encountered layers of roughly hewn limestone. Rainer Christlein (1976) recognized this structure as the remains of a Late Iron Age wall, and was able to direct excavation of a substantial portion of it. This *Altmühlwall*, as it is called, ran along the south bank of the river.

North and east of the center of Kelheim, where a new channel for the canal was to be dug, intensive excavations were carried out in an area, known as "Kanal I," where rich prehistoric finds had been recorded by the historical association. Humus was removed by machinery from 35,000 m^2, and abundant traces of prehistoric occupation activity were recognized. Between 1984 and 1986 another 5,000 m^2 was investigated, just to the south of the canal bed. Portions of a rectangular enclosure (*Viereckschanze*) that had been identified earlier were investigated at this time. Remains of occupation from all phases of the Late Iron Age were found, including a small cemetery of Late La Tène children's burials (Kluge 1985).

In 1979 excavations were conducted at the outer wall of the oppidum, resulting in documentation of the structure of the wall and the construction history of the fortification.

In 1980 excavations known as "Kanal II" undertook investigation of the landscape just outside the outer, western wall. An area of 22,000 m^2 was opened, revealing numerous pits and postholes, and some Late Iron Age materials, as well as a smelting furnace of the Late La Tène Period (Goetze 1981; Rind 1988, 51).

The Bayerisches Landesamt für Denkmalpflege investigated a number of house foundations along Mitterfeldstrasse, as new houses were constructed in open parcels of land in that growing part of the modern settlement. These small rescue excavations revealed important features of Late Iron Age settlement on the eastern part of the Mitterfeld, and yielded an abundance of cultural material attesting to the occupation and economic activities on the site. In 1984, in excavation of Parcel 2047, systematic excavation under the direction of Bernd Engelhardt revealed dense occupational debris, comparable in its richness to that from the central part of Manching. Excavations in 1985 yielded remains of a ceramic mold used for casting blanks for gold coins (Röhrig 1986), attesting to the community's role as the site of a mint.

The first major open-area excavation within the oppidum walls at Kelheim began in 1987, under the direction of Bernd Engelhardt. The purpose was a rescue excavation in connection with the construction of a high-water dam associated with the canal. A surface of about 2600 m^2 was investigated, and the results reported by Etzel (1990).

In the spring of 1988, excavations were conducted on top of the Michelsberg, near the eastern end, between the Befreiungshalle and the administration building 225 m west of it. A new underground pipe was being installed, and Michael Rind of the Excavation Office of Kelheim directed the excavation of 17 trenches, with a total surface area of about 100 m^2, to investigate the area. The modern humus was found to rest on top of the underlying limestone bedrock, and the only prehistoric materials recovered were scraps from bronze casting and a few pieces of flint. The findings have been interpreted in the context of disturbances associated with the building of the Befreiungshalle in 1842-1863 (Etzel 1990, 54-56). The bronze casting debris is likely to have been deposited at that time, since bronze was used in the monument. The excavators concluded from the results here that the entire eastern end of the Michelsberg is likely to have been leveled at the time of the construction of the monument, and any prehistoric remains that existed at that time were scraped away. Bronze Age materials were found in the garden of the administration building in 1857 and in 1916, and supposedly Late Iron Age pottery sherds were found there in 1919.

Finally, it should be mentioned that sherds of Late Iron Age pottery have been found in the area of the medieval center (the Altstadt) of Kelheim (Engelhardt 1987, 109; Etzel 1990, 60), suggesting that occupation of the oppidum extended beyond the eastern wall onto what was then an island in the Altmühl-Danube confluence. No settlement features have been reported from that area, and it is unlikely that much has survived the extensive building activity there during medieval and modern times.

Chapter 4

The Course of Excavation

Research Design

Research teams from the University of Minnesota conducted excavations on the Mitterfeld at Kelheim during the summers of 1987, 1990, and 1991. During the summers of 1989 and 1992, teams studied the excavated materials in the laboratory of the Archäologisches Museum of the City of Kelheim. Research participants included undergraduates, graduate students, and faculty members from the University of Minnesota and other universities, and volunteers, primarily from Minnesota but also from other states.

From the outset of the project, the principal aim of the research was to collect data to study the extent and character of the Late Iron Age settlement remains on the Mitterfeld at Kelheim, in order to learn more about the nature of this site. The second major aim was to gather information that pertained to the economic activities of the community, including subsistence, manufacturing, and trade. The selection of areas for excavation and of techniques of recovery was determined by these two main objectives.

Strategy

The enclosed area of the settlement at Kelheim (Figure 2.1) is enormous—about 600 hectares—and even the Mitterfeld, where most of the Iron Age settlement activity took place (Figures 4.1 and 4.2), is much too large to excavate comprehensively in a few seasons of fieldwork. The techniques of archaeological investigation thus had to be selective, and they needed to cover enough of the area to meet the project objectives. A standard random sampling procedure was not feasible, because of the current agricultural use patterns on the fields. Thus, each season it was necessary to compromise between the project goals of exploring as complete a sample of the settlement area as possible, and the practical realities of working where agricultural schedules and landowners' willingness permitted our investigations. Frequently we had to wait until crops were harvested before beginning excavation in an intended spot, and in some instances we were denied permission altogether to investigate potentially important areas.

Despite all of the compromises that we had to

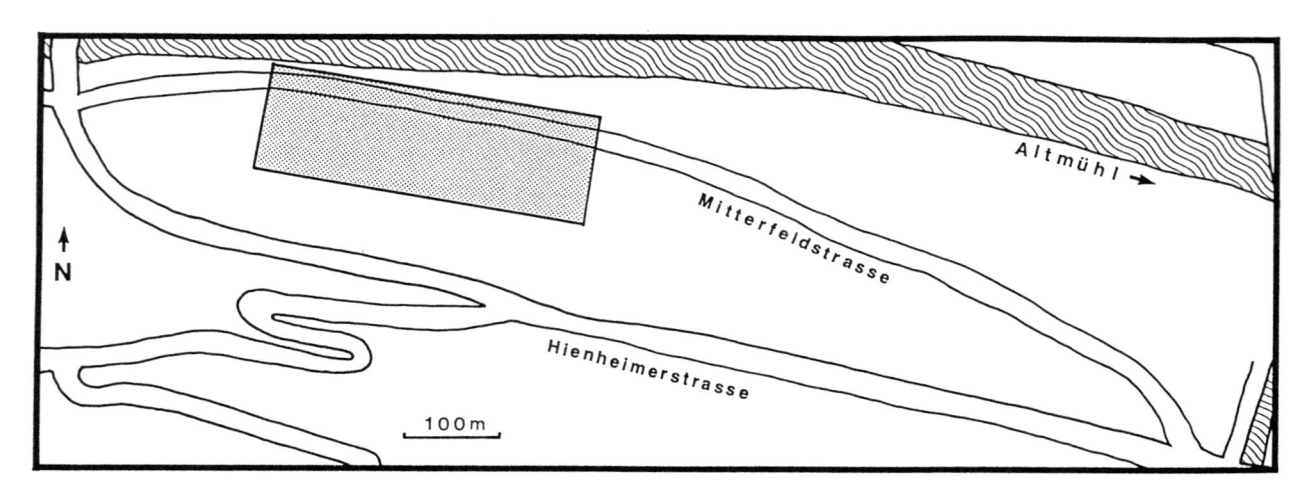

Figure 4.1. Map of the Mitterfeld at Kelheim (see Figure 2.1) showing portion (in rectangle) investigated by our exploratory trenches (see Figure 5.1).

make to work in this highly productive agricultural land, over the three seasons of excavation we were able to explore a good portion of the Mitterfeld. Across an area 350 m long from the western edge of the modern settlement toward the new road at the western end of the Mitterfeld, and 100 m wide between the road and the steep slope of the Michelsberg, we were able to excavate nine discrete trenches, totaling 614 m² (Figure 5.1). The basic unit we used for excavation, recording, and collection was a 5 x 5 m square. This unit is smaller than that generally employed on oppidum settlements, and I chose this size in order to maintain tight control over the measurement of data recovered in the course of excavation. Since a principal goal of the research was study of the spatial distribution of artifactual material, these 5 x 5 m units provided a good scale on which to collect.

Excavation Procedure

A consistent procedure was followed throughout the excavations, to assure that results would be comparable, especially as concerns the spatial distribution of artifactual materials over the surface of the settlement. In most cases, the humus topsoil was removed mechanically by backhoe. Overlying all of the Mitterfeld is a modern humus topsoil about 35 cm thick that is plowed regularly, several times a year. All materials situated in that topsoil have been severely disturbed, and thus the information lost by removing it mechanically is minimal compared to the time and expense required to remove it by hand. We excavated Sectors 1991/4 and 6 completely by hand (as well as the shallower Sectors 7, 8, and 9 situated higher on the slope) as an experiment to measure the amounts of prehistoric cultural material in the topsoil and found the quantities to be very small, as expected.

The backhoe operators had considerable experience working for the archaeologists of the Bayerisches Landesamt für Denkmalpflege, and they were able to remove the topsoil to about 20 cm above the cultural layer. At that depth, we began working with hand tools.

First, the area to be investigated was marked

Figure 4.2. View looking south across the Altmühl River at the Mitterfeld (fields in the foreground) and the Michelsberg hill with the Befreiungshalle monument at its eastern end. The building at the left is the westernmost house of the expanding settlement on the eastern end of the Mitterfeld.

out in a grid of 5 x 5 m squares, or smaller depending upon the size of the area cleared by the backhoe. The grid units were oriented to the existing field boundaries, as they provided the most convenient fixed points for this exploratory work. A map of the Mitterfeld in 1837 shows that the field boundaries (visible in Figure 4.2) have not changed between then and now (Engelhardt 1982, 6-7, Figure 1). Since the landscape on the Mitterfeld is in a state of transition with the completion of riverbank construction for the Rhein-Main-Donau Canal, secure fixed points for measurement were few. The field boundaries do not run exactly north-south and are not exactly parallel to one another, hence the excavated areas are not all on the same alignment (see plan, Figure 5.1).

After the grid was established on each area to be investigated and marked with corner stakes and string, we used spades and shovels to remove the remaining layers of humus from above the subsoil, and hoes to do the final clearing of humic material from the surface of the subsoil. In the course of the spade, shovel, and hoe work, all cultural material was collected by 5 x 5 m square. Spaders removed the soil in chunks, and dropped it such that the chunks broke open, often thereby exposing sherds of pottery or other cultural materials. Shovelers then carefully turned the soil, breaking any remaining clods, and finally shoveled it out onto the backdirt piles. Concentrations of any kind of cultural material, such as pottery, slag, and animal bones, were recorded in three dimensions and collected separately, as were all metal and glass objects. For the most part, cultural material such as pottery was scattered quite evenly and sparsely throughout the bottom of the humus layer. When denser concentrations of material were observed, we changed the excavation technique. Excavators used trowels to investigate, leaving cultural materials in situ for photographing and mapping. In the easternmost area of our excavations, explored in 1987, we found a true cultural layer with large quantities of materials in situ. In all of the units to the west, the cultural layer contained a much less dense assemblage of occupational debris.

Once we cleared all of the humus from the subsoil, subsurface features of the prehistoric settlement became apparent. On most of the Mitterfeld, the subsoil consists of a light sand, but sometimes it is a finer, silty sediment, especially higher on the valley slope, as in Sectors 1991/10 and 11. In the lower portions of the Mitterfeld that we investigated, near the road, the subsoil is gravelly. In every case, features that had been dug down into the subsoil by the prehistoric occupants of the settlement appear today as dark, humus-filled intrusions into the lighter subsoil matrix. Each cleared unit was photographed, and all features in it were mapped (Figure 4.3). The subsurface features that we encountered can be divided into two main categories, postholes and pits.

After photographing and mapping each unit, we sectioned each feature. A line, drawn onto the plan of the unit, was made across the feature with

Figure 4.3. Measuring and mapping the top of the pit in Sectors 1987/6-10. The chunks of limestone encircle the top of the pit (see Figure 5.6.) Strings have been laid over the feature to form a 10 x 10 cm grid for mapping. The students are standing on the top of the subsoil. The higher level behind them is the surface to which the backhoe cleared. View looking south.

a piece of string. One half of the feature was removed, either following natural stratigraphy or, where that was absent, in 10 cm levels, and all of the soil was screened through hardware cloth of 1/4 inch (0.625 cm) mesh. Following the removal of the one half, the resulting profile face was photographed and drawn, then the same procedure was used for the excavation of the second half of the feature (Figure 4.4). Soil samples of five liters for paleobotanical analysis were taken from many features, especially from layers that contained visible charcoal, since those layers were most likely to contain well-preserved paleobotanical remains (Chapter 8).

All cultural material was washed each day, either on the site or in the laboratory at the Archäologisches Museum of Kelheim. After it was dry, all material was inventoried, counted, and weighed, then bagged for storage until it was studied.

Progress During the Field Research Seasons (See Figure 5.1)

1987

Excavation work on the Mitterfeld began on July 1, 1987 and ended August 14. The Minnesota team excavated 280 m² in the central area of the Mitterfeld, about 60 m west of the modern houses on Mitterfeldstrasse. This part of the Mitterfeld was being investigated by the Bayerisches Landesamt für Denkmalpflege, under the direction of Bernd Engelhardt, prior to the construction of a high-water dam on the field in connection with the construction of the new canal. The University of Minnesota team excavated a portion of the area already cleared by the backhoe. The plan of the excavated features is shown in Figure 5.3, top.

Figure 4.4. Excavation of the second half of the pit in Sector 1987/3-11-12. The excavator is standing in the hole resulting from the prior excavation of one half. He is taking a soil sample for recovery of paleobotanical remains from the top of the layer 20-30 cm below the top of the pit.

1989

In 1989 a small team worked, in the Archäologisches Museum of Kelheim, on the materials excavated in 1987. Preliminary study was conducted on all categories of portable remains, especially the iron-working debris, the pottery, and the iron objects.

1990

For the excavation work this season, I wanted to investigate portions of the western part of the Mitterfeld. With the help of Bernd Engelhardt and Michael Rind, we obtained permission from the landowners and farmers to open two trenches near the road in the western portion of the Mitterfeld (Figure 4.5). The excavation ran from June 18 to July 13th, 1990. The total area of the two trenches was 107 m^2.

1991

For the 1991 field season, my aim was to explore portions of the field between the areas investigated in 1987 and in 1990, and at the same time to test portions of the field higher on the slope, to the south. Excavation work was conducted from July 12 to August 23, 1991. A total of 227 m^2 was explored during the 1991 field season.

1992

In 1992 an intensive two-and-one-half-week laboratory session at the Archäologisches Museum of Kelheim focused on a comprehensive typological and spatial analysis of all of the pottery recovered, spatial study of the metal and glass objects, and preparation of photographs for publication in this preliminary report.

Figure 4.5. View of the Mitterfeld, looking east from near the former location of the inner wall (now the location of the road that leads over the locks). Our two excavation trenches of 1990 are visible in the center, just south of the paved road (Mitterfeldstrasse). The houses in the background are at the western edge of the new settlement at the eastern end of the Mitterfeld. The Altmühl River is just beyond the bushes that flank the road on its north side.

Chapter 5
Results of Excavations

Over the course of the three summer excavation seasons—1987, 1990, and 1991, during which we excavated a total of about 16 weeks, we explored 614 m² of the settlement surface, in nine discrete trenches over an east-west extent of about 350 m of the Mitterfeld at Kelheim (plan, Figure 5.1). We encountered Late Iron Age cultural remains in three different stratigraphic contexts—in the humus on top of the site, in the cultural layer overlying the subsoil, and in the features dug down into the subsoil.

Site Stratigraphy

The basic stratigraphy on the Mitterfeld at Kelheim consists of three principal components—topsoil, old humus, and subsoil. But the stratigraphic sequence on some parts of the site is often more complex, as shown in Figure 5.2.

1. Topsoil or plowsoil. The topsoil is turned over several times a year by modern plows. On most parts of the site it is about 35 cm deep and contains a range of modern, medieval, and prehistoric materials, including corncobs, brick, modern glass, small steel pieces from tractors, medieval glazed pottery sherds, and Late Iron Age pottery.

2. Old humus. Old humus layers lie beneath the topsoil, and extend down as deep as 1.35 m on some parts of the Mitterfeld that we investigated. The old humus is brown in color, often darker at the top than further down, and is packed much more densely than the topsoil. The old humus contains some prehistoric objects, mostly pottery sherds, and occasional pieces of medieval pottery. Near the bottom of the old humus is the culture layer.

3. Subsoil. Beneath the old humus layer is subsoil. At the lowest places on the Mitterfeld that we explored, near the road, the subsoil was reddish brown in color, sandy in texture, and contained considerable gravel and rounded pebbles. Higher on the slope, the subsoil was light yellow in color and fine sand in texture. The subsoil was sterile. Random tests in the subsoil yielded no evidence of cultural materials within or beneath it. Cultural features such as pits and postholes were dug into the subsoil, and they were visible at the level of the top of the subsoil as dark intrusions into the lighter subsoil matrix.

Since the Mitterfeld is situated in a valley

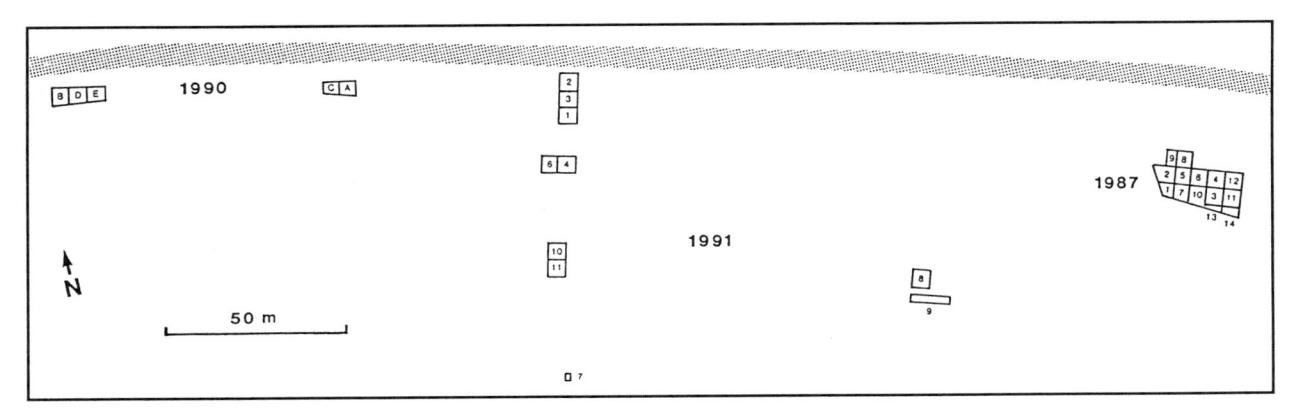

Figure 5.1. Plan of the western part of the Mitterfeld at Kelheim (see Figure 4.1), showing areas excavated by the University of Minnesota in 1987, 1990, and 1991. The narrow paved road, Mitterfeldstrasse, is indicated by the shading across the northern portion of the plan. Collection units, called sectors, are labeled. Sectors investigated in 1987, numbered 1 through 14, are situated at the eastern edge. Those investigated in 1990, designated A through E, are in the western portion. Sectors investigated in 1991, numbered 1 through 11, are in the central area.

Chapter 5 - Wells

bottom, the soil on it has been subjected to processes of erosion and deposition. Future studies of the stratigraphy on the site will need to include detailed soil analyses aimed at reconstructing the sedimentary history of the landscape in relation to the settlement history.

The Humus Layers: Topsoil and Old Humus

On the parts of the Mitterfeld settlement that we investigated, the total depth of humus overlying the subsoil ranged from about 20 cm to 135 cm. Below the topsoil, the old humus layers are unstratified, and prehistoric and, to a lesser extent, medieval materials occur at different depths in them.

In most of the trenches we excavated, we had the humus overburden removed mechanically by backhoe, down to about 20 cm above the cultural layer. In the third year of excavation (1991), however, we excavated five units from the modern surface down by hand, and thus have a sample of the quantities of prehistoric cultural material that occur high in the site stratigraphy. The sectors so excavated were 1991/4, 6, 7, 8, and 9. Sectors 1991/7, 8, and 9 were the highest on the slope that we investigated, and the humus topsoil was relatively thin in all three, apparently because of erosion of the topsoil down the slope toward the Altmühl River. In Sectors 1991/4 and 1991/6, on the other hand, between 120 and 135 cm of humus overlay the subsoil, and a good picture of the stratigraphic distribution of prehistoric materials could be obtained.

Fragments of glazed medieval pottery were common in the higher layers in Sectors 1991/4 and 6, along with various modern debris. But Late Iron Age pottery also occurred high in the sequence. In the top 20 cm of the plowsoil in the 25 m^2 of Sector 1991/6, 131 medieval and modern pottery sherds were recovered, as were four prehistoric sherds, three of them of graphite-clay ware. Glazed and other medieval pottery, as well as various types of prehistoric sherds, were found throughout the sequence from 20 cm to 90 cm below the modern surface. This result indicates considerable migration of cultural materials in the humus layers, probably largely as the result of plowing on the field over the past two thousand years, and perhaps also as a result of erosion of materials from higher on the slope. In the bottom 5-10 cm of the humus, prehistoric pottery was much more abundant than higher up, and no medieval pottery was found. No medieval or modern materials were recovered in any of the features dug into the subsoil.

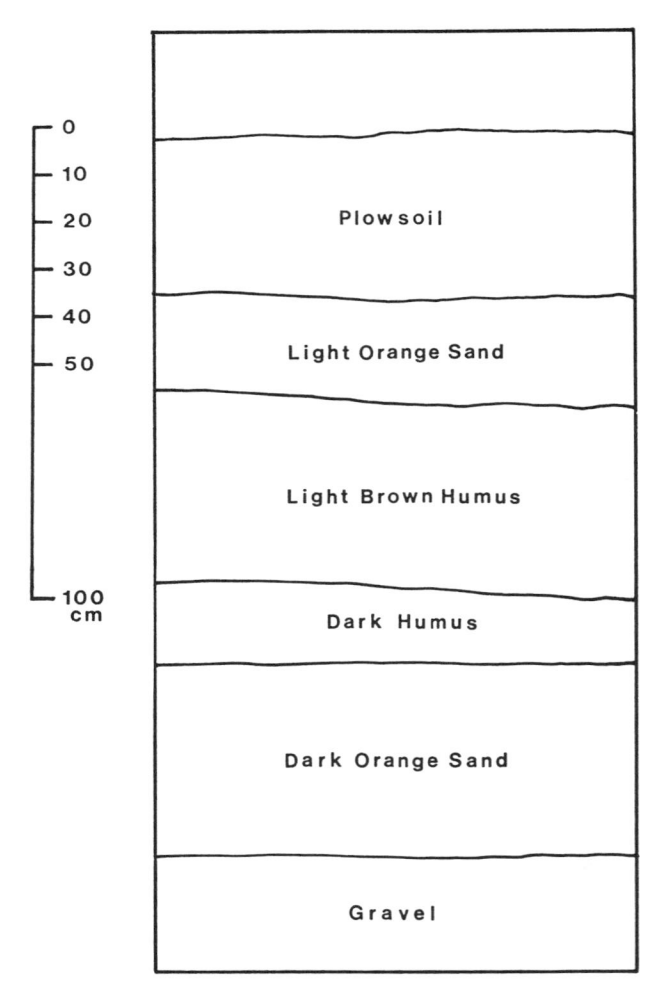

Figure 5.2. Sample stratigraphic section, from the north wall of Sector 1991/6. In this section, a light orange sandy soil separates the modern humic plowsoil from the older light brown loamy humus. The dark humus is the "cultural layer" which appears over all of the investigated parts of the site and which contains numerous small colored flecks of charcoal, daub, and pottery as well as larger, recoverable artifactual materials. The dark orange sand and the gravel beneath the cultural layer are culturally sterile. Pits and postholes are found dug into these lowest layers.

The Cultural Layer

A dark band of soil between 6 and 30 cm thick was identified in all of the cuttings north of, and including, Sector 1991/10; in other words, on the lower portions of the valley. The cultural layer was not apparent in any of the sectors higher on the slope—Sectors 1991/7, 8, 9, or 11. In those sectors, the modern plowsoil rested directly on the yellow sandy subsoil; if a cultural layer had ever existed in those areas, it has been obliterated by plowing.

In the different areas investigated on the Mitterfeld in 1987, 1990, and 1991, the top of the cultural layer occurred at depths ranging from 40 to 95 cm below the modern ground surface and it ranged in thickness from about 30 cm in the area excavated in 1987 at the eastern end of our investigations, to about 6 cm in Sector 1990/B at the western end of our research area. It is difficult to interpret the significance of the variation in depth at which the cultural layer occurs in the modern stratigraphy on the Mitterfeld as well as the variation in the thickness of the layer. The Mitterfeld is a complex surface topographically, because it is situated at the base of a slope, as well as being the bank of a river, and because it has been intensively farmed in modern times as well as in the past. Future studies of the deposits should help to clarify the conditions under which the soils were formed and the degree to which different layers have been altered as the result of human activity.

Settlement Features

Three kinds of structural features of the settlement were identified in the course of our excavations—postholes, pits, and what I shall call floors. Postholes and pits were both encountered first at the level of the top of the subsoil, while floors were identified in the cultural layer.

The distinction between postholes and other pits on the Mitterfeld is somewhat arbitrary, as is the case at many sites. Following generally accepted convention, postholes at Kelheim are round and range usually between 20 cm and one meter in diameter. They often contain a few small sherds of pottery, but rarely metal objects or large sherds. The soils at Kelheim do not preserve postmolds, thus we were not able to ascertain the actual dimensions of the posts that rested in the postholes. When several holes of about the same size occur in a pattern of rows, we can reasonably suggest that they were postholes supporting timbers that formed walls of buildings. At Kelheim, as at most late prehistoric settlements in temperate Europe, the interior surfaces of buildings for the most part are not preserved, because of subsequent agricultural activities, thus it is difficult to confirm this interpretation with supporting archaeological data.

Some pits were large—over one meter in diameter and over one meter deep below the subsoil surface—and contained abundant objects of cultural material. For these large subsurface features, we can exclude the post-holding function, on the basis of information from other sites of the period.

Each 5 x 5 m area excavated was carefully hoe- or trowel-scraped at the top of the subsoil to examine for subsurface structures, which showed up quite clearly. Photographs were taken of all cleaned surfaces, and maps were made indicating all colorations that were interpreted as possible pits and postholes.

The plans in Figure 5.3 indicate all such mapped features. Following photographing and mapping, each feature was bisected and excavated in 10-cm levels, unless natural stratigraphy was visible. In some cases, small circular subsurface structures which looked as though they might have been postholes only extended a few centimeters into the earth and contained no cultural materials. In such cases, we assume that what we observe is the bottom of the posthole which originally was cut down through the humic cultural layer and only slightly into the subsoil. Postholes and pits are not recognizable (except sometimes in the case of pits by their contents) in the upper layers on the site, because all of the soil is of a uniform dark brown color.

Figure 5.4 shows a graph of pits and postholes, represented by the total depth below the top of the subsoil (vertical axis) and the diameter at the top of the subsoil (horizontal axis). The three points on the right represent three major pits (see below). The space on the graph between these three and all of the other points suggests the special character of these pits compared to all other subsurface features. The dot at the left of the graph represents a very narrow, deep hole, perhaps for a thin post. The other dots are quite evenly spread on the graph, and they point up the difficulty in distinguishing function of most of these subsurface structures. Those toward the left are most likely postholes, those to the right most likely pits of other function, but there is considerable overlap making interpretation difficult. The dimensions alone do not serve to define postholes. We must look also at the position on the settlement surface relative to other features, and the contents of each pit.

The easternmost portion excavated, in 1987, yielded a total of 24 subsurface features (Figure 5.3, top). Two were very large pits that extended over 1.5 m into the subsoil and yielded hundreds of

Chapter 5 - Wells

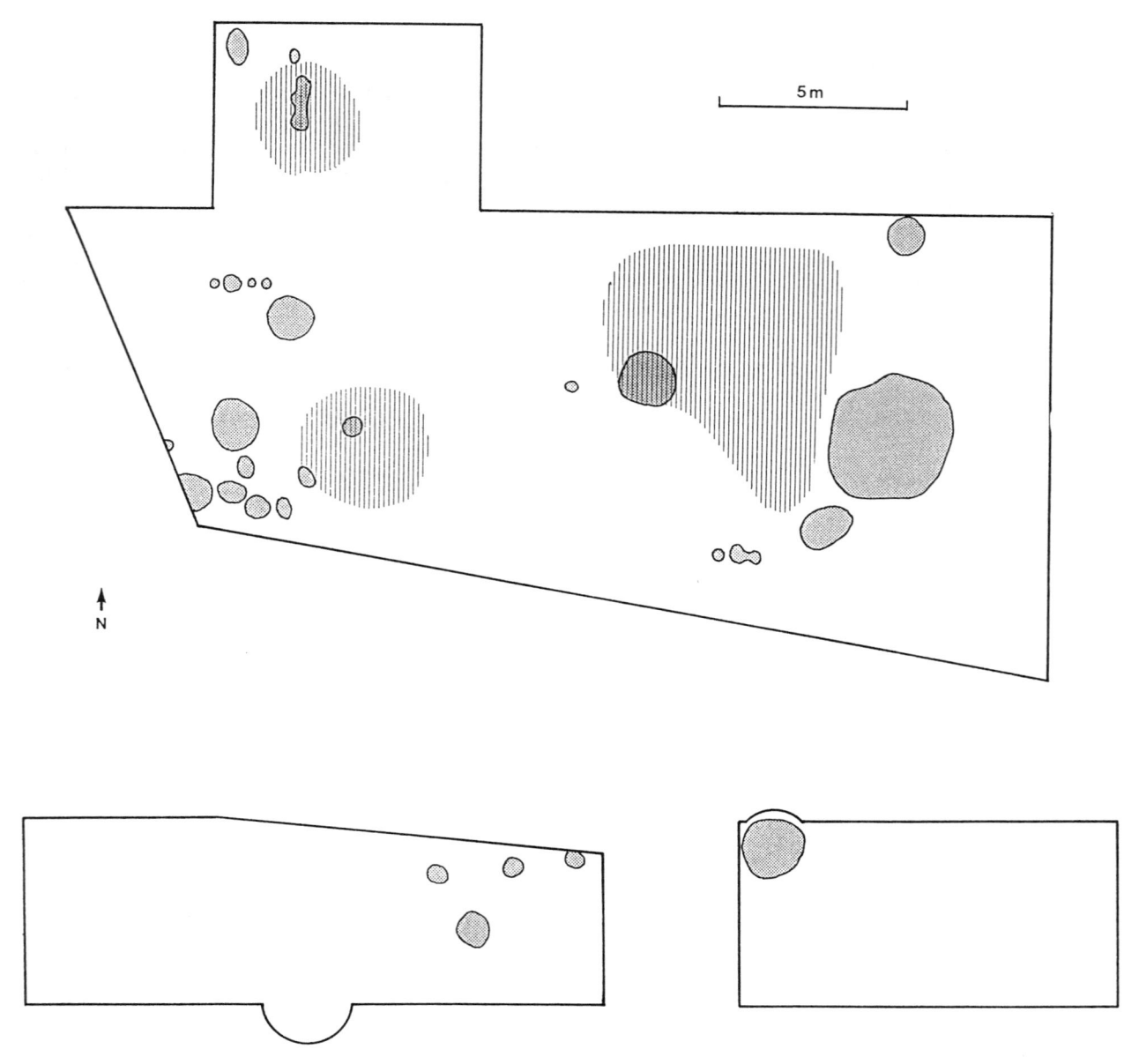

Figure 5.3. Plans of the sectors in which Late Iron Age features were found. Top: area investigated in 1987. Bottom left: Sector 1990/E. Bottom right: Sector 1991/6. Shading indicates tops of subsurface structures; hatching indicates surfaces, or floors, within the cultural layer. Hatching on top of shading indicates floors overlying pits.

objects of cultural material. Four were sizable pits that contained only modest quantities of cultural material. The other 18 ranged from features that were almost certainly postholes, to judge from their form, dimensions, contents, and position relative to one another, to shallow bowl-shaped depressions on the top of the subsoil that contained organic fill from the cultural layer but yielded no artifactual materials. Such hollows are common on settlements and could have served any number of functions. Rarely are their forms or contents distinctive enough to permit interpretation.

In the two trenches opened in 1990, four subsurface features were identified that belonged to the Late Iron Age occupation (others are of Bronze Age date and will be dealt with elsewhere). One was a pit that contained substantial settlement debris, three were postholes (Figure 5.3, bottom left).

In the six units excavated in 1991, only one major subsurface feature was identified, a large pit in Sector 6 (Figure 5.3, bottom right).

The Major Pits

The graph in Figure 5.4 shows three pits to be much larger than all the rest, especially in their diameter at the top of the subsoil but also in their depth into the subsoil. The tops of all three pits, when first clearly observed at the level of the subsoil, were of the same form—circular. At the top of the subsoil—where the pits could first be distinguished from the cultural layer overlying them—the diameters of these three pits were 1.49 m for Pit 1987/6, 2.06 m for Pit 1991/6, and 3.11 m for Pit 1987/3-11-12. Only the pit in Sector 1991/6 could be excavated to its bottom, which lay 73 cm below the top of the subsoil. The other two were excavated to a depth of about 1.5 m below the top of the subsoil, but at that point neither showed any indication of ending. (Construction safety laws in Bavaria forbid excavating beneath 1.5 m below ground level without structural supports to shore up the soil around the pit. In the time available during the excavation season in 1987, we were not able to erect such equipment. Thus we stopped excavation work at that depth. The lower parts of those two pits are well protected beneath the fields on the Mitterfeld and await future investigation.)

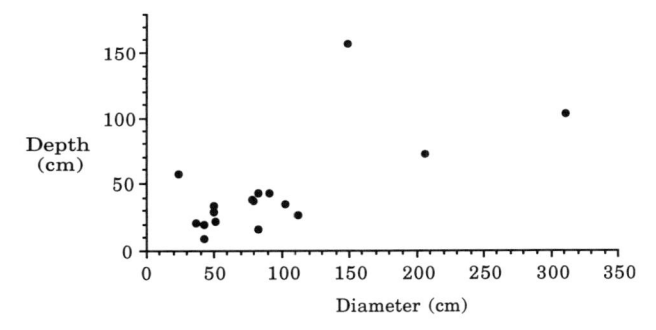

Figure 5.4. Graph showing the depth and diameter of 17 pits on the Mitterfeld settlement at Kelheim. The highest point on the graph represents Pit 1987/6-10, the point furthest to the right represents Pit 1987/3-11-12. For both, the greatest depth reached by excavation was less than the total depth of the pits. The point at diameter=206 cm and depth=73 cm represents Pit 1991/6.

All three pits showed cultural material on their surfaces at the level of the top of the subsoil (Figures 5.5, 5.6, 5.7). Pit 1991/6 had abundant pieces of charcoal on the surface, a fair amount of daub, and some pottery. Pit 1987/3-11-12 had similar materials on its surface, but less densely distributed. A small number of pieces of local limestone occurred around the inner edge. Pit 1987/6-10 had a large number of stones around the center and a few pieces of slag, bone, and pottery on the surface. The stones in the two pits from the 1987 area probably reflect material that was on the settlement surface near the pits at the time they filled in, rather than any deliberate stone structure.

In section, the principle difference between the three was the fact that the two 1987 pits extended more than 1.5 m down into the subsoil, while pit 1991/6 was just 73 cm deep from the top of the subsoil (Figures 5.8, 5.9, 5.10). Significantly, the top layer in each of the 1987 pits was very similar—in size, shape, and character of the fill—to Pit 1991/6. In profile, Pit 1991/6 and the top layers in 1987/6 and 1987/3-11-12 were all bowl-shaped, with the deepest point under the center of the pit and with gently-sloping sides. Pit 1991/6 consisted of a single homogeneous layer of dark brown humic fill containing abundant flecks of charcoal, daub, and pottery throughout, as well as larger artifactual materials. The two 1987 pits contained a more complex stratigraphy; 1987/3-11-12 contained an extensive deep pit fill below the bowl-shaped top layer; 1987/6-10 contained at least three different layers beneath the uppermost layer; 1987/3-11-12 showed in its profile distinct bedding of limestone pieces parallel to the fill pattern of the pit. In the other two major pits, limestone chunks were scattered throughout the fill, with only slight evidence for such bedding. In 1987/3-11-12, the darkest layer was not the top one, but the third one down. In 1987/6 the top layer was the darkest.

For pits 1987/6-10 and 1987/3-11-12, it is clear that the original pit was deep—more than 1.5 m deep in each case, and the top layers represent some activity or activities distinct from the earlier use of the deep original pit. Pit 1991/6 differs from the other two in having had only the single phase of deposition. In Pit 1987/6-10, an inner structure with straight sides was identifiable as a result of its darker fill, which stood out from the lighter surrounding pit fill. The color differences were subtle and showed up most clearly in the western half of the pit (the second half to be excavated) at a depth of 40 cm below the surface of the subsoil. The dark form was rectangular, with the one complete dimension measuring about 120 cm (Figure 5.11). The shape was similar to that in a pit at Manching described by Krämer (1958, 186 fig. 8 and pp. 186-188) as a rectangular frame or container of wood.

Chapter 5 - Wells

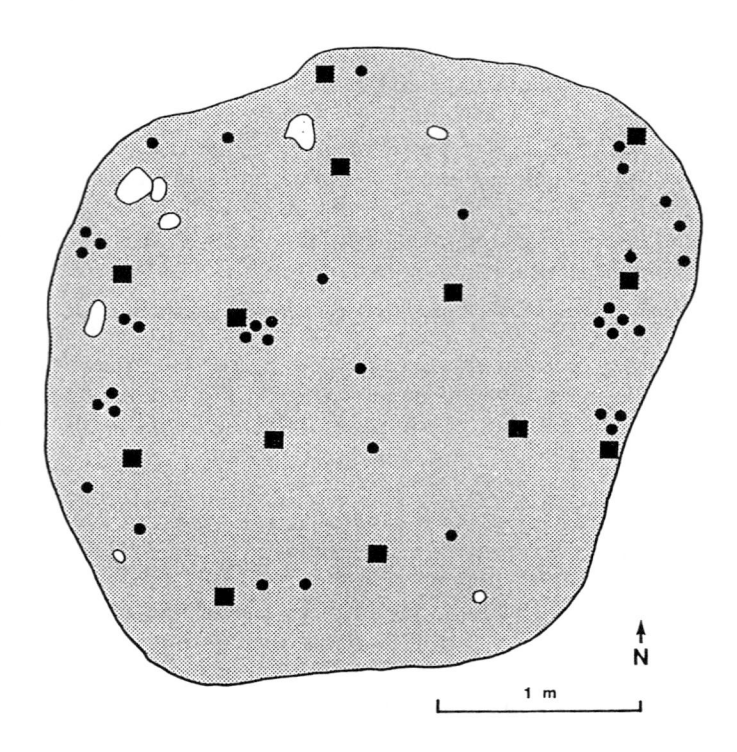

Figure 5.5. Surface plan of Pit 1987/3-11-12, showing the form of the pit and the locations of cultural materials, at the level of the top of the subsoil. Circles: charcoal. Squares: pottery. Open shapes: pieces of limestone.

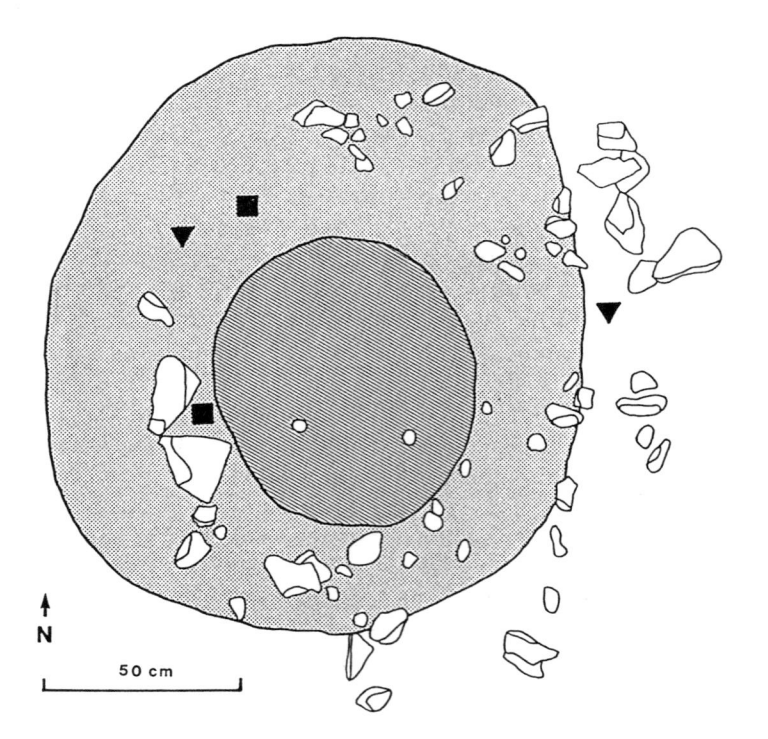

Figure 5.6. Surface plan of Pit 1987/6-10, showing the form of the pit and the locations of cultural materials, at the level of the top of the subsoil. On the top of this pit, a darker center was distinct from a lighter brown outer zone. Squares: pottery. Triangles: animal bone. Note the large quantity of limestone pieces (open areas outlined in black) in and around the pit.

24

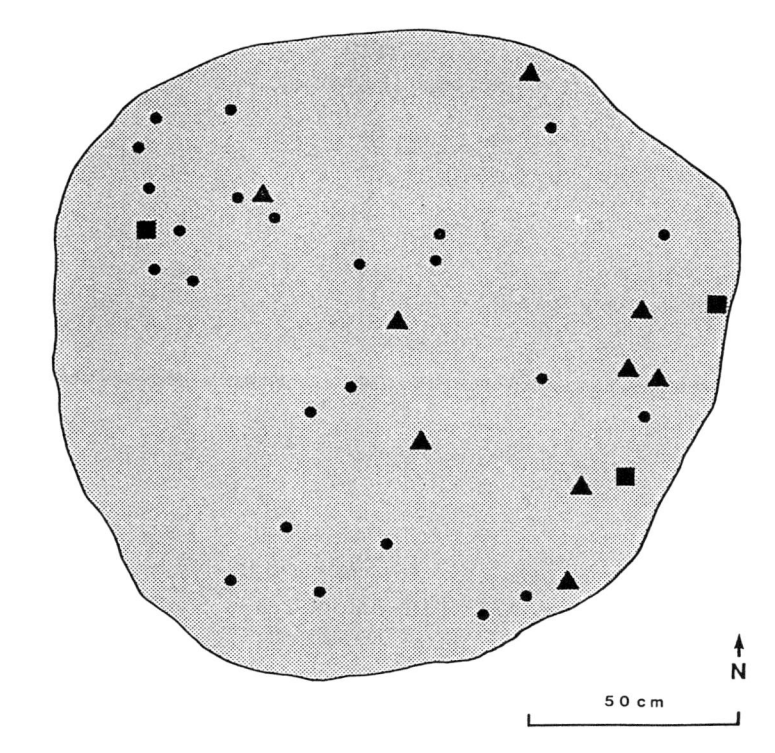

Figure 5.7. Surface plan of Pit 1991/6 showing the form of the pit and locations of cultural materials at the level of the top of the subsoil. Circles: charcoal. Squares: pottery. Triangles: daub.

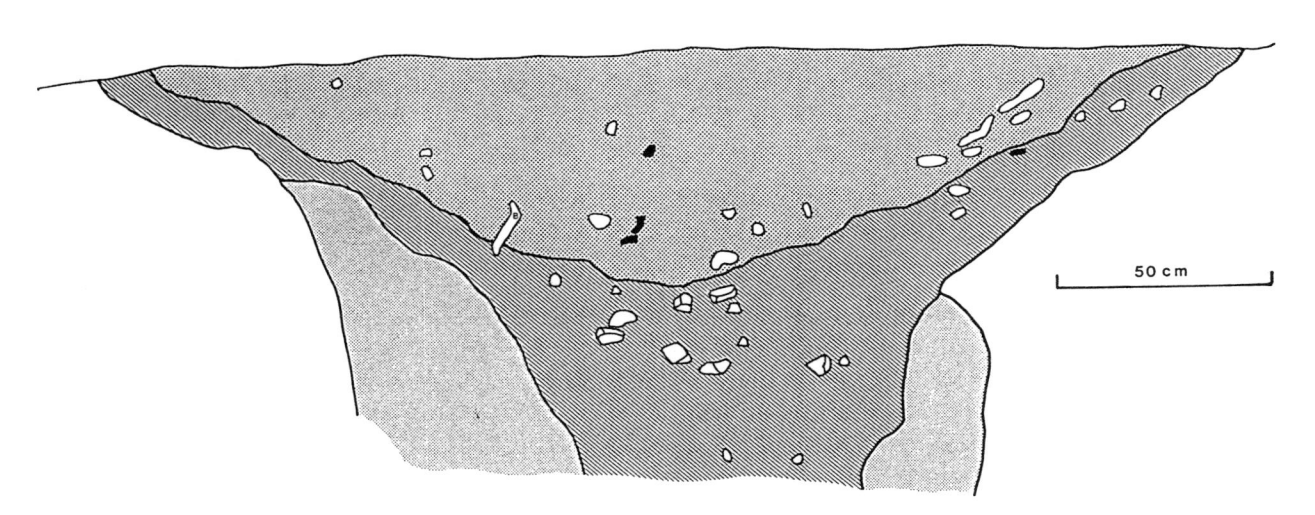

Figure 5.8. Profile view of Pit 1987/3-11-12, northeast face cut through center of pit. The top layer was dark blackish-brown humic soil, with sherds and bone in it. The bronze bird head, Figure 6.25, was found in this layer, at a depth of 20-30 cm below the top of the pit. The second layer was a lighter brown, sandy fill, containing gravel, small stones, numerous pieces of charcoal, fragmentary animal bones, and a small number of sherds. The lowest layer represented here is light brown sandy fill, similar to the preceding layer, but with abundant gravel and little cultural material. The bottom of the pit was not reached. The surrounding matrix was orange-red sand, with no cultural material in it. Open outlined shapes: limestone pieces. Filled shapes: pottery. B: animal bone.

Chapter 5 - Wells

Figure 5.9. Profile view of Pit 1987/6-10, west face of cut through center of pit. 1: Sandy grayish-brown fill with numerous limestone pieces and smaller gravel pebbles, and with some charcoal fragments and sherds. 2: Red sand mottled with brownish fill. 3: Sandy light brown fill with some fragmentary animal bones, charcoal, and limestone pieces. This layer was sandier in texture and lighter in color than layers 1 and 4. 4: Dark blackish-brown fill with substantially higher organic content than layers 1 and 3, and with larger fragments of animal bones, abundant charcoal, and fewer limestone pieces. 5: Dense red clay with coarse gravel, similar to matrix material into which the pit had been dug. 6: Dark grayish-brown fill with abundant gravel and some charcoal, very loose texture. Open outlined shapes: limestone pieces. Filled shapes: pottery. B: animal bone. Black circles: charcoal. The surrounding undisturbed matrix material from the level of layer 3 and above was red sand; the matrix below that level was dense red clay and gravel with some large pebbles.

Results of Excavations

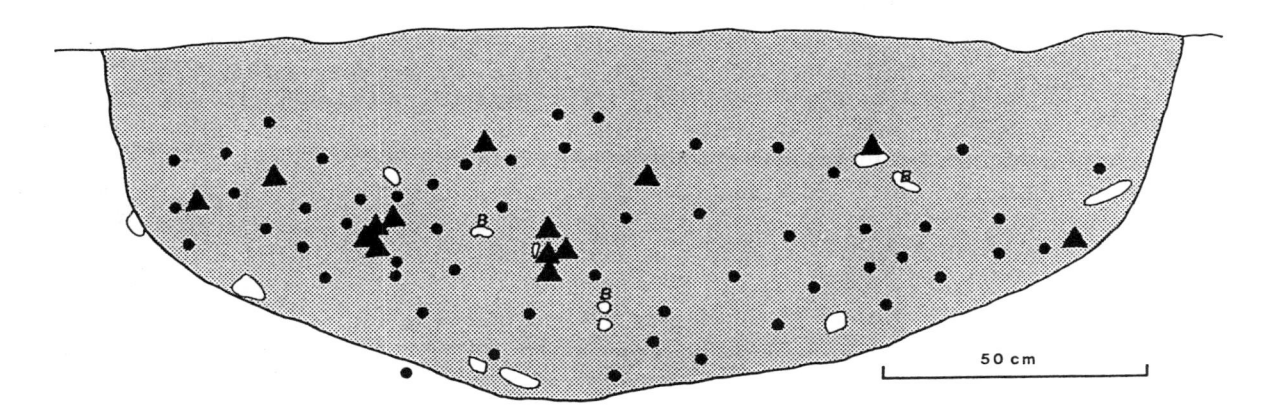

Figure 5.10. Profile view of Pit 1991/6, north profile view cut east-west through center of pit. The fill of this pit was a homogeneous dark brown sediment consisting of humus, sand, and clay. The surrounding matrix material was a light yellowish brown sand. Open shapes: pieces of limestone. Circles: charcoal. Triangles: daub.

Figure 5.11. Pit 1987/6-10 in the process of excavation. The eastern half of the pit has already been excavated (foreground), and the view shows the western half at a depth of 40 cm below the level of the top of the subsoil. Just visible in this black-and-white photograph is a rectangular (square?) area of darker fill in the center of the pit. The far side of the rectangle is about 120 cm long.

Chapter 5 - Wells

All three pits contained substantial quantities of pottery, animal bone, slag, and metal objects. Comparison of the total assemblages of materials from each of these pits, accomplished in the Kelheim Museum by laying out all of the material from each pit on a large laboratory table for close visual inspection, showed that the contents of the pits are more alike than they are different, though each differs from the other two in some respects. All three contained between 700 and 900 sherds of pottery (743 sherds in 1987/6-10, 857 sherds in 1987/3-11-12, and 898 sherds in 1991/6). Cultural materials were concentrated in the upper parts of each pit. For the two deep pits, 1987/6-10 and 1987/3-11-12, more than half of the sherds were recovered in the top 50 cm of the pit fill, though the pits were investigated to a depth of 1.5 m.

Similar types of pottery and metal objects in each pit indicate that the pits were roughly contemporaneous with one another and with the cultural layer on the settlement. All belong to the main occupation of Late Iron Age Kelheim. All three pits contained both coarsely and finely comb-decorated pottery, graphite-clay pottery, iron tools, pieces of sheet iron, fragmentary needles, and bronze ornaments. Figures 5.12-5.15 show representative sherds of pottery from each of the three major pits. The majority of the categories of metal objects represented, such as iron tool fragments, iron band fragments, and bronze buttons, are present in all three pits, and all three contained fragments of glass jewelry. Each pit seems to have contained a representative sample of material that was in use near it during the occupation of the settlement.

Differences between the contents of the pits may reflect differences in activities that took place on the settlement next to the pits. Both 1987/3-11-12 and 1991/6 contained sherds of fine painted pottery, and sherds of vessels with graphite-coated necks and fine comb decoration, but 1987/6-10 did not contain either of these types. 1987/6-10 and 1991/6 both contained large fragments of daub with branch impressions and clear surface finish, while 1987/3-11-12 did not. The two 1987 pits contained iron clamps, while 1991/6 did not contain architectural elements. 1991/6 contained the largest quantity of very fine pottery, including numerous fine painted sherds, very fine comb-decorated ware, and a unique large sherd of a thin-walled globular vessel with delicate parallel-line decoration (Figure 5.15, top left). But this pit also contained a range of coarse wares.

The degree of fragmentation in the three pits was distinctly different. The average weight of a sherd in Pit 1991/6 was 7.4 g, that in 1987/6-10 was 5.9 g, and that in 1987/3-11-12 was 3.1 g. This information suggests that the pottery in 1991/6 was considerably less broken in the course of deposition than that in the other two pits. A substantial portion of the pottery recovered from the pit in Sector 1991/6 may have entered the deposit directly from above, perhaps from the inside of a house, whereas the majority of the pottery in the other two pits may have lain on the settlement surface for a period, during which it was subjected to various forms of damage through being trodden on and kicked about.

Preliminary sorting and analysis of the sherds in each of the three major pits suggests that those recovered in Pit 1987/6-10 represent a minimum of 38 vessels, those in 1987/3-11-12 a minimum of 58 vessels, and those in 1991/6 a minimum of 64 vessels.

Other Pits and Postholes

All 29 features indicated by shading on the plan in Figure 5.3 are pits of various kinds. Figure 5.4 shows that, aside from the three major pits just discussed, the other pit features group together when graphed by diameter and depth. The majority of the pits were shallow and contained soil similar to that of the cultural layer—darker than the surrounding subsoil. In the great majority of the pits, there was no visible evidence of stratigraphy—only two of the major pits—1987/6-10 and 1987/3-11-12 contained clear stratigraphic layering. Most of the smaller pits did not contain substantial colored flecks of charcoal, daub, or pottery, except sometimes near the top. In the majority of cases, sherds of pottery confirmed association with the Late Iron Age occupation.

Besides the three major pits, 11 other pits contained 10 or more sherds of pottery, and four contained 10 or more fragments of animal bone. Other items recovered in these pits include iron objects such as nails, bronze fragments, and glass ornaments.

Floors

In three parts of the area excavated in 1987—the easternmost of our excavated areas—we encountered zones within the cultural layer where stones and cultural materials were densely packed. They are indicated by hatching on the plan, Figure 5.3. One in Sector 7 (Figure 5.3, lower left) mea-

Results of Excavations

Figure 5.12. Representative rim and decorated sherds from Pit 1987/3-11-12.

Chapter 5 - Wells

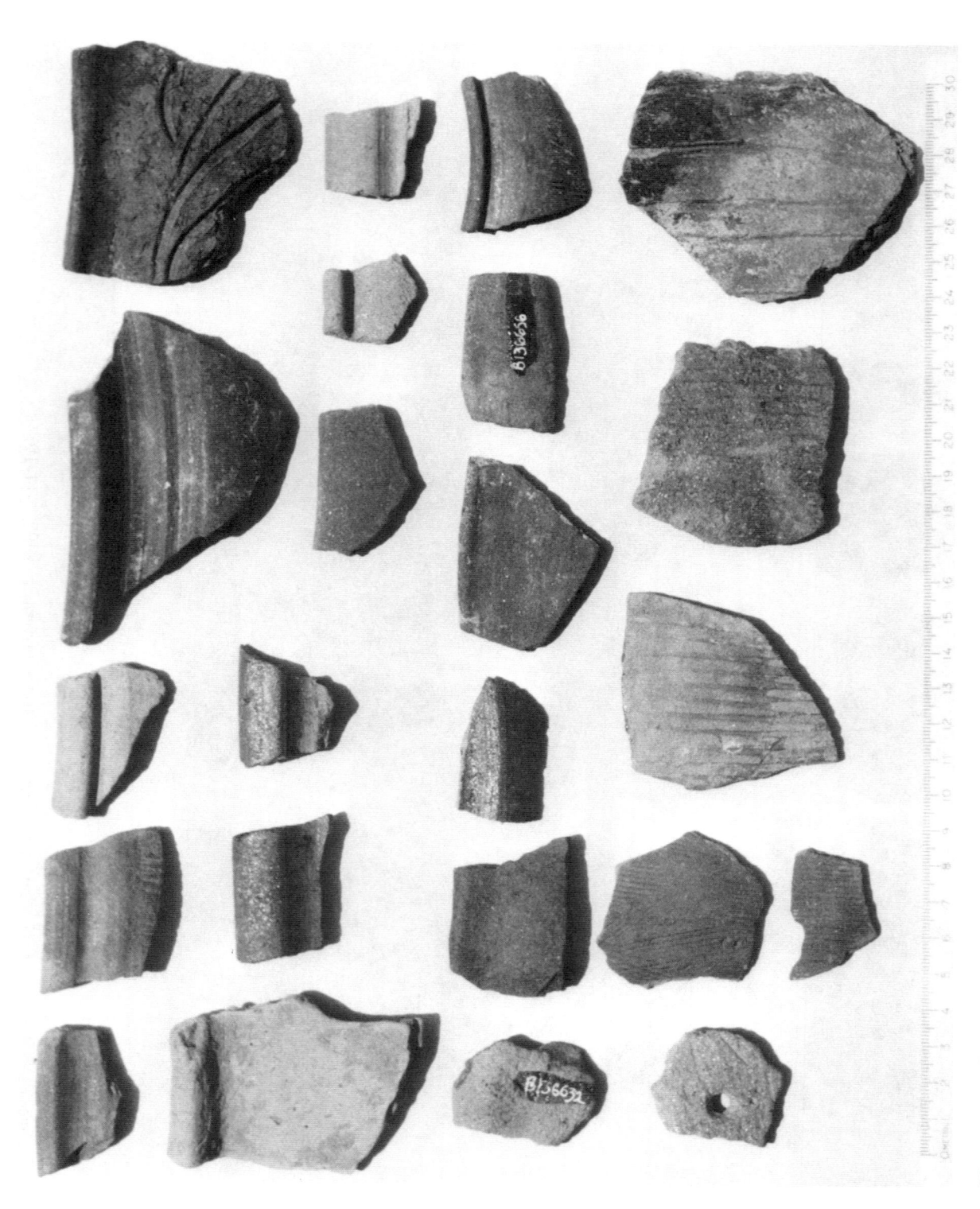

Figure 5.13. Representative rim and decorated sherds from Pit 1987/6-10.

Figure 5.14. Representative rim and decorated sherds from Pit 1991/6.

Chapter 5 - Wells

Figure 5.15. Representative decorated sherds from Pit 1991/6.

sured roughly 3 x 3 m; one in Sectors 3, 4, and 6 (Figure 5.3, right) measured about 6 x 4 m; and a circular one in Sectors 8 and 9 (Figure 5.3, top) measured about 3 m in diameter. These concentrations of material were carefully cleared with trowels and brushes, and all artifactual material was left in place for photographing and mapping.

The unusual surface in Sector 1987/7 was first noted when the large concentration of pottery sherds was observed (Figure 5.16). The dense concentration of sherds at a single level was unique, and many of them were exceptionally large. Two substantial portions of bases of thick-walled vessels were present, in each case with the bottom facing upwards (near the upper left edge in Figure 5.16), and several large rim sherds of a big graphite-clay pot were together (middle right edge of Figure 5.16). The surface also included a number of chunks of limestone, several substantial pieces of daub, five bronze objects, four iron objects including a key, and some animal bones.

The floor in Sectors 1987/3, 4, and 6 was characterized principally by numerous chunks of limestone on the same level. They ranged in size from that of a golf ball to over 15 cm in longest dimension, with the average longest dimension around 6-8 cm. In some places the stones were close together, forming almost a continuous paving, in other places they were more loosely scattered. Sherds of pottery were fairly numerous on this surface, but not as abundant or as large as in the feature described above. Animal bones were more common here, metal objects less common.

The floor in Sectors 1987/8 and 9 was formed by a much more closely arranged concentration of limestone chunks, and much larger ones. This feature was circular in shape, and the blocks piled close together and on top of one another. Pottery and animal bones were present, but in small quantities; several metal objects were found among and beneath the stones.

Figure 5.16. View of a portion of the surface within the cultural layer in Sector 1987/7, showing part of the dense concentration of pottery. Note the two large bases in upper left, and the large rim sherds of a graphite-clay pot at lower right. Another view of this feature is in Wells 1987, 404 fig. 5; plan in Wells 1988a, 85 fig. 56.

The Distribution of Cultural Remains over the Site Surface

Distribution of Settlement Features

The distribution of these settlement features over the areas investigated provides one useful means of examining spatial patterns on the site. The subsurface features first became apparent as excavation reached the sandy subsoil. The features appeared as dark, humus-filled holes in the clean yellow sand or reddish sandy gravel. If we assume that the density of subsurface features on the settlement—postholes from buildings, cellar and storage pits—is directly proportional to the density of occupation activity, then differential distribution of the subsurface features should provide a view into the spatial patterning of settlement activity. To quantify these data for comparison over different parts of the settlement, I calculated the approximate surface areas (at the level of the top of the sandy subsoil, where the features first became recognizable) of all of the 29 principal subsurface structures. (Floors were only identified in the easternmost parcel of land we investigated.)

Measuring the surface areas of pits and postholes in the units investigated yields the following results. The total area of these features is 25.64 m^2. This represents 4.2% of the total investigated surface of 614 m^2. The percentage of surface comprised by the features varies significantly on different parts of the field.

In the easternmost area investigated, a total of 21.94 m^2 of subsurface structures were identified (Figure 5.1, right and Figure 5.3, top), representing 7.8 % of the total 280 m^2. To the west, the percentages were considerably lower. In the central portion of the landscape we studied, only 2.27 m^2 of surface comprised subsurface features, just 1.0% of the total of 227 m^2. In the two westernmost trenches, 1.43 m^2 of surface was comprised of subsurface features, 1.3% of the total of 107 m^2 excavated there. Although these areas investigated to date are small, and larger-scale excavations could change the picture, these differences in the densities of settlement features on different parts of the Mitterfeld seem to indicate differences in the extent to which the Late Iron Age settlement was built up along this strip of land.

This evidence is corroborated by spatial patterns in other categories of archaeological material.

Distribution of Portable Cultural Materials

Pottery

We assume that pottery recovered in settlement contexts such as that on the Mitterfeld at Kelheim was deposited at the time that it broke and was no longer useful. Evidence from Late Bronze and Iron Age settlements in temperate Europe suggests that pottery was not systematically disposed of either in trash pits or outside of habitation areas in middens (Wells 1983, p. 29). Instead, broken pottery was tossed or kicked aside or trampled into the ground where it blended in with the surrounding soil. Some sherds came to rest in low places on the settlement surface, including disused cellar holes, storage pits, and borrow pits, while the majority remained on the surface to contribute to the build-up of the cultural layer. The fragmentation on the surface of the settlement of large quantities of pottery, together with daub from walls of buildings, would account for the widespread and often dense distribution of small pieces of reddish, grayish, and orange ceramic material throughout the cultural layer on the site. Unless post-depositional processes such as intentional clearing of surfaces, or natural erosion, take place, the distribution of pottery sherds recovered archaeologically on a settlement should reflect the intensity of activity that resulted in the breaking of the pottery—in most cases, everyday domestic activity.

In order to investigate the intensity of occupation from this perspective, we counted and weighed all pottery recovered in each unit, at the time that the material was inventoried in the field laboratory.

Figure 5.17 shows distributions, by weight, of Late Iron Age pottery in the areas studied. Some Late Iron Age pottery was recovered in every unit investigated except the highest on the slope of the Michelsberg, which is the southernmost on the plan. A general scatter of ceramics from the oppidum occupation appears to cover the whole settlement area, except on the steeper parts of the valley slope. In all but one of the central and western units the quantities were small, less than 25 g of pottery per square meter. In the eastern area, in contrast, all units yielded over 25 g per square meter. This result agrees with that from study of the subsurface features in indicating that the eastern area was

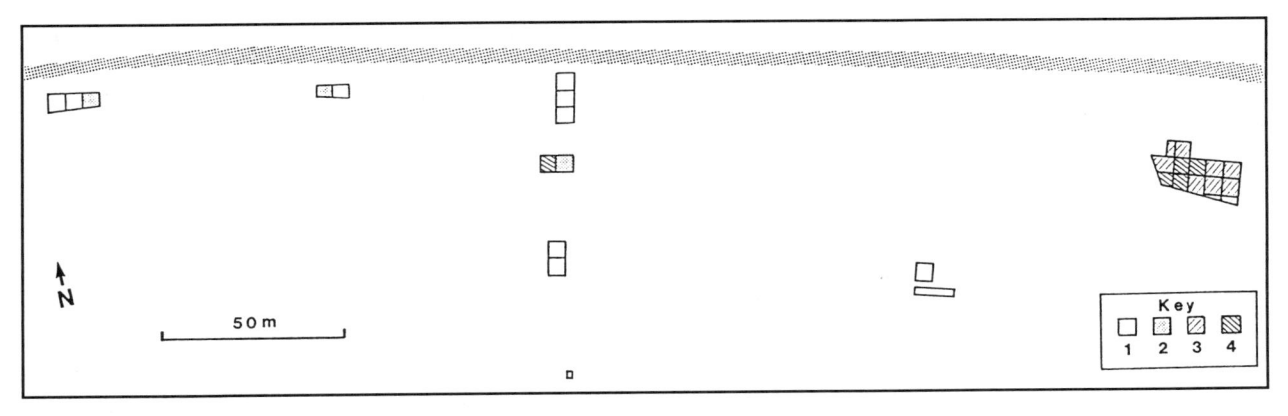

Figure 5.17. Plan of trenches excavated on the Mitterfeld showing densities of Late Iron Age pottery from all areas investigated, including old humus layers, cultural layer, and subsurface features. Key: 1 - less than 25 grams of pottery per square meter, 2 - 25–100 g/m^2, 3 - 100–300 g/m^2, 4 - more than 300 g/m^2.

part of a densely occupied settlement core, while the areas to the west were characterized by much less intensive activity. Only one unit there yielded more than 100 g of Late Iron Age pottery per square meter. Twelve units in the eastern parcel yielded over 100 g per square meter, and four of them had over 300 g per square meter.

Units that yielded large quantities of pottery also tended to have in them subsurface features, but they did not in every case. Even in units that contained rich pits, the greatest amounts of pottery did not come from within the subsurface features, but from the cultural layer above them. This evidence suggests that the presence of subsurface features and of fragmentary pottery covary with the density of Iron Age habitation activity.

Daub

Daub was represented on the settlement in very small pieces and in sizable chunks, sometimes with clear branch impressions. Throughout the cultural layer on the site and in all of the pits, small flecks of orange color attested to the presence of fragments of daub, just as small grayish or reddish flecks attested to pottery fragments and black flecks to charcoal. These were too small and too fragmentary to recover in any reasonable way. Larger pieces of daub also occurred (see Figure 6.10), mostly in the pits but sometimes in the cultural layer. These larger pieces were collected, counted, and weighed by find-unit. In general, the quantities were so small that their distribution does not provide useful information about location of structures. For the 280 m^2 area excavated in 1987, for example, a total of 1130 pieces of daub were recovered, weighing just 2173 grams. The greatest concentration in any of the 14 sectors was 19.9 g/m^2, in Sector 5—not a quantity that seems meaningful. Quantities elsewhere on the settlement were even smaller.

Of the three major pits, only that in Sector 1991/6 contained a substantial, by Late La Tène standards, quantity of daub—1354.5 g. Pit 1987/3-11-12 contained 58.5 g of daub, and Pit 1987/6-10 contained only 3 g.

Iron Working Materials

Distribution of materials attesting to the on-site production of iron is very important for understanding the settlement at Kelheim. Chapter 10 treats this subject in some detail.

Iron Tools and Equipment

Iron tools and equipment were concentrated in the eastern part of the settlement area we investigated. Very few were found in either the 1990 trenches to the west or in the 1991 trenches in the central part of the settlement area, with the important exception of the materials recovered in the pit in Sector 1991/6. This distributional evidence suggests that iron tools were used most actively in the part of the settlement represented by our eastern area, but also in the immediate vicinity of Sector 1991/6.

The great majority of iron implements recovered are small fragments of larger tools. Even the complete tools that we found are of sizes much smaller than many of the implements reported by

Chapter 5 - Wells

Jacobi (1974) from Manching. The reasons for this difference between the Kelheim and Manching tool assemblages lie in differences in the abandonment processes at the two sites (see Chapter 18).

In all, 315 more-or-less identifiable iron objects were recovered in clear stratigraphic contexts (small and highly corroded objects whose original form cannot be determined are not included in these figures). Of these, 288 iron objects were recovered in the 1987 area, four in the 1990 areas, and 23 in the 1991 areas (all in Sector 6). Only in the 1987 area did we encounter substantial quantities of metal objects within the cultural layer.

Iron objects were strikingly abundant in Sectors 1987/5 (44 identifiable objects) and 1987/6 (33 identifiable objects). Slabs of thin iron were particularly abundant in Sector 1987/5. Sector 3 was noticeably poor in iron objects, with only nine. The three iron keys recovered were all in the western half of the 1987 area—in Sectors 5, 7, and 9. Of the two major pits in the 1987 area, 6-10 contained 17 iron objects and four bronze pieces, while 3-11-12 contained 20 iron objects and eight bronze ones.

Among the iron objects from the 1987 excavation area, nails and clamps, classified by Geselowitz (Chapter 11) as architectural elements, are abundant, representing about one-quarter of all identifiable iron, suggesting substantial use of iron in construction in this portion of the settlement. Nails and clamps are not represented among the iron objects from the central and western parts of the settlement, suggesting perhaps that iron was not as much used in those areas.

Bronze-Working Materials

Lumps of bronze metal that had not been shaped into specific objects were recovered in the eastern excavation area investigated in 1987. These lumps may have resulted from pouring off excess metal from casting processes, or from storage of scrap for future casting. In either case, the presence of such pieces is strongly suggestive of bronze-working activity.

Bronze Ornaments

All of the finished bronze objects recovered can be classified as ornaments; none appear to have served as tools. A total of 41 identifiable bronze objects were recovered in clear stratigraphic contexts, 36 from the eastern area excavated in 1987, four from the central area explored in 1991 (all in Sector 6), and one in the westernmost areas, excavated in 1990. On the 1987 part of the site, bronze is concentrated in Sectors 5, 6, and 7; no bronze was recovered in the majority of the sectors (2, 3, 4, 9, 13, 14).

Glass Ornaments

Thirteen glass objects were recovered, 10 in the 1987 excavated area, one in a pit in the western area investigated in 1990, and two in the pit in Sector 1991/6. Unlike iron and bronze objects, the 10 glass ornaments found on the 1987 portion of the settlement were widely distributed across the settlement surface, seven in pits and three in the cultural layer.

Coins

We recovered four Celtic coins in the easternmost parcel of land, but none in the areas to the west (Chapter 13).

Internal Site Chronology

In the areas investigated by the University of Minnesota in 1987, 1990, and 1991, we have not been able to recognize any chronological distinctions between the Late Iron Age pits, floors, and cultural layer on the site. (Three pits of Bronze Age date discovered in 1990 will be dealt with elsewhere.)

During the museum study session in the summer 1992, when we were able to lay out and compare all of the materials recovered during the three years of excavation, it was possible to make direct comparisons between the ceramics and other objects recovered in the different settlement features. The reason for doing this was to permit comparison both of individual sherds of pottery and whole assemblages from different features, in order to ascertain similarities and differences across the site. These comparisons revealed the chronological homogeneity of the material recovered. For example, though the assemblages of pottery and metal objects from the three major pits were not identical, the presence of many common types of pottery in two of the three or in all three strongly suggests that the three pits are of similar date.

In the two major pits in the eastern portion of the excavated areas, stones of the same type, size, and form as those comprising the floor of Sectors 1987/3, 4, and 6 occurred in the top layer of the pit. The evidence suggests that the pits were open while the floor was exposed and in use, and that the pit and floor fell into disuse at the same time, with erosion causing some of the stones from the paving to fall into the filling pit.

Our degree of chronological control does not permit us to say exactly when one pit was in use relative to another—only a technique as precise as dendrochronology might allow such fine distinctions to be made. But recognizable chronological differences among the Late Iron Age settlement features on the Mitterfeld at Kelheim, such as Stöckli (1974) and Sievers (1989) identify at Manching, are, as yet, lacking.

Chapter 6

The Archaeological Material Recovered

Introduction

Here I shall present only a brief overview of the materials recovered in the course of the three seasons of excavation at Kelheim by the University of Minnesota. Studies of the individual categories of archaeological material are under way, and those will treat the objects in greater detail.

The categories used here are standard ones for classification and description of objects from Late Iron Age temperate Europe. The appropriateness of these particular groupings of material culture will be critically examined in future studies of these objects.

Most of the material culture that we recovered on the Mitterfeld is similar to that from other settlements of the period in temperate Europe. Many of our objects—sherds, iron tools, bronze and glass ornaments, and others—have very close parallels from other sites. Instead of citing numerous such parallels here, I refer the reader to the following major publications of Late La Tène settlements which illustrate many objects that compare closely to those from Kelheim: Chapotat 1970; van Endert 1991; Fischer, Rieckhoff-Pauli, and Spindler 1984; Furger-Gunti 1979; Furger-Gunti and Berger 1980; Gebhard 1989, 1991; Jacobi 1974; Joachim 1980; Kappel 1969; Maier 1970; Meduna 1970a, 1970b; Müller-Karpe and Müller-Karpe 1977; Nothdurfter 1979; Pič 1906; Pingel 1971; Stöckli 1979a.

The materials from the Mitterfeld at Kelheim also compare closely with objects from some of the cemeteries at which grave goods were still included in this period. Examples include Wederath (Haffner 1971, 1974a, 1978, 1989), Dietzenbach (Polenz 1971), and Bad Nauheim (Schönberger 1952). Many of the graves discussed by Polenz (1982) also include objects similar to our settlement finds.

Pottery: Vessel Fragments

Late Iron Age pottery was recovered in the modern humus, in the old humus layers, in the culture layer, and in the subsurface features on the settlement. A total of 14,126 Late Iron Age sherds were recovered in context. Of these, 3,283 came from subsurface features, the rest from the cultural layer and from the mixed humus layers.

The basic character of the pottery assemblage at Kelheim is similar to that at Manching and other oppida in the region. The principal kinds, following the terminology used in the Manching studies, are polished wheel-made pottery, graphite-clay pottery, undecorated coarse pottery, decorated coarse pottery, comb-decorated pottery without graphite admixture to the clay, and fine painted ware. Figures 6.1-6.8[†] show a selection of decorated sherds and rim sherds from the area excavated in 1987. (See also Figures 5.12-5.15.) Some sherds, especially of the thicker wares, show repair with iron clamps, and in a few instances remains of the clamps are still present in holes drilled through the pottery.

Pottery: Spindle Whorls

Eleven spindle whorls were recovered in the course of the excavations (Figure 6.9). Ten were made from sherds of characteristic local pottery, one is thicker and made specifically as a spindle whorl (bottom right). Of the pottery whorls, two are unfinished (bottom left and bottom center). In both cases, sherds were formed into rough circles, and a perforation was begun but not completed.

Animal Bones

Animal bones were recovered from all parts of the settlement investigated. They range from large and complete bones to small fragments of burned bone. A preliminary report on the bone is presented in Chapter 9.

Daub

Daub is abundantly represented in the cultural layer on all parts of the settlement investigated,

---

[†]All figures for this chapter are grouped together at the end, beginning on page 41.

but generally only in the form of tiny orange flecks or lumps, rarely larger than a big grain of sand. Larger fragments were few in number, especially compared to those on settlements of earlier periods (see e.g. Hancock 1983).

Only a small number of fragments preserve information about the structures of which the daub formed a part. A large chunk of daub from Sector 1987/7 (Figure 6.10) has on it impressions of four branches, and several pieces from the pit in Sector 1991/6 have layers of plaster on one surface indicative of an inner or outer surface of a wall. Comparison of larger pieces of daub from different parts of the settlement revealed a very similar texture and color among all of the daub from Late Iron Age features. It looked and felt very different from the daub from the Bronze Age pits excavated in 1990.

Iron Objects

A total of 315 iron objects were recovered from well-documented Late Iron Age contexts on the Mitterfeld settlement. With the exception of the fibulae (Figure 6.11), all can be classified as tools, even though the fragmentary nature of many precludes precise identification (see Chapter 11). They represent a variety of implements, including anvils, chisels, and perforators (Figure 6.12). Many thick, band-shaped fragments probably were parts of tools, but the original form is often not apparent (Figure 6.13). Nails of different types are well represented on the eastern part of the settlement (Figure 6.14). They vary considerably in size and in form of the head. Many shaft-shaped objects without well-defined heads seem to have served as nails (Figure 6.15); one end frequently shows signs of having been hammered, and in many cases the other end has been bent over, as is the case with many of the nails with heads. Two large spikes (Figure 6.16 top and middle) belong to the general category of nails; they may have been intended for use in connection with the wooden supports in the wall system around the settlement, or possibly for construction of buildings within the settlement. Clamps are also well represented (Figure 16.17), and they too most likely served to hold pieces of wood together. They vary considerably in size, both in length and in width. Hooks (Figure 6.16, bottom left) were probably attached to walls of buildings and used for hanging objects. It is significant that all of the iron objects that are associated structurally with buildings are concentrated in the easternmost area of our excavations.

Three keys were recovered (Figure 16.18), all in the eastern part of the settlement. A variety of different kinds of rings and objects with eyes (Figure 6.19) were probably used to attached things to one another. Fragments of sheet iron vessels may be represented by the objects in Figure 6.20, middle row center and right. The omega-shaped ring in Figure 6.20, bottom left, may have been a ring-handle from a metal caldron (as in Jacobi 1974, 147 fig. 34 and plate 39, 658. 659. 667). An end fragment of a vessel handle is shown in Figure 6.20, top left; two others from vessel handles were found in the large pit in Sector 1991/6.

Many flat pieces of iron were recovered, ranging from thick plates of metal, as in Figure 6.21, top left, to very thin sheet metal. Their purpose is not usually apparent. Some were hooks of various kinds, others fragmentary knives, and some may have been parts of locks.

Needles, some with eyes, and pins (Figure 6.22) suggest either sewing on the site or manufacture of sewing implements there.

Other readily identifiable iron objects well known from other contemporaneous sites include a strap end (Figure 6.18 second from right) and a small spearhead (Figure 6.18 right).

In general, the iron implements from Kelheim are similar to those published from Manching by Jacobi (1974) and illustrated in the other publications of excavated settlements cited above. The most important exception to this generalization is the lack of large tools and of weapons (except the small spear point in Figure 6.18) in our assemblage from Kelheim. This difference is significant in light of Sievers's (1989) recent analysis of the weapon finds from Manching. If Sievers's idea is correct, that Manching suffered a violent catastrophe at the end of La Tène C2, when most or all of the weapons were left scattered over the surface of the settlement and the site was abandoned in haste; and if the major occupation at Kelheim did not begin until La Tène D1 (see Chapter 7); then the absence of weapons and large tools at Kelheim could be explained by the peaceful and unhurried abandonment of that settlement sometime in the course of La Tène D1. These suggestions are tentative at this stage; and they are intended to help to define issues for future investigation regarding the history of occupation and abandonment at the oppida.

Kluge (1987) reports a small number of iron tools, including three complete axes, but none larger than those. The iron implements treated by Etzel (1990) are of similar size to those from the University of Minnesota excavations.

Chapter 6 - Wells

Bronze Ornaments

Our investigations recovered 41 identifiable bronze objects in Late Iron Age contexts on the Mitterfeld. We recovered 36 of them in the easternmost area excavated in 1987, and only five in the central and western parts of the site. Nine of the 41 objects are small rings (Figure 6.23, top row), seven complete and two fragmentary. Five are small hemispherical sheet bronze buttons (four in Figure 6.23, second row, third through sixth objects), another a profiled sheet bronze button (Figure 6.23, second row, left). A tack (Figure 6.23, second row, second from left) has a head similar to the hemispherical buttons. Five objects are fragmentary bands (Figure 6.24, top row). Ten are fragments of sheet bronze metal (Figure 6.24, middle and bottom rows), three of them with perforations.

Other bronze objects include a bird head (Figure 6.25; see Wells 1989), a three-part pendant (Figure 6.23, right), and four pieces of unshaped bronze metal (Figure 6.23, bottom row), apparently debris from casting.

The bronze objects are similar to those among the larger assemblage recovered at Manching (van Endert 1991). But as in the case of the iron implements, compared to the Manching assemblage as a whole, the Kelheim bronze objects are notably small. None of the larger categories of bronzes represented at Manching occurs among our finds at Kelheim.

Glass Ornaments

We recovered 13 glass objects in the course of our excavations. Most are fragments of large beads, but three are probably pieces of bracelets. Since the photograph (Figure 6.26) does not show the colors, I shall briefly describe the beads here:

Top row, left to right: Fragmentary ring-bead of brown glass with yellow bands.

Fragmentary bead (?) with white and dark blue sections.

Fragmentary bead of dark blue glass with bands of another color, perhaps originally white.

Fragmentary ring-bead of dark blue glass with bands of another color, perhaps originally white.

Fragmentary ring-bead of dark blue color.

Fragment of bright blue glass with rough surface all over, probably a piece of unworked "raw" glass.

Far right, middle row: Heavily weathered fragment of blue glass.

Bottom row, left to right: Fragment of dark blue glass, perhaps part of a bracelet.

Fragment of a bracelet of brown glass, with profiling on the outside, and with white paint in the grooves.

Fragment of a bracelet of clear colorless glass with yellow painted lines on the outside.

Glass bead of pale blue color.

Rounded droplet of blue glass.

Weathered piece of dark blue glass, perhaps from a bracelet.

The brown and yellow ring-bead, the large blue ring-bead, and the fragment of raw glass all have close parallels at Manching (Gebhard 1989, pl. 50, 753-762; pl. 54, 827; pl. 61, 889), but the other beads and the two bracelet fragments do not. Venclová (1990) illustrates many ring-beads from Bohemian sites that are similar in form to ours from Kelheim, and bracelets with profiling similar to that of the fragment in Figure 6.26, bottom row, second from left.

Flint and Stone

Considerable quantities of flint were recovered in many of the areas that we investigated. Most of the objects appear to be natural fragments or debitage from the manufacture of tools, but clear tools are also among the finds. Except for the projectile point discussed below, there were no clear associations between flint materials and settlement features. It is unclear whether most of the flint represents settlement activity on the site, or secondary deposition from site locations higher up the slope or up the Altmühl Valley. Most of the flint is not substantially abraded, suggesting that it was not transported far. Also uncertain at this stage is whether some or most of the flint represents utilization by the Late Iron Age inhabitants or by earlier occupants of the site (see Ford, Bradley, Hawkes, and Fisher 1984; and Narr and Lass 1985 on use of stone tools in later contexts). The flint materials from the site will be the subject of another study.

A white flint projectile point (Figure 6.27) 4.1 cm in length was recovered in Pit 1987/2-5, which also contained considerable pottery and other materials of Late La Tène date. The object probably dates to the Neolithic Period, but a more precise cultural and chronological ascription must await further study. It is possible that the object was deposited on the site before the Iron Age and came into association with the pit unnoticed, but it is more likely that a Late Iron Age inhabitant of the settlement found the point somewhere and brought it home, subsequently to deposit it, inadvertently or intentionally, among the Iron Age cultural materials.

The Archaeological Material Recovered

Figure 6.1. Rim and decorated sherds from Sector 1987/1.

Figure 6.2. Rim and decorated sherds from Sector 1987/2.

Chapter 6 - Wells

Figure 6.3. Rim and decorated sherds from Sector 1987/3.

Figure 6.4. Rim sherds from Sector 1987/5.

The Archaeological Material Recovered

Figure 6.5. Decorated sherds from Sector 1987/5.

Figure 6.6. Rim and decorated sherds from Sector 1987/6.

Chapter 6 - Wells

Figure 6.7. Rim and decorated sherds from Sector 1987/7.

Figure 6.8. Rim and decorated sherds from Sector 1987/10.

Figure 6.9. Ceramic spindle whorls from the Mitterfeld at Kelheim.

Figure 6.10. Daub fragment from Sector 1987/7, with impressions of four branches used in the construction of the building of which it was a part. Scale in foreground is in millimeters.

Chapter 6 - Wells

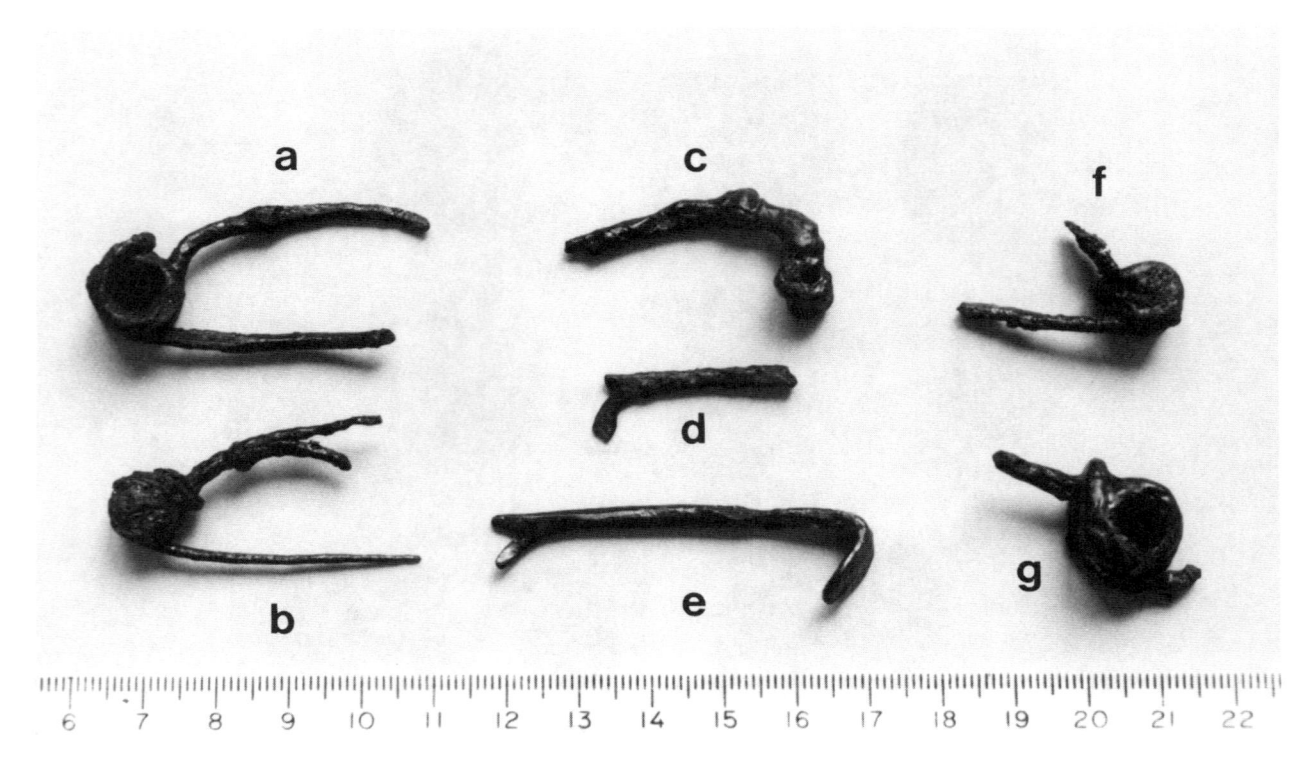

Figure 6.11. Fragmentary iron fibulae from the Mitterfeld at Kelheim.

Figure 6.12. Iron tools from the Mitterfeld at Kelheim, including an anvil (top left), a narrow chisel (second from left), and a broad chisel (top right).

Figure 6.13. Iron band-shaped fragments, probably parts of tools, from the Mitterfeld at Kelheim.

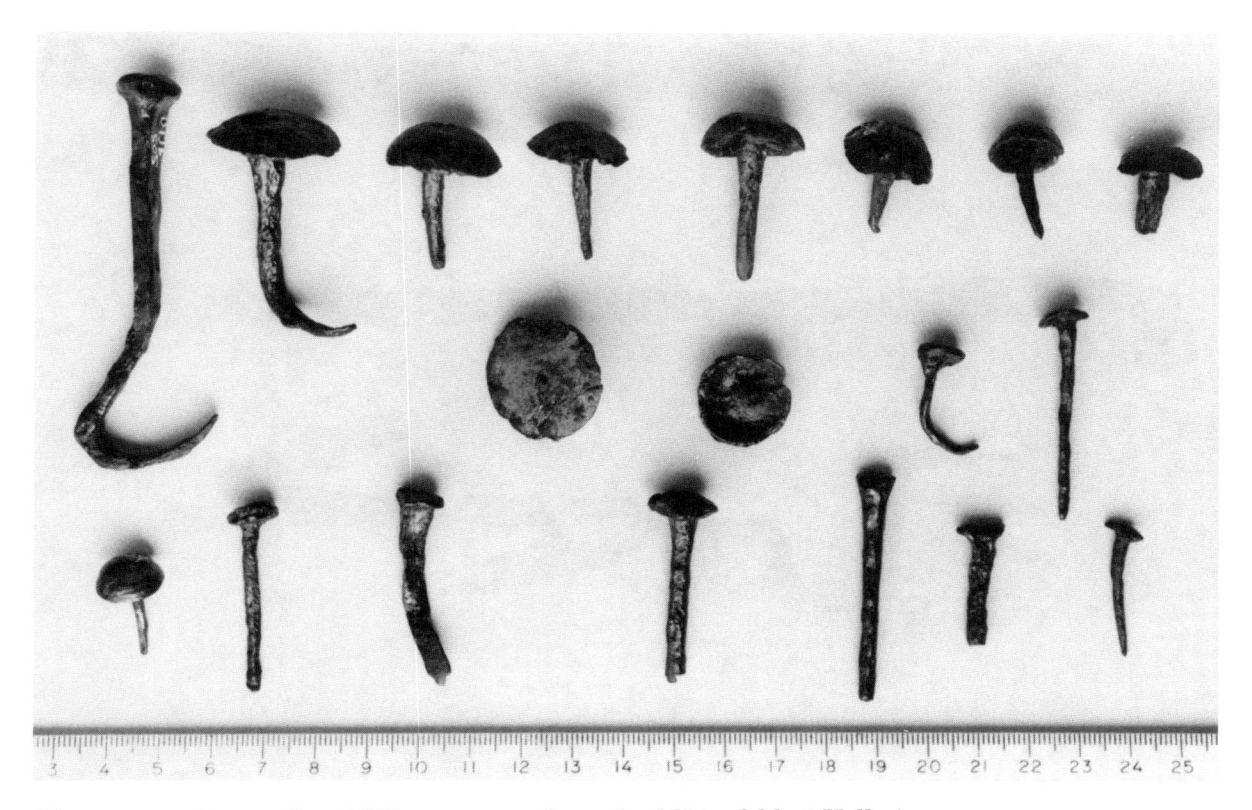

Figure 6.14. Iron nails of different types from the Mitterfeld at Kelheim.

Chapter 6 - Wells

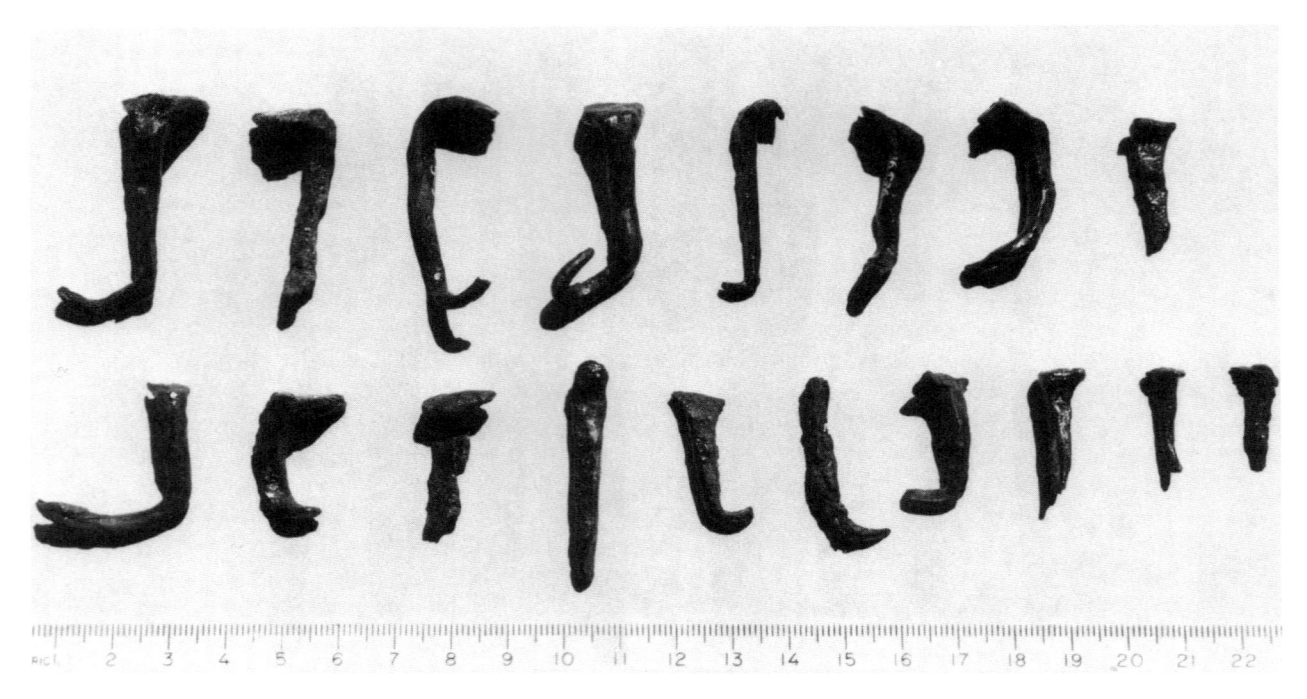

Figure 6.15. Iron shafts apparently used as nails, but without separately formed heads, from the Mitterfeld at Kelheim.

Figure 6.16. Iron spikes (top and middle) and hooks from the Mitterfeld at Kelheim.

The Archaeological Material Recovered

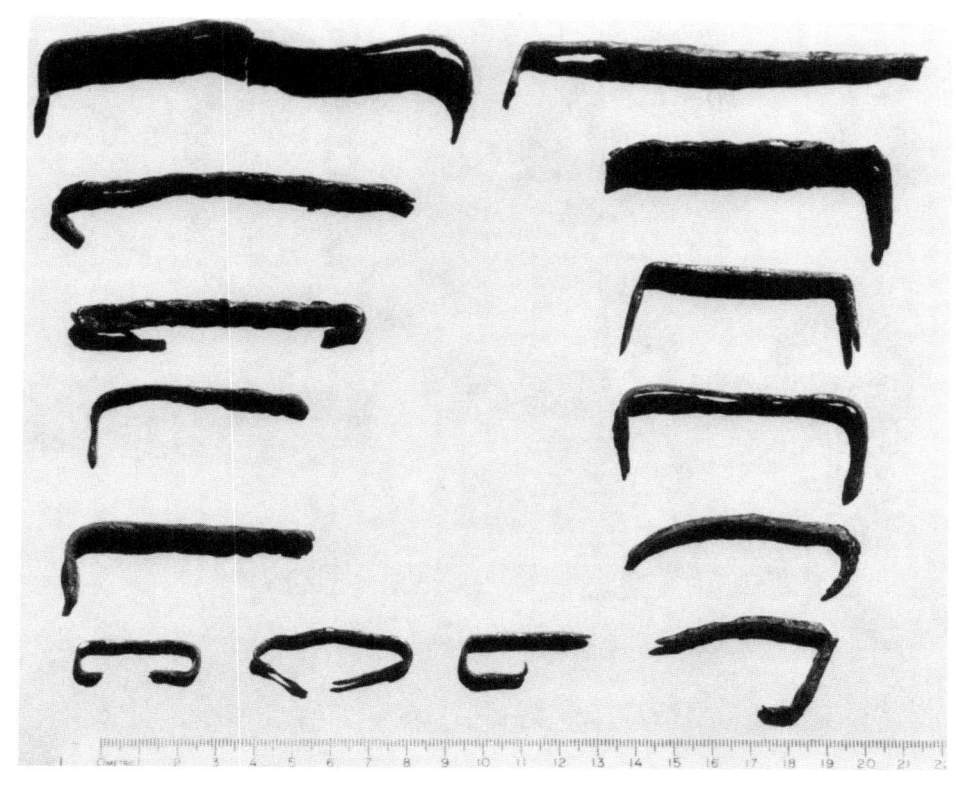

Figure 6.17. Iron clamps from the Mitterfeld at Kelheim.

Figure 6.18. Iron keys (three objects on left), strap-end, and spearhead from Mitterfeld at Kelheim.

Chapter 6 - Wells

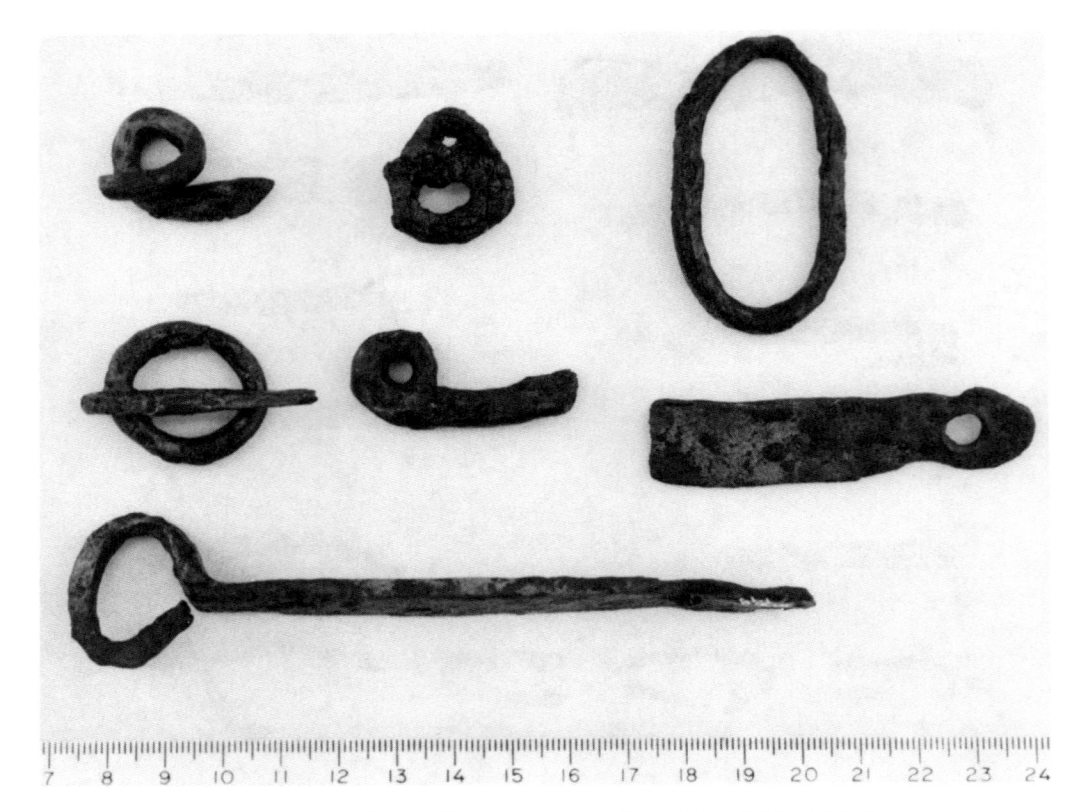

Figure 6.19. Iron rings and attachments from the Mitterfeld at Kelheim.

Figure 6.20. Iron end of vessel handle (top left), ring handle (bottom left), sheet fragments perhaps from vessel (center row, center and right), and other pieces from the Mitterfeld at Kelheim.

The Archaeological Material Recovered

Figure 6.21. Iron fragments, ranging from thick slab in upper left to thin sheet pieces. The two objects in the lower row, left and next to left, are fragmentary hooks. From the Mitterfeld at Kelheim.

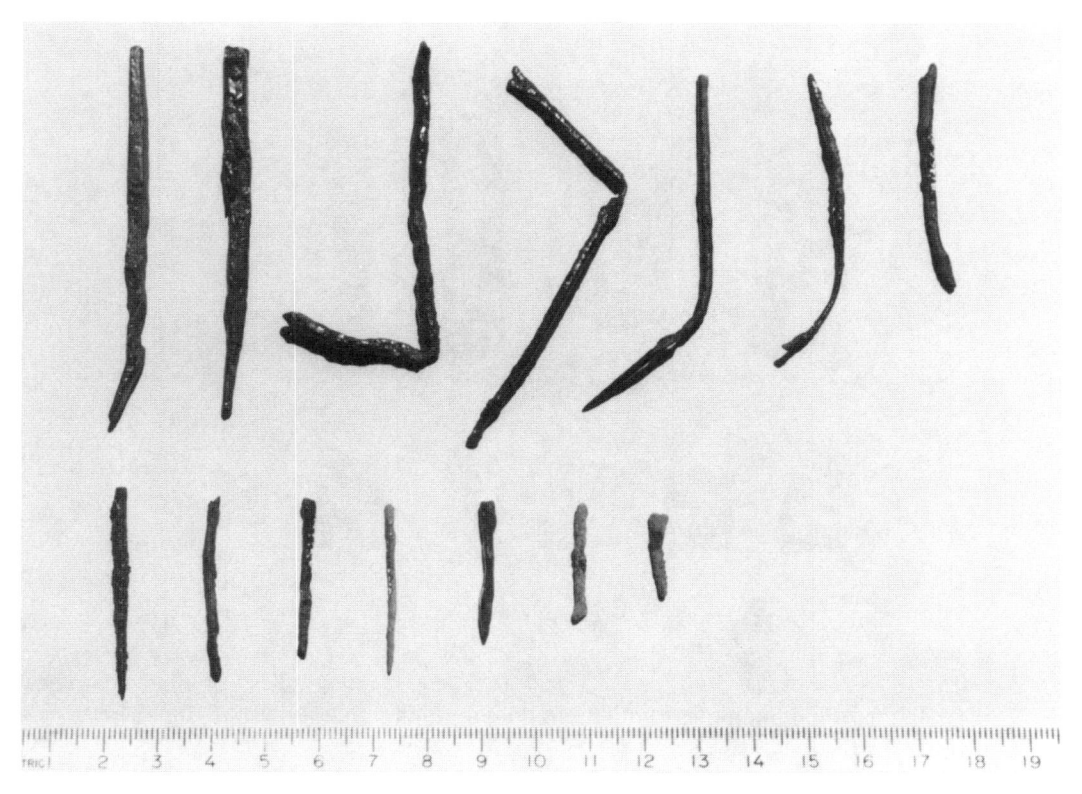

Figure 6.22. Iron needles and pins from the Mitterfeld at Kelheim.

Chapter 6 - Wells

Figure 6.23. Bronze objects from the Mitterfeld at Kelheim. The four objects in the bottom row are unshaped lumps of bronze.

Figure 6.24. Bronze objects from the Mitterfeld at Kelheim.

The Archaeological Material Recovered

Figure 6.25. Bronze bird head from Pit 1987/3-11-12 on the Mitterfeld at Kelheim. Length from back of head to point of beak 1.75 cm. (For discussion, see Wells 1989.)

Figure 6.27. Projectile point of white flint, from Pit 1987/2-5 on the Mitterfeld at Kelheim.

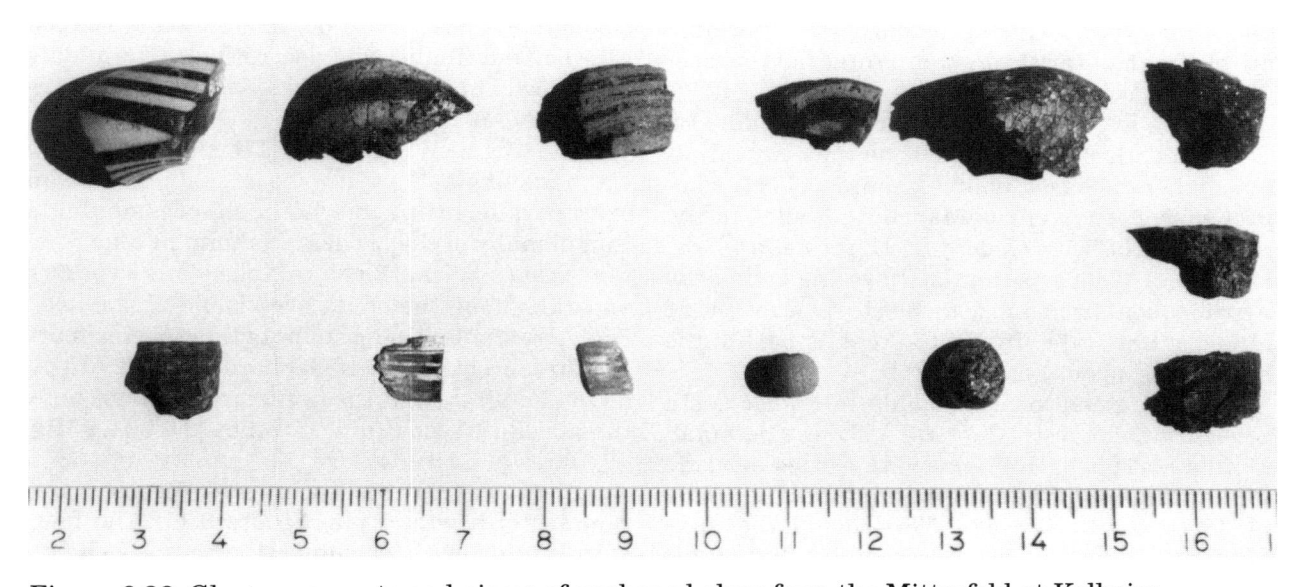

Figure 6.26. Glass ornaments and pieces of unshaped glass from the Mitterfeld at Kelheim.

Chapter 7
Chronology of the Oppidum Occupation

Introduction

The dating of the occupation of the oppidum at Kelheim can be worked out on the basis of the typology of materials recovered from the settlement excavations, compared with standard chronological markers of the Late Iron Age. Discussion here will focus on the materials recovered through the University of Minnesota excavations, but will also bring into consideration finds from the Mitterfeld settlement from earlier investigations (Kluge 1987, Etzel 1990).

The chronologically most diagnostic objects recovered in the course of the University of Minnesota excavations are fibulae, glass ornaments, coins, and painted pottery.

Fibulae

A total of 14 fragmentary fibulae were recovered during the 1987, 1990, and 1991 field seasons; the best preserved are shown in Figure 6.11. One is of bronze, 13 of iron. Only in the cases of five specimens is it possible to ascertain with confidence the probable original form of the fibula and hence the type to which it belongs; the other nine are too fragmentary to make anything but the most general of ascriptions.

Of the five, two are structurally of Middle La Tène type, three of Late La Tène type; my terminology here is based upon Gebhard's (1991) comprehensive study of the Manching fibulae in the context of fibula chronology for Europe as a whole. Middle La Tène type fibulae have the end of the wire foot bent back and attached to the bow. In the Late La Tène type, the foot is cast as part of the bow and thus not bent back.

The fragmentary iron fibula in Figure 6.11a probably belongs to Gebhard's Type 21a, small Middle La Tène iron fibulae with arched bow and with spring loop on top of the spring (21, fig. 7, 21a; pl. 38, especially 573, 574, 576), though the angle of the bow near the spring resembles that on his Type 19c, Middle La Tène iron fibula with attenuated bow and with sharply bent bow head (plate 34, 511. 512). For Type 21 fibulae, Gebhard suggests a dating in early La Tène D1, for Type 19 in the latter part of La Tène C2 and the beginning of La Tène D1 (95 fig. 42). Maute (1991, 393; 396 note 4) notes that in general, fibulae with the spring loop on top of the spring (*obere Sehne*) belong to La Tène C2.

The fibula in Figure 6.11b belongs to Gebhard's Type 21b, small Middle La Tène fibulae with arched bow and with spring loop under the bow (1991, 21 fig. 7, 21b; pl. 39, especially 590 and 591), a type he ascribes to early La Tène D1. Maute (1991, 393) notes that fibulae with the spring loop under the bow characteristically belong to La Tène D1.

The fragmentary bow and spring in Figure 6.11c probably belong to a fibula of Gebhard's Type 34, Late La Tène fibulae with knob on bow (1991, 27 fig. 9, 34a and 34b; 28). Although the specimen is very fragmentary, the form of the bow and of the knob is clear. This type Gebhard (1991, 95 fig. 42) attributes to the second half of La Tène D1.

The small fragmentary bow in Figure 6.11d resembles most closely a bronze fibula from Manching illustrated in Gebhard 1991, pl. 3, 49, belonging to his Group 6c, narrow band-shaped Late La Tène fibulae with decoration on the middle of the bow. This type he (1991, 95 fig. 42) attributes to most of La Tène D1.

The fragment in Figure 6.11e may be part of a Nauheim fibula, but I have been unable to find an exact parallel to this object. The shape is similar to that of many of the bronze Nauheim fibulae from Manching shown in Gebhard (pl. 4—his Type 6a), and rills along the edges are visible at the head end. Also similar to the shape of this specimen are the three iron fibulae of Gebhard's Type 27 in pl. 55, 844-846, though these examples do not have the rills. Both types 6 and 27 Gebhard (1991, 95 fig. 42) dates to La Tène D1.

In the case of the spring with fragmentary remains of bow and pin, Figure 6.11f, the four-spiral spring, with loop under the bow, is well preserved, but only a tiny fragment of the bow survives. The original was some type of Middle La Tène style arched-bow fibula, the parts surviving are similar to the specimen in Figure 6.11b, and perhaps it was the same type of fibula, but not enough of the bow survives to make a definite determination. In any case, its chronological position is primarily in the first half of La Tène D1.

The fragmentary four-spiral spring in Figure 6.11g may belong to Gebhard's Type 21b. It resembles fragments that he so classifies shown on his plate 40, 603-609, but so little of the bow survives than an attribution is uncertain.

The other six iron fibula fragments are from fibulae that belong to the same general spectrum of types as the seven discussed above. The bronze pin could come from a number of different types represented at Manching.

Thus the sample of fibulae from the University of Minnesota excavations on the Mitterfeld at Kelheim all can be attributed to La Tène D1, according to Gebhard's comprehensive chronology for the roughly 1850 fibulae (including fragmentary specimens) from Manching (see Gebhard for discussion of other relevant studies of fibula chronology). Some are attributed to the earlier part of D1, and possibly late C2, others more to the second half of D1, but with La Tène D1 only some 50 years in duration, finer delineation should not be expected at this stage.

The distribution of the seven datable fibulae is important in establishing the approximate contemporaneity of the settlement portions investigated. The specimens in Figure 6.11 a-d all came from the easternmost area, excavated in 1987—a from the cultural layer in Sector 5, c from the cultural layer in Sector 2, and d from the cultural layer in Sector 8. b was recovered in Pit 3-11-12, at a depth of 60–80 cm below the top of the subsoil.

Figure 6.11e was recovered in the cultural layer in Sector D of the westernmost trench.

The two fibulae f and g were recovered in the Pit in Sector 6 of the central area investigated in 1991.

It is significant to note that no fibulae were recovered of the types that Gebhard attributes at Manching to La Tène phases C1 or C2. The fibula sequence on the Mitterfeld at Kelheim thus seems to begin later than the sequence at Manching, and at about the same time as the fibula sequence at Altenburg (Maute 1991).

The other fibulae that have been recovered at Kelheim reflect a similar range of types and about the same chronological associations (Kluge 1987, 78-82; Etzel 1990, 36-37, pl. 85).

Coins

As Overbeck explains in his analysis of the four coins recovered, the two silver coins of the *Büschel* type date to phase La Tène D1, and the bronze coins in the period 80–50 B.C. The chronology of these four coins corresponds closely with that of other coins recovered at Kelheim (see Chapter 13).

Glass

Gebhard (1989, 7) observes that blue was the most common color for glass bracelets and beads in the Late Iron Age, and that such ornaments occur from the latter part of La Tène C and through La Tène D. Profiled bracelets of brown glass are dated by Gebhard in the late Middle and earliest Late La Tène phases (1989, 72-73). Clear glass with yellow surface treatment he similarly attributes to late Middle La Tène. Gebhard notes that especially colorful glass bracelets are characteristic of the Middle La Tène Period, while one-color and two-color bracelets are more characteristic of Late La Tène.

The chronology of glass beads is less well established than that of bracelets (Gebhard 1989, 168). Discussion of the beads we recovered at Kelheim will await further study of those objects and of beads from other contexts.

Pottery

Without a full analysis of the pottery from the excavations, only very preliminary and tentative observations can be made at this stage. Gebhard's (1989, 36-38) discussion of pottery at Manching is helpful in defining the chronological parameters for the Kelheim materials. Graphite-clay pottery with comb decoration occurs throughout the whole occupation at Manching, and thus the abundant occurrence of this ware at Kelheim confirms the contemporaneity of the settlement with Manching. Coarse comb decoration on pottery occurs throughout the occupation at Manching, but fine comb decoration, which is well represented in our Kelheim materials, dates principally to the Late La Tène phase (Kappel 1969, 55). Especially characteristic of the late forms is a fine, round-section rim, a shape that appears also on painted pottery and on the polished wheel-made pottery. As a whole, the polished wheel-turned ware occurs throughout the Manching occupation, while painted pottery is characteristic mainly of La Tène D1 (Stöckli 1974).

Chapter 7 - Wells

Other Materials

While other materials, such as iron tools and bronze ornaments, do not, in the present state of analysis, permit such good chronological control as fibulae, especially, but also coins and pottery, it is worth noting that the objects recovered at Kelheim correspond closely to those from other sites—both settlements and cemeteries—that are attributed in the literature to late La Tène C2, and especially to La Tène D1.

Absolute Chronology

As indicated in the preceding sections, most of the datable materials from our excavations at Kelheim can be assigned to the phase La Tène D1. The start of this phase is currently placed at around 130–120 B.C., on the basis of closed finds dated by Roman imports and especially of recent dendrochronological determinations on different sites in Germany and Switzerland. For recent discussion of the absolute dating of phases La Tène C2, D1, and D2, see Haffner 1974b, 1979; Furger-Gunti 1979; Furger-Gunti and Berger 1980; Hollstein 1980; Krämer 1985; Miron 1986, 1989; Fischer 1988; Jockenhövel 1990. Phase La Tène D1 probably ended sometime around 60–50 B.C., though both slightly earlier and slightly later dates have been suggested for different regions of central and western Europe.

If we use this currently-accepted chronology, then the majority of our finds from Kelheim date to roughly the period 125–55 B.C. Both the relative and absolute chronology of La Tène C2 and D continue to be much discussed, however, and it must be emphasized that these attributions are tentative. It is significant that no clearly La Tène C objects, nor clearly La Tène D2 objects, were recovered in our investigations.

According to these current understandings, the part of the Kelheim settlement that we investigated probably began at about the same time as the settlement at the oppidum of Altenburg on the upper Rhine, the open settlement at Breisach on the Rhine, and the open settlement at Basel-Gasfabrik in Switzerland. The settlement at Manching began considerably earlier, perhaps as much as a century earlier. The ending dates of Kelheim would appear to conform to those of Manching, and correspond to the approximate time that the open settlements of Breisach and Basel were abandoned in favor of newly fortified settlement sites (Furger-Gunti 1979, Furger-Gunti and Berger 1980, Fischer 1988).

Chapter 8
The Carbonized Plant Remains
by
Hansjörg Küster

In the course of the University of Minnesota excavations on the Mitterfeld at Kelheim, 18 soil samples for archaeobotanical analysis were taken and submitted to the laboratory of the Arbeitsgruppe für Vegetationsgeschichte of the Institut für Vor- und Frühgeschichte, Universität München. Each sample, consisting of five liters of loamy, sandy material, was soaked in water and screened in order to recover carbonized plant remains. Ewald Lukhaup and the author analyzed the specimens recovered and identified them using modern reference material.

The results are presented in Table 8.1. Crop plants identified include barley (*Hordeum vulgare*), millet (*Panicum miliaceum*), emmer wheat (*Triticum dicoccum*), einkorn (*Triticum monococcum*), spelt (*Triticum spelta*), and pea (*Pisum sativum*). Oats (*Avena* sp.) and rye (*Secale*) may also be present, but the specimens that may derive from these crops could not be identified at the species level. Since no concentration of grains or of chaff that can be considered a closed find was recovered, it is difficult to determine which plants were actually cultivated, and which existed as weeds in fields of other, cultivated crops. Each sample contains instead grains of several different species. The samples thus represent agglomerations of refuse, of which the plant seeds were a part. Examination of such contexts can also indicate which plants were cultivated and which were not (discussion in Jacomet, Brombacher, and Dick 1989). If a cereal crop plant is represented in many samples, then it is likely that it was cultivated. If it is not represented in many samples, then it is not likely that it was cultivated.

In the Kelheim samples, barley grains and spelt chaff fragments are the most common plant remains. Millet is next in frequency. Emmer and einkorn are rare. It is not clear whether oats and rye are present in the samples at all. Thus it is very likely that barley and spelt were cultivated at Kelheim, and possibly millet, but the other cereal crops can be regarded as weeds in the fields of the cultivated species. They were certainly not cultivated separately.

Cereals would have been dried near an open fire before consumption, but drying was not necessary for legumes. Thus cereal grains were often carbonized or burned, but legumes were only rarely so affected. The single pea identified therefore provides evidence that peas were grown on the fields at Kelheim.

In summary, it is very likely that four crops were cultivated at Iron Age Kelheim. This is a very small number. If one crop suffered from disease, a catastrophe resulted for the population. It would have been very difficult to find other crops to supply the lost nutrition. The fact that few crops were grown by prehistoric communities must have been one reason for the instability of prehistoric settlements. It is likely that a community would consider leaving its settlement after a bad harvest caused by disease of one of the few crops.

If we compare the results from Kelheim with those from other La Tène Period settlements in southern Germany, it becomes apparent that cultivation of only a few crop plants was the normal pattern, and the crops we recovered at Kelheim were common during this period (Küster 1991). Barley, spelt, and millet are recorded in almost all of them, and it is very likely that these three crops were cultivated in the catchment areas of most La Tène Period settlements in southern Germany.

Spelt is normally grown as a winter crop, whereas barley can be cultivated either as a summer or a winter crop. It is likely that spelt and barley were rotated on the fields, spelt cultivated as a winter crop and barley as a summer crop. It is not clear whether a fallow phase was included in the rotation system, as it was during the Middle Ages.

Millet was also grown as a summer crop. This plant was common in southern Germany from the

Table 8.1. Carbonized plant remains from the La Tène settlement of Kelheim-Mitterfeld.

Sample No.:	1987→ A	B	C	D	E	F	G	1990→ 2	3	4
Cultivated plants										
Avena sp.	–	–	–	–	–	–	–	–	–	–
Hordeum vulgare	1	–	–	–	3	–	1	–	2	–
Panicum miliaceum	–	–	1	2	–	–	1	–	–	–
Triticum dicoccon grain	–	–	–	2	1	–	–	–	–	–
Triticum dicoccon chaff	–	–	–	–	–	–	–	–	–	–
Triticum di-/monococcum chaff	–	1	–	–	–	–	–	–	–	–
Triticum monococcum grain	–	–	–	–	1	1	–	–	–	–
Triticum monococcum chaff	–	–	–	–	–	–	1	–	–	–
Triticum spelta chaff	–	–	2	15	4	–	–	–	–	–
Triticum sp. grain	–	–	–	4	–	–	–	–	–	–
Triticum/Secale sp. grain	–	–	–	–	–	–	–	–	–	–
Cerealia indet. grain	18	58	10	52	55	7	21	2	–	–
Cerealia indet. chaff	–	–	–	–	1	–	1	–	–	1
Pisum sativum	1	–	–	–	–	–	–	–	–	–
Collected plants										
Sambucus ebulus	–	–	–	–	–	–	–	–	–	–
Weeds										
Asperula arvensis	–	–	–	–	1	–	–	–	–	–
Atriplex sp.	1	–	–	–	–	–	–	–	–	1
Bromus arvensis	–	–	–	–	–	–	–	–	–	–
Bromus arvensis/secalinus	–	–	–	–	–	–	–	–	–	–
Bromus sp.	–	–	–	3	–	1	–	–	–	–
Chenopodium album	1	–	–	2	4	2	–	–	–	–
Carex sp.	–	–	1	–	1	–	–	–	–	–
Fabaceae indet.	3	–	–	1	3	–	–	–	–	–
Galium aparine	–	–	2	–	–	–	–	–	–	–
Galium spurium	–	–	–	–	–	–	–	–	–	–
Galium sp.	–	1	–	1	–	–	–	–	–	1
Phleum pratense	–	–	1	–	–	–	–	–	–	–
Poa annua	–	–	–	–	–	–	–	–	–	–
Poaceae	–	–	–	–	–	–	–	–	–	–
Polygonum convolvulus	–	1	–	–	–	–	1	–	–	–
Ranunculus sp.	–	–	–	–	–	–	–	–	–	–
Indeterminatae	2	–	1	5	5	1	–	1	–	1

Continued on next page

Late Bronze Age, Urnfield Period, on. This was also the time when horse breeding became common in the region, and it is likely that millet was cultivated more as horse fodder than for human consumption. Millet constitutes a good diet for horses, and horses are the only domestic animals that must be fed with fodder plants; cattle, sheep, pigs, and goats can browse in forests near the settlements. Horse breeding may have been one reason for establishing a settlement near a river. Horses could graze in the valley bottom areas, which were perhaps not as densely wooded as other parts of the landscape. Abundant grasses and grassy plants would have grown in such environments.

The weeds indicate that cereal crops were not cultivated in the valley bottoms. The species iden-

Table 8.1—Continued

Sample No.:	1991→							
	1	2	3	4	5	6	7	8
Cultivated plants								
Avena sp.	–	cf. 1	–	–	–	–	–	1
Hordeum vulgare	2	–	1	1	3	1	–	4
Panicum miliaceum	–	–	–	1	1	1	–	–
Triticum dicoccon grain	–	cf. 1	1	–	–	–	–	–
Triticum dicoccon chaff	–	–	–	–	–	1	–	–
Triticum di-/monococcum chaff	–	–	–	–	–	–	–	–
Triticum monococcum grain	–	–	–	–	–	–	–	–
Triticum monococcum chaff	–	–	–	–	–	–	–	–
Triticum spelta chaff	–	–	–	1	2	6	–	1
Triticum sp. grain	–	–	–	10	–	2	2	3
Triticum/Secale sp. grain	–	1	–	–	–	–	–	–
Cerealia indet. grain	1	7	6	14	26	21	3	11
Cerealia indet. chaff	–	–	–	–	1	–	–	–
Pisum sativum	–	–	–	–	–	–	–	–
Collected plants								
Sambucus ebulus	–	1	–	–	–	–	–	–
Weeds								
Asperula arvensis	–	–	–	–	–	–	–	–
Atriplex sp.	–	–	–	–	–	–	–	–
Bromus arvensis	–	–	–	–	–	1	–	–
Bromus arvensis/secalinus	–	–	–	1	1	–	–	–
Bromus sp.	–	–	cf. 1	–	–	–	–	3
Chenopodium album	–	–	–	–	1	–	–	–
Carex sp.	–	–	–	–	–	–	–	–
Fabaceae indet.	–	–	–	1	1	2	–	–
Galium aparine	1	–	2	–	–	–	–	–
Galium spurium	–	–	–	–	–	2	–	–
Galium sp.	1	–	–	–	–	–	1	–
Phleum pratense	–	–	–	–	–	–	–	–
Poa annua	–	–	–	–	2	–	–	–
Poaceae	–	–	–	–	–	1	–	–
Polygonum convolvulus	–	–	–	–	–	–	–	–
Ranunculus sp.	–	–	–	–	1	–	–	–
Indeterminatae	–	–	–	–	–	1	–	–

tified (e.g. *Chenopodium album*, *Polygonum convolvulus*, *Bromus arvensis*, *Galium aparine*) are common on dry, fertile, arable land. They are well represented from Neolithic times on. Their presence indicates that fields were situated on the higher valley lands above the settlement. Since land for fields is very restricted in the Altmühl Valley, we must assume that fields were also situated in the hilly regions nearby. Crops must have been transported from such fields down to the settlement. It is likely that the cultivation of crops was done by the Kelheim farmers themselves. There is no good reason to assume that a more "urban" community in the Kelheim oppidum obtained its subsistence from "rural" settlements in the surrounding area. As far as we know, there was no separation between urban and rural populations during the La Tène Period (Küster 1992). Farmers lived in the oppidum, and they grew cereals for their own consumption. Perhaps they gave a portion of their harvest to specialized crafts workers, who also lived in the settlement. This reconstruction is based on the fact that weed seeds had not been separated from the grain before the crop arrived at the Kelheim oppidum settlement. If crops had been transported from a rural to an urban settlement, they would have been winnowed and sifted, and weed seeds would have been thus separated from the crops.

Thus, four principal crops were grown by the farmers at Kelheim—barley, spelt, millet, and pea. Spelt was grown as a winter crop, barley as a summer crop. The cultivation of millet may have been connected with production of fodder for horses. The fields were probably situated above the settlement higher on the valley slopes, but perhaps also farther away. It is probable that farmers who grew the crops represented by the recovered seeds lived in the oppidum settlement. The results show that the community at Kelheim practiced typical La Tène Period agriculture. It is significant to note that the same crops were grown in southern Germany during the Roman Period, when they were consumed not only by the local population, but also by the Roman soldiers stationed in the area.

Acknowledgements

The author thanks Ewald Lukhaup and Peter Wells for their help.

Chapter 9

Vertebrate Faunal Remains from Kelheim
by
Pam J. Crabtree

Introduction

This report includes the animal bones recovered from the 1987 and 1990 seasons at Kelheim, the faunal remains recovered during the first half of the 1991 excavation season, and the animal remains recovered from the 1987 excavations by the Bayerisches Landesamt für Denkmalpflege on the Mitterfeld at Kelheim (Table 9.1). For each animal bone fragment information on animal species, body part, side, fragmentation, age at death, butchery, and osteometry was recorded using the ANIMALS program (Campana and Crabtree 1987). The ANIMALS program is a data-base manager for faunal analysis which is written in the "C" computer language. Bone measurements were recorded following the recommendations of von den Driesch (1976). Estimates of ages at death for the domestic mammals were based on both epiphyseal fusion of the long bones (Silver 1969) and dental eruption and wear (Grant 1982).

Composition of the Faunal Assemblage

The vast majority of the faunal remains are those of the domestic mammal species: pig, cattle, sheep and goat, horse, and dog. Evidence of hunting was rare, although the bones of red deer (*Cervus elaphus*) and hare (*Lepus* sp.) were recovered from the 1987 Landesamt für Denkmalpflege excavations. Species ratios (Figure 9.1) for the domestic mammals were based on fragment counts or the number of identified specimens per taxon (Grayson 1979, 1984). Pigs were the most common species (38.4%), followed closely by cattle (33.6%). Sheep and goats made up just under one-quarter of the identified domestic mammal bones (24.1%), and

Table 9.1. Animal bones identified from the Kelheim Mitterfeld excavations.

Species Identified	1987	1990	1991	BLfD
Cattle (*Bos taurus*)	125	23	21	323
Sheep (*Ovis aries*)	8	6	0	35
Goat (*Capra hircus*)	1	1	0	3
Sheep/Goat	90	12	1	196
Pig (*Sus scrofa*)	188	35	7	332
Horse (*Equus caballus*)	7	1	0	25
Dog (*Canis familiaris*)	8	0	0	16
Red deer (*Cervus elephus*)	0	0	0	2
Hare (*Lepus* sp.)	0	0	0	1
Small mammal	99	28	2	185
Large mammal	70	7	1	142
Bird	0	5	0	6
Fish	0	43	1	0
Unidentified	3046	412	59	1847
Total	3642	573	92	3113

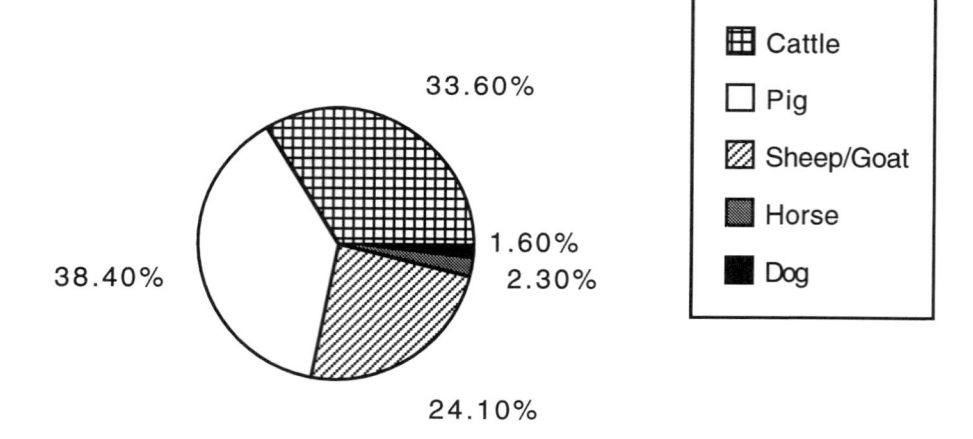

Fig. 9.1. Species ratios for the domestic animals from Kelheim Mitterfeld.

horse (2.3%) and dog (1.6%) bones were relatively rare. A small number of bird and fish bones were recovered from the Kelheim excavations, but these have not yet been identified to species. The vast majority of the fish bones were recovered from the 1990 excavations on the Mitterfeld.

Ages at Death

Analysis of ages at death focused on the cattle and pigs, since these animals made up the vast majority of the identified animal bones from Kelheim. Twenty-one pig mandibles were recovered from the excavations at Kelheim, and the vast majority are immature individuals. While some of the mandibles are incomplete and cannot be aged precisely, 15 mandibles came from pigs with worn second molars and unworn third molars or pigs whose third molars are just coming into wear. In the pig, the second molar erupts between 7 and 13 months, and the third molar erupts between 17 and 22 months (Silver 1969, 298-299). Most of the Kelheim pigs therefore appear to have been killed during the second year of life. The Kelheim assemblage also included a single mandible from a suckling pig, and a mandible from an adult pig with a heavily worn third molar. Two mandibles came from pigs with unworn second molars that were probably killed during their first year.

The data on epiphyseal fusion (Table 9.2) can provide a more detailed picture of the ages at death of the Kelheim pigs. To produce a harvest profile for the pigs, the epiphyses were grouped into early fusing (those that fuse by one year), middle fusing (those that fuse by 2.5 years), and late fusing (those that fuse by 3.5 years) categories. The epiphyseal data (Figure 9.2) indicate that about two-thirds of the pigs (68.8%) survived to more than one year of age, while less than one quarter of the pigs (23.3%) survived to more than 2.5 years of age. Less than 3% of the pigs survived to more than 3.5 years.

The ageing data for cattle present a strikingly different picture. Of the 12 cattle mandibles that were recovered from the Kelheim excavations, seven come from adult animals with worn permanent teeth. The others come from immature animals, probably killed at about 1.5 years of age.

The data on epiphyseal fusion for cattle are presented in Table 9.3. The cattle epiphyses were grouped into early fusing (by 1.5 years), middle fusing (by 3 years), and late fusing (by 4 years) categories (Figure 9.3). The epiphyseal data suggest that nearly all the cattle (95%) survived to more than 1.5 years. An additional 20% of the cattle were killed between 1.5 and 3 years, and approximately three-quarters of the cattle survived to adulthood (more than 4 years).

The critical archaeological issue is whether the inhabitants of the oppidum at Kelheim were raising their own livestock, or whether they were provisioned by farmers from the surrounding countryside. In a self-contained economy, harvest profiles should include all age classes, from neonatal mortalities to mature adults. When urban dwellers are provisioned with animals which were raised elsewhere, the harvest profiles may include an abundance of market-age animals and relatively few neonatal or older breeding-age individuals (Wapnish and Hesse 1988, 84).

The ageing data for cattle from Kelheim suggest that the residents of the oppidum may have been provisioned with cattle raised elsewhere. The

Table 9.2. Epiphyseal fusion data for all pigs from Kelheim.

Element	Age of Fusion (in years)	Number Fused	Number Unfused
Proximal Humerus	3.5	0	4
Distal Humerus	1	3	2
Proximal Radius	1	7	1
Distal Radius	3.5	0	4
Proximal Ulna	3.5	0	6
Distal Ulna	3.5	0	1
Proximal Femur	3.5	0	7
Distal Femur	3.5	1	5
Proximal Tibia	3.5	0	6
Distal Tibia	2	1	5
Proximal Fibula	3.5	0	1
Distal Fibula	2.5	0	4
Calcaneus	2–2.5	0	5
Proximal 1st Phalanx	2	1	4
Proximal 2nd Phalanx	1	1	2
Distal Metapodia	2–2.5	5	5

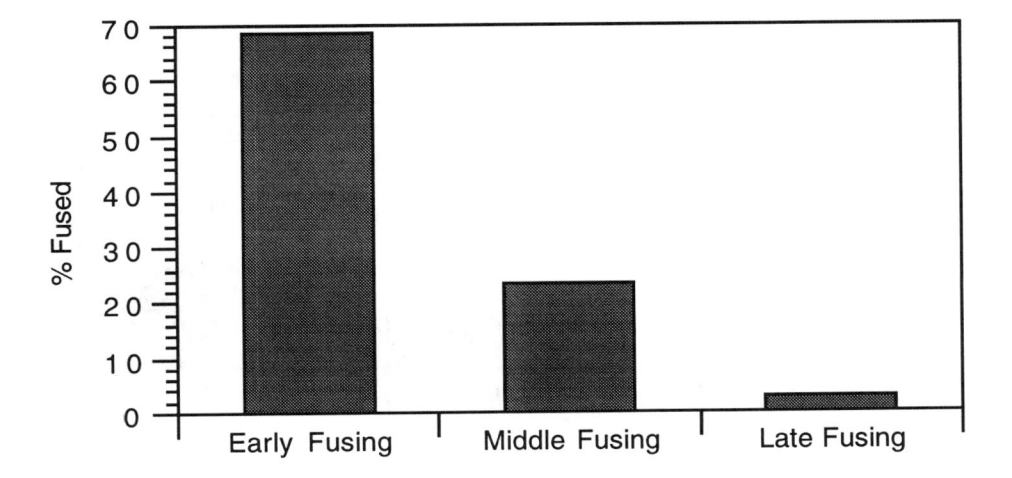

Fig. 9.2. Epiphyeal fusion data for pigs from Kelheim Mitterfeld.

Chapter 9 - Crabtree

Table. 9.3. Epiphyseal fusion data for cattle from the Kelheim excavations.

Epiphysis	Age of Fusion (in years)	Number Fused	Number Unfused
Proximal Humerus	3.5–4	1	1
Distal Humerus	1–1.5	9	0
Proximal Radius	1–1.5	8	0
Distal Radius	3.5–4	3	0
Proximal Ulna	3.5–4	0	1
Proximal Femur	3.5	4	2
Distal Femur	3.5–4	1	3
Proximal Tibia	3.5–4	2	1
Distal Tibia	1.5–2	8	2
Calcaneus Tuber	3–3.5	4	3
Distal Metacarpus	2–2.5	2	0
Distal Metatarsus	2–2.5	2	3
Distal Metapodial	2–3	1	0
Proximal 1st Phalanx	1.5	16	2
Proximal 2nd Phalanx	1.5	5	0

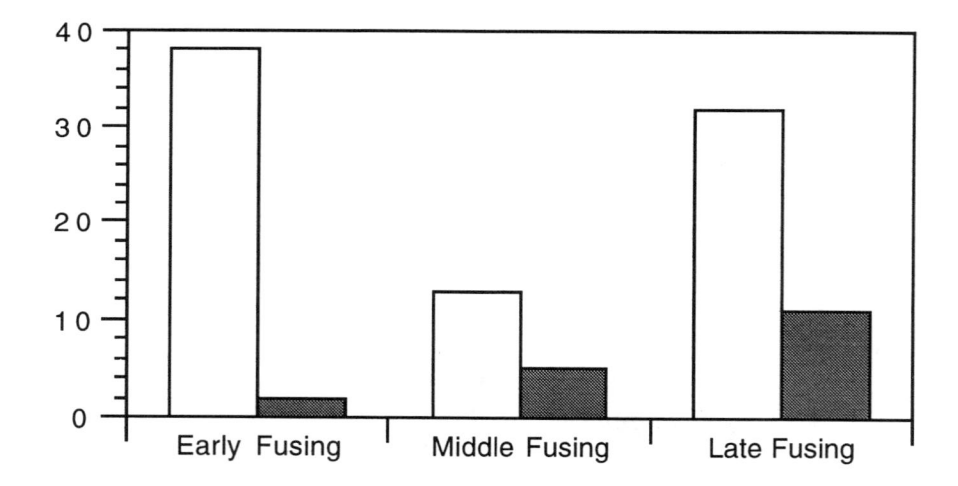

Fig. 9.3. Epihyeal fusion data for cattle from Kelheim Mitterfeld.
White bars: number fused. Black bars: number unfused.

vast majority of the cattle consumed by the inhabitants of the oppidum were mature individuals, and most of the immature animals that were consumed at the site were between 1.5 and 3 years of age at time of death. No neonatal or young juvenile cattle were recovered from the excavations at Kelheim.

The pigs, on the other hand, may have been raised within the oppidum. All age classes, from suckling pigs to mature adults, are represented in the Kelheim faunal assemblage. As Zeder (1991, 37) has recently suggested, "Pigs...would be the animal of choice for supplementary production by urban households."

Conclusions and Future Research

In general, the species ratios seen at Kelheim are quite similar to those calculated for the nearby oppidum at Manching (Boessneck et al. 1971, 145, 152; see also Gamble 1978, 339-340). The major difference is that cattle slightly outnumber pigs at Manching, while pigs outnumber cattle at Kelheim. At Manching, as at Kelheim, domestic animals made up the vast majority of the identified faunal remains, indicating that hunting played a very minor role in the urban economy of Late La Tène Bavaria. In a general survey of La Tène faunal assemblages from Europe, Bökönyi (1991, 429) has argued that hunting played only a minor role in Late Iron Age subsistence and that this is especially true of the oppida.

In this interim analysis, the entire faunal assemblage from the Kelheim Mitterfeld excavations has been treated as a single unit to maximize the data available on taxonomic abundance and ages at death for the main domestic species. Future analyses will include a more detailed contextual analysis of the faunal remains, in order to determine whether there is any significant intrasite patterning in the distribution of species and/or body parts.

Chapter 10
Iron Production at Kelheim
by
Carl Blair

Introduction

The production of iron in and around the oppidum of Kelheim has long been recognized by archaeologists as being of great local and even regional importance. Early archaeological reports focused upon the artifactual remains found within the oppidum's walls, in particular furnace bottoms (Behaghel 1940) and ore pits (Reinecke 1935). More recent work has sought to include the production of iron at Kelheim in regional inter-oppidum trade networks, particularly with the oppidum of Manching (Collis 1984a). Despite the long-term archaeological interest in iron production in and around Kelheim, there is a remarkable dearth of actual artifactual data relating to iron production. This lack of data may be partially explained by the limited amount of excavation which has occurred in and around the oppidum and partially by a lack of appropriate artifact recovery and study focused on iron-working debris in the course of many of the rescue operations.

The artifacts which allow for the study of early iron production include: iron slags, ores, smithing debris, and the remains of smelting furnaces and smithing hearths. These form a diverse assemblage of materials that can tell much about methods, scale, and organization of early iron production. Henceforth collectively referred to as IAMs, or Iron Associated Materials, these artifacts have generally been the focus of only limited attention in archaeological investigations. Among the few researchers who include IAMs as an integral part of their investigations are Peter Crew (Snowdonia National Park, Wales) and Brigitte Cech (Vienna, Austria). Crew, in the course of comprehensive excavations at small Welsh Iron Age hill settlements, has used IAMs to quantify and detail iron production (Crew 1986). Cech, through a mix of remote sensing and limited excavation, has demonstrated the possibilities of using restricted assemblages of IAMs to estimate a total level of iron production activity at a small Iron Age settlement (Cech 1988). Aside from these examples, IAMs have rarely been incorporated into site studies. A more common use of IAMs has been to focus upon a specific category of artifact, such as furnace bases, for a limited, descriptive purpose, as was done at West Brandon, Durham (Joby 1966). In other situations the existence of IAMs is virtually ignored, aside from a brief mention of their presence in association with the metallographic analyses of the iron objects themselves.

In the University of Minnesota excavations at Kelheim, a conscious effort has been made since the beginning of the project to recover fully and study the IAMs. The purpose of this recovery and study has been to develop a model of the scale and organization of the iron industry in and around the oppidum. In the three seasons of excavation, 2,534 IAMs have been recovered. These artifacts range in size from 702 grams to less than one gram, and they represent all phases of iron production from unprocessed ore to slag cakes from smithing hearth bottoms. Unfortunately, to date, no smelting furnace bottoms or smithing hearths have been recovered in situ. Over 90% of the IAMs, a total of 2,308 pieces, have been found in clear Late La Tene contexts, dated by associated pottery and metal objects. Without associated artifacts it is extremely difficult to date IAMs resulting from direct process iron production. In the Kelheim region IAMs from direct process iron production are recovered from sites ranging over an almost 2,000 year period, from c.400 B.C. to A.D. 1500. Direct process iron production, in the current archaeological context, may be defined as the reduction of an iron oxide ore to metallic iron in a smelting process in which the charge—ore and fuel—is in actual contact, and in which the operating temperatures are below the melting point of iron.

Along with the IAMs from the University of Minnesota excavations, the author studied those recovered by earlier investigations and by recent rescue excavations by the Bayerisches Landesamt für Denkmalpflege. Access to these materials was generously provided to the author by the Kelheim Archaeological Museum.

Methods of Analysis

The methods of study have been chosen to best distinguish the major characteristics of the different types of IAMs. The most significant differences have proven to be features of structure, color, chemical composition, and mineral phases present. Since it is possible to distinguish the Kelheim IAMs on the basis of major physical, chemical and mineral differences, the trace elements present and the minor mineral phases have not been expressly studied.

Two principle means have been employed to analyze the IAMs recovered. Physical methods of examination were applied in the field, and instrumental methods at the University of Minnesota. At the Archaeological Museum of Kelheim, a series of physical measurements were made of every IAM. These included determining gross surface morphology, weights, density, and colors. When identifying the IAMs' colors, both wet and dry, the Munsell Soil Color Charts were used. Such charts provided a permanent, albeit subjective, means of comparing colors of IAMs from year to year and from place to place within the areas excavated. In order to minimize the inevitable variation which occurs when determining such a subjective characteristic as visible color, a similar procedure was used with all the IAMs. The artifacts were examined in a consistent mix of natural, southern exposure, and artificial, florescent light, and the color determinations were made by one individual, the author.

A selected sample of IAMs was subjected to chemical and mineral phase analyses. Fifty-nine IAMs have been so tested, 2.6% of the prehistoric IAMs recovered. They were chosen to reflect the range of artifact types present and their distributions throughout the excavated areas. The sample was skewed towards larger IAMs. The average weight of tested IAMs is 48.8 grams, while the average weight of all IAMs is only 6.7 grams. The range in weight of tested samples is from 702.0 grams to 3.0 grams. The justification for making this skewed selection was that it was possible to select artifacts that would not be consumed by destructive testing, leaving a portion for future analysis. It was felt that allowing artifact size to be a factor in the choice of tested samples would not invalidate the results, since physical characteristics of the smaller and larger artifacts were very similar in gross morphology, colors, and density. Testing larger artifacts allowed a greater proportion of the total artifact mass to be examined. The 59 samples tested represent 17.4% of the total mass of the artifacts.

A mix of instrumental methods was used to perform the analyses. The mineral phases present were determined through powder x-ray diffraction, XRD. In XRD the sample, reduced to a fine powder, is bombarded with a stream of x-rays of constant wavelength and strength. As the sample is rotated in relation to the initial beam of x-rays, the angle and intensity of the diffracted beam of x-rays is recorded and analyzed to reveal the characteristic patterns of angle occurrence and intensity for each mineral phase present (see Goffer 1980).

Two instrumental spectrographic methods were employed to determine the chemical, or oxide, composition of the samples. These methods were induced coupled phase spectroscopy, ICP, and semi-quantitative scanning electron microscopy, SEM. In both methods the sample is bombarded with beams of varying wavelengths. When appropriate energy levels are achieved, the oxides present in the sample are excited and the presence and strength of the characteristic spectra emitted are noted.

In the 1987-1988 academic year, 10 IAMs were tested using the XRD/SEM mix. Between 1990 and 1991, 49 IAMs were tested with the XRD/ICP mix. Two samples from different parts of each artifact were taken and tested from each of the first 10 IAMs analyzed. The results were compared. Because great similarities were found in the chemical and mineral phase compositions within each pair, in the later analyses only one sample was taken from each artifact. Although only approximately 2.0 grams of sample were needed from each artifact, an average sample size of 6.0 grams was taken and powdered. This larger sample and the powdering procedure combined to minimize the potential of a particularly heterogeneous portion of an individual artifact distorting the overall results.

Data relating to artifact distributions and compositions were analyzed by a variety of statistical methods. Two competing factors influenced the level and amount of analysis. The first factor was that the sample available represented the total population of recovered artifacts. The second, and ultimately more significant, factor was that this sample population came from a minute area of the oppidum, an area equivalent to 0.01% of the total. This fact would render any detailed statistical analysis premature, particularly in view of the principle research goal of understanding iron production throughout the site. As a result, only relatively simple measures of variable normality, regression, and variance have been made which allow for reasonable, yet not excessively detailed, conclusions to be drawn.

Experimental Data and Results

Combined, the results of the physical and instrumental analyses provide a wide range of experimental data relating to characteristics and distributions of the Kelheim IAMs. On the basis of the physical data, four principle classes of IAMs were initially defined. The four classes are: tap slags, slags, slag linings/heated or fused materials, and ores. Tap slags are the remains of the molten, largely silicate waste products which were removed—tapped—from a furnace in a liquid state during the course of the smelting process. A tap slag will have clear physical signs of the frozen slag flow and often a high MnO concentration. The latter is a necessary defining characteristic of Kelheim tap slags. Slags are a catch-all classification which includes the largely silicate debris from both smelting and smithing operations. Aside from a generally glassy and/or porous appearance, slags as a whole have few specific distinguishing physical or chemical characteristics. Slag linings/heated or fused materials—I shall call them slag linings for short—are defined as the by-products of ore processing or smelting operations in which an object, generally a piece of ore, was heated but neither fully reduced nor thoroughly slagged. Many slag linings incorporate large quantities of fused and vitrified sand, while some show signs of the re-oxidation of bloom or slag fragments. Slag linings are often physically weak and very heterogeneous with visible variations between the incorporated materials. The ores are the essentially chemically unmodified raw materials of iron smelting. Both physically processed and unprocessed ores are found at Kelheim. A range in ore quality may be observed, although most sampled are of excellent quality, with high FeO and low SiO concentrations.

The instrumental analyses have served to reinforce these physically based classes and to indicate further refinements and potential subclasses. Developing reliable and distinct artifact classifications has been an essential goal of the research program. Once such classifications are established, the distribution studies necessary to explore the scale and organization of the iron industry may be carried out. I decided to make these artifact classifications in such a way as to reflect the functional divisions of iron production including ore acquisition and preparation, smelting, and bloom consolidation and forging. It was not the purpose of these analyses to further refine and explore the characteristics of the varying types of slags and ores. Such studies already exist, and indeed provided much of the basic understanding of IAMs necessary for this project (see Bachman 1982, Tylecote 1987).

The characteristics of the four classes, summarized in Table 10.1, suggest the utility of the divisions. While any given characteristic may be shared with or similar to those of another artifact class, cumulatively each class is distinct. In addition to the characteristics listed in Table 10.1, a few other features need to be emphasized. In the tap slags a very high concentration of MnO is found, an average of 8.2%. This high concentration is an indication that these slags are indeed from initial smelting operations; because of differences in the relative heats of reaction, Mn is preferentially incorporated into the slag over Fe.

The slag linings and slags are quite mixed artifact classes. While distinct from the other classes, each has a wide range of materials included within it. The slag linings tend to be heterogeneous artifacts which can include fragments of ore or slag in a fused sand matrix. Not surprisingly, the slag linings often exhibit little structural integrity and tend to be among the smallest IAMs. The slag category includes both smithing and smelting slags. The artifacts vary in composition and structure. Some of the most interesting are a few fragments of plano-convex smithing hearth bottoms, or PCBs. PCBs, as defined by Peter Crew, are slag accumulations found below the tuyeres in smithing hearths (Crew 1990). The PCBs are composed of slag nodules and drips, bloom fragments, and ash. Their characteristic plano-convex form is a result of the shallow bowl shape of most smithing hearths. Just as the presence of tap slags demonstrates smelting activities, PCBs unequivocally show that smithing operations were being carried out.

The artifacts classed as ores tend to be one of three types of material. A few, less than 5% of the total, are very poor grade goethite ores, with FeO contents of below 10%. These are interpreted as most likely either rejects or materials which entered the valley soil matrix from the ore-bearing strata in the adjacent hills through erosion. The

Table 10.1. Characteristics of Kelheim IAMs.

Artifact Class	Total Number of LaTène C/D IAMs	Total Weight	Density g/cc.	Principal Dry Colors Munsell Colors	Principal Wet Colors Munsell Colors	Gross Morphology By Observation	Number Instrumentally Tested	Ratio of FeO+MnO/SiO From SEM and ICP	Characteristic Mineral Phases From XRD
Ore	890	4,299 g	2.54	2.5 YR 4/2 2.5 YR 4/0 weak red dark gray	2.5 YR 3/2 7.5 YR 3/0 dusky red v. dark gray	solid surface with small pores, often banded colors, red	22	16.87:1	$FeO(OH)$ Fe_2O_3
Tap Slag	444	3,804 g	3.52	7.5 YR 3/0 2.5 YR 3/0 v. dark gray	7.5 YR 2/0 Black	smooth, very hard surface shiny, few pores	10	2.80:1	Fe_2SiO_4 $(Fe,Mn)_2SiO_4$
Slag Lining	344	1,678 g	2.92	7.5 YR 4/2 5 YR 4/1 dark brown dark gray	5 YR 3/1 v. dark gray	flat, solid with some signs of melting, grainy	13	0.69:1	SiO_2 $FeO(OH)$
Slag	630	5,618 g	2.52	10 YR 5/4 10 YR 5/1 yellowish brn. gray	10 YR 3/3 10 YR 3/1 dark brown v. dark gray	porous, variable hardness, strength inverse to entrapped sand	14	1.76:1	Fe_2SiO_4 FeO SiO_2

latter possibility is suggested because most of these pieces are relatively large and smooth-sided, or even rounded, suggesting a long exposure to weathering processes. The majority of the ores are very high grade, with total FeO and MnO contents of over 85%. These ores are either goethite, or a mix of hematite (syn.) and goethite. Many of the high grade pieces are quite angular, or even sharp-sided pieces about two cm in diameter. Perhaps not surprisingly this size is one which has been found to be particularly suitable in experimental smelting trials for use in direct process smelting furnaces (Gilles 1958, Crew 1991, Blair n.d.).

Artifact Distributions

Since the excavation sectors from which the IAMs were recovered ranged in size from 5 m^2 to 25.6 m^2, all the IAMs totals were recalculated using an ideal 20 m^2 sector for the purposes of the distribution studies. A 20m^2 sector was chosen rather than a 25m^2 sector, even though the standard excavated sector was 5m x 5m, because when the total area excavated was divided by the actual number of sectors the average area was closer to 20m^2 than 25m^2. The actual artifact numbers and weights were multiplied by the ideal, 20 m^2, area and then divided by the actual excavated area. This recalculation resulted in some distortion in the artifact quantities, although the relative amounts remained similar (see Table 10.2).

For each artifact class five variables were examined: total numbers, dry weight, wet weight, average weight, and density. These five variables were examined for each of five artifact groups, tap slag, slag linings, slag, ore, and the total assemblage. The distributions of these variables were examined for the areas excavated both in the units investigated in each of the three years individually and then in all of the units combined (see Figure 10.1).

The first tests were for normality. The assumption was made that a normal distribution would represent an essentially random distribution of IAMs. If a non-normal distribution was found, it would justify searching for further patterning and relationships between the variables, representing perhaps intentional activities related to iron production. The test for normality used was a rank sum equation with normality accepted or rejected at the 90% confidence level. When the materials from all excavated units were examined together, by artifact group, none of the 25 variables showed evidence for a normal distribution. But when just the units excavated in 1987 and 1990 were considered, six of the variables showed a normal distribution. These include numbers, dry weights, and wet weights from the slag lining group. The most extreme evidence for normality appeared when the units excavated in 1990 were examined alone. Of the 25 variables 18 showed evidence for normality. Only the tap slag distributions were substantially non-normal. Of the five tap slag variables only dry weight showed a normal distribution. In sum, while

Table 10.2. Effects of recalculating IAM totals.

Area/Class	Actual	Corrected for Area	Difference
Total Area	613.5 m^2	580 m^2	- 5.5%
1987	279.5 m^2	280 m^2	+ 0.2%
1990	107 m^2	100 m^2	- 6.5%
1991	227 m^2	200 m^2	- 11.9%
Ore			
Number	890	779.1	- 12.5%
Weight	4,299 g	3,717.5 g	- 13.5%
Tap Slag			
Number	444	403.5	- 10.0%
Weight	3,804 g	3,382.8 g	- 11.1%
Slag Lining			
Number	344	294.2	- 14.5%
Weight	1,678 g	1,515.4 g	- 9.7%
Slag			
Number	630	623.9	- 1.0%
Weight	5,618 g	5,386.2 g	- 4.1%

Iron Production at Kelheim

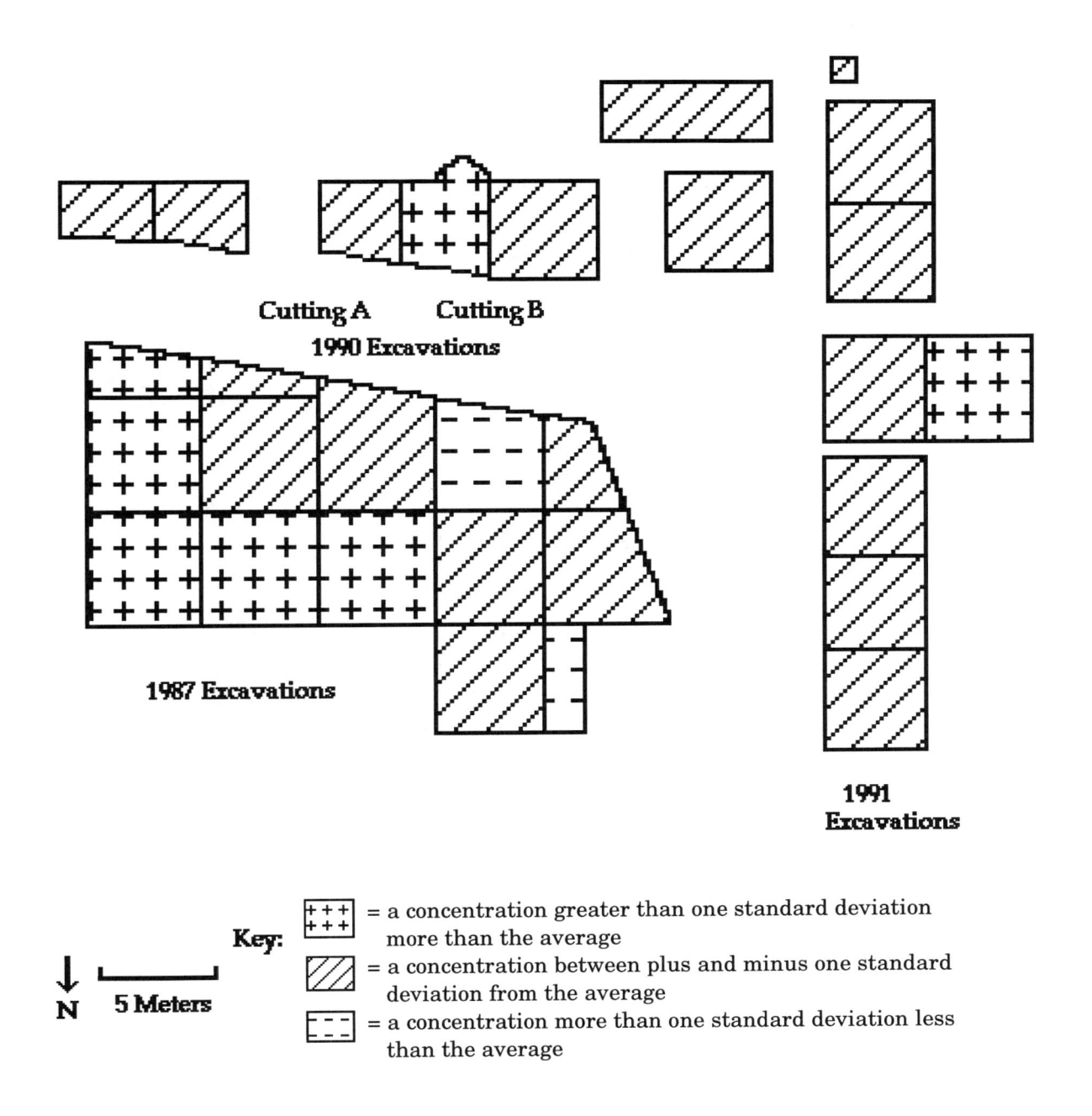

Cutting A   Cutting B
1990 Excavations

1987 Excavations

1991 Excavations

Key:
↓ N   5 Meters

+++ / +++ = a concentration greater than one standard deviation more than the average

/// = a concentration between plus and minus one standard deviation from the average

- - - = a concentration more than one standard deviation less than the average

Figure 10.1A. In this, and the succeeding two figures, 10.1B and 10.1C, the effects of plotting the IAMs either individually by each year's excavation unit or with multiple years plotted together will be illustrated. In Figure 10.1A, the distribution of the dry weight of the excavated ore is plotted, with each year's total plotted independently. One result of this approach is that a maximum of variation within each excavation area may be seen, however, the relations between the excavated areas are difficult to envision. In 1987 the average ore weight, per sector, was 254 g with a range of 10 g to 580 g. In 1990 the average weight was 105 g with a range of 21 g to 256 g. In 1991 the average weight was 11 g with a range of 0 g to 102 g.

Chapter 10 - Blair

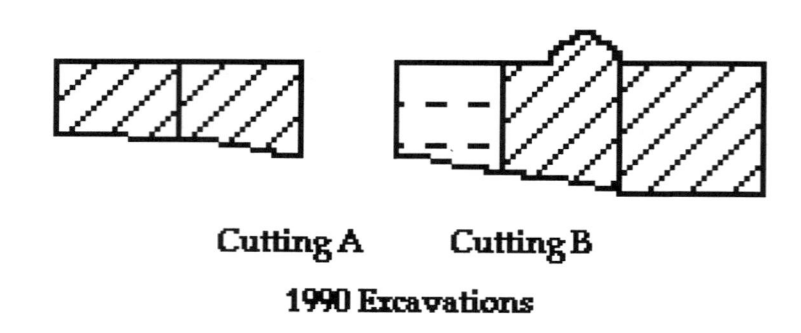

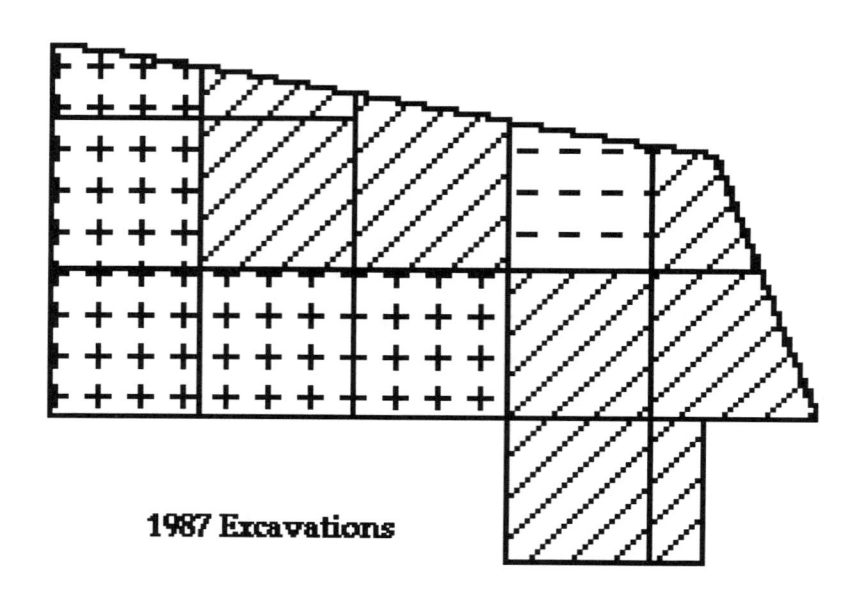

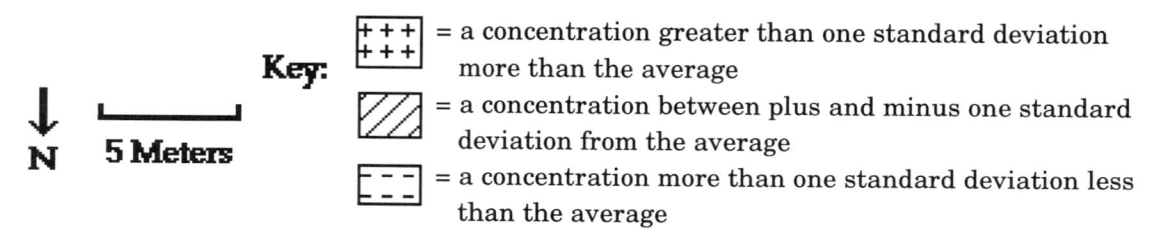

Cutting A **Cutting B**
1990 Excavations

1987 Excavations

Key:
- +++ / +++ = a concentration greater than one standard deviation more than the average
- ▨ = a concentration between plus and minus one standard deviation from the average
- - - - = a concentration more than one standard deviation less than the average

↓ N   5 Meters

Figure 10.1B. In this figure the ore weights from the years 1987 and 1990 are plotted together. As may be seen the amount of variability within each year's excavated area is decreased compared to Fig. 10.1A. In this plot the average weight is 215 g with a range of 21 g to 580 g.

Iron Production at Kelheim

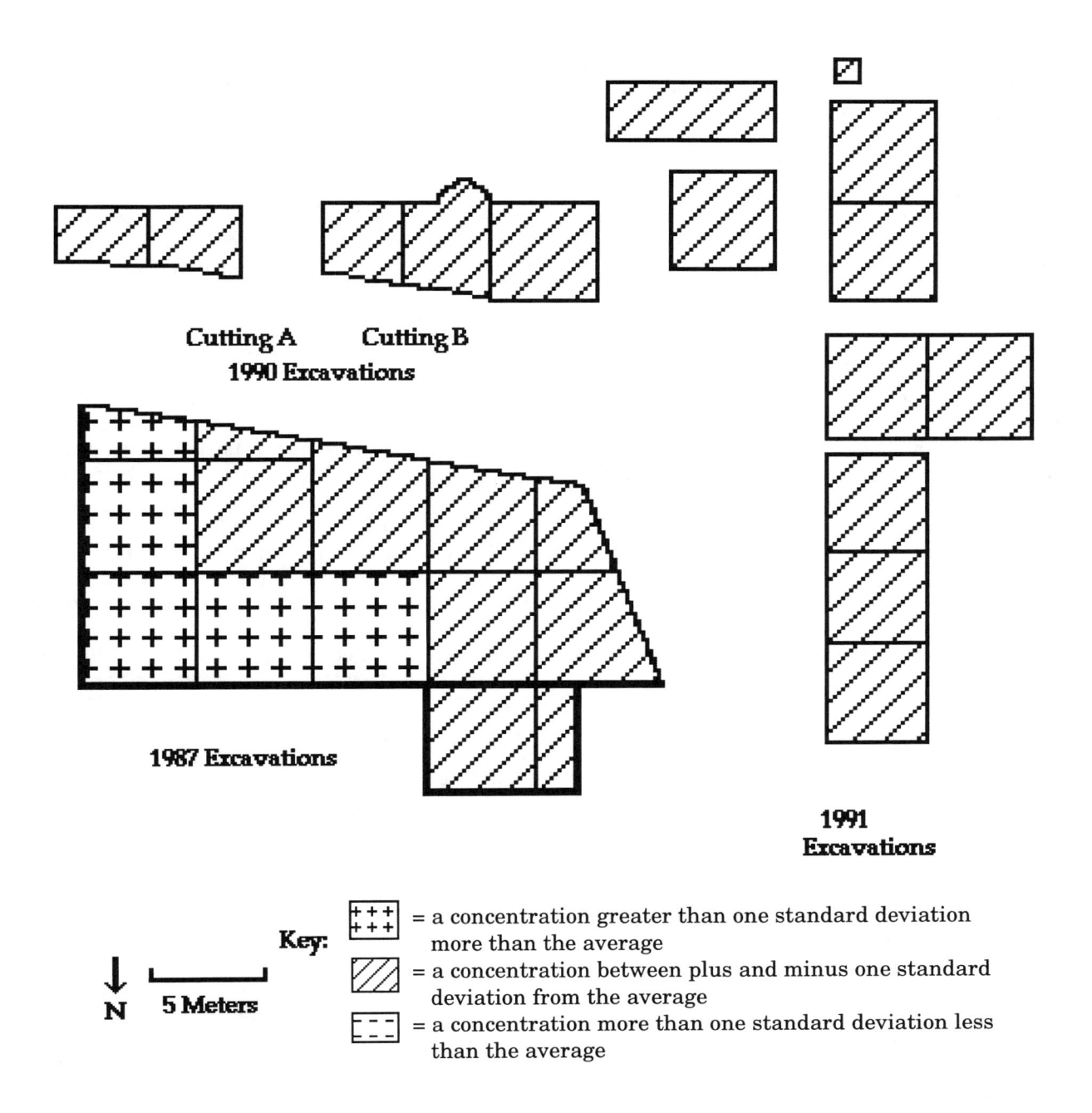

Cutting A   **Cutting B**
1990 Excavations

1987 Excavations

1991 Excavations

↓ N   5 Meters

Key:
⊞ = a concentration greater than one standard deviation more than the average
▨ = a concentration between plus and minus one standard deviation from the average
▢ = a concentration more than one standard deviation less than the average

Figure 10.1C. In this figure the dry ore weights from all three years are plotted together. The masking effect of combining multiple years reaches a maximum compared with the initial plots in Figure 10.1A. However, the variation which is still apparent may be used for complete site comparisons. In this figure the average weight is 145 g with a range of 0 g to 580 g.

for many variables, normal, or random, distributions characterize IAMs within a portion of the site when all excavated units are looked at together, non-normal, or patterned, distributions are characteristic. These distributions may reflect iron production activities on the site.

To ascertain which variables may have been related once the potential for patterned artifact distributions was demonstrated regression analyses were carried out. Strong evidence, with a minimum of a 95% confidence level, was seen for a relationship between many variables. A particularly strong relationship was consistently found between the variables for dry weight and wet weight. Within each artifact class r^2 values as high as .9872 occurred, and r^2 values in the .9000 range were standard where a value of 1.000 indicates a perfect relationship. (r^2 is the coefficient of determination, which is a dimensionless number relating to the measured variation in two variables, x and y, which expresses the proportion of variation in y which can be attributed to a linear relationship between x and y in the statistical sample (Devore and Peck 1986).) Such high values suggest that the experimental procedures for determining weights in the field were consistent and reliable. Consistent relationships were also found between certain variables in the different artifact classes, such as numbers, dry weights, and wet weights. With density and average weights, few such inter-class relationships were noted. This pattern further suggests that the defined classes represent distinct varieties of artifacts.

When analysis of variance was attempted, particularly multi-variant analysis, to test the model of whether or not the artifact distributions represent distinct patterns, clear signs emerged that such was indeed the case. Strong positive relationships exist for all the artifact classes, particularly for the tap slags. An illustration of these relationships may be seen in the distributions in Figure 10.2. When comparing the variance among the different variables strong relationships were seen for many, especially artifact numbers. Density, on the other hand, showed little to no positive evidence for a relationship.

The statistical analyses of the data strongly suggest that real differences exist in the IAM distributions. A significant concentration of tap slag is seen in the southwestern portion of the area excavated in 1987. A smaller concentration lies in the western portion of the area excavated in 1990. Slag linings are found particularly in the central portions of the 1990 area. Concentrations of ore are apparent in the northeast and eastern portions of the 1987 area. Slags are distributed relatively evenly across most of the areas investigated in 1987 and 1990, with a significant decrease in their concentration in the middle of the 1987 area. In all of the categories, IAM concentrations in the 1991 area are especially low. This low quantity of IAMs in the 1991 area may represent a space between iron production areas. In quantitative terms, the IAMs recovered in the University of Minnesota excavations are dominated by categories directly associated with the initial production of iron, ore and tap slags. The areas in which these artifacts were recovered are ones without much evidence for large post-built structures, such as those at Manching. These are areas with significant human activity, as evidenced by, for example, the ceramic assemblages. The absence of large, permanent structures, the presences of IAMs, and the distribution of ceramics suggest that these areas may have been primary production zones, virtual industrial areas. It would be reasonable to hypothesize therefore that if additional areas were excavated in the immediate vicinity, further evidence for primary production, especially the iron smelting furnaces, would come to light.

Examination of iron-working debris collected during earlier excavations and now in the Archaeological Museum at Kelheim suggests a pattern of distributions similar to that described above. Significantly assemblages with abundant tap slags, including remains of smelting furnaces, are most common near the outer wall, and on top of the Michelsberg. Both are areas thought to have been lightly settled (see Chapter 3). Assemblages with abundant PCBs and other apparent smithing slags are more common towards the east end of the oppidum, where we think the center of the settlement was located.

This distribution pattern of primary production in the settlement periphery and bloom consolidation (smithing) near the settled core of the oppidum, suggests a significant relationship between the location of the specific iron-related activity and the value of the materials worked. The primary production, the smelting, is based on the exploitation of a relatively low value material, iron ore. The smithing of the iron bloom, on the other hand, represents work done with materials into which considerable time and value have already been invested. It is hardly surprising therefore that the smithing activities are concentrated in the settled, and presumably more secure, portions of the oppidum (see Figure 10.3).

Iron Production at Kelheim

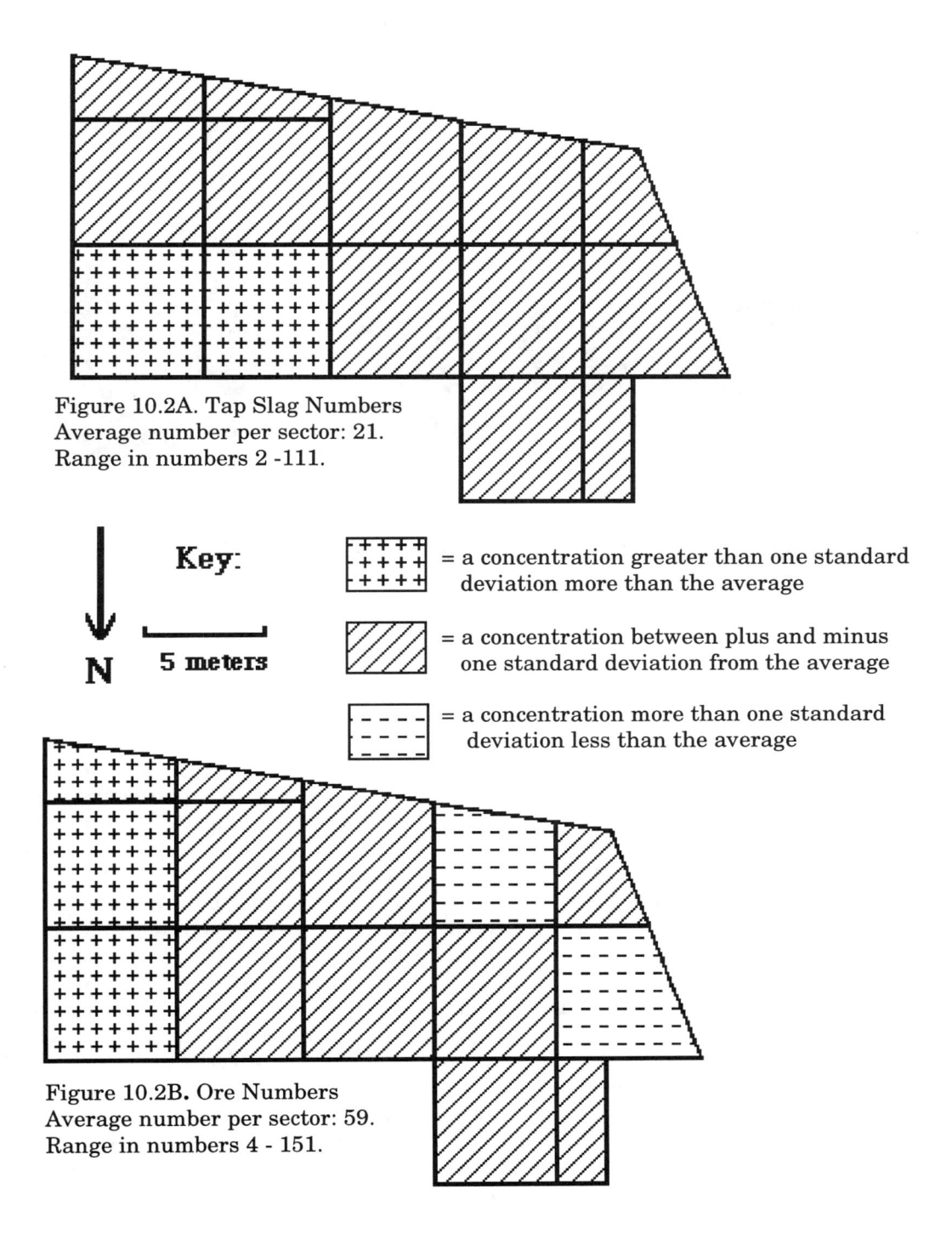

Figure 10.2A. Tap Slag Numbers
Average number per sector: 21.
Range in numbers 2 -111.

Key:

↓ N   5 meters

┼┼┼┼ = a concentration greater than one standard deviation more than the average

▨ = a concentration between plus and minus one standard deviation from the average

┄┄┄ = a concentration more than one standard deviation less than the average

Figure 10.2B. Ore Numbers
Average number per sector: 59.
Range in numbers 4 - 151.

Figure 10.2. Distribution maps of selected Kelheim IAMs from the 1987 excavation season. All totals have been corrected to the ideal 20 m² excavation sector. These two maps provide a demonstration of the variability which may be found in the distributions of the artifact types excavated during each of the seasons at Kelheim. Each artifact class in and of itself provides indications of the overall IAM patterns. This information may be expanded through the combination of many of these individual maps and also through the consideration of all five variables studied for each artifact class.

75

Figure 10.3. Representative samples of Kelheim slags and ore. From left to right they are: racked slag, ore, slag lining, and tap slag.

Conclusions

The University of Minnesota excavations do not yet provide detailed evidence as to the scale of iron production at Kelheim. A few published sources furnish some clues, especially to the location, number, and size of slag heaps located by survey and rescue work carried out from the 1930s to the 1980s (Reinecke 1935, Burger and Geisler 1983, Rind 1988). These sources provide undoubted evidence for several tens of thousands of tons of slag in and around the oppidum dating from the La Tène C/D period, an amount of slag as great as or greater than that found at any contemporary site in central or western Europe. When these quantities are viewed in association with the evidence from the University of Minnesota excavations which suggest that the different activities related to iron production were occurring in different portions of the site, a model of a dispersed, yet regionally integrated, iron production industry may be advanced. This iron production industry would have been on a greater scale and shown more integration than any previously suggested in Iron Age Europe.

Details of such a model are beyond the scope of the current work, but will be explored elsewhere (Blair n.d.). A brief summary will indicate the outlines of this model. Archaeological evidence for large-scale production slag heaps, separated work areas, and artifact distribution patterns, needs to be combined with experimental evidence regarding iron smelting, smithing, and raw material consumption (Crew 1991, Blair n.d.). When all the tasks involved in producing consolidated iron bloom are considered—mining, wood cutting, charcoal burning, furnace operations, and bloom smithing—the amounts of labor involved and materials consumed are staggering. As an example of the labor required, the following estimates are presented; they are based upon the results of an experimental iron smelting project, Smelt 1991, which I directed. In Smelt 1991 a replica iron smelting furnace, of the type used at Kelheim, was run in a full scale production smelt for eight days. To produce a single ton of consolidated bloom would require 7.4 tons of iron ore, 170 tons of wood (mostly used as charcoal), and approximately 5.5 man-years of work. If this total is expanded by the hundreds of tons of consolidated bloom assumed to have been produced each year, the economic and social impact of the iron industry on the Kelheim region can be seen to have been tremendous. An industry of such a scale would have been a defining element of the character for the entire region.

Chapter 11

Labor Specialization in Late Iron Age Temperate Europe: The Evidence from the Kelheim Iron
by
Michael N. Geselowitz

Introduction

It has long been felt that iron production played a significant role in the economy of the Late Iron Age oppida. Models to explain the rise of the oppida have emphasized either the productive capacity of iron or its role in trade with the Mediterranean region (Collis 1984b, 151-156; Wells 1984, 143-182).

Ironworking technology, introduced and developed from the Late Bronze Age onward, clearly had the potential to transform the society. Although the properties of plain wrought iron are similar to those of bronze, the raw materials for iron production are much more common than those for bronze, the previous metal of choice. The limiting factor in iron production is the intensity and specialization of labor required, especially owing to the fact that in prehistory iron could not be melted and cast like bronze but had to be hot-forged in the solid state. However, when specialization enabled the achievement of a sufficient level of technical expertise, the iron produced could become greatly superior to bronze, opening up new avenues for the use of metal in society (Geselowitz 1988; Rostoker and Bronson 1990).

One of the attractions of investigating the oppidum site of Kelheim is that earlier research and chance finds suggest that rich evidence for every aspect of iron production is present there (Collis 1984b, 151; Wells 1987, 401). The excavations by the University of Minnesota have uncovered large quantities of slag and partially processed iron ore (Wells 1987, 405; Blair, this volume) as well as some 400 objects of iron, mostly unidentifiable fragments (Wells 1987, 405; Lehman 1991).

Although the distribution of iron artifacts in the archaeological record of temperate Europe has long been a focus of study, important advances have been made in the last decade (Pleiner 1981, 1989; Scott 1990). During the Early Iron Age (ca. 800–400 B.C.), iron was used mainly for weapons which are recovered from male graves (i.e. axes, spears, knives, and, rarely, swords), small tools (knives, styli), and decorative objects (fibulae, beltplates) which are recovered from graves and settlements. These iron objects are found in limited quantities, and still do not surpass bronze objects in the archaeological record. We now know that the quality of this metal was poor. The smiths applied what was essentially a bronze-working technology to the new metal and therefore had limited control over the mechanical properties of the finished objects (Pleiner 1962, 1980, 1988; Geselowitz 1988).

By the time of the oppida, however, although cemeteries are not well known from much of temperate Europe, iron is ubiquitous on the settlements, and occurs in the form of nearly every element of the toolkit that is to characterize the European economy until the end of the medieval period (Wells 1984, 145). Furthermore, we know from the archaeometallurgical study of the major types of tools (scythes, sickles, axes, scissors, chisels, files, saws), the occasional weapon (swords, spears), and the commonplace knife (which may have been, situationally, a tool or weapon) that the smiths of the oppida had a range of techniques at their disposal for improving the mechanical properties of their finished products (Pleiner 1980, 1982; Ehrenreich 1985; Geselowitz 1988). The smiths could produce an object made of a complex combination of pure wrought iron and steel (carburized iron), heat-treated to take advantage of the properties of the two materials. This procedure seems to have been done about half the time in the case of the large tools and weapons that have been the primary focus of analysis, with no difference in the frequency of the finishing techniques observed in regards to object type or place of manufacture (Pleiner 1980, 404; 1982; Ehrenreich 1985).

The Kelheim Iron Objects

What is most striking about the Late Iron Age, however, is the range and number of small commonplace, everyday objects of iron recovered from every oppidum (Wells 1984, 145). Among the approximately 180 iron objects from the recent excavations at Kelheim that were identifiable by type, none were large tools, making the distribution somewhat different from Manching and other partially excavated oppida (Jacobi 1974; Wells 1984, 143-146); this anomaly could easily be due to the small sample size. About one-quarter of the Kelheim objects are small tools (needles, knives) and about one-quarter are decorative objects (fibulae, belthooks, rings). Over one-half of the objects are architectural elements (nails, rivets, clamps, keys), and this distribution does agree with the data from contemporary sites.

In other words, one of the major technical innovations of the Late Iron Age was the use for the first time of metal, in the form of iron, in construction. This fact must surely influence our understanding of an Iron Age society and the role of iron in the development and functioning of the oppida. Yet almost none of this class of objects has been analyzed archaeometallurgically.

The exception is Ehrenreich (1985) who analyzed 26 nails as part of his study of 503 iron objects from Iron Age (550–50 B.C.) southern Britain. Much of his overall material was from the end of this time period, which coincided with the Late Iron Age on the continent, and during which large hillforts appeared in southern England, although 22 of his 26 nails come from a poorly dated context at the small site of Winnal Down. Furthermore, it is debatable whether these English hillforts are comparable with oppida (Wells 1984, 158). I will return to Ehrenreich's results below.

I have therefore undertaken the preliminary study of the iron from the recent excavations at Kelheim by focusing on the architectural elements and analyzing metallographically three knives (to be able to compare with knives from other oppida for control), six nails, three rivets, two clamps, and a key.

Results

The metallographic data are summarized in Table 11.1. The microstructures of the knives (Figure 11.1) indicate that each was made by piling together alternating sheets of iron and steel, and quench-hardening the resulting blade. This technique represents the height of the craft of the Late Iron Age blacksmith, and the result would have been a superior object for use as a weapon or, more importantly, as an everyday tool for a great variety of purposes.

The architectural elements, on the other hand, were made of very inhomogeneously carburized steel, some of which, for example rivet KI-2 (Figure 11.2), were completely pure wrought iron. These would have had inconsistent mechanical properties, and the best of them would not have been very hard.

Discussion

These results are unsurprising, however, as such elements would have needed to be only hard enough to enter wood once, perhaps with the aid of a pilot hole. After that, hardness would even be a handicap if accompanied by brittleness. In fact, we know from historical studies of nails that if a nail deforms slightly upon entering the wood, it holds the wood more firmly. Barring that, a carpenter will often "cinch" a nail by bending over the tip, something that could not be done to brittle steel without breaking it (Geselowitz 1991).

In other words, the Kelheim smiths had a wide range of techniques that they could apply, but chose to use "appropriate technology" for architectural elements. This technology enabled them to turn out larger numbers of these objects than if they produced them with more complex techniques, and it enabled them to conserve superior raw material that could be put to better use elsewhere.

These data match those of Ehrenreich's (1985) study of Iron Age English iron objects from both large oppidum-like sites and their smaller neighbors. Ehrenreich, like other researchers, does not focus on architectural elements. His discussion of the other artifact types indicates that the state-of-the-art of iron production in England was behind that of the Continent, but that, while heat-treating was unknown, many objects had significant carbon contents, and piling was sometimes employed. One must go to the complete table of results in his appendices to learn of the microstructure of the 26 nails he studied, and it turns out that only one had any appreciable carburization.

Interestingly, Ehrenreich's only comment on the nails is to note that they tended to be made from an ore considered superior because it produced low-phosphorus iron, a less brittle, though incidentally less hard, final product (1985, 79). In his sample this raw material is otherwise used only at large sites for producing artifact types which Ehrenreich perceives to be of greater social value than average. Ehrenreich attributes this pattern to the idea that iron nails "may have been regarded as prestige items during the Iron Age" (1985, 79-80).

I consider such a suggestion unlikely, given the number and distribution of nails in the archaeological record. Either this result is due to geographical skewing (85% of Ehrenreich's nails are from one site, while the other artifact types in his sample have better distribution) or else, despite the low social value of nails, it was necessary to use the better iron to produce them, because high-phosphorus iron would have been too brittle to perform as described above.

From these data Ehrenreich suggests that there were groups or families of smiths, each with proprietary secrets, and that some of these were better at ironworking than others. Some may even have been good enough to support themselves by specializing in certain tool types. The larger sites would have been better able to attract and maintain the better and/or more specialized smiths. However, poor quality artifacts were produced on even the largest sites, and a small site might be fortunate enough to have a master smith (Ehrenreich 1985, 73-83).

Ehrenreich (1985, 83) warns against supposing "an established hierarchy of blacksmiths in the Iron Age" as has been proposed by others. His model matches that of Wells (1984, 148), who also points out that the archaeological evidence from the Late Iron Age does not support the existence of complete specialization of production, but admits that there were probably superior smiths or groups of smiths, and that these would have been attracted to the oppida.

Certainly the overall evidence from Kelheim suggests at least partial site specialization in iron production. Such site specialization from "free Europe" during the Roman period is well attested (e.g. Piaskowski 1985). In addition, one cannot rule out the possibility that the specialists making the high-quality knives were different from the individuals producing the architectural elements. We know that from at least early post-medieval times in England, nail-making was a regionally-based cottage industry dominated by women and children (Willets 1987). When the raw material for

Figure 11.1. Photomicrograph of section of edge of iron knife from Kelheim showing piled structure and heat treatment, with light bands of relatively pure iron alternating with dark bands of moderate carbon steel, and needle-like martensite structure at tip. Etched in nital, 100X.

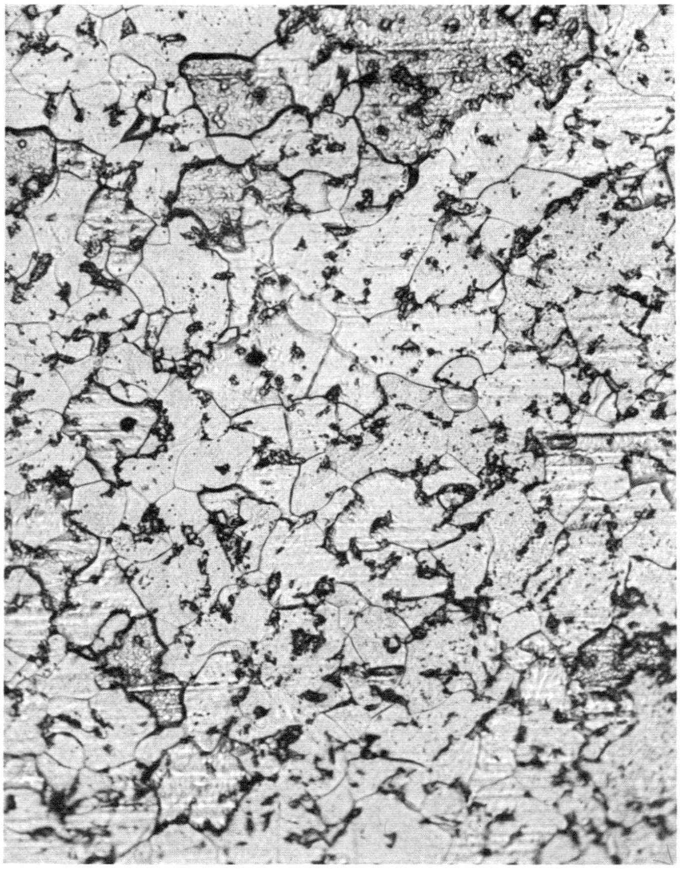

Figure 11.2. Photomicrograph of cross section of shaft of nail from Kelheim showing plain wrought iron structure of light, polygonal crystals of relatively pure iron interspersed with numerous dark slag inclusions. Etched in nital, 100X.

nails was supplied in the form of rods, the series of movements necessary to produce them was not complex, and even children could be easily trained to carry out the task. Such production can be performed during times when subsistence activities are minimal (i.e. winter in an agricultural society), and the objects easily stored.

Thus the evidence from Kelheim might suggest that there were specialized iron-smelters who supplied raw material both to master smiths, who would have been full-time specialists, and to part-time producers of more mundane objects. The master smiths could have varied in their own abilities. Since the iron would have been supplied to part-time producers already partially processed, there is the possibility that the master smiths were also the smelters, and that they distributed some partially processed raw material to part-time specialists, while keeping for themselves the material they wanted and needed to produce better objects. Such patterns of production are known ethnographically (e.g. van der Merwe and Avery 1988).

If this was the case in the Late Iron Age, the smelters/master smiths are likely to have resided at the oppida, while the part-time specialists could have been distributed throughout the society. It particularly makes sense for each small settlement to have had an individual who could make or repair simple agricultural tools, as well as architectural elements, but small settlements may not have been able to support smelting operations.

Conclusions

The tentative discussion of craft specialization above must wait for further evidence so that it can be tested and refined. Certainly what is needed are further analyses of the full range of iron artifacts from several oppida as well as from related smaller sites, and also a continued search for and study of production areas. However, the very general picture of the Iron Age development of iron technology is clear and of interest to archaeologists and historians of technology alike.

The level of technology later applied to nails was available in the Early Iron Age, yet architectural elements of iron were not produced. At the same time, iron knives and axes, whose superiority to bronze would have to await the technical developments of the Late Iron Age, were produced

Table 11.1. Summary of metallographic results. Microhardness is Rockwell scale, measured with a load of 100 grams and a load time of 30 seconds. All sector numbers refer to 1987 area.

Object # (lab)	Object Type	Field #	Context	Structure	Microhardness
KI-1	clamp	B136555	Sector 10 top; surface 50-75 cm	case-hardened	150-200
KI-2	rivet	B136576	Sector 5 top; surface 50-75 cm	pure wrought iron	100-120
KI-3	clamp	B136730	Sector 9 top; surface 50-75 cm	pure wrought iron	100-120
KI-4	knife	B136578	Sector 7 top; surface 50-75 cm	piled steel, quenched	150-200 (iron) 700-750 (steel)
KI-5	nail	B136555	Sector 10 top; surface 50-75 cm	inhomogeneous steel, P present	160-340
KI-6	nail	B136561	Sector 6 top; surface 50-75 cm	pure wrought iron	100-120
KI-7	nail	B136752	Sector 3 Pit 1987/3-11-12	inhomogeneous steel	160-260
KI-8	rivet with sheet	B136543	Sector 3 top; surface 50-75 cm	rivet pure wrought iron, sheet piled steel	100-120 (rivet) 160-220 (sheet)
KI-9	knife	B136525	Sector 3 top; surface 50-75 cm	piled steel, quenched	150-200 (iron) 700-750 (steel)
KI-10	rivet with sheet	B136562	Sector 10 Pit 1987/6-10	rivet case-hardened, sheet piled steel	100-180 (rivet) 190-270 (sheet)
KI-11	key	B136477	Sector 10 top; surface 50-75 cm	pure wrought iron	100-120
KI-12	nail	B136506	Sector 5 top; surface 50-75 cm	pure wrought iron	100-120
KI-13	knife	B136504	Sector 5 top; surface 50-75 cm	iron-to-steel welded	120-150 (iron) 200-250 (steel)
KI-14	nail	B136583	Sector 6 top; surface 50-75 cm	inhomogeneous steel	200-250
KI-15	nail	B136732	Sector 9 top; surface 50-75 cm	pure wrought iron	85-100

in the Early Iron Age. It would seem that rather than the iron technology somehow causing the growth of the oppida, we have to see Iron Age society as having developed to the point where there was sufficient specialization, organization, communication, and level of production that it was worthwhile for the existing technology to be used to spend a great deal of time making many simple objects as well as fewer objects of greater complexity. This point holds true even if the new producers were not full-time specialists and not particularly well-versed in the full range of ironsmithing techniques. At the same time, the decision to produce iron nails and other architectural elements in bulk would have enabled an increase in the scale and speed of construction and therefore would have fed back into the increasing social complexity that was occurring at the oppida.

Chapter 12

Paste Groups as a Unit of Analysis: Preliminary Report on the Ceramics from the 1987 Excavations on the Mitterfeld
by
Susan Malin-Boyce

Introduction

My objective here is to classify the ceramics recovered during the 1987 excavation by the University of Minnesota on the Mitterfeld at Kelheim. My typology is drawn particularly from the research at Manching. I rely principally on paste groups as the basis for analysis for two reasons. First, paste can be identified on even very small sherds. Second, a strong correlation exists between paste groups and vessel forms. Thus, paste groups may provide a means of studying individual vessels represented at the site.

This research follows closely the work of four investigators who published analyses on ceramics from Manching. Kappel (1969), Maier (1970), Pingel (1971), and Stöckli (1979a) provide the basic reference for classification of ceramic types for Late Iron Age Bavaria.

During the 1987 excavation season, the University of Minnesota team recovered a total of 11,722 sherds of Late Iron Age pottery from an investigated area of 280 m^2 on the settlement. The study upon which this paper is based included 10,918 sherds with good provenance information. Those sherds without clear contexts are not considered in this analysis.

Research Design

Data recorded for each sherd are as follows:
1. Provenance of the sherd.
2. Characteristics of paste.

This determination is based on visible inclusions. They are comprised of both mineral and organic tempering materials. Individual paste groups were divided into six categories listed in Table 12.1, and described in more detail below. Observations were also made with respect to paste color.

3. Vessel part.

In many cases large pieces of ceramics made it easy to ascertain what part of the vessel was represented. However, 52.9% of the sherds were designated as unknown during recording. The majority of these were too small or too badly exfoliated to warrant confident identification. In addition, some sherds, while sufficiently large, were broken in such a way as to make it impossible to say whether they were portions of base, beaded shoulder, or lid. This problem arose especially in the case of fine wheel-thrown ceramics with pastes including mica.

4. Vessel form.

Several vessel forms are readily identifiable. These include the so-called *Kochtopf* ("cooking pot"; Kappel 1969) (Figure 12.1), and *Wulstrandtopf* ("bulging-rimmed jar"; Stöckli 1979a), as well as the ubiquitous bowl with an in-turned rim (Pingel 1971; Stöckli 1979a) (Figure 6.1, top left).

5. Decoration.

This includes slip paints, incised patterns, and plastic features.

6. Condition of preservation.

Measurements of size and weights were taken for selected sherds. These data were gathered for future analysis of deposition. In addition, rim sherds greater than 3 cm in length were measured for inside rim diameter.

All Late Iron Age sherds were sorted by context into groups divided first by paste type and then by categories of vessel part for the purpose of correlating paste groups with morphological types. Comments on decorative features and the appearance of sherds were collected with a view toward patterns of use, discard, and deposition of these ceramics. The data were entered into the database management program Paradox 3.5 (Borland International 1990) and subsequently imported into

Figure 12.1. Sherd of a characteristic *Kochtopf* with comb decoration from the Mitterfeld at Kelheim.

Access (Microsoft Corporation 1992). Four database tables were developed for this analysis. The first contains records for all 10,918 sherds, and includes clusters for sherds with like characteristics. A second contains information for the 619 rim sherds regardless of whether or not they can be associated with particular vessel forms. A sample of 126 sherds comprises the third database table. Bernd Engelhardt of the Bayerisches Landesamt für Denkmalpflege kindly allowed me to bring these to the United States for microscopic analysis. The fourth database table contains context information throughout the excavated area in order to maintain artifact provenance. The rationale for separating these datasets was to prevent the collected information from becoming unwieldy. Because both Paradox and Access are relational database management systems, these separate sets of data may easily be cross referenced. These tables are the basis for the ceramic data outlined below.

Paste Groups

Of all the sherds, 66.2% contain a mineral coarse fraction. This fraction consists primarily of mica, quartz, and feldspar, in varying quantities. In some cases small specks of what appears to be iron ore may have been utilized as temper. Even occasional bits of worked iron have found their way into these pastes. In addition, 6.4% of all sherds contain some portion of the graphite-bearing clays described in Kappel (1969). Finally, 27.4% of all sherds contain organic materials in the form of chaff and seeds (Table 12.1).

Mineral Inclusions

Distinctions between the following minerals are preliminary.

Mica

There are few pastes from which mica is absent. This paste group, represented by 4,879 sherds, is a catch-all for pastes that do not exhibit another dominant substance and that contain little coarse fraction. Pastes of this type appear to have been used for both hand-built and wheel-thrown vessels. Mica is especially common in vessels of the burnished wheel-thrown type (*glatte Drehscheiben-*

keramik; Figure 6.4, top left), and in vessels with red and white slip decoration. Jars and everted-rim pots and bowls of the types discussed by Pingel (1971) are present at Kelheim. Red and white slip painted vessels are primarily open and closed mouthed jars, or *Flaschen* ("bottles") in the German literature (Maier 1970). Sixty-five sherds bearing paint were recorded in the sample. Without exception there was much visible mica in each of these sherds. Concentrations of mica are also present in fine wares. These are wheel-thrown, burnished or comb decorated, typically thin-walled small pots and bowls. Unlike the slip painted paste, which was in all but one instance orange, these small vessels are generally gray or dark brown—sometimes appearing almost black. Smooth pastes containing quantities of visible mica were also used for in-turned rim bowls though generally with the addition of small amounts of organic material (chaff). The single example of a sieve bottom bowl is of this paste type.

Fine Sand

Approximately 2.7% (298 sherds) of the specimens contain fine sand of the type that Stöckli (1979a) notes for Manching. Of 52 rim sherds of this paste group, the majority are the bulky rounded type associated with *Kochtöpfe*. At this time the source of this fine sand has not been identified.

Coarse Sand

A total of 2,053 sherds contain varying quantities of mica, quartz, and feldspar, along with other as yet unidentified sands. The basis for differentiating fine and coarse sand is grain size. At this stage I am unable to distinguish between natural coarse fraction and temper. The deliberate and consistent use of quartz in pastes of the *Kochtopf* vessels, however, suggests that the makers used quartz to resist thermal shock. This advantage would be especially important in vessels that were heated regularly. Additional data were collected on 247 sherds from vessels of the *Kochtopf* type. These vessels are readily identified by both their unique rim style and the presence of a vertical comb decoration over the entire pot. As such, they present an opportunity to isolate the relationship between paste type and vessel form. Potters of the Late Iron Age utilized some pastes preferentially for certain types of vessels. Of the 247 sherds, 98 exhibited the coarse fraction of this paste group (Table 12.2).

Graphite

Graphite-clay deposits are located to the east at Passau on the German-Austrian border and in southern Bohemia (Kappel 1969, 28-29). Clays containing graphite appear to have been utilized in two ways. The earlier use, which is less observed during the period under discussion, is as an external application, burnished onto the surface of vessels. The more common use of graphite-clay in the Late La Tène Period was as an additive to other clays. The exclusive use of graphite-clay and blended clay mixtures in the Mitterfeld ceramics appears in the *Kochtopf*. Of the aforementioned subset of 247 sherds displaying characteristics identifiable with the *Kochtopf* form, 56.7% contain varying quantities of graphite.

Kappel (1969, 19) found graphite content to

Table 12.1 Paste groups.

	Number of Sherds	Percent
I. Mineral Inclusions		
Mica	4879	44.7
Fine sand	298	2.7
Coarse sand	2053	18.8
Graphite	691	6.4
II. Organic Inclusions		
Chaff/Seed	2862	26.2
Fine seed	135	1.2
Total Sherds:	10918	100.0

Table 12.2 Data subset collected on *Kochtopf* vessel form reflecting use of graphite and quartz temper.

	Number of Sherds	Percent
1. Quartz temper	98	39.7
2. Surface graphite	9	3.6
3. Moderate graphite blend	19	7.7
4. Dominant graphite blend	41	16.6
5. Graphite-clay	80	32.4
Total Sherds:	247	100.0

vary from 1 to 83%. While examining *Kochtöpfe* I distinguished five categories of graphite content:

1. No visible graphite.
2. External application of graphite.
3. Graphite blended with other clays such that the color of the paste was not dominated by graphite. This category includes blends in which graphite has been reprocessed as a grog temper that appears as specks throughout the paste.
4. Concentrations of graphite such that the color is dark metallic gray. The paste retains a hardness and mineral coarse fraction that differentiate it from category 5.
5. Graphite-rich pastes that are soft, very dark (Munsell 2.5YR 4/0) and metallic in appearance, and can be used to write with, like a pencil. Kappel (1969, 24) contends that the graphite is conducive to uniform heating as well as heat retention. Also, graphite reduces drying time of vessels during production and is an excellent temper to increase resistance to thermal shock (Arnold 1985, 97). All of these qualities would make it a suitable additive for use in cooking pots. Of the subset of *Kochtöpfe* 32% contain this category of graphite.

Organic Inclusions

In all of the pastes described below, organic inclusions occur together with the mineral inclusions identified above. The distinction between them was made on the basis of the predominant material observed.

Chaff/Seeds

Chaff temper occurred in 2,862 or 26.2% of the sherds. Identifying this material as temper assumes that it was deliberately added to the paste. This inference was made based on the uniformity in size (approximately 5 mm x 1 mm), of the chaff and seeds included. Uses for chaff-tempered pastes in the Late Iron Age included manufacture of the large *Wulstrand* jars, as well as bowls with in-turned rims. The advantage of adding organic materials to pastes is an increased porosity that lowers firing temperature, reduces firing time, and reduces the risk of thermal shock during the firing of large, thick-walled vessels. However, this same quality may have made these vessels unsuitable for purposes other than dry storage. They would have required additional internal preparation, such as the application of pitch, in order to make them less permeable for storage of liquids. Sherds of this type are poorly preserved because of their extreme porosity. Often these sherds are fractured through the profile, making it difficult to determine the original thickness of the vessel. Bowls with in-turned rims made of this paste generally contain far less organic material with little or no coarse fraction. In addition, both the exterior and interior surfaces of the bowls are frequently scraped or smoothed, thereby thinning the walls and reducing porosity.

Fine Seeds

A second type of paste with somewhat less porosity includes small round seeds. Sherds with these seeds do not contain visible chaff. This paste appears infrequently, in 1.2% of the sherds. It was used primarily for bowls with in-turned rims.

Surface Treatment

The dominant decorative technique for ceramics in this assemblage is a vertical comb-incised pattern. This pattern appears on *Kochtöpfe* and thin-walled fine wares. Of the fine ware sherds, 15.2% exhibit an elaborate criss-cross comb decoration (Figure 12.2). Most of the comb-decoration can be divided into one of three patterns.

1. Crude, freehand incising of wide vertical parallel lines, often made when the paste was still wet and soft.
2. Medium-width comb incising done when the vessel was partially dry or "leather hard" (Figure 12.1).
3. Fine comb pattern also incised when the vessel was leather hard.

Combs of the type used to apply the decoration have been recovered in Late Iron Age contexts at other sites and are made of bone, wood, or metal. The total number of comb decorated sherds in my sample is 764; 237 of these are of the mica-bearing fine ware type, and 160 contain graphite.

A second decorative technique, represented by only 65 sherds, makes use of red and white slip paints. These slips (Cumberpatch and Pawlikowski 1988, 188) are clay based and rely on inorganic substances for coloring (Figure 12.3). They are particularly vulnerable to moisture and abrasion upon excavation. Very few substantial portions of slip decorated pattern are present in the sherds utilized for this analysis.

Figure 12.2. Sherd with fine criss-cross comb decoration from the Mitterfeld at Kelheim.

Figure 12.3. Sherd with slip decoration from the Mitterfeld at Kelheim.

Conclusion

My goal has been to carry out an initial classification of one assemblage of ceramics recovered on the Mitterfeld. The evidence demonstrates the presence of a variety of vessel types that were in use at the oppidum. These include *Kochtöpfe* tempered with quartz and graphite, wheel-thrown jars and bowls, red and white slip painted jars and bottles, small decorated fine ware vessels in the form of pots and bowls or cups, and large organic-tempered jars. The limited array of Late Iron Age ceramic types, and the preference of Iron Age potters for certain pastes for specific vessel forms, facilitates quantification. The diagnostic sherds recovered during the 1987 excavation are chronologically consistent with a La Tène D1 occupation of the Mitterfeld.

Acknowledgments

I gratefully acknowledge the following individuals for their contribution to this research: Professor Peter S. Wells for his support in providing me with the opportunity to work with this material, Professors Rita P. Wright and Pam J. Crabtree for their encouragement and advice, and Doctors Bernd Engelhardt and Michael M. Rind for their guidance and continued interest in my work.

Chapter 13

The Four Celtic Coins

by

Bernhard Overbeck and Peter S. Wells

Circumstances of Recovery

In the course of the excavations conducted in 1987 by the University of Minnesota, four Celtic coins were recovered; none were found on the parts of the settlement explored in 1990 and 1991. The same techniques of excavation were employed during all three seasons, thus coins were equally likely to be recovered throughout the course of our investigations.

Figure 13.1 shows the locations at which the four coins were recovered. The contexts in which coins are found on settlements may help us in understanding the economic significance and the function of Celtic coins (on function, see Overbeck 1980; Kellner 1990; Steuer 1987, 410-423). I list the coins in the order in which they were recovered.

1. July 3, 1987, on the surface of the cultural layer in association with abundant pottery and iron slag.

2. July 13, 1987, high in the cultural layer in association with a layer of limestone pieces ranging from the size of an egg to that of a fist, together with pottery, animal bones, and a small number of iron and bronze objects.

3. July 23, 1987, just west of the circle of large limestone pieces in the lower part of the cultural layer.

4. August 14, 1987, near Number 3, at about the same depth.

Discussion

All four coins were recovered in association with the cultural layer, either within it or on its surface. None were found in the settlement pits, although the pits contained substantial quantities of pottery and animal bones. All soil from all pits was screened through hardware cloth of 0.25 inch (0.635 cm) mesh, hence it is unlikely that coins in the pits were missed. Although four coins constitute only a very small sample, the consistent occurrence of these specimens in the cultural layer raises important questions.

Could the occurrence of the coins in the cultural layer, but not in the pits, be explained chronologically? Stöckli (1974) and Sievers (1989) have shown that at Manching the differential distribution of different types of objects on the settlement surface can be interpreted in terms of chronological distinctions. Different parts of the settlement at Manching were built up at different times, as chronologically diagnostic objects indicate. We must ask therefore whether the pits at Kelheim could possibly be earlier than the cultural layer, and whether the coins could have come into regular use after the pits had already been filled. According to present evidence, such a situation seems unlikely. The pottery and other materials from the cultural layer appear to be chronologically indistinguishable from those from the pits, though future studies, especially of the ceramics, could alter our understanding of the fine chronology of the settlement features. For Manching, Gebhard (1991, 52-70) argues that the pits contain the same materials as the cultural layer, and that situation seems to pertain to Kelheim as well.

The distribution of the coins at Kelheim more likely depends upon the use to which they were put. The pits contain mainly rubbish, especially pottery sherds and animal bones. We do not yet know what purpose each pit served, but hope through ongoing analysis to ascertain the function of each. The small pits in the southwestern and southeastern parts of the surface in Figure 13.1, for example, were probably postholes. One of the larger pits may have served as a well. When the pits no longer served their original purposes, rubbish accumulated in them. The inhabitants of the settlement may have thrown rubbish into the disused pits; or broken pottery, animal bones, and

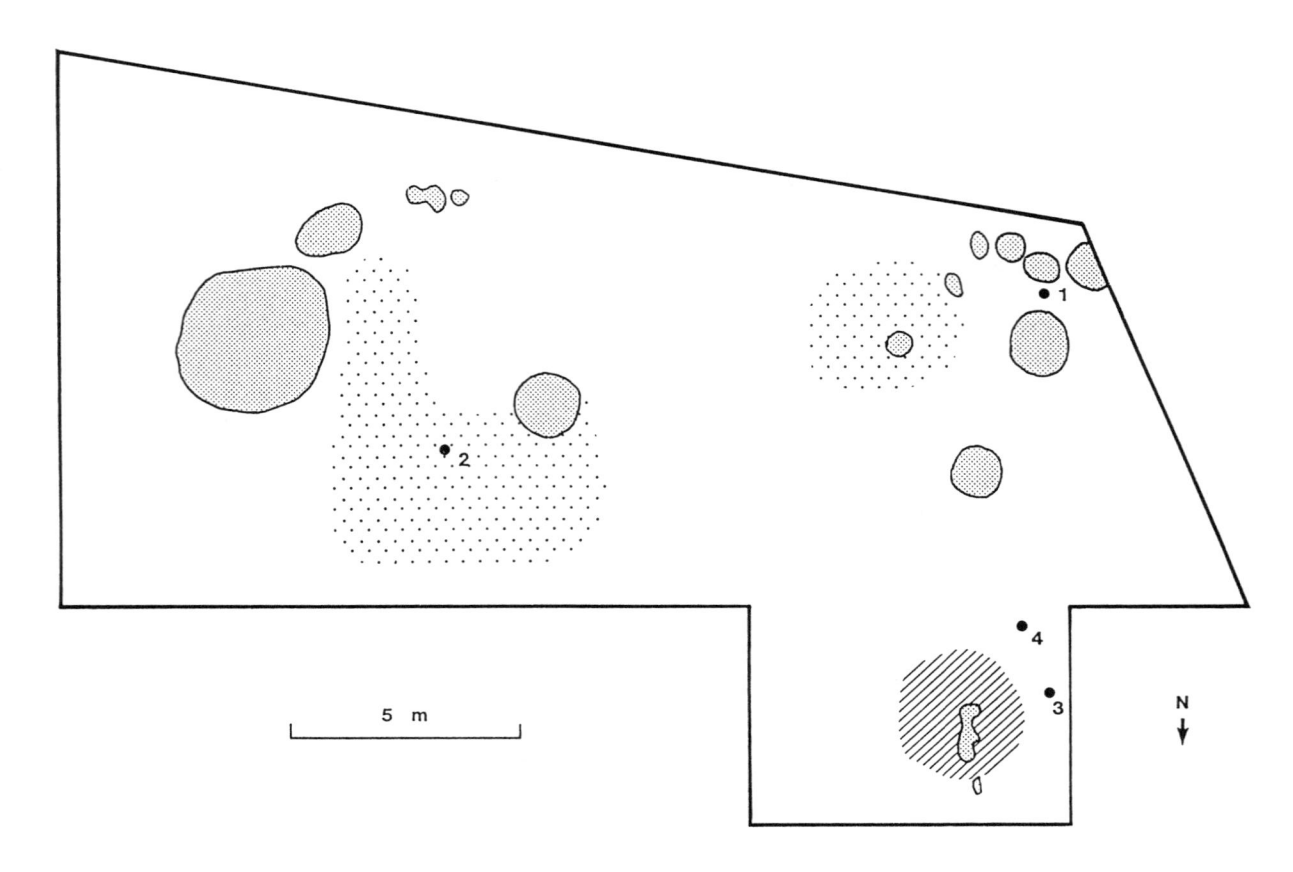

Figure 13.1. The locations at which the four Celtic coins were recovered.

fragments of daub from the settlement surface may have simply collected in the pits as a result of the movement of humans and animals and of erosion. If pits had been dug specifically to serve as rubbish containers, we would expect substantially denser accumulations of debris in them than we find. Whether the rubbish in pits was thrown into them intentionally or not, we would not expect to find coins in them.

All four coins were recovered in contexts indicative of habitation activity. Coin 1 was near six pits which may have been postholes, just west of a surface comprised of unusually dense concentrations of pottery sherds (Figure 5.16). To judge by both the exceptional quantity of pottery and the above-average sizes of the individual sherds, it is likely that a house stood on this spot. Coin 2 was found together with abundant pottery and animal bones, as well as a few bronze and iron objects, and with many pieces of limestone that formed a loose paving. The circle of limestone blocks in the northwestern part of the area, where Coins 3 and 4 were found, may have been the floor of a building. Significantly, no coins were found in the open parts of the surface between these features, in the eastern part of this area, nor in any of the areas explored to the west in 1990 and 1991.

We know relatively little about the use, transport, storage, or loss of coins in the Late Iron Age. If the three complexes in Figure 13.1 discussed above were indeed sites of dwellings, then perhaps in these coins we see objects that were dropped and lost inside houses. Perhaps they fell between floorboards, or between a floor and a wall (as, for example, Hope-Taylor 1977, 57) or they may have been trodden unintentionally into a dirt floor between the limestone pieces. The finds indicate that at least some of the occupants of the oppidum settlement could use coins in their everyday lives. Additional information about the contexts in which coins have been recovered on other settlement sites would surely contribute important insight toward our understanding of these questions.

P.S.W.

Figure 13.2. The four coins from Kelheim-Mitterfeld. Scale 1:1.

Analysis of the Coins (Figure 13.2)

Catalogue:

1. "*Quinarius*," coated and consequently a contemporaneous counterfeit (copper with thin silver coating, now partly scraped away), so-called *Büschel* type, weight 1.02 g, die orientation 12 o'clock. (The die orientation, and for the potin coins the mold orientation, is indicated with reference to the position of the hour hand on a clock; the number refers to the orientation of the reverse side of the coin.)

    Obverse: Stylized head with still recognizable face and tuft-like stylized hair, (in German called *Büschel*), facing left.

    Reverse: Stylized horse facing left, above it sphere.

2. As 1, silver, weight 1.33 g, die orientation 11 o'clock.

    Obverse: as 1.

    Reverse: as 1, but sphere surrounded by torc, above the horse.

3. Cast potin coin, of so-called Sequani type, weight 5.10 g, orientation of mold 4 o'clock.

    Obverse: head facing left.

    Reverse: steer on base line facing left.

4. As 3, weight 4.54 g, orientation of mold 2 o'clock.

    Obverse and reverse: as 3.

Interpretation

All four coins can be classified well. "Quinarius" is actually a Roman domination, one half of a denarius. In the field of Celtic numismatics, this term is used to characterize a small silver coin of about the same size and weight as its Roman model. The "*quinarii*" are typical silver coins in the southern German-Bavarian area, probably minted in Bavaria. It is not possible, however, to locate the site of the mint (on general evidence for minting at Kelheim, Manching, and other sites, see Overbeck 1987a, especially note 12; 1986). These two types are also represented in the great hoard from Neuses, Gde. Eggolsheim, Ldkr. Forchheim in Oberfranken (Overbeck 1982; on the *Büschel* type in particular, Overbeck 1987b). At Manching, this type is also common, hence its presence at Kelheim is not surprising (Egger 1984, numbers 12-43; Kellner 1990). The "Sequani" type potin coins, which were doubtless cast somewhere to the west, also occur at Manching (Egger 1984, numbers 87-92; Kellner 1990, numbers 16 and following). Apparently they were accepted as small change in circulation far from the region in which they were minted.

It is important to place these four coins chronologically. The silver coins of *Büschel* type can be reasonably well dated (for complete interpretation, the two already-known *Büschel quinarii* from Kelheim must also be considered—see Overbeck 1987a, 245 numbers 1 and 2 [also among these is a contemporary counterfeit coin with copper core]; on general issues for dating, see Overbeck 1987b). They definitely belong to phase La Tène D1, and thus, if we follow the reasoning of Polenz (1982, especially 127 table 1, 159 table 4), in the period around 100–80 B.C., in any case before the second half of the final century B.C. As a result of the studies by Furger-Gunti and von Kaenel (Furger-Gunti 1975; Furger-Gunti and Kaenel 1976, especially 54 fig. 5 and 60 fig. 8), the "Sequani potin" coins can also be dated. Coins 3 and 4 belong to their Class A1, which, on the basis of archaeological and historical considerations relative to the pre-Caesarian coin types from Basel-Gasfabrik and the later, post-Caesarian coins from Basel-Münsterhügel, clearly belong to the earlier group. In this case, the origin and the principal period of circulation lie between about 80 and 50 B.C. This dating is supported directly by the above-mentioned occurrence of Sequani potin coins of type A1 at Manching, the occupation of which ended in the context of the historically-documented movements of peoples (Christlein 1982, Overbeck 1987b) that Caesar called the migration of the Helvetii and that led to his intervention in Gaul.

These four coins, along with the already published finds (Overbeck 1986, 1987a), make clear that the end of the oppidum of Alkimoennis-Kelheim needs to be seen in the same historical context as the end of Manching (Christlein 1982, Overbeck 1987b).

B.O.

Acknowledgment

This chapter is based on an article published in *Bayerische Vorgeschichtsblätter* (Overbeck and Wells 1991). Minor changes were made to include information from the 1991 field season and to make the text conform to the rest of the volume. We thank Dr. Jochen Garbsch for permission to translate the original article and to use the figures again here.

Chapter 14
Trade at Kelheim

Introduction

The subject of trade at the oppida of the Late Iron Age is a large and complex issue, and I can do no more than to introduce some of the important topics here. In our preliminary studies at Kelheim, we have not yet undertaken the investigations of materials through sourcing that may help us to pinpoint the origins of the some of the traded goods recovered on the settlement. Yet since the subject of trade is essential for our understanding of the oppida in general, and of Kelheim in particular, it is necessary to review the evidence in this report.

Commerce and the Oppida

The oppida of the Late Iron Age functioned as centers of commercial activity, including both manufacturing for trade and importation of materials from outside (for summaries see Collis 1984a, Fischer 1985, Steuer 1987, Maier 1991; on the textual evidence, Timpe 1985). The clearest evidence for this activity is in the imported manufactured goods that regularly occur at the oppida, including coins from many different sources (Kellner 1990) and Roman imports such as bronze vessels, fine pottery, jewelry, and many other items (Werner 1978; Stöckli 1979a; Svobodová 1985). Trade is also readily apparent in the variety of raw materials that circulated to the oppidum settlements. Copper and tin for bronze, graphite and graphite-clay for pottery (Waldhauser 1992), stone for grindstones (Waldhauser 1981; Fröhlich and Waldhauser 1989), are among the most common materials that are well represented at oppidum sites and that in most instances were brought from considerable distances.

At least four different commercial networks that involved the oppida can be distinguished, all of them interrelated. One was trade between oppida and smaller communities in their hinterlands. We do not know as much about this kind of interaction as we would like to (Meduna [1980] includes a good discussion of this subject, and Murray's study in Chapter 15 is an important contribution in this direction), but it seems likely that smaller communities depended upon the specialized production at the oppida for goods such as bronze and glass ornaments, and trade goods from outside their regions.

A second network was between oppidum communities in different parts of temperate Europe. These interactions are best demonstrated by the coins recovered archaeologically, since they often reveal long-distance communication through coins minted at other oppida (Allen 1980, Kellner 1990).

The links with the Mediterranean world, including Italy and southern Gaul, are apparent in the Roman imports—bronze vessels, fine pottery, transport amphorae, and a variety of other objects. Links with northern regions of continental Europe are becoming increasingly apparent. Metal vessels manufactured at the oppida have been found widely on the North European Plain (Redlich 1980, Hachmann 1990), and Celtic coins (Berger 1985) and glass ornaments (Peddemors 1975, Lappe 1979), and iron weapons (Frey 1986) also circulated widely in the regions to the north of the oppida.

The evidence for commercial interaction between the oppida and other communities is thus abundant, but it has not been comprehensively evaluated in recent years, since large quantities of new data have accumulated. Part of the long-term goals of our research a Kelheim is to use that community as the basis for such a reevaluation.

Imported Materials at Kelheim

A number of different materials recovered in the excavations at Kelheim were produced elsewhere and thus attest to "trade," in the broadest sense. The evidence at Kelheim is similar to that at other oppidum settlements. The bronze objects recovered indicate trade in copper and tin. The glass suggests importation of raw glass, though the source(s) of that material is unknown (Haevernick 1960, Venclová 1990). Graphite or graphite-clay was brought from the region east of

Passau or from Bohemia (Kappel 1969). The two potin coins from our excavations were cast somewhere to the west (see Chapter 13) and probably arrived at Kelheim through some form of commerce; other coins recovered at Kelheim indicate commercial relations with other parts of temperate Europe (see references cited in Chapter 13).

Interaction with the Roman world before the conquest is apparent in the bronze jug found on the eastern end of the Mitterfeld in the last century (Werner 1954, 1978). A fragment of a bronze seive may also be a Roman import, but the origin of such pieces is disputed (Kluge 1987, 94). A dolphin attachment may also be Roman in origin (Kluge 1987, 95). Although ceramic amphorae from the Roman world have been reported from Manching (Stöckli 1979a, Will 1987) and other oppida, none have been identified at Kelheim as yet. Since the numbers of amphorae recovered at oppida east of the Rhine are very small relative to those at sites in Gaul, and since so little of the Kelheim settlement has been investigated, this absence of amphora fragments may not be significant.

All of the imports and likely imports from the Roman world at Kelheim were recovered at the eastern end of the Mitterfeld. In his rescue excavations and test trenches, Herrmann did not report any Roman imports, and none were reported from the excavations just outside the western wall. Nor did we encounter any such objects in our excavations between the middle of the Mitterfeld and the inner wall.

The Question of Iron Trade

The extraordinarily abundant evidence for iron production at Kelheim has been noted since the beginning of this century (Reinecke 1935; Kluge 1987, 166), and both Kluge's (1987) and Blair's (this volume, Chapter 10) studies support the idea that the community at Kelheim produced quantities of iron far exceeding what its members would have needed for their own use. With evidence currently available, it is not possible to prove or to disprove that export trade in iron was important at Kelheim. The location of the site on the Altmühl and Danube Rivers certainly offered an ideal means of transportation of heavy materials, and there is every reason to think that substantial export trade of the metal probably occurred at the site, but any information about scale, direction, or mechanisms of the trade is hypothetical at present. Perhaps future research could identify diagnostic features of Kelheim iron and test iron objects from settlement and cemetery sites in the surrounding landscapes, and beyond, to ascertain whether or not iron from Kelheim might be identified. Although no direct evidence for boats or wharfs from Late Iron Age Kelheim has been reported, evidence from other places attests to a strong tradition of ship-building and shipping during the period (Ellmers 1969, Timpe 1985).

Kelheim and Danube Traffic

Several authors have noted the strategic location of Kelheim with respect to the Danube Gorge and drawn attention to the possibility that the community at the site may have controlled river traffic (Engelhardt 1982, 8). Just across the Danube from the southwest corner of the oppidum is the peninsula of Weltenburg (see Figure 16.1), with the steep hill of the Frauenberg rising behind it. The Frauenberg has also yielded materials of the Late Iron Age, including Late La Tène pottery and other objects contemporary with the Kelheim oppidum. The Frauenberg can be viewed as an extension of the main oppidum (Koch 1991, 141-142), and the two may have formed a complex from which the inhabitants could monitor traffic along the Danube. The southwest corner of the Kelheim oppidum and the Frauenberg are situated at the beginning of the Danube Gorge, and the eastern end of the Kelheim oppidum is located at the end of the gorge. Just 100 m upstream from the Frauenberg is an important ford at Stausacker, and the location of the Frauenberg would have afforded control of the ford as well.

Oppida as Trade Centers

In the study of oppida, it has long been thought that oppida played the role of centers of manufacture, distribution, and long-distance trade in the Late La Tène landscape. With recent excavations conducted at many small unfortified settlements, such as Berching-Pollanten (Fischer, Rieckhoff-Pauli, and Spindler 1984) and Aulnat (Collis 1975, 1980), it has become apparent that much significant production and commerce was also occurring at communities other than the major oppida, but the sheer quantity of material recovered, and of industrial debris, at Manching, Kelheim, and other oppida still indicates that more manufacturing and trade was carried out at these oppida than at smaller sites. Some categories of objects represented at the oppida are not common at the small settlements, as for example the fine painted pottery (Kluge 1987, 186). For Gaul, Timpe (1985), in his analysis of the Greek and Roman textual sources, argues for this strong central role of the oppida in the Late Iron Age economy. While we always need to bear in mind differences between the Gallic sites and those east of the Rhine, all of the evidence suggests a special role of the oppida in production, distribution, and trade.

As Kluge (1987, 186) observes, the material culture recovered at Kelheim corresponds closely with that from the other occupied oppida. The same fibula types, the same iron tools, and the same forms and types of pottery occur at Kelheim as occur at oppidum sites as far west as Gaul and as far east as Moravia. Our knowledge of the material culture of the Late La Tène period is not yet sufficiently precise to say which objects were produced locally at each major oppidum and which were imports from some central location or locations, but the striking uniformity of material culture in this period (Rieckhoff-Pauli 1980) bespeaks very close and regular interactions between the communities.

Chapter 15

The Landscape Survey, 1990–1991
by
Matthew L. Murray

Introduction

The large fortified settlements (oppida) that appeared during the second century B.C. in temperate Europe are often cloaked in an aura of mystery that pervades discussion of their social and spatial contexts (Collis 1984b, 149). This apparent inexplicability is related to poorly defined perceptions of the archaeological landscapes from which the Late Iron Age settlements emerged and to which they belonged. Late Iron Age oppida are interpreted broadly as "towns" or "cities" that were home to thousands of inhabitants, busy places of industry and commerce which commanded large hinterlands (Collis 1984a; Wells 1984). However, these hinterlands are rarely the focus of archaeological research.

This report details the rationale, methods, and preliminary results of a research project designed to collect data concerning the archaeological landscape of a massive Late Iron Age oppidum on the Danube River at Kelheim, Lower Bavaria, in southern Germany. The project combines a literature and archival search with archaeological field survey.

Work was undertaken as part of an interdisciplinary research effort to investigate the Late Iron Age settlement at Kelheim and its physical, cultural, and social context (Wells 1987, 1988b, 1991). It is part of a doctoral dissertation exploring the archaeological landscape of the final millennium B.C., a period of significant social change that culminated in the emergence of a Celtic civilization across western and central Europe. The study stresses the interplay of archaeological place and social discourse over time that incited, encoded, and was manipulated to create the Late Iron Age landscape.

Kelheim and its Physical Landscape

The city of Kelheim is situated in the southern German state of Bavaria within the department of Lower Bavaria (Niederbayern). A small center of industry and trade today, the city on the Danube River is located between the larger cities of Nuremberg and Munich. The Late Iron Age settlement at Kelheim was built around the Michelsberg, a massive limestone spur above the confluence of the Altmühl and Danube Rivers (Figure 15.1). Earthen and stone walls enclosed part of the spur and river terraces in the Altmühl Valley below.

The Michelsberg above Kelheim overlooks an important trade and travel nexus. Passing through Kelheim, the Altmühl River flows from the Central German Uplands into the Danube, which threads through the central European landscape to bind Western and Eastern Europe. The Altmühl meanders in the confines of its narrow valley (now part of a major new canal connecting the Rhine with the Danube) past numerous caverns and rock shelters. Before reaching Kelheim, the Danube lazily flows past rich agricultural fields and moors near Neustadt and Hienheim, and then roils through a scenic gorge carved out by the river over 200,000 years ago. Beyond the confluence of the two waterways, the river valley opens into a broad basin. The Kelheim Basin expands to about three kilometers at its widest point, before narrowing as the combined energies of the Altmühl and Danube pass once again between dramatic sedimentary cliffs.

Kelheim occupies a special geomorphological position astride three very different landforms (Figure 15.1). These landforms endow the region with a variety of resources, such as iron, limestone, flint, timber, and major waterways, all plentiful and accessible within a short distance of Kelheim. In contrast, access to good arable land is limited in the narrow, steeply-sloped river valleys and on the sandy floodplains. The best tillable soils overlie deposits of loess between 4–7 km south and east of the oppidum.

Every region is a mosaic of local environments and conditions. The landscape around Kelheim can be conveniently divided into three primary landforms: 1) the Jurassic Upland plateau north of the Danube, 2) the Tertiary Hills south of the Danube, and 3) the broad Kelheim Basin between the plateau and the hills. This description simplifies what is in actuality a very complex situation (Rutte 1990). The Jurassic Upland also extends south of the Danube at Saal and in the vicinity of Weltenburg, where the Danube races between massive limestone cliffs. Characteristics of the Tertiary Hills, such as extensive loess deposits, are found north of the Danube on the Jura between Marching and Hienheim, where some of the richest agricultural land of the region is situated. Southwest of Kelheim the Abens River meanders slowly through bog and marsh before joining the Danube in the extensive fens of the Donaumoos.

The Jurassic Upland at Kelheim is the southern extremity of the Central German Upland. It is a karstic landscape based predominantly on sedimentary deposits from the Jurassic geologic period. Upland topography is characterized by high relief with rolling plateaus dissected by steep and narrow valleys. Near Kelheim elevations range from 400 m in valleys to over 500 m on the plateau. Soils of the area tend to be poor clays and clay loams, although there are scattered thin "islands" of loess along the edge of the Danube Valley. A large percentage of the Jura is forested, including much of the Fränkische Alb west of Regensburg and the Bavarian Woods to the east.

The Tertiary Hills of southern Germany were created by the crumpling of the Alpine Foreland as a result of tectonic instability during the early Tertiary geologic period. In the ensuing Miocene epoch, great deposits of alluvial sediment washed into the area and later were sculpted by numerous rivers. Late Pleistocene loess deposits and sand dunes accumulated along southern slopes and drainages, completing the gently rolling landscape of the present day. Relief is fairly consistent in the hills, and elevations near Kelheim range from 380 to 420 m. Near Kelheim south of the Danube there are Jurassic outcrops in the hills. Soils are fair to excellent, particularly those developed on thick loess deposits. Much of the area is currently under the plow. South of Kelheim at Abensberg begin the famous hops gardens of the Hallertau region.

The Kelheim Basin is a natural and historic focus of settlement in the region. The basin comprises alluvial deposits, sand, and gravel terraces, enclosed by Jurassic formations. Elevations range from about 340 m at the Danube surface to over 460 m. The southern slopes of the basin between Kelheim and Saal bear the imprint of two major abandoned waterways: the Altabens, which emptied into the Danube west of Saal, and the Urdonau, which flowed in a sharp meander around the present location of Saal (Rutte 1990). Loess deposits and aeolian sands partly overlie old Danube terraces along the northeastern slopes of the basin. Soils in the basin vary from sands to sandy clay loams and loams. They range from poor to good quality. Although heavily modified in the west and south by the city of Kelheim and neighboring town of Saal, the basin still supports many farmers, particularly in the river bottoms and along the terraces north of the Danube.

Aspects of the prehistoric landscape of Kelheim may have differed significantly from the present day, particularly the local vegetation, soil, topography, and weather conditions. Palynological tests undertaken during excavation of Neolithic settlements at Hienheim produced data for an environmental reconstruction of early farming communities in the Kelheim landscape (Bakels 1978). This reconstruction also focused on changes in microtopography which are relevant for much of the landscape around Kelheim. Studies of climatological change and prehistoric cultural modifications to the landscape elsewhere in southern Germany provide a basis for interpolation for later prehistoric periods (e.g. Küster 1986a, 1986b, 1988a, 1988b, 1988c).

Landscape Archaeology and Socio-Spatial Dynamics

The Kelheim field survey was designed to unite two different, but complementary, theoretical approaches to the archaeological landscape. The two approaches are based on different theoretical constructions about the "landscape" and the role of spatial structures in human settlement and social life. The first approach is the study of the immediate hinterland or "catchment area" of a large Late Iron Age settlement. In southern Germany, studies of Late Iron Age settlement systems have traditionally focused on the relations between larger population aggregates and commercial centers which are often separated by distances of 50–100 km or more. Too little attention has been paid to the landscapes around the oppida themselves, so that we lack adequate information about the size and character of rural populations, the exploitation of local resources, and changing patterns of land-use associated with oppida development. By using a diachronic approach to the study of the landscape around Kelheim, I hope to elucidate

Chapter 15 - Murray

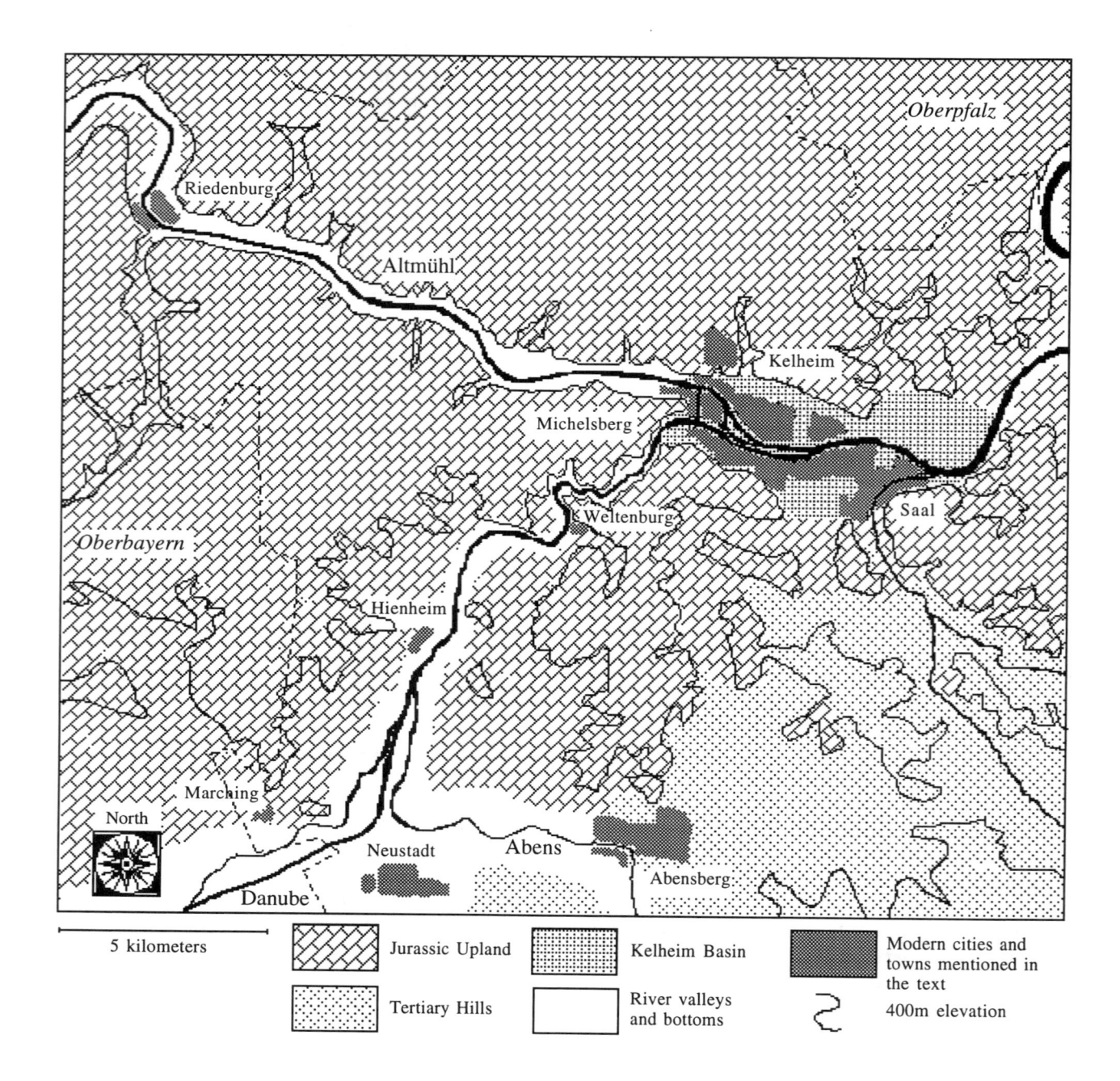

Figure 15.1. Location of Kelheim at the confluence of the Altmühl and Danube Rivers in the southern Bavarian department of Niederbayern. This is the arbitrary area selected as the "region" for a records search to collect data on prehistoric cultural resources. The three major geomorphic units of the Kelheim "region" are indicated. The Jurassic Upland is characterized by limestone, chalk, dolomite and heavy, loamy *Albüberdeckung*. Large loess fields are located in the vicinity of Marching and Hienheim. The Tertiary Hills are characterized by loess and Miocene sands and gravels. The Kelheim Basin is composed mainly of alluvial sediments with areas of loess and aeolian sands. The extensive fens at the confluence of the Abens and Danube rivers (Donaumoos) is also indicated. Political boundaries of neighboring departments of Oberpfalz (north) and Oberbayern (west) are indicated with a dashed line. These areas were not included in the records search.

general historical trends associated with the evolution of Iron Age societies. This approach will use the methods of traditional site catchment analysis and will employ a primarily ecological and processual approach to the landscape, in which the Late Bronze and Iron Age communities are visualized as conscious participants in a dynamic relationship with their physical surroundings. The landscape is an ecological backdrop providing the material basis for social development but also creating physical constraints on those developments.

The second approach explores Late Bronze and Iron Age landscapes in the context of new directions in critical social and spatial theory. Recent critical social theory revolves around the central concepts of "practice" and "discourse." Practice refers to a cognitive system through which human groups represent their social relations, in effect creating their own versions of social reality (Bourdieu 1977, 21). When contradiction between these constructions exists, people engage in discourse, a form of mediation in which participants reflect on, interpret, and represent their particular social conditions (Leppert and Lincoln 1989, 7). Discourse can be either reproductive, reaffirming existing dominant structures (Lincoln 1989, 73-74), or revolutionary, challenging dominant structures and acknowledging rival versions of social reality (Kertzer 1988, 40).

Discourse has a material and spatial dimension which makes social practice palpable and opens the process of social reproduction to critical analysis. The current reaffirmation of the spatial dimension of critical social theory was spearheaded by French scholars in the 1970s, such as Henri Lefebvre (1976) and Manuel Castells (1977), and has been further developed by, among others, British sociologists Anthony Giddens (1984) and John Urry (1984), and by American geographer Edward Soja (1989). According to Soja, socially created spaces possess an ideological content that provides a material form and expression to society. Space, therefore, is the concrete manifestation of practice; places and their relationships are laden with meaning and cultural value and become the material structures of social realities. These spatial relations in turn structure society, producing what Soja (1980) terms the "socio-spatial dialectic."

Some prehistorians have developed arguments to link the spatially-informed notions of practice and discourse with the material residues of past societies (e.g. Hodder 1986; Barrett 1988). The material resources of discourse are situated in space and time and these temporal spaces are places rich in social meaning. Landscapes are mosaics of places and are the ideal venue to explore long-term changes in places and their associated human dramas. This argument has been developed differently in provocative new studies, such as Hodder's (1990) analysis of Neolithic domestic structures and the sublime examination of the Cranborne Chase landscape (Barrett et al. 1991). Cranborne Chase, we learn, is a series of places in which people routinely engaged in social discourse, during which they transmitted knowledge, reinforced authority structures, or negotiated alternative social strategies through the manipulation of the ideological content of everyday materials. The landscape was routinely "read" during the cycles of agricultural reproduction which established social relations, based on age, gender, and inheritance structures (Barrett et al. 1991, 223). All forms of settlement, cemetery, cultivated plots, and non-habitation sites are the material representations of biological reproduction (Barrett et al. 1991, 236) and were the stages for social discourse, both reproductive and contentious. Therefore, cemeteries establish a topography of the dead as a social road map for the living, and internal ordering of settlements, processing and consumption of food, consumption of metalwork, and even presence of human remains in informal burial contexts were all means of social discourse (Barrett et al. 1991, 236-240). The prehistoric landscape and the monuments that are the focus of archaeological research today were active participants in the structuring of prehistoric social conditions (Barrett et al. 1991, 6-8). The landscape is an important social resource; it operates as a frame of reference for social behavior and, therefore, as a force of and participant in historical event.

The socio-spatial dialectic informs us that through time social and spatial structures are continually negotiated and reproduced or transformed. This provides a new theoretical framework within which to investigate the changing landscape of the final millennium B.C. in southern Germany. Through the study of different socio-spatial contexts through time, the discourses that comprise social relations may become apparent and open avenues of interpretation and discussion on the nature of prehistoric social relations. The changing structure of different social contexts through time is the essence of social landscape archaeology. When these contexts, such as ritual, are examined over the *longue durée*, they help to underscore the contradictions that fuel social discourse and make these contradictions visible at the levels of geographic and social time (Bradley 1991). This has already been illustrated for changes in burial ritual and mortuary spaces from the Late Bronze Age to the Late Iron Age in southern Germany (Murray 1992).

The goal of the Kelheim survey project is the construction of long-term history for the Kelheim region. The study incorporates two approaches that operate within different theoretical spheres and ask different questions about the role of the landscape. A traditional approach in landscape archaeology studies different land-use patterns over time, the distribution of site types and functions across the landscape, and the changing relationships between sites. The second approach explores the landscape as a force of social history, as a social resource, and as a dialectic rather than as a static source of material resources and physical constraints. According to Pred (1990), the fundamental purpose of landscape history is the study of the local transformations of social practice and power relations. I suggest that both approaches are valid and that a multifaceted landscape analysis can yield data to serve both approaches.

Literature and Archival Research

Examination of the Kelheim landscape began with a study of the physical surroundings. The initial step was to gather environmental information about the Kelheim area, including mapped geological, soil, and vegetation data. These data largely reflect modern analytical criteria, and their use should be tempered by existing data on the prehistoric environment. Information on pre-modern conditions is available from palynological data and through a consideration of site formation and post-deposition dynamics. This involves consideration of post-depositional modification to the prehistoric landscape, especially via intensive modern agriculture, managed forestry, flood control, settlement, warfare, soil erosion and accumulation. The second step involves the recording of known prehistoric find spots through a search of various sources for published and unpublished reports, including excavation protocols, find notices, aerial photographs, field collections, and cultural resource inventories of communities within the search area.

Rationale and Method

Prior to the literature and archival search, four issues were considered that affect the process and results of data collection: 1) selection of an appropriate study region, 2) determination of the scale of analysis, 3) choice of data criteria, and 4) determination of temporal analytical units.

Archaeological concepts of region have been the focus of recent critical dialogue (Marquardt and Crumley 1987). Archaeological regions often have more to do with our research goals and methodological limitations than prehistoric realities. What size landscape is sufficient to treat the proposed research questions? In the absence of a clearly delimited natural region at Kelheim or any evidence that natural boundaries and social or cultural boundaries overlap, a choice was made to combine research interests with pragmatic considerations.

The oppidum at Kelheim is located conveniently at the center of the official 1:50,000 topographic map (Figure 15.1). This map covers nearly 550 km^2 in Lower Bavaria, Upper Bavaria (Oberbayern) and Upper Palatinate (Oberpfalz). It includes several significant geomorphological areas. It was decided to limit the collection of reported data to the area on this map, in effect, to make this map the arbitrary "region" around the site of Kelheim. To further streamline data collection, only data within the borders of Lower Bavaria would be collected, comprising 453 km^2. Terrain belonging to Upper Bavaria (west-southwest of Kelheim) and Upper Palatinate (north and northeast) involves mainly Jurassic Upland landforms similar to those found north of the Danube at Kelheim, so the exclusion of this territory from study does not remove unique or otherwise significant terrain from consideration.

The selected region should not be confused with a bounded prehistoric reality. However, it offers certain advantages to the study of long-term landscape history around Kelheim. The region contains land up to 17 km from the Michelsberg, an area whose inhabitants would have been in close contact with the oppidum during the Late Iron Age. Within this hinterland we can assume that the oppidum inhabitants obtained their daily bread and other necessities, as well as raw materials for production and trade, such as iron, stone, and clay. The region extends over 15 km up the Danube River from Kelheim, incorporating nearly one-half the territory between Kelheim and the oppidum at Manching, which is situated 36 km to the southwest. The selection of this region also will allow the study of local landscape history prior to oppidum construction and occupation.

The scale of analysis is determined by the selected region and the proposed research questions. Since the project goal is to construct a local cultural and social history of the landscape around Kelheim, the analytical scale has to be at a detailed local level. The selected scale determines the kinds and quality of data to be collected. During archival and literature review, all known remains of prehistoric activity in the landscape were noted, including the results of unsystematic investigations, surface collections, and even isolated finds. Details of recovered materials, extant features, and other data pertinent to the recognition of prehistoric behavior were collected from available records. Information concerning discovery contexts is important to the critical appraisal of the data and also was noted. A variety of environmental data was determined for each location recorded during the search. Geomorphological data were studied on two levels: 1) the local situation and 2) the surroundings within a one-kilometer radius of the locale. Data included the geological substratum, topography, soil type and quality, vegetation, and modern land-use. Additional data recorded for each locale included elevation, slope, aspect, water source(s), and location within nested natural regions and sub-regions based on German government land divisions.

The final issue was the selection of temporal units of analysis. Although the project is intended to focus on events of the final millennium B.C. (Late Bronze to Late Iron Age), the locations and descriptions of Neolithic and Early–Middle Bronze Age sites were also recorded, since these would be encountered during field survey. Important Palaeolithic and Mesolithic remains are known in the study region, primarily from caves and abris below river bluffs and along river terraces. Their locations were noted but are not included in this report.

Neolithic remains from the study region comprise a detailed sequence of archaeological cultures and regional type groups, from the Early Neolithic (Linearbandkeramik) through the Middle Neolithic (Stichbandkeramik, Oberlauterbach group, Münchshöfen) to Late Neolithic and Eneolithic cultures (Michelsberg, Altheim, Cham group, and the Schnurkeramik–Glockenbecher facies). For the purposes of this report, these remains have been generalized as "Neolithic," although specific cultural affiliations were recorded during data collection. In future work it may prove fruitful to examine data for discrete Neolithic archaeological cultures and groups for the Kelheim region. The Neolithic sequence in southern Germany spanned about four millennia, from 5800–1800 B.C. Bronze Age remains belong to the Early (A–B1 horizons) and Middle (B2–C horizons) Bronze Age periods following the south German chronology established by Reinecke and modified by several generations of German prehistorians. The Early and Middle Bronze Ages lasted approximately 500 years, from 1800–1300 B.C.

At the end of the Bronze Age and the beginning of the Iron Age there are two chronological groups: the Late Bronze Age (Bronze Age D horizon) and the early Hallstatt period (Hallstatt A–B horizons), commonly refered to as the "Urnfield" Bronze Age culture. These two groups are combined under the term "Late Bronze Age" because of the similarities in material culture, especially ceramic forms, that make their separation difficult and because of the establishment of flat cemeteries and cremation rites in the Bronze Age D horizon which become a hallmark of the subsequent Urnfield culture. The Late Bronze Age spanned about 550 years, from 1300–750 B.C.

Traditionally the Early Iron Age in Central Europe begins with the later Hallstatt horizons (Hallstatt C–D). These assemblages are associated with changes in the mortuary and settlement behavior of the Late Bronze Age which are related to important social, political, and economic developments. In spite of the appearance of a new art style during the Early La Tène (A–B1 horizons), there is an unmistakable continuity in burial and settlement pattern during the Late Hallstatt and Early La Tène. In the Kelheim region, this continuity is illustrated by excavations in the Altmühl River Valley which recovered several pottery assemblages with mixed Late Hallstatt and Early La Tène attributes (Rind 1988), allowing the identification of a "transitional" period during which established Late Hallstatt populations absorbed new La Tène cultural innovations. For these reasons, Hallstatt Iron Age and Early La Tène are identified as "Early Iron Age," which lasted about 400 years, from 750–350 B.C.

At the start of the Middle La Tène period (B2–C1 horizons) in southern Germany there is a break in burial patterns and settlement occupation. This period marks the end of mound burial and the establishment of flat inhumation cemeteries. Burial changes correspond with the abandonment of most habitation sites of the Early Iron Age. The ensuing Late La Tène period (C2–D2 horizons) marks the appearance of the oppida and the virtual disappearance of organized burial places in southern Germany. There are relatively few Middle La Tène cemeteries in southern Germany and settlements are almost non-existent. The apparent lack of archaeological material is usually explained by reference to the historical migration of Celtic peoples south of the Alps and eastward as far as Asia Minor. But this is not a very satisfactory explanation, since it fails to explain how very large, complex fortifications were established at the end of the Middle La Tène and beginning of the Late La Tène if the territory had been so heavily depopulated. The lack of Middle La Tène settlement remains is more likely related to weaknesses within established pottery chronologies. Not until the Late La Tène are typologically important metal objects (such as fibulae) common finds within habitation sites, so that ceramics remain the primary basis for establishing cultural affiliation. The general absence of pottery in cemeteries of this period, with their associations of jewelry and weapons, constrain the relative ceramic chronologies. Middle La Tène domestic pottery can rarely be separated from Early, or more importantly, Late La Tène assemblages, so that extant Middle La Tène sites are probably not identified and are therefore underrepresented. For these reasons, Middle and Late La Tène assemblages are combined under the term "Late Iron Age," which spanned nearly 350 years, from 350–15 B.C. Data collection ends with the final La Tène phase (La Tène D2) prior to Roman occupation at the end of the first century B.C.

Sources

After the consideration of methodological issues, data collection began with literary sources and archival records. Regional studies in prehistoric archaeology long have been popular in southern Germany, although the regional approach there has a somewhat different connotation from that in Anglo-American circles. German regional studies tend to have a strong culture-historical philosophy and are often painstakingly detailed discussions of the typology and chronology for a particular area (e.g. Kossack 1959; Torbrügge 1979). Until recently, regional studies largely have been based on archival data collection (Schmotz 1989; Schier 1990), and extensive systematic field survey is not as common as it is in American or British archaeology.

One result of this tradition in German regional archaeology is the compilation of excellent culture resource inventories for selected areas. Some volumes are catalogs of known monuments and sites of all periods in a particular region (e.g. Pätzold 1983), while others specialize on a particular period (e.g. Hochstetter 1980). For the Kelheim region there exist numerous catalog sources useful to this investigation, including works by Torbrügge (1959), Stroh (1975), Stork (1983), and Bayerlein (1985).

Archaeological field work in and around Kelheim is reported in a variety of professional journals, both local (e.g. *Vorträge der Niederbayerischen Archäologentages, Archäologische Denkmalpflege in Niederbayern*) and international (e.g. *Archäologisches Korrespondenzblatt, Das archäologische Jahr in Bayern, Bayerische Vorgeschichtsblätter, Bericht der Bayerischen Bodendenkmalpflege, Germania*), as well as in other journals, monographs, and unpublished theses.

Literary sources were consulted at Widener and Tozzer libraries in Cambridge, Massachusetts; Wilson Library in Minneapolis, Minnesota; the Bayerisches Landesamt für Denkmalpflege in Landshut and Kelheim; and the Archäologisches Museum in Kelheim. The majority of the archival research was conducted during the summer of 1990 at the Lower Bavarian repository of archaeological site records at the Landesamt für Denkmalpflege in Landshut. Follow-up research was conducted during the spring of 1991 prior to field work. The repository contains site files, aerial photographs, and cultural resource inventories of the Kelheim area. Additional information about local collectors, private collections, and Rhein-Main-Donau Canal excavations in the Altmühl River Valley was obtained at the Bayerisches Landesamt für Denkmalpflege and the Archäologisches Museum in Kelheim.

Results

Literary and archival sources reveal the rich cultural tapestry of the landscape around Kelheim (Figure 15.2). The data represent nearly 6000 years of continuous settlement from the earliest farmers of central Europe to the pre-Roman Celtic peoples. They also reflect a long history of amateur and professional interest in prehistoric monuments and other remains in the area beginning early in the 19th century.

A total of 490 prehistoric locales[1] are known within the 453 km^2 of archival search area (Table 15.1). This is an average of more than one locale per square kilometer, but the average is slightly distorted by the fact that some locations of prehistoric activity have produced remains from more than one chronological period. Unconfirmed reports of prehistoric remains are not included. The total also does not include 10 locations within the Danube Gorge that were frequented by a private collector for many years (Rind 1991b). These materials are curated at the Landesamt für Denkmalpflege in Kelheim and were not available for analysis. They are from a mix of primary and secondary contexts along the river banks and document prehistoric activity in the gorge from the Palaeolithic to the Middle Ages.

Each locale represents a single archaeological component; some are components of multi-function occupations, such as a habitation with coeval burial remains, or of multi-component occupations, such as a location producing artifacts from several distinct chronological periods. For example, a place known to contain Late Bronze Age burials and yielding coeval domestic pottery, as well as producing Early Iron Age domestic debris from pits, is counted as *three* locales: a Late Bronze Age cemetery, a Late Bronze Age ceramic scatter, and an Early Iron Age settlement.

Three particular qualities of the archival and literary data are explored below: 1) distribution of remains from different archaeological periods, 2) distribution of different kinds of prehistoric remains and associated behavior through time, and 3) contexts of discovery for different kinds of remains and archaeological periods. Italicized terms refer to categories presented in the respective figures.

The occurrences of known prehistoric finds are summarized in Figure 15.3. Locales that could not be affiliated with any specific chronological unit (such as locales with generic "prehistoric" or "latènoid" artifacts) have been removed from the sample. There are 120 reported Neolithic locales, representing the entire Neolithic sequence for southern Germany. Highpoints in locale occurrence are the Bronze Age with 86 locales and the Early Iron Age with 78 locales. There are 58 known locales of Late Bronze Age remains and considerably fewer Late Iron Age find spots (only 43) around the oppidum at Kelheim. The large number of Neolithic locales is striking when compared to the occurrences of later prehistoric cultures, but this is a distortion caused by the greater span of time represented by Neolithic remains. When time is factored into the total locale occurrence for each chronological period (Figure 15.4), the Neolithic data emerge as a significantly smaller set.

Prehistoric locales can be divided into 10 rudimentary categories with formal and functional characteristics (Table 15.2). The categorization of each locale is based on associated materials, features, and the context of discovery.

Settlements are associations of domestic, industrial, and architectural residues with subsurface features, such as ditches, pits, hearths or furnaces, and postholes. These features may be recorded during excavation or noted as soil stains in plowed fields, construction sites, or quarries. A "settlement" usually connotes domestic behavior, but evidence of industrial activities, such as iron smelting, has also been included in this category. Settlements account for only 14% of the prehistoric locales.

Cemeteries include locations of funerary monuments, burials, or materials characteristic of funerary contexts. Unexcavated tumuli are included in this category. Cemeteries account for nearly one quarter (23%) of the known locales.

Ceramic scatters are finds of pottery sometimes with varying quantities of flint and metal. These locales are not associated with features. They may be surface collections from plowed fields, salvaged remains from construction sites, or stray finds made during the excavation of a locale from a different cultural context. For example, stray Late Iron Age sherds collected during the clearing of a Late Neolithic enclosure are identified here as a ceramic scatter. Ceramic scatters are the most numerous recorded prehistoric locale (32%).

Flint scatters consist entirely of worked lithic debris without other cultural remains. Like ceramic scatters, they may derive from surface collection, construction, or excavation. Scatters of flint account for 4% of the recorded locales.

Many cave and rock shelter sites in the Kelheim region have yielded cultural resources. This category also includes cliff top or cliff base deposits. Some mixed materials date to excavations at the turn of the century or earlier and can be related only to a group of neighboring caves, such as artifacts from the Schulerloch series in the Altmühl Valley or the Franzhöhle group in the Danube Gorge. Each of these series is counted here as a single locale. Caves total 9% of the known prehistoric locales.

Earthworks are monuments such as defensive walls and enclosures. Existing earthworks on the Michelsberg, Frauenberg, and Ringberg are included in this category, as are eight characteristic Late Iron Age rectilinear enclosures, *Viereckschanzen,* that are scattered across the landscape (Schwarz 1959). Trenches cut into earthworks on the Michelsberg (Herrmann 1973) and Frauenberg (Sage 1975) have revealed the ages of some monu-

Chapter 15 - Murray

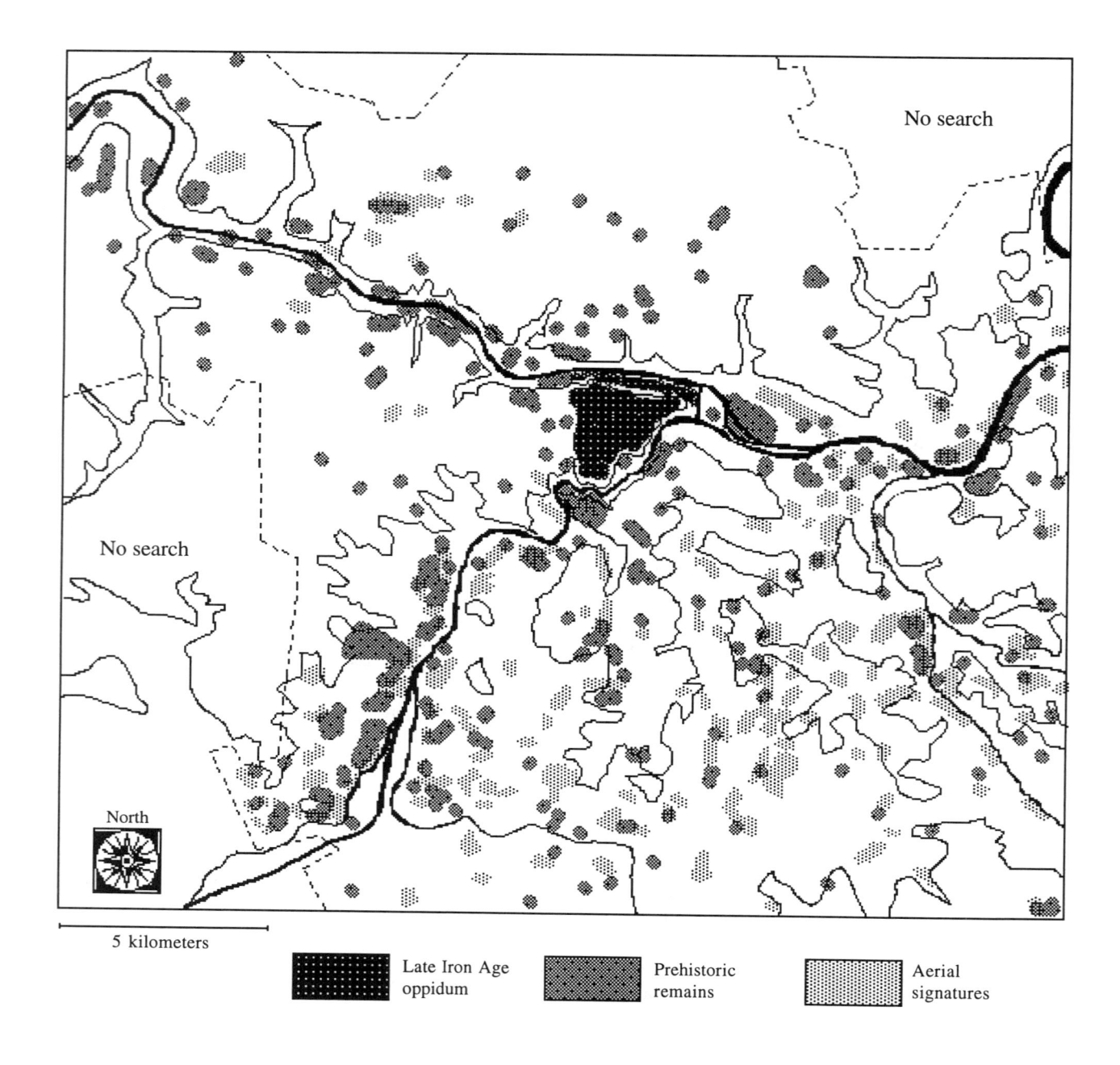

Figure 15.2. Distribution of post-Mesolithic prehistoric remains in the Kelheim region, based on a literature and archival search. All 490 recorded prehistoric locales are indicated, representing about 6000 years of landscape history. Some locales have more than one cultural or functional component. Areas with crop or soil marks identified in aerial photographs are also indicated.

Table 15.1. Reported prehistoric locales in the Kelheim region.

Locale Type	"Prehistoric"	Neolithic	Bronze Age	Late Bronze Age	Early Iron Age	Late Iron Age	"La Tène"	Total	%
Settlement	2	13	14	17	18	6	0	70	14
Cemetery	50	3	17	11	26	5	0	112	23
Ceramic Scatter	6	67	22	16	25	13	9	158	32
Flint Scatter	18	0	0	0	0	0	0	18	4
Cave	0	13	14	5	7	2	4	45	9
Earthwork	9	0	0	0	0	9	0	18	4
Hoard	0	0	5	4	0	0	0	9	2
Isolate	2	18	10	5	1	8	4	48	10
Unknown	0	4	4	0	1	0	1	10	2
Flint Mine	0	2	0	0	0	0	0	2	0
Total	87	120	86	58	78	43	18	490	100

Table 15.2. Discovery contexts of reported prehistoric locales in the Kelheim region.

Find Context	"Prehistoric"	Neolithic	Bronze Age	Late Bronze Age	Early Iron Age	Late Iron Age	"La Tène"	Total	%
Excavation	1	17	20	22	33	17	1	111	23
Salvage	0	11	28	7	14	3	5	68	14
Agriculture	21	78	19	16	20	7	9	170	35
Construction	5	9	15	9	8	7	3	56	11
Visible	58	0	0	0	0	8	0	66	13
Unknown	2	5	4	4	3	1	0	19	4
Total	87	120	86	58	78	43	18	490	100

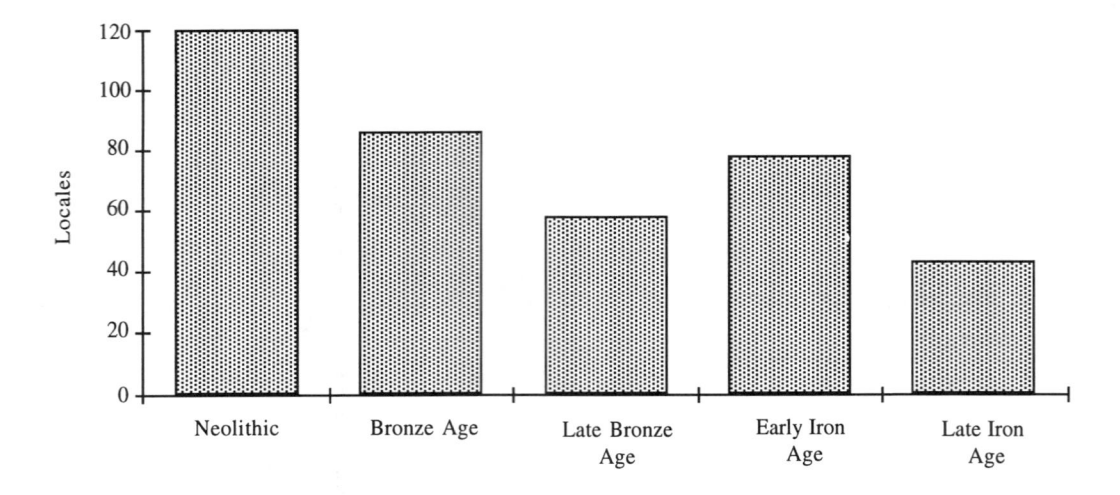

Figure 15.3. Counts of reported prehistoric locales in the Kelheim region for each chronological period. The graph does not include 87 "prehistoric" and 18 "La Tène" find spots. The "prehistoric" locales consist of material of unknown pre-Roman cultural affiliation; "La Tène" finds may belong to the Early or Late Iron Age.

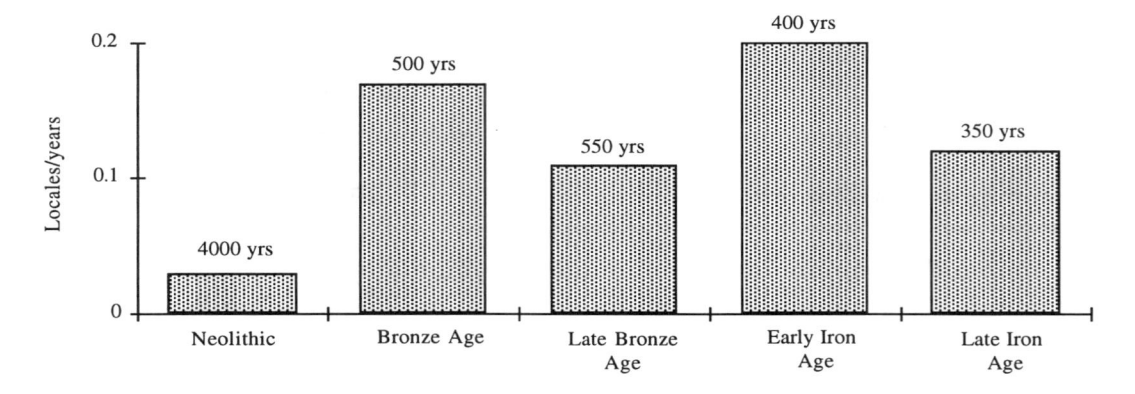

Figure 15.4. Relative numbers of locales in the Kelheim region corrected for the temporal duration of each chronological period (ratio of number of locales to years). Taken as a crude measure of the intensity of prehistoric activity, the data suggest a significant increase in intensity during the Bronze Age, a slight decline in the Late Bronze Age, and another marked rise in the Early Iron Age. Density of activity declined again during the time of oppidum construction and occupation in the Late Iron Age.

ments, but other remnant walls and enclosures in the region are not securely dated. Earthworks account for 3% of the known locales. Two kinds of monument have been omitted from the discussion because of difficulties posed by the identification and dating of the remains. These remains are open-pit iron mines and slag heaps that are known to dot the Jurassic landscape around Kelheim and probably date to the Late Iron Age and medieval periods (Schwarz et al. 1966; Burger and Geisler 1983). Only a few pits and heaps have been investigated. From the surface, the mines easily can be confused with natural karstic features. In the absence of archaeological tests to establish their nature and date, most mines and slag heaps remain dubious cultural resources.

Hoards are closely associated materials in contexts that may indicate intentional deposition, such as in cliff fissures, bogs, and pits (Stein 1976). Often the contents of the find are a clue, such as broken metal objects and scrap characteristic of a "founder's hoard." The find context is crucial in the interpretation of this locale category, but context information is not always available in archival records. Isolates or materials interpreted as domestic (settlements or ceramic scatters) actually may be hoards, so this category could be underrepresented. Finds that are interpreted as hoards comprise 2% of the total locales.

Isolates are the reported discoveries of single objects. This category encompasses a broad variety of materials, from individual sherds to a coin, bronze axe, or single iron sword. Isolates make up 9% of the total locales.

A small number of locales cannot be categorized. Their locations and contexts are recorded but details of the cultural resources are *unknown*. Information about these locales comes from vague notes in the archives, for example a brief notice concerning the unearthing of unspecified Early Iron Age finds in a turnip garden. These materials were often found many years ago and are now missing. Only 2% of the locales are unknown.

There are two known prehistoric *flint mines* in the record search area. The mines account for fewer than 1% of the total reported archaeological locales.

Figure 15.5 summarizes the occurrence of specific locale categories across all archaeological periods. Eighteen find spots with "latènoid" pottery have been excluded from the graph because the ceramic may belong to the Early or Late Iron Age. Settlements make up a fairly even proportion of locales from the Neolithic to the Early Iron Age, but are less common for the Late Iron Age. Neolithic and Late Iron Age cemeteries are rare, but burial materials are plentiful from other periods. The largest single category for nearly every period is surface scatter. Flint scatters are by definition "prehistoric," because of the lack of diagnostic material in a scatter of lithic debris. Cultural deposition in caves apparently was significant during the Neolithic, Bronze, and Early Iron Ages, but declined markedly in the Late Iron Age. Earthworks are either "prehistoric," i.e. they are unexplored but appear to be pre-Roman, or date from the Late Iron Age (the *Viereckschanzen*). Earthen monuments that are probably Roman or medieval have been eliminated from the study. Hoards are known from the Early and Late Bronze Age.

The large number of burial mounds and cave sites around Kelheim attracted an early curiosity in the archaeological landscape. Amateur explorations began as early as 1800, when a certain *Forstmeister* Schmid hacked holes into wooded tumuli. In recent years, the area has witnessed numerous large-scale professional excavations and salvage operations as archaeologists struggle to recover the past before it is destroyed by modern development (Engelhardt 1987; Rind 1988). A strong local amateur interest remains, and numerous collectors visit their favorite hunting grounds to gather surface materials. Most individuals report these finds to the archaeologists, and the locations are then documented in the archives.

Fewer than one quarter (23%) of the known locales were discovered by professional *excavation* (Table 15.2). Find contexts of these excavations are secure, and records are published or preserved in the state archives. About 14% of the locales were explored during *salvage* operations, which are typically abbreviated. Reported materials and contexts are secure, but records are often inadequate. This category also includes older, amateur excavations, of which records have been lost or are incomplete. More than one third (35%) of the locales stem from *surface* collections. Construction accounts for the recovery of 11%, and a further 13% of the locales are visible monuments that have never been investigated. The discovery contexts of 4% are unknown.

Figure 15.6 summarizes the discovery contexts for each archaeological period (excluding "La Tène" locales). The graphs reveal several patterns with important implications for the interpretation of archival data. The high number of "prehistoric" monuments visible on the surface reflects the inclusion of 50 uninvestigated tumulus groups in this

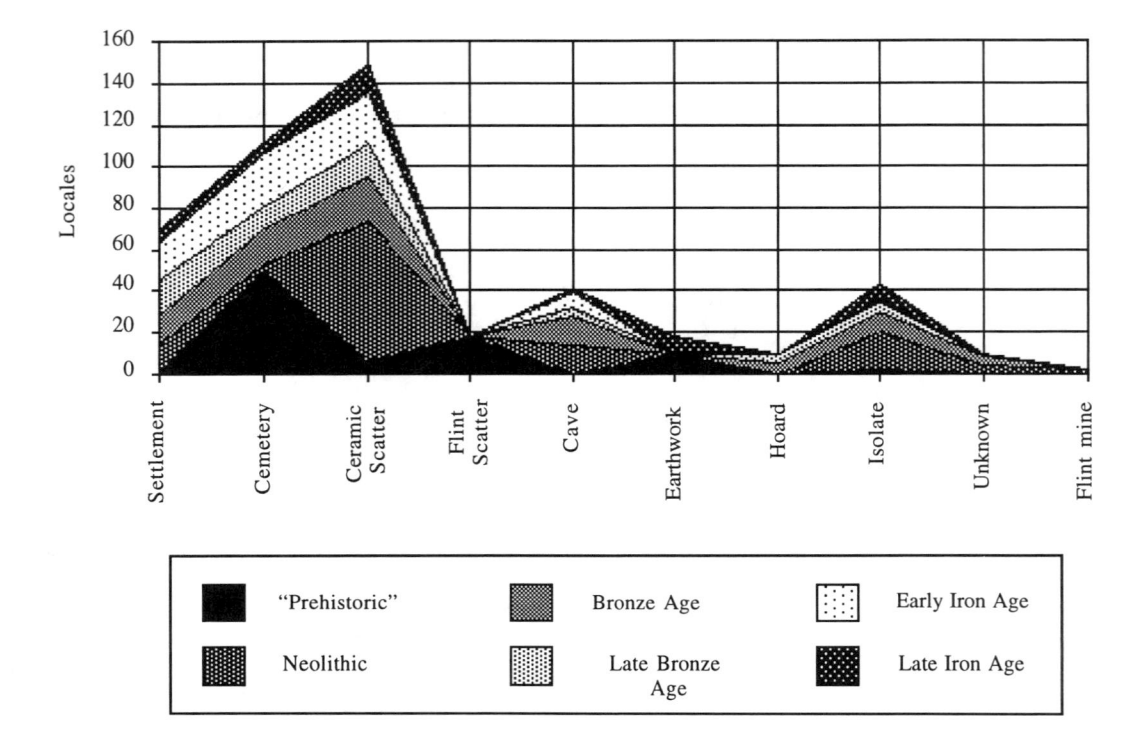

Figure 15.5. Area graph showing numbers of reported prehistoric locales in the Kelheim region plotted against locale category. The graph presents a comparison of the varying numbers and proportions of locale categories through time. A few patterns deserve brief comment. The large number of "prehistoric" cemeteries reflects the presence of many uninvestigated groups of tumuli in the region (at least 50 known groups). Cemeteries from the Neolithic and Late Iron Age are poorly represented, but burial grounds are more common during the Bronze, Late Bronze, and Early Iron Ages. Ceramic scatters without associated features are the most numerous category and constitute the largest single category for nearly every period. Cultural residues in caves are common during the Neolithic and Bronze Age, and occur also in the Late Bronze and Early Iron Ages, but are rare during the Late Iron Age. With the exception of several undated "prehistoric" earthworks, most monuments date to the Late Iron Age (the *Viereckschanzen* and oppidum fortifications). Eighteen "La Tène" find spots are not included in the graph.

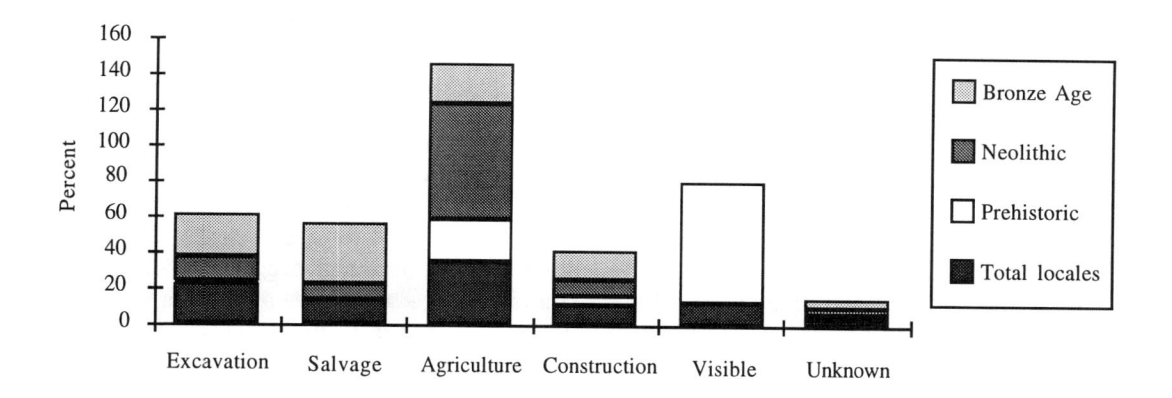

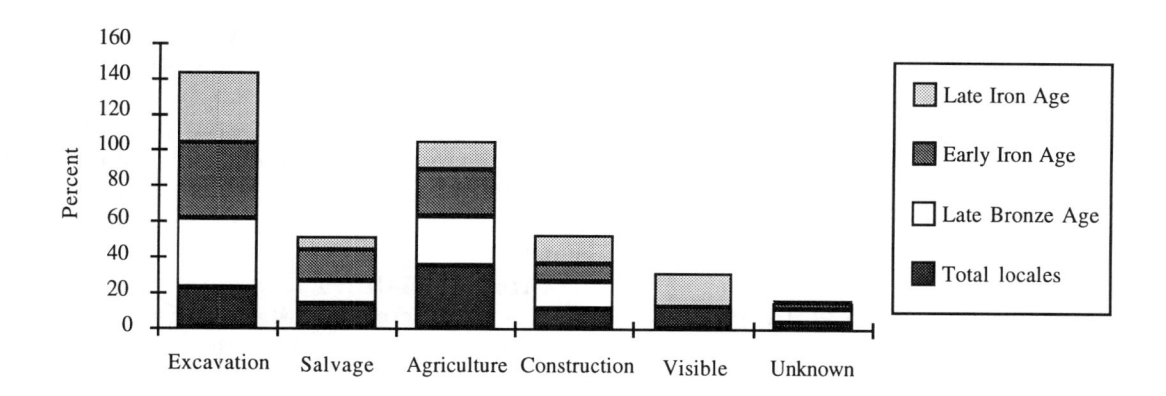

Figure 15.6. Summary of discovery contexts for reported prehistoric locales in the Kelheim region according to their chronological period. Values are presented as percentages of the total for each period. The graphs exhibit certain patterns with intriguing implications for the interpretation of archival data. A majority of locales affiliated with early prehistoric periods (top) have been discovered through agriculture and salvage (including old and amateur excavations). The fact that 65% of all Neolithic locales stem from surface collections in plowed fields may indicate a preference for good land that continues to be cultivated today. The discovery of one third (33%) of Bronze Age locales through salvage reflects early amateur interest in the numerous tumulus cemeteries of the Kelheim region, many of which have produced Middle Bronze Age burial materials. In contrast, locales of later prehistoric periods (bottom) have been recovered mainly through professional excavation. Thirty-eight percent of Late Bronze Age finds, 42% of Early Iron Age locales, and 40% of Late Iron Age locales are the results of excavation. This pattern suggests concentrated later prehistoric activity in river valleys, where recent professional excavations have been conducted.

context category. A large percentage of Neolithic locales has been found through surface collection in cultivated fields. Perhaps this is related to a prehistoric preference for good soils, such as loess, that are still cultivated today. Similarly, numerous Late Bronze and Early Iron Age locales are discovered as a result of modern agricultural activity. The predominant role of salvage and amateur excavations in the creation of the Bronze Age assemblage is a factor of the early local interest in tumulus cemeteries, many of which contain Middle Bronze Age remains. The set of locales from the Late Bronze to the Late Iron Age is mainly the product of professional excavations. This pattern of discovery is very different from earlier prehistoric periods and suggests differences between the nature of earlier (Neolithic, Bronze Age) and later (Late Bronze to Late Iron Age) prehistoric remains in the region. Were later prehistoric activities most intense in areas currently targeted for excavation (such as river valleys), or do the nature of the remains and the site formation processes peculiar to later prehistoric cultural resources possess some quality that makes them more likely to be discovered through excavation rather than surface collection? It is not clear if this pattern results from prehistoric cultural choice or archaeological bias; it is probably a combination of both factors.

Since the late 1970s, the Bavarian State archaeologists have closely scrutinized much of Bavaria from the air (Christlein and Braasch 1982). The Landesamt für Denkmalpflege in Landshut houses several thousand photographs of the Kelheim region. Aerial photo reconnaissance during the past 12 years has identified traces of over 200 possible prehistoric or historic occupations within the archival search area around Kelheim. These signatures consist of crop marks and soil stains. They range from positive images of ditched enclosures or post-built structures in ripe wheat fields, to negative images of stone-built burial tumuli in maize stands. Earthworks and mounds are also revealed through shadow in oblique light or snow cover.

Caution must be exercised in the interpretation of aerial photographs, particularly in a karstic and cultivated region such as Kelheim. Sink holes, underground springs, and filled drainages often mimic the aerial signatures of buried cultural remains. Aerial reconnaissance fails to provide adequate information about cultural affiliation, although attempts often are made to relate the particular forms of remains (such as a ditched enclosure) to specific functions and time periods. Aerial photos are effective only for cultivated land, meadow, or construction sites and therefore are biased toward currently open terrain. For the present research project, aerial signatures were used only as a reference for field walking. Attempts during fieldwork to identify surface remains that could be related satisfactorily to aerial signatures yielded little success.

While the known archaeological material around Kelheim reveals a prehistoric landscape of considerable diversity and density, the data are largely the result of accidental discovery. Large-scale organized archaeological reconnaissances in the area have been rare and have focused on salvage work or the study of specific local areas. Rhein-Main-Donau Canal construction along the Altmühl River in the 1970s and 1980s led to archaeological prospecting and numerous large clearing operations in the valley between Kelheim and Riedenburg (Rind 1988; Engelhardt 1989a). A small-scale pedestrian survey of loess fields along the Danube's northern bluff south of the Michelsberg was undertaken in 1974 in conjunction with the excavation of Neolithic settlements at Hienheim (Modderman 1977, 1986). Particular fields often are visited by amateurs and professionals for surface collection, but these efforts usually are guided by knowledge gained from non-rigorous methods of detection.

Archival data comprise an archaeological sample as valid as any other (Schier 1990), but it is a sample that must be reconstructed through methods of source criticism. It is not a sample that the investigator can influence, beyond the initial steps of selecting a search area and collection criteria. In order to improve the reliability of available data concerning the prehistoric landscape around Kelheim, I designed and implemented a modest scheme of rigorous extensive and intensive field survey.

Field Survey

The Kelheim Survey Project was intended to balance work efficiency, economy, and effectiveness. Although so-called "full coverage" surveys recently have been proposed as the best approach to regional archaeological studies (Fish and Kowalewski 1990), their great expense still relegates them to ideals that have been only partly realized through long-term projects in some parts of the world. The realities of archaeological fieldwork usually demand less grand designs to produce meaningful results within existing financial and personnel structures and acceptable time limits.

Rationale and Sampling Method

The Kelheim survey was bounded by certain practicalities. It was conceived as an exploratory project, combining a wealth of existing data with small field samples, to prepare a reasonable data base for constructing a long-term history of social and spatial dynamics for a selected region. During design of the survey it was imperative to create an efficient research program for maximum economy, i.e. to maximize the production of meaningful data at a minimum of cost.

The specific goals of the field survey were to supplement previously recorded information, address questions raised by that information, and explore particular areas close to the oppidum at Kelheim. There were two important limitations to fieldwork: 1) data gathering was restricted to surface collection because of the considerable expense of systematic subsurface testing, and 2) work was to be performed by a single individual during two months in the spring of 1990.

Since field work was restricted to surface collection, a survey would be feasible only in terrain where surface visibility was adequate. About 60% of the landscape surrounding Kelheim and the Michelsberg presently is forested (Figure 15.1). To address this problem, field survey was preceded by an experiment in forest visibility.

The forest experiment was designed to determine the relative economy of a pedestrian survey in the managed forests of Bavaria. In heavily populated Germany, timber resources and woodland fauna are carefully monitored. State forest agencies constantly maintain woodlands, keeping paths cleared, regularly harvesting uprooted trees, and repairing disturbances to the forest floor. Many forests around Kelheim consist of tall, straight stands of conifers, planted in regular rows as a quick crop to replace harvested hardwoods. Forest canopies are dense, and undergrowth is inhibited, but a thick layer of leaf mold and vegetal detritus completely obscures the undisturbed forest floor and inhibits or hides the work of burrowing animals.

In the carefully maintained German woods, few opportunities exist for a visual evaluation of the forest floor and subsurface. Numerous forest paths are frequented by many hikers and local pedestrians, but the paths are old and established, and tend to be covered with the same detritus as elsewhere. Surface visibility is afforded only in occasional low-lying rutted areas or along isolated cut banks. A violent storm in the spring of 1989 caused extensive damage throughout Lower Bavaria, uprooting hundreds of trees and disturbing the forest floors. By the following year, clean-up efforts by forest workers and farmers had already removed most of the tree falls.

Because of regular recreational and economic activity in the forests, the long tradition of German map-making, and an established history of local interest in prehistoric mounds and earthworks preserved in the forests of Kelheim, it is doubtful that a systematic pedestrian survey of the woodlands would produce any significant unreported prehistoric surface features. The intensive mapping of iron mines may be an exception to this, but it would prove very difficult to distinguish between natural (i.e. sink holes) and cultural features without some form of subsurface prospecting. The utility of a modern investigation in the forests would lie primarily in the discovery of subsurface cultural deposits. This goal was beyond the modest scope of the present survey design.

Although preliminary assessment suggested that forest evaluation would not prove successful, fieldwork began with a test of forest versus field survey economy. This test was designed to compare the efficiency and expense of surface evaluation in forested and open field conditions. Two adjacent one-quarter-square kilometer parcels were selected as survey areas at the interface between the Tertiary Hills and Jurassic Upland. One parcel was located entirely in crop conifer forest. The second parcel was situated in open, agricultural terrain. The two parcels were selected because of their geomorphic and topographic similarity. Both are situated on reasonably good loess soil, and they share a similar aspect and elevation. In addition, the forested parcel contains a large pre-Roman earthwork (a Celtic *Viereckschanze*) and lies between an extensive Bronze Age tumulus cemetery and the remains of a Roman fortification, so there is a potential for buried cultural resources on the parcel. The test was based on the assumption that if the forest offered acceptable opportunities to view surface and subsurface cultural deposits, then materials would be recorded during a pedestrian survey.

Both parcels were investigated on the same day, to avoid any significant differences in weather conditions. Field walking was conducted along parallel 10 meter intervals in each parcel; direction varied depending upon the terrain (this close interval was expanded to 15 meters during later field investigations to increase efficiency). Cultivated fields within the open parcel provided excellent surface visibility, allowing an unobstructed view of 75–100% of the surface, weathered and washed by winter rains and snow. Fields in the open parcel yielded prehistoric and modern artifacts, but no subsurface features were evident. Prehistoric artifacts were even collected from animal burrows in a meadow. Visibility in the forested parcel was limited to rutted tracks and about a dozen tree throws. All were negative, including several uprooted trees within 50 meters of the *Viereckschanze*.

The forest economy test results showed clearly that pedestrian survey in the woods around Kelheim would be a slow, unproductive job, and would probably not increase our knowledge of prehistoric activity in the region. It also indicated that surface conditions in the cultivated fields were generally excellent and that burrowing animal activity allowed the location of buried prehistoric remains in meadows. Survey in the forests was not a productive or economical approach for the proposed fieldwork, so investigation was further restricted to open lands, including cultivated fields and meadows.

Time and personnel limitations meant that fieldwork had to be conducted at a modest level. Information on known sites was collected for an area of over 450 square kilometers around the oppidum (Figure 15.1). This area was clearly too large for a small-scale archaeological field survey. Therefore, an adequate sample of the area had to be determined that would address the research goals but conform to available time and support. The basis for sample selection was the desire to systematically investigate portions of all three geomorphological units at Kelheim. These units were chosen as sample strata, and survey areas were established on open parts of the Jurassic Upland, Tertiary Hills, and almost the entire Kelheim Basin (Figure 15.7).

The body of literature dealing with sampling issues in archaeology, and in archaeological survey in particular, is extensive (e.g. Mueller 1975; Plog 1976; Cherry et al. 1978). Sampling priorities for the Kelheim project were 1) the investigation of different landforms (sample strata) to provide a basis for comparison, 2) systematic data collection to ensure complete and representative coverage of varying local conditions within each stratum, and 3) the addition of a randomizing element to reduce selection bias and help overcome possible periodicity in the data. The present field work was inspired by Shennan's (1985) archaeological survey in East Hampshire, Britain. Shennan stresses the utility of transect survey in the exploration of an environmentally varied, archaeologically poorly known landscape. In addition, the transect method poses fewer managerial problems in a landscape divided into small agricultural fields such as at Kelheim, in contrast to quadrat or other approaches.

Each survey area was first divided in half and then further separated into parallel transects one-half kilometer wide and varying in length depending upon area dimensions (Figure 15.7). A random systematic transect sample was chosen for each survey stratum. A sample size of 50% was selected for maximal coverage while maintaining a manageable scale. The starting point of each systematic series was determined randomly. This series then was offset in the other half of each area to partly overcome any periodicity in the archaeological remains. This method does not possess much randomizing "power;" however, it does have the advantage of ensuring optimal coverage of each area. This coverage was desired because of the absence of such systematic work in the formation of the known data base.

Field Walking and Surface Collection

Within each selected transect all open (i.e. accessible) fields were investigated, including plowed, harrowed, and seeded plots, as well as meadows where the labors of burrowing animals allowed some visibility. Fields were walked at regular intervals along parallel transects. Prehistoric surface materials were collected and recorded; surface features, such as soil stains or artifact concentrations, were mapped, and associated artifacts were collected separately.

The first several days of fieldwork were used to experiment with different techniques to "fine tune" the survey to local conditions. During this period, issues of surface collection and coverage intensity were addressed. Surface collection techniques involve total or sample (controlled) collection of present cultural resources. Sample techniques are appropriate for the investigation of large sites with extensive amounts of surface debris (Redman 1987). However, they are poorly suited to a project involving the discovery and identification of new sites, particularly in an area such as Kelheim. Total surface collection was used in the Kelheim project

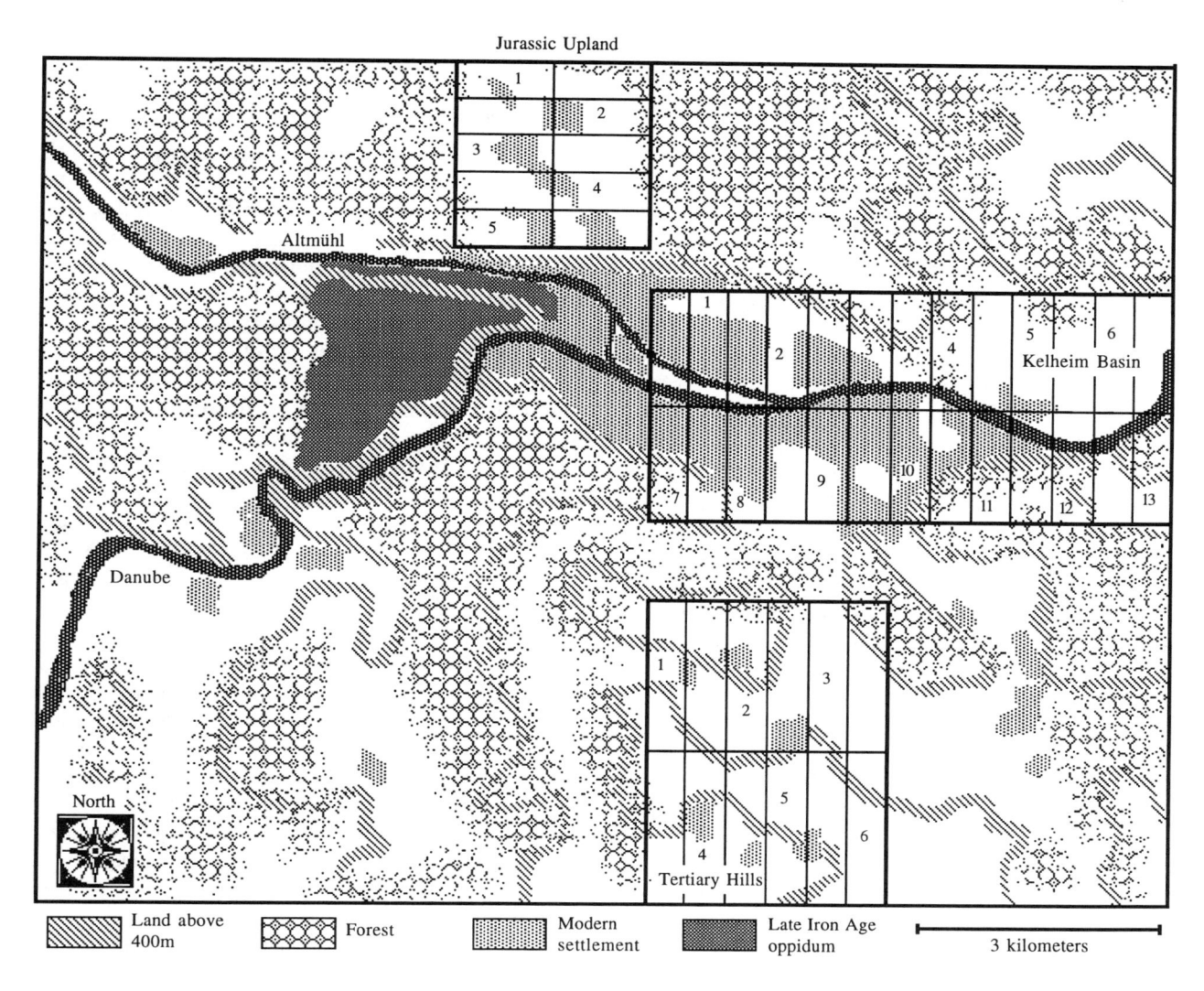

Figure 15.7. Archaeological field survey areas at Kelheim. Sample strata in the Jurassic Upland, Tertiary Hills, and Kelheim Basin are shown. Numerals identify actual transects investigated in each stratum.

for two reasons: 1) the relatively small average number of artifacts encountered per survey parcel, and 2) the importance of recovering diagnostic materials. Diagnostic materials, such as decorated sherds, are not immediately obvious among surface debris. Often, crucial artifacts are not identified until after washing in the laboratory. Under these conditions, total collection effectively speeds survey by avoiding the field search for diagnostics or the time-consuming process of gridding out features for partial collection. Surface features were mapped and intensively collected; larger features were collected along one- or two-meter transects.

In agricultural fields throughout Germany centuries of plowing have eroded many soils, destroying ancient living surfaces and leaving intact only features excavated into the subsoil. The presence of subsurface features, such as large postholes, pits, and ditches, may be revealed when plowing disturbs buried feature fill. Subsurface features were located by two means during field survey. Under damp, cloudy conditions the organic fill of disturbed subsurface features is easily visible on the surface. Dark feature fill contrasts with the light-colored sandy and loamy soils that predominate in the survey area, and under appropriate conditions the fill can be observed from a distance of several hundred meters. These soil stains usually are associated with a discrete concentration of artifacts on the surface, often including burned clay, bone, and charcoal. When strong sunlight or dry soils prohibit the observation of features, the artifact concentrations still mark their location. This method of locating buried features is made possible by surface erosion and regular subsurface disturbance, processes that are active on cultivated hilltops and slopes. In situations where alluvial or colluvial deposition occurs, such as in floodplains or at the base of slopes, prehistoric features and living floors may be deeply buried and untouched even by modern chisel plows. These features cannot be located without subsurface testing.

Coverage intensity is related to transect orientation and the distance between transects. Once established, these practices were kept consistent during fieldwork. Enhanced visibility was afforded by a field walking technique parallel to plow furrows and conforming to the local topography, so that survey orientation varied depending upon the field. Transects were parallel to maintain horizontal control during collection. Paced intervals of 10 to 20 m between transects were tried in the field. Visibility in a typical field (plowed and weathered) was excellent within a 5–10 m radius of the walker, depending upon furrow depth, and soil and light conditions. Within this radius most surface cultural material was easily visible. At a distance of 10 m and beyond, the ability to recognize surface artifacts dropped off sharply. A 15 m interval was established as the most economical alternative, balancing survey speed with acceptable coverage.

Field collection around Kelheim was conducted by the author between March 11 and April 28, 1991. German law protects the public right of access to private land, so permission from each private landowner was not necessary to perform the survey. While field walking, the author had the opportunity to interview many owners and tenants in their fields about archaeological remains on the properties, land history, and farming schedules and techniques. Artifacts collected during field work were cleaned and analyzed in the Archäologisches Museum in Kelheim.

Surface visibility was generally excellent during the first two weeks of survey. Winter snows had melted in the warmer spring rains and sun. Fields plowed after the autumn harvest were cleansed by months of inclement weather. Some fields planted in winter cereals already sported greening crops and were closed to investigation. By the end of March, dry, sunny weather predominated, inhibiting visibility and slowing field investigation. The friendly conditions prompted farmers to begin preparation and seeding of their fields one to two weeks earlier than usual. This activity reduced the number of fields open for collection, but experimentation proved that cultural deposits in freshly seeded or raked plots were still visible, and field walking continued. Survey was halted in late April, when all cultivated plots were either prepared or planted, and the spring sugar beet crop began to sprout.

Detailed records were kept of soil, light, and weather conditions, as well as the time of day, farming activities, and other factors that influence surface visibility and investigator performance. These data will allow a critical evaluation of the survey's effectiveness under varying field conditions. Conducting field survey alone is not always ideal, although it suited the project's scale and economy. A significant advantage of the solitary approach is that it limits investigator bias during collection to a single individual.

Results

Results of the fieldwork are summarized in Table 15.3. A total of 256 survey parcels, incorporating 541 individual fields, were walked in all three survey strata: Kelheim Basin, Jurassic Upland, and Tertiary Hills. This amounted to approximately 4,000,000 m^2 or four km^2 of area. The mean proportion of land walked in all three strata was 10%. More than 87% of the parcels were plowed and the remaining 13% were meadow or pasture. Most of the meadow and pasture was located on the floodplain of the Danube River within the Kelheim Basin.

Prehistoric remains, mainly scattered pottery fragments and worked stone debris, were discovered on 158 parcels. Features or associated cultural material concentrations were observed on 29 parcels. Observation of soil stains became a casualty of the arid weather that presided over the latter part of the survey. Soil stains could be identified on only two parcels; 27 parcels yielded discrete concentrations of artifacts that probably mark the location of subsurface features.

A total of 1566 prehistoric sherds and a fragment of a fired clay spindle whorl were collected from survey parcels. A small proportion of the pottery, 251 sherds, is potentially diagnostic, including decorated pieces, rims and near rims, basal fragments and body sherds with graphitic pastes, which are typical of specific archaeological periods or cultures. Preliminary ceramic analyses suggest that over 69 ceramic locales may be related to specific archaeological periods, from the Early Neolithic Linear Pottery culture (Linearbandkeramik), through the Early Bronze Age, to the Iron Age

Hallstatt and La Tène periods.

Lithic debris was recovered from most plowed parcels and a few meadows. Over 23.5 kg of lithic debitage, cores, hammerstones, tools, and utilized pieces were collected. Of the 59 assorted tools and utilized pieces in the assemblage, at least six specimens are representative of particular Neolithic or Early Bronze Age periods. In most instances, flint debris was clearly foreign to parcels and appeared culturally modified. However, flint nodules occasionally occur in fluvial gravel deposits or chalk bedrock outcrops in the region. Fractured flint from parcels on these deposits should be treated with skepticism. Suspect materials have been removed from the assemblage discussed here.

Survey results show that a blanket of flint debris covers the landscape around Kelheim. Two important prehistoric flint mines are situated in the project area at Baiersdorf above the Altmühl Valley (Binsteiner 1987) and Arnhofen near Abensberg (Binsteiner and Engelhardt 1987), as well as at four other known sites (Reisch 1974; Engelhardt 1983). Lithic remains indicate a considerable and widespread exploitation of flint that was not evident from archival data. Since every piece of debitage observed was collected, the survey results will allow the flint content of each field to be compared, enabling relative frequencies of lithic debris in different areas to be assessed.

The survey produced only a few metal or glass objects of established prehistoric origin. These include an incised bronze ring from the Early Iron Age (see below, Figure 15.12, 6), and a small translucent blue glass bead with parallels from Late Iron Age settlements in Bavaria. The majority of the iron and bronze/brass items collected are unidentifiable fragments and cannot be ascribed to specific archaeological cultures.

Large amounts of medieval, recent, or unknown detritus were also collected during the course of the survey, including ceramics, glass, brick, slag, ore, and various metal objects.

Kelheim Basin

The survey area in the Kelheim Basin was sited to incorporate a variety of landforms within the broad river valley. It measured 6.5 by 3 km, and involved 19.5 km^2. The survey area was divided into 26 transects measuring 0.5 km wide and 1.5 km long.

In recent years, the Kelheim economy has boomed, attracting new inhabitants, industries and transportation facilities along the Danube. This growth is most evident on the face of the river bottoms and pleasant terraces east of the city. Currently about 15% of the basin within the survey area has been modified by construction. These areas were closed to the present field survey. In some western and southern transects, the amount of

Table 15.3. Preliminary results of archaeological field survey at Kelheim.

	Kelheim Basin	Jurassic Upland	Tertiary Hills	Total
Total area (km^2)	19.5	6.25	12	37.75
Total survey transects	26	10	12	48
Transects surveyed	13	5	6	24
Sample size	50%	50%	50%	50% (mean)
Survey parcels	165	19	72	256
Fields	431	35	75	541
Area surveyed (km^2)	1.81	0.36	1.79	3.96
Portion of total area surveyed	9.28%	5.76%	14.92%	10% (mean)
Identified locales	86	5	67	158
"Prehistoric"	53	5	36	94
Neolithic	2	0	4	6
Bronze Age	4	0	2	6
Late Bronze Age	1	0	4	5
Early Iron Age	1	0	5	6
Late Iron Age	3	0	6	9
"La Tène"	22	0	10	32
Prehistoric sherds (qty.)	238	1	1327	1566
Lithic debitage (kg)	5.505	0.098	17.946	23.549

modified terrain approaches 80%. Destruction of cultural resources through urban expansion is continuing at a rapid rate, despite Herculean salvage efforts by local archaeologists. Forest covers less than 10% of the basin survey area, largely in the southeast where the survey area includes a portion of high ground.

All open fields (cultivated and meadow) were investigated in one half (13) of the transects. One hundred sixty-five parcels were surveyed, comprising 431 individual fields. An area of 1.81 km² was actually walked. This is nearly 10% of the total survey area in the basin.

According to the literature and archival search, there are 39 known prehistoric locales within the limits of the survey area in the Kelheim basin. In addition, aerial photographs reveal 24 locations of possible cultural activity. Most known locales were recorded through excavations or salvage operations required by rapid urban growth and canal construction.

Field walking yielded an additional 86 prehistoric locales. These results more than triple the number of known prehistoric find spots in the basin. Prehistoric cultural remains collected in the basin include 5.5 kilograms of stone debitage and tools, and 238 sherds. Most of the material is undiagnostic, but preliminary analysis revealed extensive areas of Neolithic and Bronze Age activity on upper terraces of the basin. Diagnostic lithics and pottery indicate the presence of at least two Neolithic locales (Figure 15.8, 1). Four Bronze Age locales produced decorated ceramics (Figure 15.8, 2-3).

Sherds with typical Late Bronze Age decorative motifs (Figure 15.8, 4) were identified from one locale. Combined archival and survey data indicate that settlement and burial activity during the Late Bronze Age was concentrated in the northwest corner of the basin on a former island between the Altmühl and Danube Rivers (Figure 15.9). Elsewhere, remains are lightly though evenly distributed and consist of ceramic scatters and cemeteries.

During survey, the discovery of fragments of highly decorated impressed and painted pottery (Figure 15.8, 5-6) from a surface feature revealed the presence of an Early Iron Age cemetery on a terrace along the Danube's northern edge. The archaeological landscape of the Early Iron Age in the basin (Figure 15.10) is similar to the Late Bronze Age. Intensive occupation of the island continued, and there is a regular distribution of burial places and ceramic scatters throughout the basin.

Twenty-two survey parcels yielded La Tène ceramics with graphite pastes, and characteristic Late La Tène pottery was recovered from three parcels (Figure 15.8, 7-8). In contrast to the preceding periods, occurrences of Late Iron Age residues in the basin appear high compared to the Late Bronze and Early Iron Ages (Figure 15.11). This appearance belies the transitory nature of most remains. While the Altmühl island just outside of the oppidum walls continued to be a location of intensive cultural activity, the remaining occurrences are markedly thin, as indicated by the modest sum of 32 sherds recovered from 25 survey parcels. Most occurrences consist of one or two sherds. Some plain graphite wares may be Early Iron Age; only three sherds can be dated securely to the Late Iron Age. The ceramics are scattered across the floodplain, on adjacent sand and gravel bars, and along the bluff top. Two distributions of graphite sherds and Late Iron Age pottery in adjacent survey parcels may indicate the presence of more substantial buried remains. One scatter (five sherds) occupies a sandy terrace south of the Danube above Saal; the second scatter (eight sherds) is sited on loess soil on the southern exposure of a narrow ridge that divides the basin from rolling hills to the south. Overall, the results suggest widespread but very low-intensive activity in the basin beyond the oppidum during the Late Iron Age.

Jurassic Upland

The survey area in the Jurassic Upland at Ihrlerstein above Kelheim measured 2.5 x 2.5 km, incorporating 6.25 km² of typically abrupt, rocky terrain. The area was divided into 10 transects measuring 0.5 km wide and 1.25 km long. All exposed terrain in five transects (50% of the area) was investigated.

Although the land is marginal, farmers till nearly 75% of the ground around Ihrlerstein. About 10% of the survey area is built-up or otherwise disturbed and inaccessible to field survey techniques. Nearly 10% of the area consists of stony grassland, particularly along the plateau's southern edge. The shallow soil is unfit even for burrowing animals, so the lack of visibility prevented these meadows from being included in the survey. Forest covers approximately 5% of the area, mainly along the western and eastern edges. Many fields around Ihrlerstein had been planted with winter crops which were already sprouting during survey, prohibiting the scrutiny of a large portion of

The Landscape Survey, 1990–1991

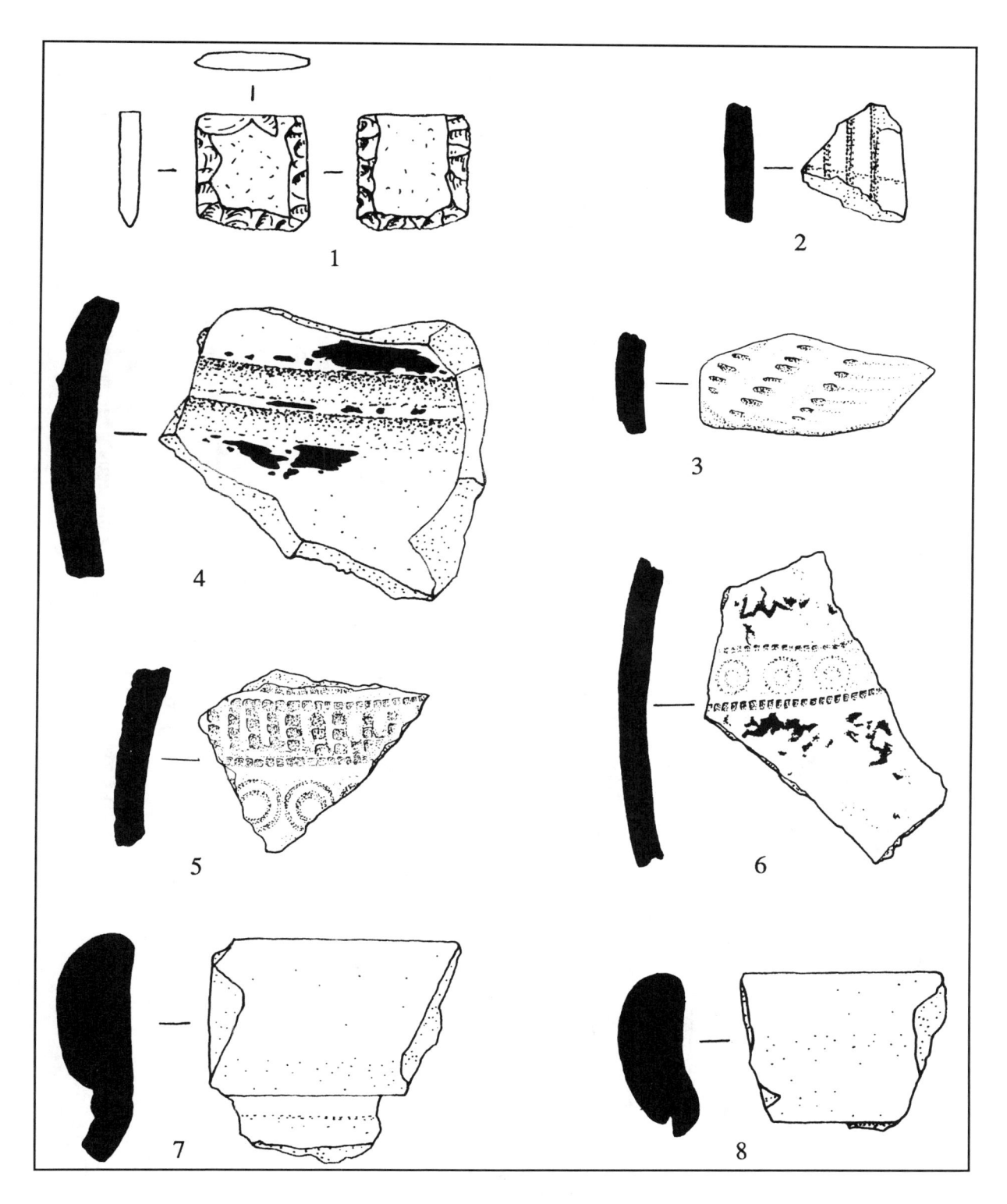

Figure 15.8. Representative artifacts recovered in the Kelheim Basin during surface collection: 1 is flint, 2-8 are ceramic. Scale is 1:1. 1: projectile point fragment (base), Neolithic; 2-3: decorated sherds, Bronze Age; 4: decorated sherd with graphite, Late Bronze Age; 5-6: impressed and painted sherds with graphite, Early Iron Age; 7-8: rim sherds, *Graphittonkeramik*, Late Iron Age (drawings: M. L. Murray and V. Woelfel).

Chapter 15 - Murray

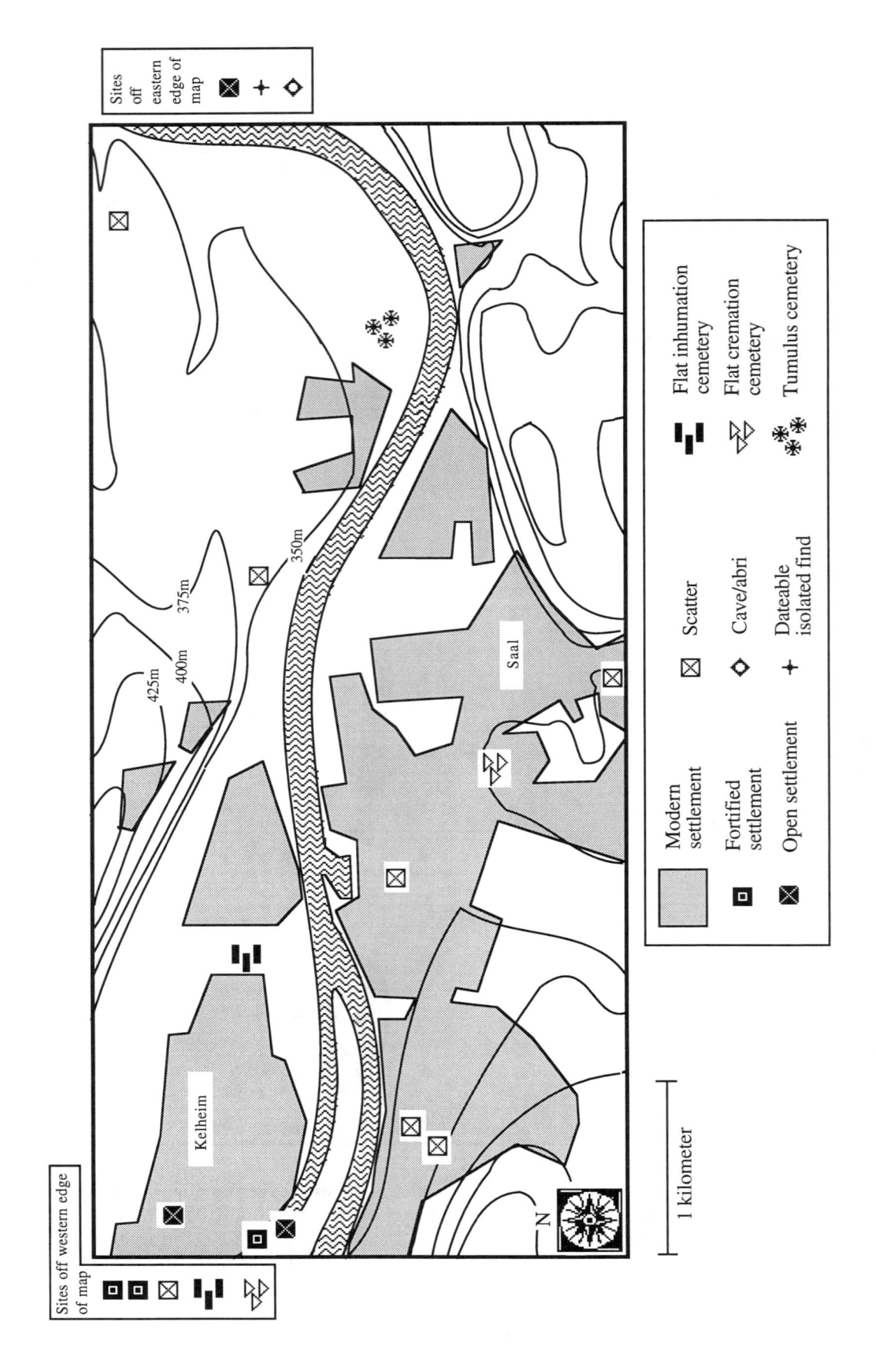

Figure 15.9. Late Bronze Age (1300-750 B.C.) remains in the Kelheim Basin, including previously recorded finds and results of field survey in 1991.

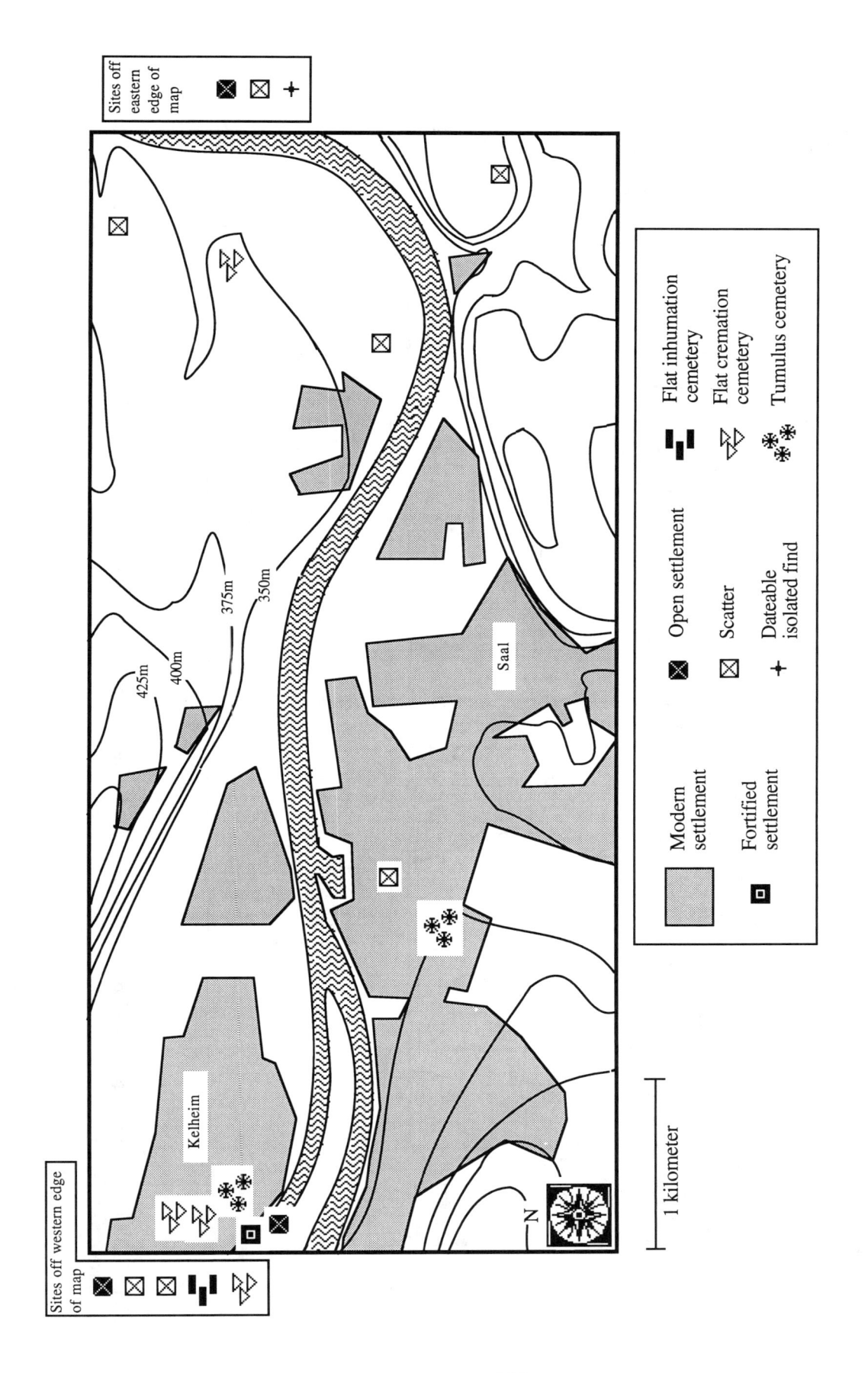

Figure 15.10. Early Iron Age (750-350 B.C.) remains in the Kelheim Basin, including previously recorded finds and results of field survey in 1991.

Chapter 15 - Murray

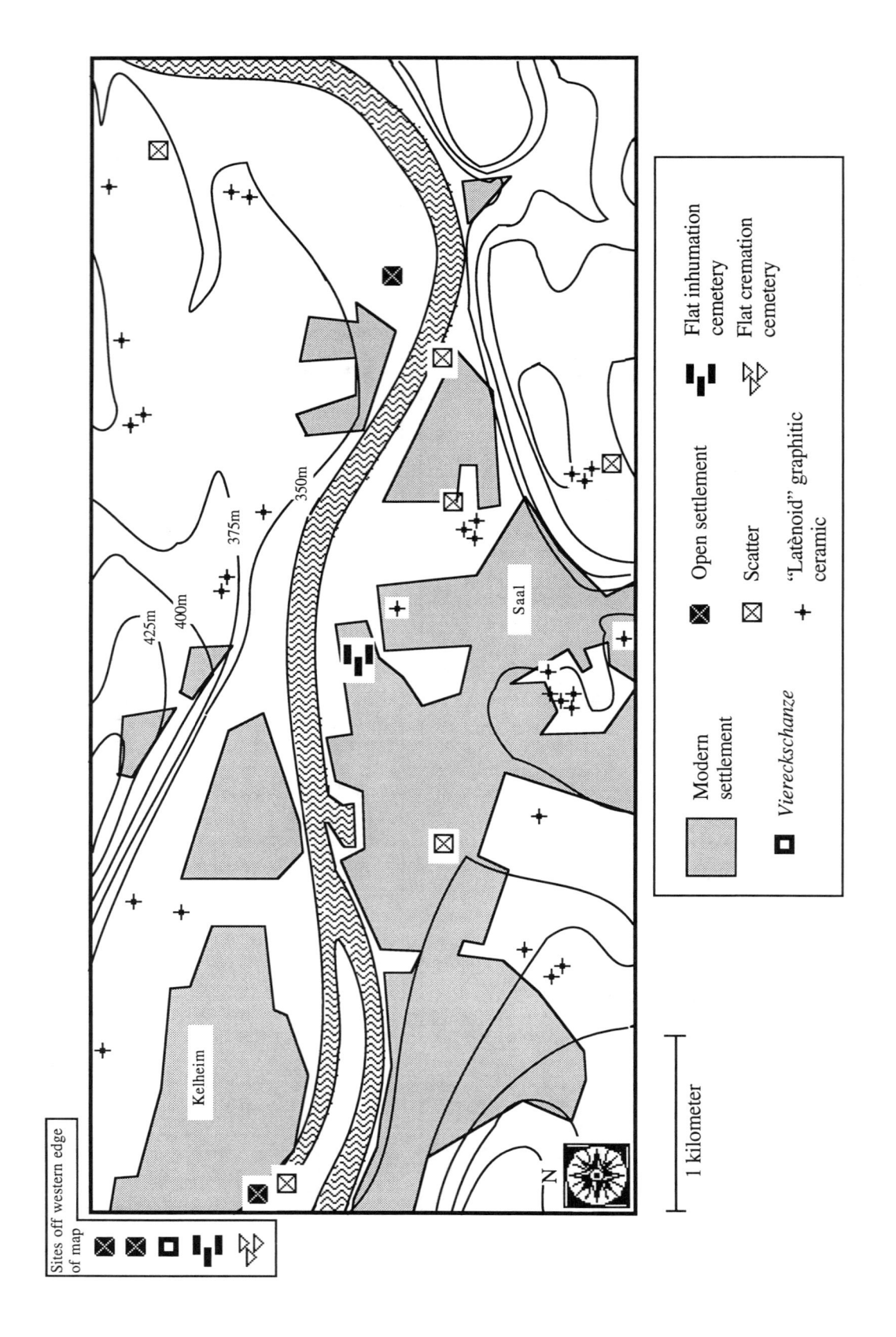

Figure 15.11. Late Iron Age (350-15 B.C.) remains in the Kelheim Basin, including "latènoid" graphitic sherds (ca. 450-15 B.C.); data include previously recorded finds and results of field survey in 1991.

the Jurassic Upland sample. Nineteen parcels were investigated, comprising 35 individual fields and an area of 0.36 km². This is about 6% of the survey landscape in the Jurassic Upland.

Only two known prehistoric locales were identified within the survey area on the Jurassic Upland. Both places consist of a small grouping of visible monuments assumed to be prehistoric tumulus cemeteries, although no finds are known from the earthen and stone mounds. Similar mounds nearby have produced characteristic funerary remains from the Middle Bronze and Early Iron Ages. No other prehistoric cultural resources have been recorded for the entire area, in spite of continuous building and intensive agriculture. Aerial photographs fail to reveal traces of cultural activity.

The paucity of previous evidence gives the impression of little remnant cultural activity in the upland. But the presence of cemeteries would suggest that this is a distorted view. Field survey identified five new prehistoric locales. These locales are of questionable quality, since they consist of a handful of lithic fragments (nine pieces) and a single undecorated and undiagnostic prehistoric body sherd.

Because of the small number of fields in the Jurassic Upland available for study, we should exercise caution, so as not to overreach the evidence. A handful of finds may suggest some prehistoric use, but the overall sterility of the investigated parcels is dramatic when compared to other survey areas. Field and weather conditions during survey in the Upland were similar to those in effect during surface collection in portions of the Tertiary Hills (see below), so the negative results are not the result of survey bias.

Tertiary Hills

In the Tertiary Hills, the survey area measured 3 x 4 km, incorporating 12 km² of gently rolling farmland. The survey area was divided into 12 transects measuring 0.5 km wide and 2 km long. All open fields in 50% of the transects (six) were walked. Occasionally, parcels outside the transects also were investigated to take advantage of opportunities afforded by good conditions and open terrain. Seventy-two parcels were walked, involving 75 individual fields and 1.79 km². About 15% of the total survey area actually was walked.

Modern settlement in the area is relatively sparse and consists of a regular pattern of small villages based on one or more farmsteads sited 1–2 km apart. This pattern is typical for the southern Bavarian hills and probably was established already by the early Middle Ages, if not earlier. Only about 5% of the survey landscape has been modified by construction. Less than 1% of the terrain is forested, mainly along the northern edge where the survey area adjoins Jurassic outcrops. The remaining 94% of the landscape is cultivated, and the soils are considered fair to good. Agricultural fields are considerably larger in the hills than in the Basin or on the Jurassic plateau; the tilled land is not as intensively subdivided.

There are 13 known prehistoric locales within the survey landscape in the Tertiary Hills. Also, 16 locations exhibit soil or crop marks. Field survey in the hills produced 67 new prehistoric locales (an in rease of over 500%). These results suggest that previously recorded data represent a very small portion of existing prehistoric cultural resources in the hills.

Recovered cultural material comprises mainly lithic debris and ceramic fragments from surface scatters and features. Nearly 18 kg of flint were collected. Flint residues are so common in the fields that only six of 72 surveyed parcels produced no lithic material. A total of 1327 prehistoric sherds were collected. At least four Neolithic locales have been identified. One Neolithic locale yielded classic pottery of the Linearbandkeramik culture (Figure 15.12, 1). Numerous pieces of fine Bronze Age pottery were recovered from two parcels (Figure 15.12, 2).

Combined archival and survey data reveal two clusters of Late Bronze Age activity on the southern aspects of gentle loess hills in the survey landscape (Figure 15.13). During survey, four parcels yielded evidence of subsurface features with associated artifacts (Figure 15.12, 3-4). Finds associated with these loci suggest various domestic activities, textile production, metal working, ceramic production, and trade in graphite. One locale on the southern edge produced fine decorated pottery (Figure 15.12, 5), burned bone, and bronze debris and may mark the place of destroyed Late Bronze Age cremation burials.

The mixing of Early Iron Age materials (Figure 15.12, 6-7) with Late Bronze Age sherds on most parcels indicates that occupation of most locales continued during the Early Iron Age (Figure 15.14).

Similar to survey in the Kelheim Basin, field collection in the Tertiary Hills yielded scattered La Tène graphite sherds and a small amount of Late Iron Age pottery in several thin scatters (Fig-

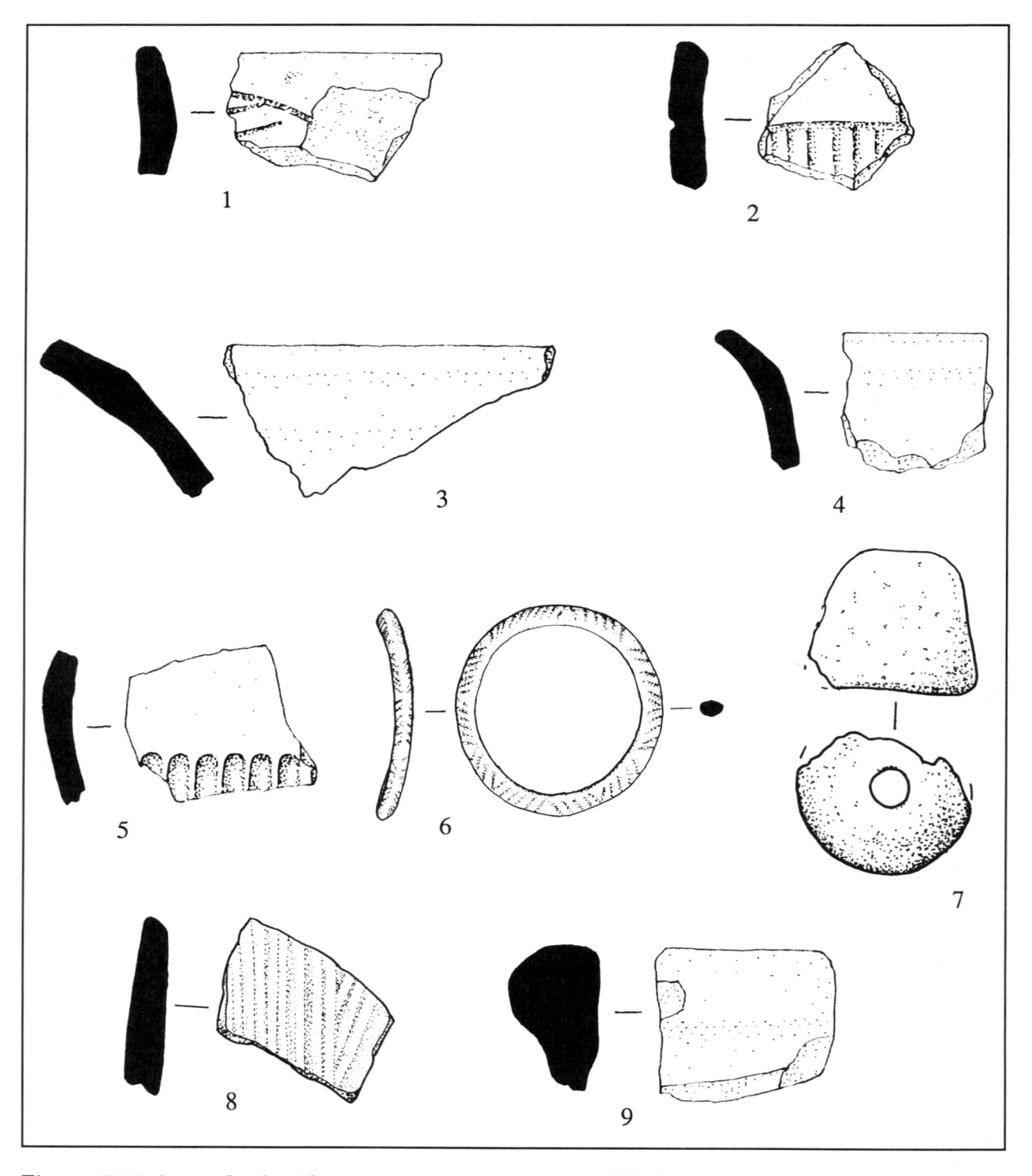

Figure 15.12. A sample of artifacts recovered in the Tertiary Hills during surface collection: 1-5, 7-9 are ceramic, 6 is bronze. Scale is 1:1. 1: decorated rim sherd, Linearbandkeramik culture, Early Neolithic; 2: decorated sherd, Bronze Age; 3-4: rim sherds, Late Bronze Age; 5: decorated sherd, Late Bronze Age; 6: decorated bronze ring, Early Iron Age; 7: fired clay spindle whorl, Late Bronze Age or Early Iron Age; 8: decorated sherd, *Kammstrichkeramik* ("combed ware"), Late Iron Age; 9: rim sherd, *Graphittonkeramik*, Late Iron Age (drawings: M. L. Murray and V. Woelfel).

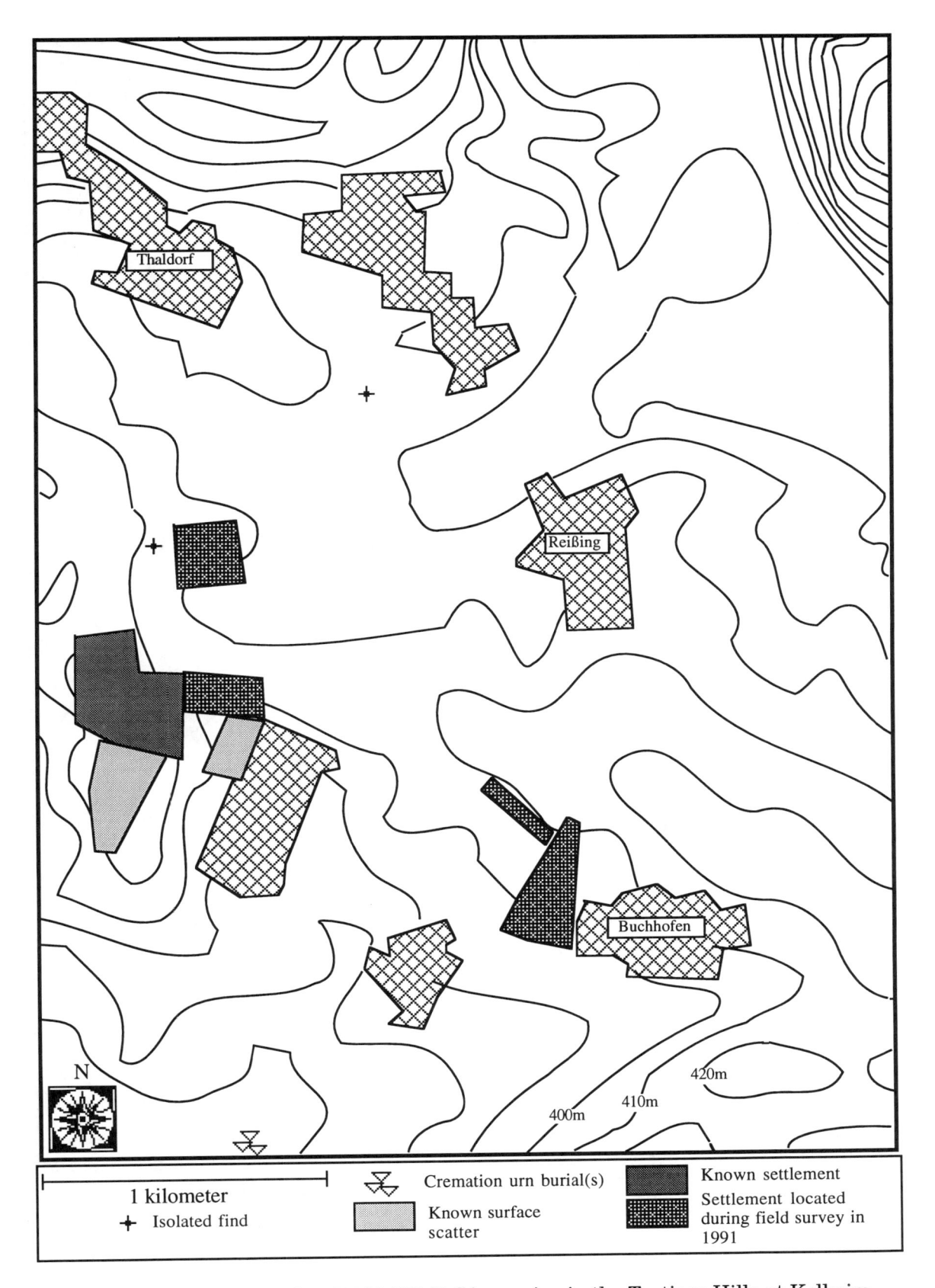

Figure 15.13. Late Bronze Age (1300-750 B.C.) remains in the Tertiary Hills at Kelheim.

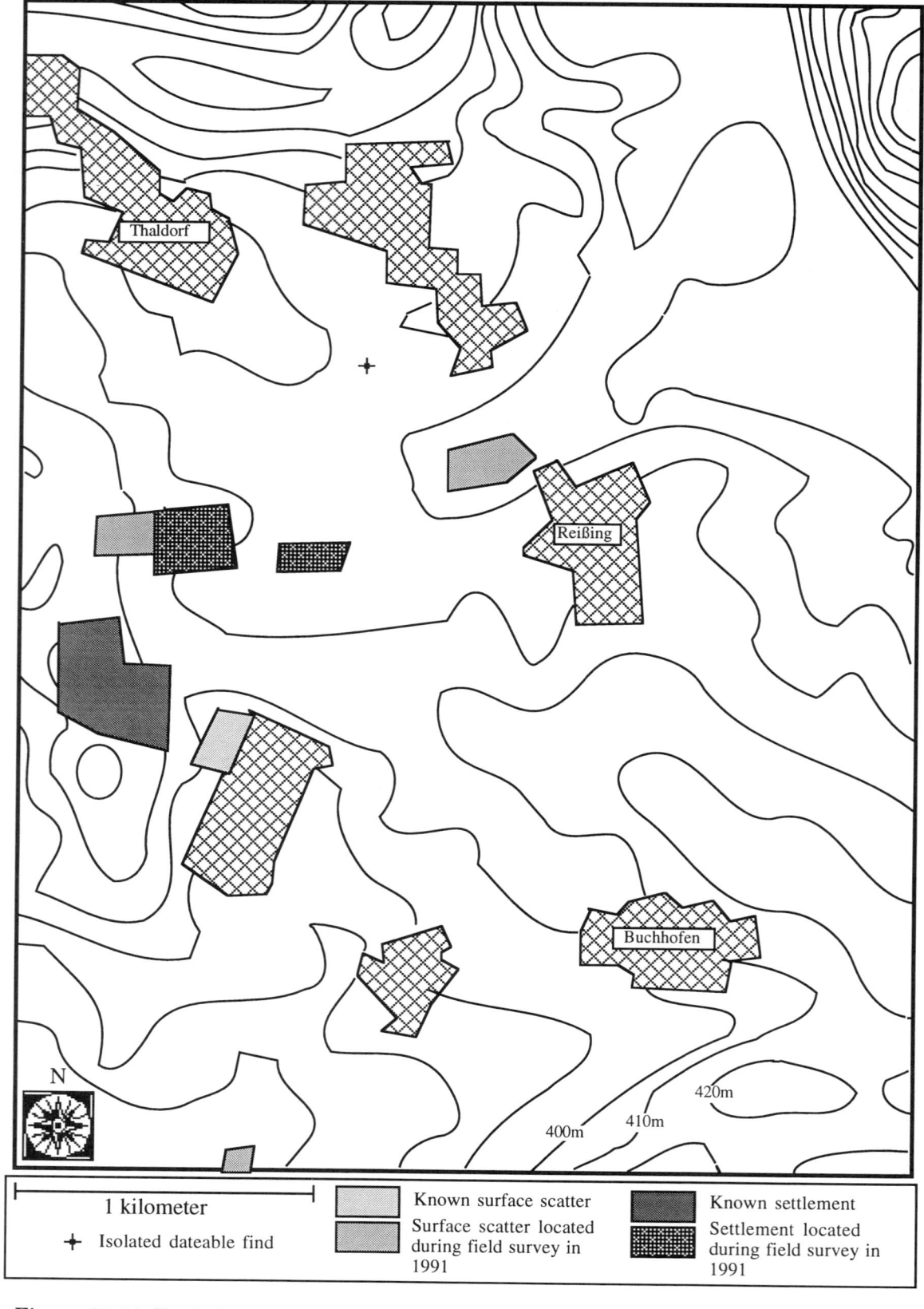

Figure 15.14. Early Iron Age (750-350 B.C.) remains in the Tertiary Hills at Kelheim.

Figure 15.15. Late Iron Age (350-15 B.C.) remains in the Tertiary Hills at Kelheim including "latènoid" graphitic sherds (450-15 B.C.).

ure 15.12, 8-9). There is no evidence of associated subsurface features, dense surface scatters, or other indicators of more intensive occupation (Figure 15.15). This lack of evidence for intensive Late Iron Age activity is in sharp contrast to a wealth of evidence from the Late Bronze and Early Iron Ages.

Discussion

The Kelheim survey project has produced a broad, integrated data base to study the local history of a landscape. For the purposes of this report, discussion will focus on the final millennium B.C. and the development from the Late Bronze to the Late Iron Age. Some preliminary conclusions are suggested, but like most archaeological fieldwork, the results pose more questions than they answer.

Historical Development and the Hinterland of the Oppidum

The Late Bronze Age (Bronze Age D and Hallstatt A–B horizons) at Kelheim is preserved in a fairly even distribution of settlements, ceramic scatters, and cemeteries (Figure 15.16). Cave occupations and hoards are also common residues of this time. Cemeteries are characteristically flat cremation burial grounds, sometimes containing hundreds of graves (Müller-Karpe 1952). Several locales at cliffs along the Altmühl appear to be the places where ritual activity involved intentional destruction of ceramic vessels. Thick sherd deposits at the base of cliffs indicate that pots were either tossed from the cliffs or shattered at their bases (Maier 1984). Late Bronze Age sites are found throughout the Altmühl River Valley, Kelheim Basin, and the Tertiary Hills. Field survey confirmed this pattern, locating particularly extensive areas of settlement and some funerary activity on loess deposits in the hills. There are no known finds from the Jurassic Upland north of the Altmühl and Danube. Late Bronze Age remains have been found mainly through excavation and surface collection, an indication that they correspond with modern archaeological interest and agricultural activity in the area, focused respectively on the Altmühl River Valley and on the relatively good soils of the Tertiary Hills.

The Early Iron Age (Hallstatt C–D horizons) is preserved as an assemblage of burial remains, ceramic scatters, and settlements (Figure 15.17). Burial grounds of the Early Iron Age are either far more numerous or more visible than from the preceding period. The act of burying the dead beneath stone and earth mounds increases the chances of survival and visibility of these remains. Many of the 50 known prehistoric tumulus groups in the area date to this time period. Like the preceding period, Early Iron Age remains have been found along the Altmühl, in the Kelheim Basin, and in the Tertiary Hills. The mute presence of tumuli in the Jurassic Upland speaks of activity on the plateau, although both archival search and field survey failed to locate significant settlement remains there. Field survey discovered remains of extensive settlement in the Kelheim Basin and Tertiary Hills, often mixed with Late Bronze Age residues. A new location of funerary remains was discovered above the northern bank of the Danube in the eastern Basin. There is increased activity within caves and rockshelters during this period. The contexts of discovery for Early Iron Age remains at Kelheim are similar to those for Late Bronze Age locales. This pattern suggests certain similarities in the relationship between the nature of archaeological remains and methods of discovery.

By the Later Iron Age, there appears to have been a constriction of settlement around the Michelsberg (Figure 15.18). During the second century B.C., the time of oppidum construction, activity in the surrounding landscape either does not seem to have matched the apparent intensity of the late eighth to early fourth centuries B.C. or was of a very different nature. Exceptions to this are the Mitterfeld in the Altmühl River Valley within the oppidum walls, and the western Kelheim Basin at the foot of the Michelsberg. These are the only known locations of extensive Late Iron Age remains. Subsurface features are associated with Late Iron Age artifacts at two locales in the Altmühl Valley and at one locale in the eastern Basin, but these "settlements" consist only of one or two pits. Late Iron Age sherd scatters were commonly found during excavation of other prehistoric settlements. Fertile terrain of the Tertiary Hills and loess islands on the Jurassic Upland near Hienheim are particularly devoid of settlement. No Late Iron Age features were observed during field walking in the Hills or Basin. The oppidum seems to command a rather empty "hinterland."

Landscape data from regions in Germany without large Late Iron Age defended sites contrast with those from Kelheim. Archaeological survey undertaken at the extensive open-pit coal mines of the Rheinland (Simons 1989) reveal a pattern of diffuse Late Bronze and Early Iron Age settlement, with regular site displacement over time. There was no observable regularity in settlement size or spacing. In contrast, Late Iron Age settlement was concentrated in larger "villages" with increased longevity and regular spacing at one km intervals. Similar patterns of intensive rural settlement during the Late Iron Age are apparent in data from the lower Schwarzach River Valley (Schmidt 1986; Bockisch 1987) in northern Bavaria, the Danube River Valley near Regensburg 20 km east of Kelheim (Schier 1985), and the Danube-Isar confluence about 80 km downstream (Schmotz 1989).

Extensive extra-murus settlement remains similar to Kelheim are known from numerous Late Iron Age fortifications, such as on the Kleiner Gleichberg bei Römhild (Spehr 1971) and at the Moravian oppidum of Staré Hradisko (Meduna 1970a). At Závist in Bohemia, there is a *Viereckschanze* in close proximity to the oppidum walls (Břeň 1971), and there is a similar Late La Tène enclosure within the walls on the Donnersberg in western Germany (Engels 1976). Similar rectilinear enclosures have been identified in aerial photographs of the interior of the Manching oppidum, and the recent find of a miniature gold "cult-tree" suggests a ritual place at the core of the defensive enclosure (Maier 1990).

The discontinuous occupation of the surrounding hills and eastern basin during development of the Kelheim oppidum is reminiscent of the rural settlement implosion known from prehistoric urban settings such as Teotihuacan (Sanders et al. 1979) and the Uruk countryside (Adams and Nissen 1972). There is evidence at the Manching oppidum, 36 km southwest of Kelheim, that rural communities combined during the second century B.C. into a single intramural population (Krämer 1985). Archaeological survey data from central France also reveal a sharply constricted pattern of Late Iron Age settlement around the oppidum at Levroux (Buchsenschutz et al. 1988). Similarly, several areas in central and western Europe have revealed a process of abandonment of open settlements in favor of defended agglomerations during the final century B.C. This process is suggested for Aulnat and Gergovie in south-central France (Collis 1975, 1980) and has been documented in Switzerland at Basel-Gasfabrik and Basel-Münsterhügel (Furger-Gunti 1980). It may also have occurred in southwestern Germany at Breisach-Hochstetten and Breisach-Münsterberg (Collis 1984a).

At Kelheim, this "implosion" may be evidence of the urban agglomeration of rural population at the oppidum. To maintain such an agglomeration, intensive food production and raw material extraction beyond the settlement walls would be necessary. Compared to the numerous Late Bronze and Early Iron Age settlements with pit features, a few thin sherd scatters from the Late Iron Age seem scant evidence of this exploitation. On the other hand, they may reflect transitory occupations, for example those of food producers housed within the oppidum who tended the fields and flocks by day and returned to the oppidum at night. In this manner, the daily needs of the Late Iron Age community were addressed by individuals or groups living within or near the oppidum in the Altmühl Valley and western Basin. The sherd scatters in the surrounding countryside may be the residues of seasonal migrations by food producing groups into the hinterland, or may indicate the manuring of fields (Wilkinson 1988) using dung collected within or near the oppidum. The oppidum, then, did not serve as a redistributive center or market for surrounding communities (up to a distance of 16 km), and there was no extensive network of rural villages providing agricultural or raw material surplus. The only central function that the oppidum served on a local level was as a focal point for habitation, iron production, and other craftwork. This interpretation has independent confirmation from the palaeobotanical analysis of plant remains from the Mitterfeld within the fortification (see Chapter 8).

An alternative interpretation is that the sherd scatters are the residues of small mobile or semi-mobile groups that roamed the Late Iron Age countryside, such as specialized pastoral communities. Such herding groups may not leave behind remnant features such as storage pits or post-hole structures that are used to identify "intensive" settlement. The oppidum population may have interacted with specialized pastoralists in the surrounding countryside, so that the settlement functioned as a central place for the interface between permanent oppidum and extra-murus communities and mobile herding communities. Patterns of cattle remains from the Mitterfeld suggest that beef stock was raised and processed outside of the oppidum (see Chapter 9).

Landscape and Social Reproduction at Kelheim

While traces of Late Iron Age activity in the surrounding landscape are few, there are numerous rectilinear enclosures (*Viereckschanzen*) that probably date from the Late Iron Age. Four *Viereckschanzen* are still preserved south of the

Chapter 15 - Murray

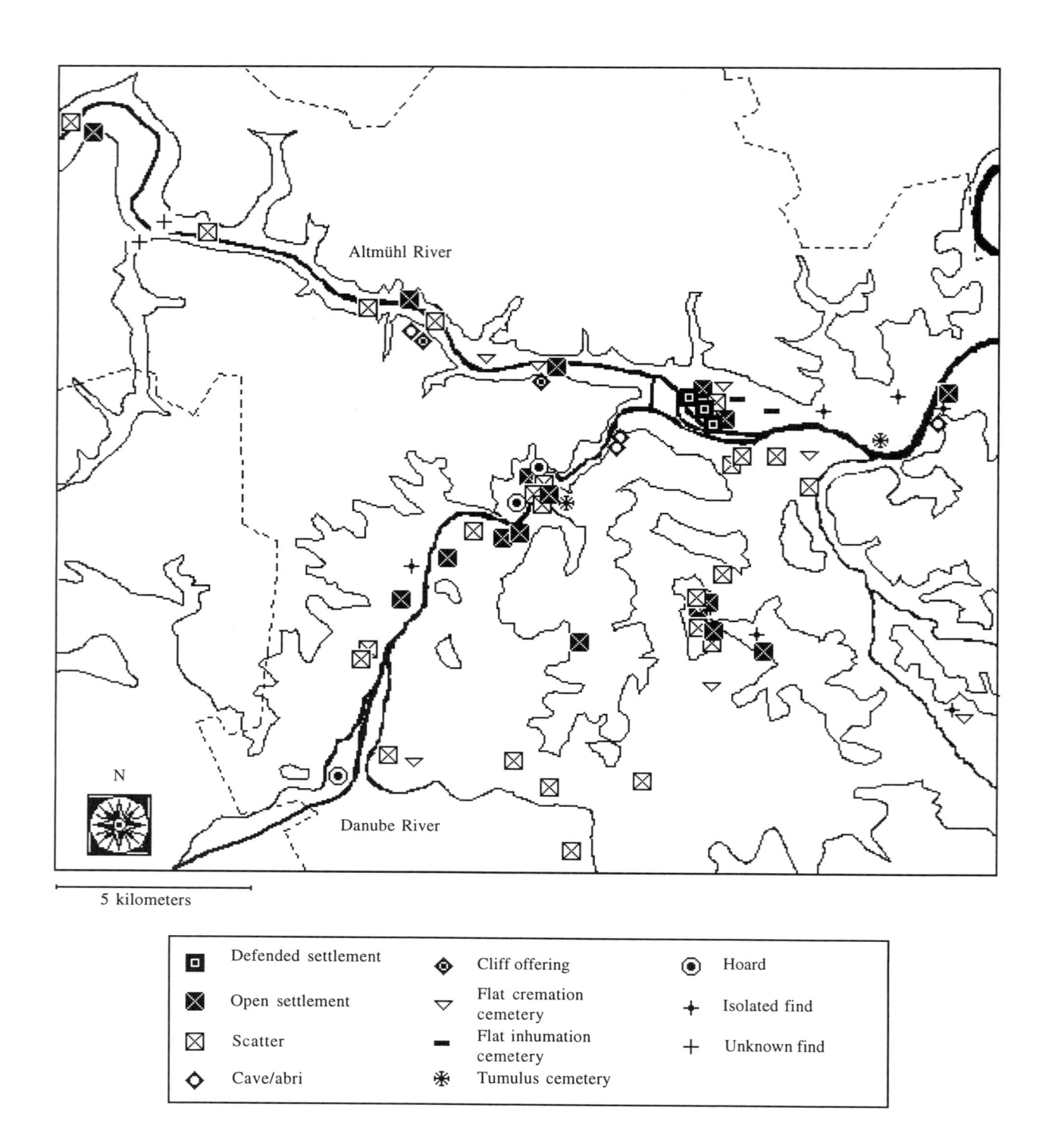

Figure 15.16. The Late Bronze Age archaeological landscape at Kelheim (ca. 1300-750 B.C.).

The Landscape Survey, 1990–1991

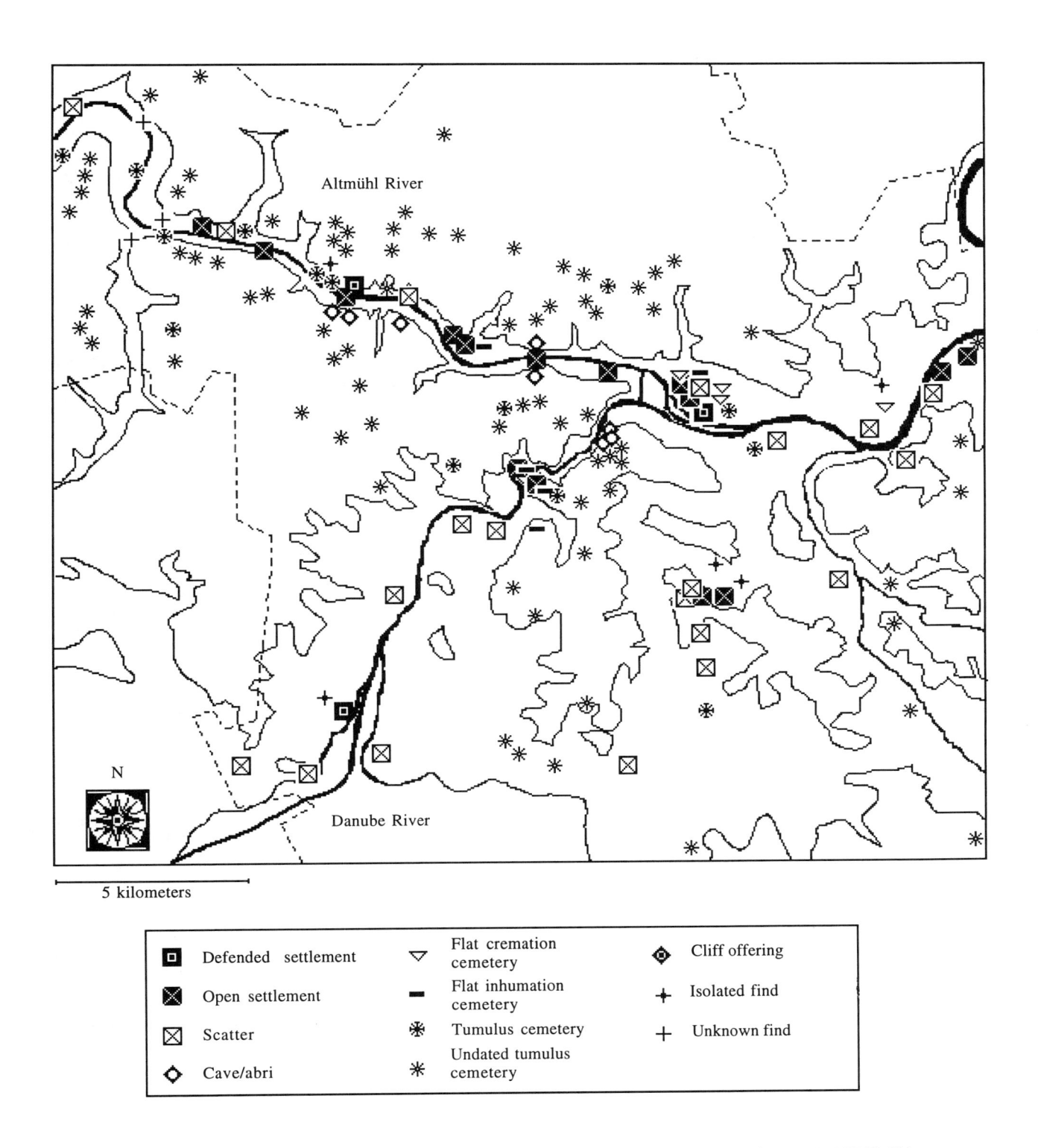

Figure 15.17. The Early Iron Age archaeological landscape at Kelheim (ca. 750-350 B.C.).

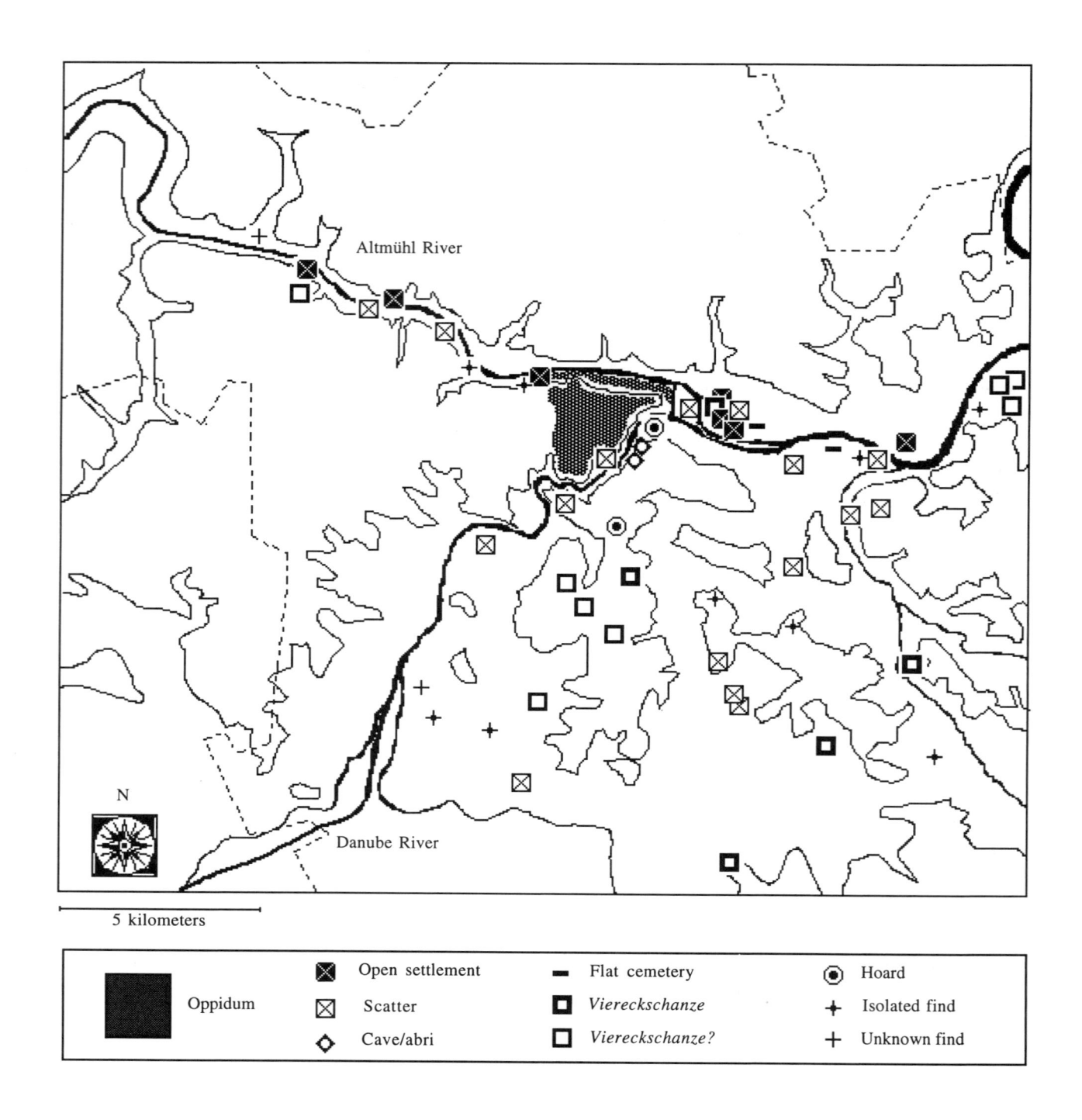

Figure 15.18. The Late Iron Age archaeological landscape at Kelheim (ca. 350-15 B.C.), not including generic "laténoid" finds.

Danube, and one is known from excavation immediately east of Kelheim's old city. The subterranean outlines of several others appear in aerial photographs of the Tertiary Hills and the eastern Basin, and one possible enclosure occupies a small spur above the Altmühl River Valley east of Riedenburg. If these sites were the focus of Late Iron Age ritual activities, as is currently believed (Schwarz 1975; Planck 1982; Bittel et al. 1990), then clearly the "hinterland," while sparsely occupied, was incorporated into the Late Iron Age sociospatial frame of reference. The social and ritual contexts of the *Viereckschanzen* are poorly understood, and unfortunately none of the structures at Kelheim have been adequately studied; it is not clear if the enclosures were in use at the same time. Were these sites used by a small rural population, each enclosure constructed by an independent community, or were they visited seasonally by a united population? Were they established by oppidum elite to bring the surrounding landscape into their control? Each enclosure occupies a particular ecological niche in the landscape, from infertile Jura outcrop to good loess soil. Perhaps one or more communities erected these specialized structures for the worship of different natural agencies in the Celtic religious pantheon (Brunaux 1988).

Deposition of cultural remains in caves or in association with cliffs was common from the Neolithic to the Early Iron Age at Kelheim. In the Late Iron Age, cave deposition declined markedly, although it did not cease entirely, particularly in caves along the cliffs of the Danube Gorge below the Michelsberg (Nadler 1986). This pattern of deposition is found throughout Germany (Behm-Blancke 1976; Weissmüller 1986; Züchner 1977). In his analysis of post-Mesolithic cave occupations in the southern Nördlinger Ries, Weissmüller (1986) notes that deposition in caves is linked to the intensity of settlement in the surrounding landscape and the ways in which people used and discarded their materials (i.e., how they became part of the archaeological record). Post-Mesolithic cave occupations often have an extra-domestic, "ritual" character. While usually composed of artifact types associated with habitation (ceramics, metals), cave deposits lack the breadth of domestic refuse (Weissmüller 1986) or possess qualities that otherwise differentiate them from habitations, such as the mixing of debris with select human remains (Maier 1965; Schauer 1981; Leja 1991).

When cave and cliff use declines in the Late Iron Age, a new formal structure, the *Viereckschanze*, appears in the landscape. This change may herald a restructuring of Iron Age ritual life, from practice in natural places to the formal incorporation of nature into built places. Whereas practice was previously governed by nature (such as natural boundaries and existing places such as caves and cliffs), nature was now artificially bounded and incorporated into the process of social reproduction. Was this incorporation of nature a form of natural legitimation for new social, political, and religious structures?

These changes in the structuring of nature and ritual parallel transformations in mortuary ritual and burial place from the Late Bronze to Late Iron Ages in southern Germany. Typical flat cremation fields of the Urnfield Late Bronze Age are found throughout the Kelheim region. There are seven known cremation cemeteries. There are also two known flat inhumation cemeteries of the Late Bronze Age D horizon in the Kelheim Basin. In addition, Early Urnfield funerary materials were found in a Middle Bronze Age tumulus on the Wurzberg above Weltenburg, and several Urnfield cremation burials were recovered under destroyed tumuli on the Danube shore near Herrnsaal. Urnfield cemeteries tend to be very uniform and densely packed, and the typical grave comprises a simple pit with two or three ceramic vessels and occasional bronze objects (Pfauth 1989). Like the Urnfield cemetery located on the eastern outskirts of the Kelheim old city (Müller-Karpe 1952), these cemeteries may contain many hundreds of graves. Mounds, ditches, and posts occasionally delimited grave space in some cemeteries (e.g. Rochna 1965), but grave monuments demarcating burial space within the larger urnfields are usually absent or consist only of flat stones placed over each pit. While the burials of the Urnfield Late Bronze Age contain little material wealth, objects were deposited in hoards and votive contexts in large quantities during this period. Three Late Bronze Age hoards were found along the shores of the Danube within the study region. Late Bronze Age metal hoards comprise single items to over 100 objects. The Kelheim hoards are small and consist of bronze axes and sickle fragments. Following Rissman's (1988) analysis of the patterns of Harappan wealth consumption, hoards and votive deposits may represent ritual consumption of private wealth, whereas the consumption of materials in funerary contexts represents public display. I have argued elsewhere (Murray 1992) that the contradiction evident in the consumption of the materials of social discourse between private and public ritual arenas during the Late Bronze Age in southern Germany represents a mystification of social inequality by a dominant ideology.

Burial places of the Early Iron Age are especially numerous within the Kelheim region. There are 13 known tumulus cemeteries, four flat cremation fields, and five flat inhumation burial plots. In addition, many of the more than 50 unexplored tumulus cemeteries visible in the forests and in aerial photographs probably contain funerary remains from this period (as well as Middle Bronze Age graves). The Early Iron Age is traditionally associated with the practice of inhumation under and within mounds, but there is actually a striking variety of burial formats in southeastern Germany, often within the same cemetery. For the Oberpfalz, Torbrügge (1979) charted at least 20 different kinds of burial from the Hallstatt Iron Age, with different funerary rites and structures. This change does not necessarily represent the introduction of new cultural norms (Barrett et al. 1991, 224), but a reworking of the existing material resources of social reproduction. Older traditions of cremation burial in nondescript pits with few offerings continued side-by-side with the new emphasis on monumentality in many cemeteries. Hoards and votive deposits are rare from the Early Iron Age, and no such finds are known within the study area. Many of the same kinds of materials, such as metalwork, that had been deposited in very large quantities in hoards and votive deposits during the Late Bronze Age were now worked into the transformed burial practices and appeared in graves as complements of jewelry, weapons, metal vessels, and other appurtenances. The material resources of private ritual were thus transformed into the resources of public ritual. This transformation may be interpreted as contentious discourse between social groups with conflicting versions of their social conditions, in which the dominant structures of age, gender, and inheritance were open to public debate rather than euphemized through a uniform funerary ritual (Murray 1992).

In contrast to the Early Iron Age, there are very few funerary remains from the Late Iron Age. A couple of graves from an early phase of the Middle La Tène were found at the Weltenburg cloister opposite the Michelsberg at the southern end of the Danube Gorge (Koch 1991), and objects from two graves were salvaged from gravel pits on a lower terrace at Saal in the Kelheim Basin. Older salvage work and excavations for the Rhein-Main-Donau Canal at the confluence of the Altmühl and Danube Rivers in the western Basin uncovered a series of at least 19 Middle and Late La Tène burials just east of the oppidum in Kelheim-Gmünd (Kluge 1985). At least two burials are suspected from the Mitterfeld within the oppidum on the basis of older finds (Krämer 1952). Pottery recovered intact from a sand pit south of Saal may be from a Late La Tène cremation burial. Finds of bronze belt hardware near Eining may also be from destroyed Late Iron Age graves (Krämer 1968). Except for Kelheim-Gmünd, the burial places contain very small numbers of graves and appear to lack any formal structuring. In spite of the lack of formal burial from the Late Iron Age, there are many finds of human remains within settlements in central Europe, both from structural features and as scattered finds (Wiedemer 1963; Ruoff 1964). Although such remains have not been identified at Kelheim, they have been recovered from the oppidum at Manching and cannot be associated with warfare (Lange 1983; van Endert 1987, 56-58). These finds and the general absence of formal burial places in southern Germany represent dramatic transformations in the treatment of mortuary remains and the reproduction of social relations during the Late Iron Age. It appears that the discourses relating to classification of the dead and the structuring of inheritance, kinship, and social obligations previously undertaken within separate burial places may have shifted to the settlements themselves.

Conclusions and Prospects

Both archival data and field survey results reveal that the remnants of Late Iron Age life in the landscape around Kelheim are light and scattered, in contrast to dense patterns of activity and deposition in the Late Bronze and Early Iron Ages. Not only are there fewer Late Iron Age locales, but the deposits tend to be surface scatters without associated subsurface features. By the second century B.C., settlement was concentrated within or near the large fortification on the Michelsberg. There is little evidence of intensive habitation up to 16 km from the oppidum, in spite of the presence of numerous rectilinear ritual structures. This observation is more significant when we note that nearly one-half the distance to the Late Iron Age oppidum of Manching is included in the study region. In other parts of Germany that have been carefully studied through large-scale archival or survey research, rural Late Iron Age settlement is dense and often regular. The decline of rural populations at Kelheim represents a process of population centralization in large fortified settlements that occurred throughout central and western Europe. In southern Germany, these changes were associated with transformations of the social and spatial contexts of ritual and the use of the material resources of social reproduction to represent alternative strategies.

Two interpretations of Late Iron Age landscape have been presented, based on a preliminary overview of the archival and field survey evidence. One interpretation is that the daily needs of the Late Iron Age community were addressed by the inhabitants of the oppidum itself. The sherd scatters in the surrounding countryside may be the residues of seasonal migrations by food producing groups into the hinterland or may indicate the manuring of fields using dung collected within or near the oppidum. In this case, the oppidum was not a local redistributive center or market for an extensive network of rural villages. The only local central function of the oppidum was as a focal point for settlement. Palaeobotanical analysis of plant remains from the Mitterfeld indicates that crops were grown and processed by farmers living within the fortification. Alternatively, the sherd scatters may be the residues of small mobile or semi-mobile cattle pastoralists. In this scenario, the oppidum may have functioned as a central place for the interface between settled communities and mobile herding groups. Patterns of cattle remains from the Mitterfeld suggest that beef stock was raised and processed outside of the oppidum.

The interpretations outlined above are not exhaustive nor mutually exclusive, but they provide a direction for future examination of the historical development of the Iron Age landscape and the nature of oppida-hinterland interaction. Finds of graphite and painted pottery, metal work, coinage, and Roman imports within the oppidum are evidence that the settlement participated in an extra-regional circulation of goods, probably enhanced by its location at the confluence of two important waterways (Kluge 1986), but on the local level the settlement was apparently self-sufficient, with the possible exception of stock farming. The low-intensive rural settlement around the large Late Iron Age oppidum at Kelheim has important implications for the study of social and spatial dynamics of Iron Age societies, especially if the oppidum is interpreted as a thriving settlement of several thousand souls. The results of the Kelheim survey project may give pause to reassess the "urban" nature of Kelheim or rethink traditional notions of prehistoric urban settlement and consider alternative structures, such as clustered settlement (McIntosh 1991).

The analysis and interpretation of the Kelheim landscape is an ongoing research program. Part of the program is the examination of important bias issues in the use of archival and surface collection data to study archaeological landscapes. The three major bias issues are: 1) the visibility of archaeological deposits, 2) the use of surface collections to establish cultural affiliation and develop functional interpretations, and 3) the accuracy of field work. A brief analysis of the relationships between discovery context and archaeological period and locale type presented above suggests that there are biased conditions operating on the formation, preservation, and recovery of certain archaeological deposits. In particular, a greater proportion of later prehistoric locales were recorded through modern excavations in contrast to earlier archaeological periods. The nature of these biased conditions is not clear and should be investigated in greater depth. Focal points for a source criticism of the landscape project are the history and process of archaeological discovery in the region and the analysis of archaeological accumulation and post-depositional processes specific to the Kelheim landscape.

A second important bias issue is the nature of assemblages composed of surface collected artifacts and the use of artifact scatters to establish cultural affiliation and function. Graphite rim sherds and one "combed ware" sherd make up the limited evidence of Late Iron Age activity from the Kelheim survey. While graphite pots are archetypal for the La Tène archaeological culture, they constitute only about one third of ceramic assemblages from Late Iron Age oppida (Kappel 1969; Stöckli 1979a). Perhaps fewer graphite wares were in use at rural sites than at the oppida. If this was the case, then some undecorated, non-graphite pastes in the surface collection may be Late Iron Age, and our inability to recognize them may lead to a misunderstanding of the relative intensity of Late Iron Age activity around Kelheim. However, ceramic assemblages from sites such as Berching-Pollanten (Fischer et al. 1984), Altendorf (Stöckli 1979b), and Köfering-Egglfing (Osterhaus 1988) show that graphite wares also were widely used in undefended Late Iron Age communities in Bavaria, so we would expect these ceramics to be present in rural sites at Kelheim. Ceramic paste characterization studies from excavations at Kelheim (Schaarf 1988; see Chapter 12) may provide future assistance in the identification of non-graphite undecorated Late

Iron Age ceramics from surface collections. The problems and promises of interpreting artifact scatters have been examined in recent publications (Schofield 1991). Continued research at Kelheim will examine the implications of artifact scatters to the study of patterns of later prehistoric behavior at Kelheim.

Finally, a variety of managerial data were recorded during field walking, such as surface visibility, field condition, light and cloud cover, weather, and time of day. Analysis of these data will allow the evaluation of external interference during survey that may have affected the accuracy of the results.

In addition to the ongoing source criticisms described above, research continues to address the two theoretical approaches to the archaeological landscape outlined earlier. The first approach involves the analysis of manifold data concerning the physical location of cultural residues—i.e., landform, geology, soils—collected during the archival search. The relationships between the physical landscape and the cultural landscape of the Late Bronze and Early Iron Ages as well as the patterns of land-use around the oppidum in the Late Iron Age will be examined. The second approach involves visualizing the archaeological landscape as a resource in prehistoric structures of social discourse. Some preliminary observations on the utility of this approach have been presented. On-going work involves the integration of archival and field survey data into a program of social landscape archaeology.

Acknowledgements

I am indebted to Professor Peter S. Wells, who appreciated the value of a landscape approach to the interdisciplinary study of Iron Age society at Kelheim. The survey project was funded through Wells' National Science Foundation grant. Access to regional archives and permission to conduct field work were generously provided by Dr. Bernd Engelhardt of the Bayerisches Landesamt für Denkmalpflege, Landshut. Numerous individuals offered friendly support and advice during my study of the archives in Landshut, and I would especially like to thank Stuart Aitchison, Tommy Dannhorn, Helen Manley-Jones, Robert Pleyer, Günter Wullinger, and Werner Weber. Werner Hübner shared his expertise in the detection and collection of surface remains in the German landscape.

During field work at Kelheim, Dr. Ingrid Burger of the Archäologisches Museum generously offered space to clean and analyze artifacts, and opened the museum's collections and archives to study. Dr. Michael Rind, Kreisarchäologe for the district of Kelheim, allowed access to his unpublished data from archaeological investigations in the Kelheim region and was a valuable advocate of the field project; he also offered helpful observations on many of the ceramics collected during survey. Bettina Arnold, Peter S. Wells, and Nancy L. Wicker offered helpful comments on earlier drafts of this report. Any omissions or errors are entirely my responsibility.

My heartfelt thanks to the many farmers and landowners in Kelheim, who accepted my fieldwalking and queries with good humor and curiosity, and shared with me a personal knowledge of their landscape.

Notes

[1] The term "locale" is used here to avoid problems of defining an archaeological "site," particularly when the data consist of surface collected materials. It is meant to identify a *locus of prehistoric deposits* while avoiding any gross functional interpretation.

Chapter 16
Material Culture and Settlement: Site Structure, Economic Behavior, and Communication

Introduction

This chapter examines the evidence for human behavior and material culture on the Kelheim settlement. Three interrelated topics are considered. The first is the spatial patterning of settlement remains, including both features and portable objects, on the site. The second is the residue from economic activities carried out by the inhabitants, including subsistence production, manufacturing, and trade. The third is the relation between the material culture that survives archaeologically on the settlement and information that it was intended to communicate, about relationships between people, about social statuses, and about identities.

The Late La Tène Occupation at Kelheim

Occupation activity of different kinds is represented in many different parts of the Kelheim Basin and its vicinity (see map, Figure 16.1). Present evidence from early accidental discoveries and from recent systematic excavation suggests that the densest occupation remains are located on the Mitterfeld, specifically on the eastern half of the Mitterfeld. Other remains have been recovered along the south bank of the Altmühl between the inner and outer walls. Remains of activity associated with the Late La Tène occupation of the site have also been investigated outside the outer wall, where significant traces of iron-smelting activity have been recovered (Goetze 1981), but no indication of dense habitation.

Late La Tène pottery has been reported from the center of medieval Kelheim (Engelhardt 1987, 109), though with the densely built up landscape there and intensive medieval and modern settlement activity, it is unlikely that any settlement features survive intact. East of the medieval city, substantial remains of Late La Tène settlement activity have been found, including a settlement site, a small cemetery with the infant burials reported by Kluge (1985), and a *Viereckschanze* (Etzel 1990, 61).

Late La Tène pottery has been reported from surface collecting at Wipfelsfurt, a low-lying semicircular area on the north bank of the Danube between the outer wall and the eastern end of the oppidum. The presence of such pottery must indicate some kind of settlement activity, but no structures have been ascertained there as yet.

Finally, Late La Tène materials have been reported from the Weltenburg monastery area, especially in the garden of the monastery, and small amounts of pottery of the period have been recovered at many different locations on the Frauenberg (Koch 1991). If a settlement existed during the Late La Tène Period on the land now occupied by the Weltenburg monastery, its remains would probably have been obliterated by the intensive activity on the site since around A.D. 600.

The eastern promontory of the Michelsberg, where the Befreiungshalle now stands, has long been regarded as a potential location for remains of Late La Tène date, possibly from a place of ritual, political, or strategic importance (Engelhardt 1987, 107). The location offers a panoramic view of the Kelheim Basin to the east and of the two valleys, the Altmühl to the north and west and the Danube to the south and southwest. If the promontory were cleared of trees, the site would provide visibility over most of the areas from which we have Late La Tène settlement remains, as well as an extensive view of the Danube in its gorge. The promontory would also be visible from all of the surrounding locations on the ground and would offer an ideal location to display signs of power and authority. Indeed King Ludwig I took advantage of just this aspect in deciding to construct the Befreiungshalle on this spot, between 1842 and 1863.

Late Iron Age pottery has been found in the garden of the administrative building on the promontory (Engelhardt 1982, 11), indicating some kind of activity there. Test excavations conducted between that building and the Befreiungshalle in 1988 yielded no Late Iron Age settlement remains, but rather confirmed the general suspicion that in the course of the construction of the Befreiungshalle in the middle of the last century, the topsoil layers on the promontory were scraped away, probably obliterating most if not all traces of prehistoric activity there (Etzel 1990, 54-56).

The Structure of the Settlement on the Mittlerfeld

Settlement Features

All of the evidence available from chance finds and from systematic excavations suggests that the densest occupation remains of the Late La Tène Period are on the Mitterfeld on the south bank of the Altmühl, within the inner wall system and especially at the eastern end of the Mitterfeld. The Archäologisches Museum of Kelheim has in its collections abundant materials from the Late La Tène occupation on the Mitterfeld, especially materials recovered during the construction of houses at the eastern end at the end of the last century and the beginning of this one. Röhrig (1986), Kluge (1987), and Etzel (1990) provide useful plans of portions of the Mitterfeld that have been investigated since 1980 by the Bayerisches Landesamt für Denkmalpflege, prior to the construction of new houses there.

Their reports indicate settlement remains that are consistent with the findings presented here from the University of Minnesota excavations of 1987. Pits and postholes on the areas reported by them are similar in shape, size, and character to those we encountered, and the density of settlement features is comparable (see especially Etzel 1990, Figure 10). Features that Kluge and Etzel interpret as remains of houses are similar in area to the "floors" that we identify (Chapter 5). Postholes reported by them compare closely in size to pits that we identify as postholes, and the spacing of the postholes is in many instances similar to that of our row of holes in Sector 1990/E (Figure 5.3, bottom left). From this evidence, it is fair to say that based on present information, the eastern half of the Mitterfeld was the site of a relatively uniform settlement during the Late La Tène period, with structures including houses and storage pits indicating a densely built up habitation area, of a character similar to that of the central region at Manching (Krämer 1962) and of the portion of Staré Hradisko reported by Meduna (1970a). The pattern on the western half of the Mitterfeld is different, with substantial thinning-out of settlement remains, as our excavations of 1990 and 1991 demonstrate. These parts of the Mitterfeld settlement can be compared with the excavated parts of Manching that lie south and north of the central area (Schubert 1972; Maier 1985, 1986).

Chronology of the Settlement

All of the cultural materials recovered at the Late Iron Age settlement on the Mitterfeld indicate occupation during the phase La Tène D1, with no clear evidence of occupation during La Tène C2 and none for La Tène D2 (see Chapter 7). Study of the wall systems around the settlement reveals that the outer wall was renewed twice, the inner one once (Engelhardt 1987, 105; Kluge 1987, 54), suggesting that the settlement persisted at least long enough to require repair of the defenses. Estimates for the length of time that timbers sunk in the ground remain useful before rotting in the central European environment average around 25 years. If the determining factor in the renewal of the walls was the condition of the timbers, then we might suggest that the repair sequence indicates that the outer wall was in use a minimum of 50 years (requiring two repairs). But deterioration of the stone facing may have necessitated repair first, and I know of no experimental research that suggests how long such stone facing remains intact.

Character of the Settlement Deposits

The topographical situation of the Mitterfeld settlement in a valley bottom and on the slope between the Michelsberg and the Altmühl River makes the site susceptible to deposition and erosion from water washing down the slope from the south and down the valley from west to east. A complete investigation of the site must include a study of the sedimentation patterns on the Mitterfeld, to study the processes of build-up and erosion that have taken place. We were not able to undertake such an investigation in the preliminary research reported here, but such an undertaking should be part of future research at the site.

The character of the cultural layer on the settlement suggests that no major erosional disturbances occurred during or shortly after the Late Iron Age occupation. As noted in Chapter 5 (see also Herrmann 1969), the cultural layer is of consistent character, though of varying thickness, across most of the areas of the site that we investigated, with similar distributions of pottery, daub, and char-

Material Culture and Settlement

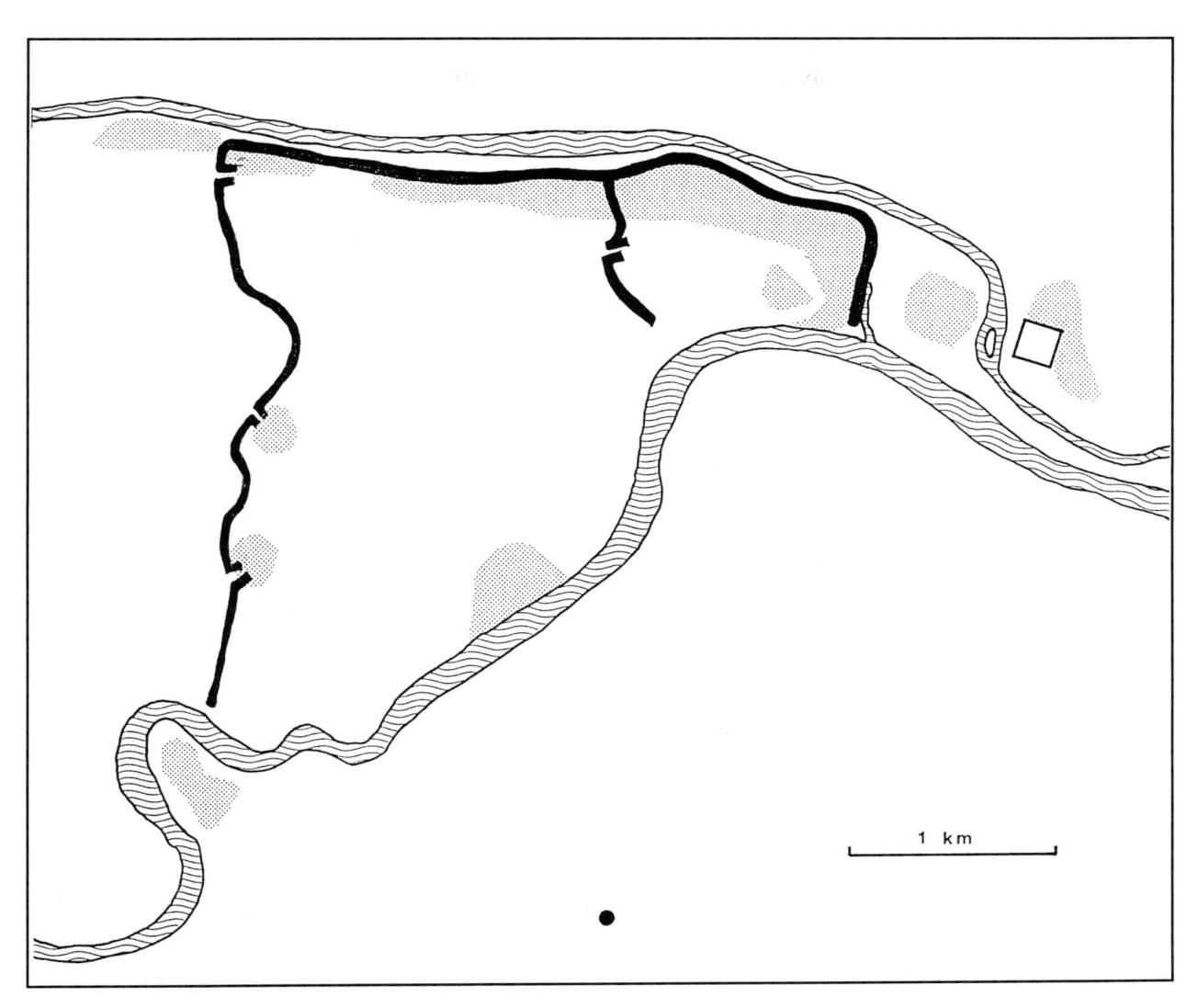

Figure 16.1. Map showing locations of Late La Tène settlement remains at Kelheim. The Altmühl River is shown at the top, the Danube at the bottom. The heavy dark lines represent the oppidum walls. Areas where traces of Late La Tène settlement have been found are represented by shading. The square at the right is the *Viereckschanze*. The large dot at the center bottom marks the place at which the bronze bull figurine (see Chapter 17) was found. Map based on Engelhardt 1987, 104 fig. 59 and Koch 1991, 143 fig. 25.

coal throughout. This layer is similar in character to that at Manching (Krämer 1962, 296-297), though in most places on the Mitterfeld it is thinner and less densely filled with cultural materials. If major erosion had occurred during the Late Iron Age occupation, or shortly after that occupation before sediment built up on top of the cultural layer, I would expect the cultural layer to vary more in character and to be absent on some parts of the settlement. We did not observe either of these patterns in the areas that we investigated.

The subsurface features—the pits and postholes—were certainly not disturbed by erosion. Their contents—the humic fill and the cultural debris in that matrix—were intact and showed undisturbed depositional patterns similar to those at other settlements, including stratigraphic layering in some of the larger pits (Figures 5.8 and 5.9).

Spatial Patterning

The results of our excavations on different parts of the middle and western portion of the Mitterfeld

137

(see Chapter 5) suggest that the character of settlement activity on the western portion was very different from that on the eastern. The eastern part of the site had on it densely built-up and intensively occupied settlement, comparable in density of habitation remains (but not in the size of structures identified so far) to the central area at Manching. The western part of the site shows a very different character, with settlement features and distributions of material culture much sparser, suggesting a rural rather than an urban aspect. Here comparison can be made with the recently-reported outlying areas of Manching, north and south of the densely occupied center. In addition to the marked differences in the distribution of settlement features and in quantities of settlement debris on different parts of the site, it is significant that iron objects relating to architecture (see Chapter 11), including nails, clamps, and keys, were abundant in the eastern part of the settlement that we investigated, but absent, except for one atypical nail, from the central and western parts. This fact suggests that not only was settlement activity much less intensive on the western half, but also that the character of the buildings on the different parts of the settlement was different. The structures on the eastern part of the Mitterfeld were built more substantially, employing the latest in architectural technology. Pottery, metal, and glass objects from our eastern and western trenches indicate that the occupation on these different parts of the Mitterfeld was contemporaneous.

Kelheim and Other Oppida

The plans of settlement features and data on the density of cultural materials recovered from different parts of the Mitterfeld enable comparison to be made with other excavated oppida, particularly with those for which plans of excavated features and numerical data regarding material remains have been published. Manching, which is both the most comprehensively excavated oppidum and the closest to Kelheim, offers important points of comparison. The early excavations of the late 1950s and 1960s at Manching were conducted in the center of the site, and they yielded rich settlement features, including pits, postholes, and foundation trenches, as well as vast quantities of pottery, animal bones, metal tools and ornaments, glass jewelry, and other materials. In the 1970s and 1980s, the Manching excavations extended southward and northward from the central area, and the character of the settlement remains uncovered in those areas was quite different (Schubert 1972; Maier 1985, 1986). Settlement features of all kinds were much sparser. No very large structures, such as those that characterize the central part of Manching, are apparent in the outlying areas. And the distribution of cultural material as a whole was found to be considerably less dense than it was in the center. This pattern at Manching closely resembles what we have found in our excavations at Kelheim, though of course the areas we have investigated so far are much smaller than those excavated at Manching.

In the present state of our knowledge, it is difficult to compare Kelheim and Manching, mainly because so little of Kelheim has been systematically investigated. Whereas the central area of Manching, where the richest occupation materials have been recovered, has been open land and thus permitted extensive systematic excavation, the area at Kelheim where occupation was densest—the eastern part of the Mitterfeld—has been covered by houses and other buildings in modern times, thus preventing extensive investigation. Yet even with limited parts of the Kelheim settlement available for study, I think we can make comparisons that bring out useful information. The results of the salvage excavations reported by Kluge (1987) at the eastern end of the Mitterfeld (see her pl. 253) and those reported by Etzel (1990) just east of our 1987 excavations suggest dense occupational debris at Kelheim comparable to that of the central area at Manching.

In order to compare the density of cultural material recovered in our 1987 excavation area with that at the central area at Manching, I compared the numbers of sherds of Late Iron Age pottery recovered in our excavations, 11,722 from an investigated surface of 280 m^2, with the 147,894 sherds reported for the 16,235 m^2 of the central area of Manching, excavated between 1955 and 1961 (Gebhard 1991, 65). The result is that that portion of the Kelheim settlement yielded more sherds per square meter (41.9 sherds per square meter) than the central area of Manching (9.1 sherds per square meter). Since the portion of the Kelheim site compared was very small, the comparison does not have much statistical meaning, but it suggests the possibility that the eastern part of the Mitterfeld at Kelheim was the site of a settlement at least as dense as that in the center at Manching, though it was probably substantially smaller. Perhaps the eastern part of the Mitterfeld at Kelheim was more densely occupied that the central portion of Manching because the amount of available settlement land was so restricted, by the steep slopes of the Michelsberg to the south and the Altmühl River to the north. Perhaps this issue could be addressed at Kelheim by excavating small sounding trenches in any available undisturbed land around the periphery of the modern Mitterfeld settlement, for example in yards along Hienheimerstrasse and Kanalstrasse. It is not clear, however, whether much undisturbed land exists in those locations.

Another major question with respect to Kelheim is the extent and character of settlement remains that may lie under (if they survive) the medieval center of Kelheim and to the east, north and south of the new canal. Traces of Late La Tène occupation activity have been found in those locations (see Chapter 3), but in the absence of substantial systematic excavations it is not possible to know their character. Medieval and modern construction activity may have obliterated most traces of the Late Iron Age settlements.

In their investigations at Staré Hradisko in Moravia, Meduna (1970a) and Čižmář (1989a) interpret their results to indicate an oppidum settlement comprising an agglomeration of units akin to farmsteads similar to those in smaller settlements in the countryside. Staré Hradisko lacks the very large structures that have been identified in the central area at Manching. To judge by areas excavated and published to date, the organizational principle at Staré Hradisko was based upon these individual settlement units, each with a range of economic activities carried out by its residents, separated from others by fences.

In her recent study of the oppidum of Hrazany in Bohemia, Jansová (1986, 70) interprets the settlement evidence to indicate distinct enclosed units, which she calls *Gehöfte*, similar in character to those of Staré Hradisko.

At Závist in Bohemia, the recent synthetic study by Motyková, Drda, and Rybová (1990) shows the settlement to consist of different kinds of settlement units, dispersed over the area within the walled enclosure. Perhaps a central area of denser habitation comparable to the center of Manching and the eastern end of the Mitterfeld at Kelheim is yet to be found. These results from Závist appear to be similar to the peripheral areas of settlement at Manching and the central and western parts of the Kelheim Mitterfeld, including the three house foundations on the terrace reported by Herrmann (1969).

The existence of Late La Tène settlement traces outside of the oppidum wall, but contemporaneous with the oppidum settlement on the Mitterfeld, is a pattern that has been identified at other oppidum sites. At Stradonice, for example, Motyková-Sneiderová (1962) reports a settlement at the foot of the hill on which the great oppidum is situated. The author notes (p. 154) the excavation of four iron smelting furnaces in this settlement, along with extensive deposits of slag, a situation similar to the iron-smelting evidence just outside the outer wall at Kelheim (Goetze 1981; Rind 1988, 51). In fact, the placement of iron-working facilities just outside of the settlement, or just inside the wall but removed from the main settlement area, is characteristic of many oppida. At Hrazany, Jansová (1986, 71) notes the concentration of evidence for metalworking in areas near the walls. This spatial arrangement is probably attributable to the desire to keep the noxious fumes and danger of fire associated with metalworking away from the principal areas of settlement. At Závist, also, a settlement has been reported at the base of the oppidum fortified site (Čižmář 1989b), yielding remains of habitation, metalworking, and textile production. A similar situation has been identified at the Steinsburg (Spehr 1971).

Evidence for Economic Behavior on the Settlement

Activities Represented in the Archaeological Evidence

Analyses of the plant remains (Chapter 8) and of the animal bones (Chapter 9) provide important information about the subsistence economy of the community at Kelheim and about possible locations at which the plant foods were grown and the livestock raised. Future analyses will examine distribution patterns of these subsistence remains on the settlement surface, to test for special activity areas in the preparation or consumption of meals.

Spatial patterning in the debris of manufacturing processes yields insight into locations of industrial activities on the settlement. The most abundant evidence of this type is in the iron-working remains, treated in Chapter 10. Carl Blair is able to distinguish local concentrations of debris that can be associated with specific processes in iron production.

Four small lumps of bronze metal which may have resulted from spillage during bronze casting were recovered, all from the easternmost of our excavation areas, investigated in 1987 (Figure 6.23, bottom row). The largest was found in Pit 1987/3-11-12, the smallest (second from right in the figure) in a small pit in Sector 1987/1, and the other two in the cultural layer in Sector 1987/6. These fragments are good evidence that bronze casting was carried out on this part of the Mitterfeld, but the scattered distribution of such small pieces does not allow us to identify the precise location of such activity.

Similarly, all three fragments of glass that may relate to manufacturing processes were found in the easternmost of our excavation areas. They are two fragmentary pieces of what may be "raw," unshaped cobalt-blue glass (Figure 6.26, top and center right) and a complete rounded droplet of the same color (Figure 6.26, bottom row, second from right). The droplet and the first of the two fragments cited came from Sector 1987/6, the other fragment from Sector 1987/5.

No pottery kiln has been reported from the Kelheim settlement as yet, though sherds were recovered in the 1987 excavations that may constitute debris from misfired pottery. A fragment of graphite or graphite-rich clay found in Sector 1990/B may be connected with the manufacture of graphite-clay pottery on the site, or with the storage of the raw material in preparation for such production. The piece was recovered near the location of a test trench in which Herrmann found two similar fragments (1969 pl. 16, 20.21).

Meaning of the Patterns Observed

Analysis of spatial patterning with respect to subsistence remains has not yet been completed. For the manufacturing evidence, the information gathered so far permits the stating of preliminary conclusions about the arrangement of that category of economic behavior on the settlement.

Debris from iron-working is distributed over all of the areas that we investigated, suggesting that that activity was carried out on many different parts of the settlement and supporting the idea that iron production was a major activity at Kelheim and perhaps the principal source of export value to exchange for the imported raw materials and finished goods at the site. As Blair (Chapter 10) demonstrates, different categories of iron-working remains have different spatial distributions on the settlement, suggesting that different processes were carried out in different locations. If future research should confirm this preliminary observation, then that evidence would support a model of the Kelheim settlement as the site of an integrated, centrally-managed iron production operation rather than the location of many small-scale workings. Different processes may have been carried out at different places, with a managed integration of the whole operation.

For pottery manufacture on the site, the evidence is too sparse to make any more than the most tentative of observations. The discovery of misfired pottery in the 1987 excavation area could suggest that a kiln was nearby (though certainly not in the part of the settlement that we excavated), and the finding of a lump of graphite or graphite-clay in Sector 1990/B, near the location at which Herrmann recovered similar pieces, could be from a production area of that category of pottery on the western part of the Mitterfeld.

The fact that remains of bronze casting and glass production processes were recovered only in the easternmost area explored is significant. The 280 m^2 of that area constitutes about 46% percent of the whole surface of 614 m^2 that we excavated at Kelheim, and all seven traces (four of bronze, three of glass) of manufacturing in these materials came from that one area. This pattern permits us to state that, as far as the present evidence is concerned, the eastern end of the Mitterfeld was the location of craft production in bronze and glass, while the central and western portions of the site investigated by us yielded no trace of such activity.

The most important generalization that I would draw from this evidence is the following. The largest-scale manufacturing activity in evidence at Kelheim—iron production, is represented by manufacturing debris across the whole of the settlement. This evidence adds considerable support to the suggestion that iron-working was an activity of major economic signficance to the community at Kelheim. In fact, from the very widespread and relatively dense distribution of debris from iron production (Chapter 10), we might hypothesize that the entire settlement was organized around the production of that material on a scale far exceeding the needs of the local community.

The manufacture of ornaments of bronze and glass, on the other hand, was restricted in its spatial distribution on the settlement. Such material remains occurred only in the easternmost excavation area, and only in a few sectors there. The small scale of the crafts that produced ornaments in those substances suggests that they were made for local use only and not for export to other communities, at least not on a sizable scale.

Material Culture and Expression at Kelheim

Material Culture and Settlement

Our knowledge of late prehistoric societies in Europe derives principally from two sources of information—settlements and graves. For the most part, our understanding of economy and settlement organization is gleaned from study of settlements, while we derive information about costume, gender distinctions, wealth and status distribution, and ritual from burials. I wish here to depart from traditional approaches to the analysis of settlement material and to consider the Kelheim settlement as a source of information about material culture and everyday life. In order to do this, I need to use available cemetery evidence for comparison.

As is the case with most of the oppida, we do not have the burial population of Kelheim, except for the very small cemetery east of the medieval city (Kluge 1985) and the possible grave(s) at the eastern end of the Mitterfeld from which the Roman jug and iron weapons may have come (Krämer 1985, 136).

As I wish to suggest here and to argue on the basis of our material from Kelheim, settlement evidence can provide a different and potentially valuable source of information about everyday life that graves do not. For the Late Iron Age, we do not know why particular objects were placed in graves with the dead. The grave goods may or may not have been objects that were worn or carried by the buried individual in everyday life. They may represent items worn only on special occasions, or they may even constitute signs of status that were only worn at the funerary ceremony.

Burials represent conscious deposits—the objects in them were selected by the burying parties to communicate specific kinds of information to the portion of the community that participated in the funeral, including both humans and deities. Materials recovered on settlements, on the other hand, represent primarily debris from everyday life. Most such objects were not consciously selected for deposition on the settlement, but instead entered the ground after their use-life had ceased, most often because they were broken (as in the case of pottery, iron tools, and ornaments of bronze and glass) but also sometimes because they were lost (as in the case of coins and unbroken ornaments). At Kelheim we encountered no evidence for the systematic clearing or removal of materials from the settlement surface, such as pits that were purposefully filled with trash or middens of debris. Pottery and fragmentary tools and ornaments were scattered throughout the settlement deposits. It is reasonable to suppose that the distributions of materials recovered on the settlement reflect the locations of activities in which they were last used (see Gebhard 1989, 26-36).

One of the principal goals of our research was to study such distribution of materials on the settlement surface in order to gather information about spatial patterning of various activities. Pottery will be an important source of such information, but the study of the Kelheim pottery is still in its early stages. A future goal of the pottery studies is to ascertain the locational patterning of vessels of different functions over the settlement surface, in order to understand the spatial patterning of different behaviors.

The material culture that is represented by the objects that we recover on settlement sites is not identical to that in graves, and the differences can be significant. Because of the change in burial practice that occurred with the beginning of phase La Tène D1, we know of very few graves in Bavaria that are contemporary with the occupation at Kelheim. For comparisons, we must make use of cemeteries at which the practice of placing objects in graves continued through La Tène D1. A number of useful cemeteries have been studied in the region around the Main River and in the lands east of the middle Rhine. They include Bad Nauheim (Schönberger 1952), Dietzenbach (Polenz 1971), and Wederath (Haffner 1971, 1974a, 1978, 1989), along with a series of richly outfitted burials such as those studied by Polenz (1982) and those at Hoppstädten-Weiersbach (Haffner 1969) and Neuwied (Joachim 1973).

The most abundant objects that we recovered at Kelheim were pottery, iron-working debris, iron implements, bronze ornaments, iron fibulae, and glass ornaments (I exclude animal bones from consideration here). In the graves of the period, pottery is the most common object, and second most frequent are fibulae. Analysis of the pottery from Kelheim is not yet sufficiently advanced to permit detailed comparison between the types of pottery in the settlement contexts and those in graves. Glass ornaments, especially ring beads, are also common in graves of the period. Spindle whorls and coins sometimes occur in graves as well. Wealthy burials often contain objects that we did not recover on the Kelheim settlement, such as bronze vessels, iron weapons, and remains of wheeled vehicles.

Industrial debris such as iron slag, bronze lumps, and raw glass do not occur ordinarily in burials in these cemeteries.

Iron implements, well represented from our settlement excavations, are not common in graves. Nails and clamps occasionally are reported from burials, where they must have been part of wooden structures—coffins perhaps, or chests—placed in the burials, but they too are uncommon. Some of the nails and clamps that we recovered at Kelheim are very similar to those associated with wagons in burials of the period (e.g. Joachim 1973). This similarity could mean that these metal objects on the settlement represent wagon-building on the site, or it could simply be that standard types of nails and clamps were employed for many different purposes. Not enough research has been conducted on Late Iron Age nails to enable us to distinguish the purpose of nails of the different shapes and sizes with respect to specific functions.

Somewhat surprising is the general lack in the burials of the miriad kinds of small bronze objects that we recovered on the Kelheim settlement—small rings, ring beads, buttons, studs, and sheet bronze attachments. Such items occasionally occur (e.g. Haffner 1971 pl. 85, 1), but they are rarely reported. It is not clear whether they are simply rare, or whether they are often not recovered for one reason or another.

What do these similarities and differences between the objects found on the settlement and those found in graves of the period mean? On the one hand, one is struck by the similarities of objects on the settlement and in the graves. All of the categories of pottery that occur in graves of this period are also represented on the Kelheim settlement. This point suggests that there was no "funerary ware" made exclusively for burial. Graves were outfitted with pottery that was in use in everyday contexts. (This is not to say that people did not reserve special vessels for special occasions, including burial, only that pottery was apparently not made just for burial.)

The second most common grave good, the fibula, is also represented on the Kelheim settlement, in every case in fragmentary condition. The occurrence of these fibulae in the settlement deposits can be attributed to one of two processes—either they broke in the course of a person's daily life, fell from the garment to which they had been attached, and were thus lost; or a person disposed of them—apparently by simply tossing them aside—after they broke. The occurrence of such broken fibulae on the settlement indicates that they were a regular part of everyday life, not special items worn only in the funerary context. The regularity of their occurrence in burials points to their importance as part of the standard outfit of the persons with whom they were buried. Fibulae served the practical purpose of holding together garments, but they also served important message-bearing functions in communicating information about status, gender, and fashion (see e.g. Pauli 1972).

Like the fibulae, all of the glass objects that the University of Minnesota investigations recovered from the settlement are fragmentary, though Kluge reports complete ring beads found earlier on the site (1987, pl. 181,2; 222, A1). Like fibulae, they were worn by individuals and they occur frequently in burials, though not as regularly as fibulae. Their appearance in fragmentary condition in the settlement deposit indicates their use in everyday life. Unlike fibulae, glass ornaments did not function to fasten garments, but served purely communicative (and "decorative") roles.

Spindle whorls, keys, and coins occur both on the Kelheim settlement in the burials of the period, and they need to be considered differently from fibulae and glass ornaments. None of these three categories of objects are primarily items of personal adornment, to judge from the evidence of burials, and all three play significant roles in economic processes. Spindle whorls served as flywheels for spinning fiber in the manufacture of textiles, coins were a standard of value used in exchange, and keys were part of the expanded security system required in the urban context of the Late La Tène oppida to keep accumulated property secure. Each of these three kinds of objects also occurs in burials with some regularly, though not as frequently as fibulae or glass ornaments.

Women's and Men's Grave Goods, and Material Culture on the Settlement

All three of these categories of objects tend to occur in women's graves. In his study of Late Iron Age burials containing coins, Polenz (1982) found that they occur almost exclusively in women's graves. Spindle whorls also are most frequently in the burials of women. Keys, often found together with thin slabs of iron that represent the plates on the outside of locks, also occur most often in graves of women.

It is thus apparent that these three categories of objects, which in settlement contexts are most associated with particular aspects of economic activity, also had strong symbolic-expressive links, particularly with women. The characteristic feature of men's graves in this period is weaponry, and, as noted above, the only clear weapon that we recovered at Kelheim was the small spearhead, and it is not of a type that characteristically appears in burial contexts. Thus objects associated in graves with women occur in the settlement context, but those with men do not. The reasons behind this pattern merit further investigation.

Material Culture and Expression of Status

Among the settlement features at Kelheim, no clear evidence for the material expression of status differences has been identified. To date, no exceptionally large dwellings or buildings associated with objects that might denote special status have been observed (for examples of such situations at other sites see Haarnagel 1979 for Feddersen Wierde, and Hvass 1985 for Hodde). In the very limited areas investigated so far, it is difficult to discern any patterns in the occurrence of different categories of objects that might express status differences. Still, some patterns are worth noting, though their significance is not yet clear.

One special characteristic of some parts of the settlement but not others is the fine polychrome painted pottery. From the 1987 Landesamt für Denkmalpflege excavations, Etzel (1990, Figure 38) was able to show a distinct concentration of painted sherds in the northeast corner of the investigated area, though a sparse scatter of painted sherds occurs over most of the surface explored. In the areas that the University of Minnesota teams investigated, painted pottery was best represented in the pit in Sector 1991/6 and in Sectors 1987/1 and 1987/2. If fine painted pottery was used mainly or exclusively by persons of high status in the Late Iron Age, and the burial evidence suggests that it was (e.g. Haffner 1971, 1974a, 1978), then this characteristic may be useful in identifying where individuals of higher-than-average status lived on the site.

Other items of material culture that may be associated with high status also occur in the same areas where fine painted pottery was most abundant. The three keys and three of the four coins were recovered in the same portion of the easternmost excavation area, from 1987, as the painted pottery. In the pit in Sector 1991/6, along with the painted pottery, was the unique thin-walled, finely incised sherd of a globular vessel (Figure 5.15, top left) and an exceptionally large quantity of metal objects, including handles of metal vessels, as well as two glass ornaments. I interpret this pit as a cellar beneath a house, and suggest that it was the house of a family of above-average status. No objects that can be associated with elevated status occur in either of the westernmost trenches, nor in any of the central trenches except Sector 1991/6.

The most distinctive evidence of special status at Kelheim remains the Roman bronze jug found in 1863, unfortunately without clear context. If it came from a grave, as is likely, then that may have been the burial of a significant political leader in the Kelheim community at some point during its existence (Kellner 1990, 13).

Size and Character of the Social Unit

For Gaul, the evidence from Caesar enables us to associate the major oppida with particular tribes, as their capitals. For regions east of the Rhine, for which textual sources are much less complete, links between the archaeological settlements and tribal entities are much more difficult to make. Manching has been identified as the capital of the Vindelici tribe of Celts, and Kelheim as a sub-tribe of them. But we have very little solid textual information to go on in trying to identify the rank of the Kelheim community with respect to other oppida in temperate Europe east of the Rhine.

Population estimates for all oppida are difficult to make (discussion in Wells 1984, 164-166), in part because of the lack of cemeteries associated with the settlements. For Kelheim the difficulty is compounded because most of the eastern end of the Mitterfeld, where the densest settlement remains are situated, was built on before systematic excavation could be carried out. Based solely on the evidence of the density of settlement features and habitation debris found in our excavations in 1987, together with the earlier findings reported by Kluge (1987) and Etzel (1990), I would make an educated guess that the population of the Mitterfeld may have been between 1000 and 3000 persons at any one time. As we have seen, the densest habitation remains are on the eastern half of the Mitterfeld, and from about the middle of the Mitterfeld westward, they thin out markedly, as our excavations in 1990 and 1991 demonstrate.

Chapter 16 - Wells

Only the eastern end of the site could merit the term "urban" with respect to considerable traces of structures and the rich deposits of pottery, animal bone, and industrial debris. The western half of the Mitterfeld appears, from present evidence, to have been much more "rural" in aspect, with scattered buildings, fewer subsurface features, and a much less dense distribution of cultural materials of all categories except some types of iron-working remains.

The relationship between Kelheim and Manching is an important issue, and it bears directly on the question of the status of the Kelheim community. Since Kelheim and Manching are quite close together and linked by the Danube River, the question has been posed whether Kelheim could have been a community that was in some respect subservient to Manching, since the settlement remains appear to be less abundant at Kelheim. Much work needs to be done on this matter, and in our preliminary analyses of the Kelheim materials we did not address this question. But a few remarks on the issue are in order.

The general character of the material culture at the two sites is similar—the same kinds of pottery, similar patterns of animal bones, similar iron tools and bronze and glass ornaments, and similar coins occur on both sites. The absence so far of ceramic amphorae at Kelheim may result from the very small proportion of the settlement that has been investigated. The Roman bronze jug makes clear that the Kelheim community also was in contact with the Roman world. There is thus no compelling evidence in the character of the material culture to suggest that the community at Kelheim was in any way of lower status than that at Manching.

Expression of Community Identity: The Wall at Kelheim

Oppidum walls are important and have received considerable attention. At Kelheim, the wall system has been explored at a number of locations, especially by Herrmann (1975), and we have good information about its character and construction. Several observers have noted that the walls seem too extensive—some seven km in total length—to have been adequately defended by the residents of the community there, even if we reckon the addition of substantial numbers of people from the surrounding countryside who might have fled to the fortified site in times of danger. If we were to imagine the western wall alone, about 3.2 km in length, with one defender every two meters along its course, 1,600 fighters would have been required as a first line of defense on that one part of the site. The settlement at Kelheim and smaller ones in the surrounding area would have been unlikely to have mustered so many armed and able defenders.

A more realistic approach to the questions concerning the wall is to view it not strictly in terms of defense, but rather as an expression of territoriality and power, as several investigators have suggested (Herrmann 1973; 1975, 305; Burger 1984a, 64; Kluge 1987, 53-54). It served as a boundary between the community's defined area and the outside world. The outer face of the wall was constructed of quarried Kelheim limestone, with vertical supports of tree trunks every 1 or 1.5 m along its course. At a total height of five or six meters, it would have presented a striking gleaming white appearance when new (Burger 1984a, 64) and may have served as a potent symbol of the community, its power, and its claim to the site.

Chapter 17
Material Expression of Ritual and Cult

Introduction

Although most archaeological studies of settlement sites typically focus on economic issues and questions of spatial organization, a settlement is not just a place where people dwell and carry out their daily tasks of food and craft production. Human culture possesses an important symbolic and ritual dimension, and in any archaeological investigation of a settlement this aspect must be considered. Victor Turner (1967, 1969), especially, has argued that ritual is an integral part of all human culture, and that in order to understand any aspect of human behavior in an anthropological framework, ritual must be considered. In study of Iron Age settlements, it is not easy to identify evidence for ritual activity, but with what we know about the importance of ritual and symbolism in human life, it is essential that we make an attempt, however tentative, to come to terms with this realm of human experience. Renfrew and Bahn (1991, 359) also note that cult behavior is often a part of regular everyday activity. Therefore by trying to recognize the material evidence for such behavior, we come closer to the possibility of understanding the totality of the patterns of behavior that resulted in the archaeological remains we recover. In the past two decades, anthropological archaeologists have become increasingly interested in confronting questions of ritual, cult, and symbolism in prehistoric societies, and even applying information about these subjects to the study of cultural change (e.g. Conrad and Demarest 1984, Renfrew 1985). Anthropology teaches us that all material culture serves, at some level, as means of communication (Clarke 1968, Douglas and Isherwood 1979, Richards 1992), and much of this communication relates to interactions between humans and the powers of the other world. Our challenge is to develop ways of understanding the media employed and the messages transmitted. As Renfrew suggests (1985; Renfrew and Bahn 1991, 358-363), we can systematically study ritual and cult activity by identifying recurring patterns in specific contexts of activity in relation to particular locations and objects.

There exists a considerable body of research on the subject of ritual and religion in the Celtic world of Iron Age Europe, much of it based primarily on textual sources of information, but with important connections made to the archaeological record (e.g. Ross 1967; Brunaux 1988; Davidson 1988; Green 1989, 1992). Though this literature does not generally deal specifically with settlement evidence, much of it can aid in the interpretation of patterns that we observe at the Mitterfeld at Kelheim and in its vicinity.

In this preliminary report on our excavations at Kelheim, I wish to briefly call attention to the rich variety of evidence on and near the settlement that bears on issues of ritual and symbolic expression. A full interpretation of the Kelheim settlement from this perspective is in progress. All of the evidence from Kelheim that I cite below has parallel evidence at other sites of the period and is thus part of a broad ritual and symbolic context in the Late Iron Age of temperate Europe.

Earlier Ritual and Cult Sites in the Kelheim Area

Suppe's paper (Chapter 19) emphasizes religion and ritual as aspects of human experience that show continuity in the Kelheim area. Evidence for ritual activity at and around Kelheim dates back at least to the Early Bronze Age. Bronze objects deposited in a hoard near a spring at Weltenburg (Koch 1991, 136), in the Danube near Weltenburg (Spindler 1984a, 212), and on the Michelsberg (Burger 1984a, 33) probably represent offerings. In the Altmühl Valley just west of the oppidum at the Schellnecker Wand, a deep deposit of pottery, animal bones, and bronze objects at the base of a cliff has been interpreted as an offering site of a type characteristic of the Late Bronze Age (Burger 1984a, 45; Maier 1984, 208). Just east of the medieval city center of Kelheim, in the region known as Gmünd, enclosures and burial grounds that were in use from the Late Bronze Age to the Late Iron Age illustrate a continuity of ritual tradition at that location (Engelhardt 1987). The situation of this part of Kelheim, at the confluence of the Altmühl into the Danube, is consistent with much ritual behavior of the Bronze and Iron Ages (Torbrügge 1971).

Late La Tène Ritual and Cult Materials

Four kinds of archaeological evidence at Kelheim can be associated with presumed ritual or symbolic activity; each kind has parallels at other oppidum sites.

Viereckschanzen

A *Viereckschanze* (rectangular enclosure) has been well documented in the area of Gmünd, east of the medieval city center at Kelheim (see Figure 16.1). Its form and size is typical of this category of sites in temperate Europe, and it is one of 11 known in the Landkreis (county) of Kelheim. Unfortunately, most of the structure had been destroyed by gravel-quarrying operations before it could be researched in detail. The internal area of this enclosure has not been explored.

Research on many *Viereckschanzen* throughout Europe has shown that these enclosures were almost certainly ritual sites (Schwarz 1975, Bittel 1981, Brunaux 1988). At some *Viereckschanzen*, large quantities of animal and human bones have been found, as well as weapons, especially swords. The evidence suggests that a kind of sacrifice or offering was carried out at the enclosures. Excavation at several *Viereckschanzen* in southern Germany, including Fellbach-Schmiden (Planck 1982), Holzhausen (Schwarz 1975), and Tomerdingen (Zürn 1971), has revealed deep vertical shafts within the enclosed areas, sometimes containing objects that were probably deposited in the course of ritual activities.

The situation of the Kelheim *Viereckschanze* in the low, sandy lands at the confluence of the Altmühl into the Danube is significant, since many of these enclosures have been found closely associated with water. As part of their ritual function, these enclosures have been interpreted as gathering places for communities for the performing of community rituals. It is noteworthy that the *Viereckschanze* is close to the unusual small cemetery of infant burials of the same period (Kluge 1985; on infant burials and ritual see also Scott 1991), and to the enclosures and cemeteries of earlier periods, extending back to the Late Bronze Age.

Animal Representations

A number of animal representations in bronze have been recovered at and around Kelheim. While it is rarely possible to assert with certainty that a specific figurine was of ritual significance, the recurrence of particular animals in the artistic tradition of late Celtic Europe, and the special contexts in which many are recovered, make such associations likely. In many cases, subsequent traditions recorded during Roman times or later support ritual attributions of Iron Age iconography (Klingender 1971, Green 1992).

The cast bronze bull figurine found near a once-active spring at Weltenburg is a characteristic type of animal representation from this period (Krämer 1950). Koch (1991, 136) notes that a hoard of bronze objects of Early Bronze Age date was recovered close by. Cast bronze bulls, boars, horses, and stags are common on sites of this period (Krämer 1989, Megaw and Megaw 1989, Gerlach 1990), and specimens have been recovered at most of the oppida. (On the special role of bulls in Celtic iconography, see Green 1989, 149-151; 1992, 51-52.)

The sheet bronze plaque with two opposing stylized horse heads from a pit on the eastern end of the Mitterfeld has attracted considerable attention from the perspective of Celtic art (De Navarro 1959, Megaw 1970). The object was found in 1937 in the course of house construction, in a settlement pit that also contained abundant pottery, a purple glass ring bead with yellow lines, and an iron chisel (De Navarro 1959, 131). The piece, 6.1 cm high, had holes that suggest that it was originally attached to a wooden object, perhaps a box or chest. Like bulls, horses too played a significant role in Celtic iconography and mythology (Bahn and Ullmann 1986; Green 1989, 146-149; 1992, 120-122).

Excavations on the Mitterfeld conducted by the Landesamt für Denkmalpflege in 1986 recovered a bronze spout in the form of a dog's head (Engelhardt 1987, 107 fig. 63). The piece closely resembles a find from Manching (van Endert 1991, pl. 9, 237). Both have a single hole underneath the spout through which a nail or rivet was presumably hammered to attach the object to a wooden vessel. Like bulls and horses, dogs occupied a special place in Celtic tradition (Green 1989, 144-146; 1992, 82-84).

The cast bronze bird's head (Figure 6.25) that

we recovered in Pit 1987/3-11-12 is the smallest object of this group. As I have argued elsewhere (Wells 1989), the bird represented here is probably a vulture, a creature that occurs often in Celtic iconography, for example on coins minted in Bavaria during this period (e.g. Kellner 1990, pl. 22, 526; 45, 1211-1219). In a number of mythological traditions of ancient and medieval times, vultures played a special role as messengers between gods and humans.

Of these four animal representations, the bull was found near a spring, a type of place at which ritually deposited objects are often recovered (Torbrügge 1971; Green 1989, 155-164; 1992, 197-198). It was a cast figurine, and it appears to be complete. At least two of the other three objects (the plaque with horse heads and the bird head) were found in settlement pits on the Mitterfeld, together with characteristic settlement debris from the La Tène D1 occupation. All three had been attached originally to other objects which had apparently been used on the settlement. In our excavations, the majority of bronze objects, like the majority of the pottery sherds, were recovered in the cultural layer, not in the pits. The discovery of these animal representations in pits on the settlement suggests that their deposition may have been deliberate. This sample of animal motifs from Kelheim is too small to draw any conclusions, but a systematic examination of the contexts in which animal representations occur at all oppidum settlements would indicate whether it was deliberate practice to deposit such objects in pits on the site (on depositions made in disused settlement pits in Britain, see Cunliffe 1992).

The Hoard from the Mitterfeld

Behaghel (1952) reported a pit found in 1939 on Mitterfeldstrasse in the course of construction associated with canal work. The pit was about 1.1 m in diameter at the top of the subsoil and extended some 0.8 m deep into the underlying gravel. It contained 10 sizable iron implements, most cutting tools, two objects that appear to be keys, three rings, a fibula, and other scraps, along with pottery of characteristic types from the settlement and some bones. Behaghel interpreted the deposit as a tool kit relating specifically to mining and forest work, and thus the cellar contents of the house of a miner. The pottery and bones would conform to the general character of settlement pits on the Mitterfeld.

Another possible interpretation of this find is in the context of hoard deposits of iron metal of the Late Iron Age, a group of finds studied by Rybová and Motyková (1983). They interpret such hoards as votive in function. In this particular case, the implements intended for excavating into the earth and for cutting down the trees of the forest could have served a particular purpose in the votive context, if we follow the argument of Rybová and Motyková.

Kluge (1987, 70-71), however, casts some doubt on Behaghel's report and on his interpretation. As she observes, the report is vague about some important details concerning the find, and no plan or profile of the pit was published. Kluge calls attention to other finds in the Archäologisches Museum of Kelheim with the same inventory number as the iron objects reported by Behaghel, and they include skeletal remains of a child seven or eight years of age. She suggests that the find may have been a child's grave.

As Kluge makes clear, there is much confusion about this find, and without a plan of the pit it is impossible to make a good judgment as to its character. Behaghel's general description of the pit (1952, 106) corresponds well to the settlement pits that we excavated on the Mitterfeld, but Kluge's observations about the child's skeleton raise concerns. With the available information, we cannot confidently interpret the significance of this find. But future discoveries of other deposits that may be similar to this one may help to clarify the situation.

Deep Pits on the Settlement

From earlier rescue excavations on the Mitterfeld, two deep pits have been identified as wells (Kluge 1987, 72-73; Etzel 1990, 14-16). The first appeared at the top of the subsoil as a round, humus-filled hole 2.6 m in diameter. Inside this circle was another round discoloration 1.0 m in diameter. The form of the pit was cylindrical, and layers of fill could be distinguished around the vertical shaft, though no wooden structure was identified. The cultural materials recovered in the fill of the shaft are described as very rich. The second pit was characterized at the top by a shallow basin about 4 m in diameter. At a depth of 1.7 m, the shaft reached the limestone bedrock, and it cut into the bedrock about 5 m. No interior framework was identified. In this case also, layers of fill could be discerned that were added to the outer part of the shaft, apparently between an inner structure and the outer rim of the hole. An iron handle of a pail was found at the bottom of the well, along with wood fragments that may have been remains of a wooden pail.

The two major pits that our excavations uncovered in 1987 (Figures 5.5, 5.6, 5.8, 5.9) were similar to these wells described. Similar pits interpreted as wells have also been identified at other oppida (e.g. Jansová 1960). At Manching, Krämer (1957, 1958) reports the existence of internal rectangular structures—perhaps well linings of wood—very like that identified in pit 1987/6-10 in our excavations.

Wells in prehistoric and historic Europe were frequently sites at which special deposits were made (Beck 1981), and connections have been drawn between *Viereckschanzen* and wells. The deep shaft in the *Viereckschanze* at Fellbach-Schmiden may have been a well originally (Planck 1985). In mythology, wells were believed to provide healing and nourishment, and to offer insights into the future. Gods and goddess who could influence the future course of events were thought to inhabit wells.

For the present, it is not clear whether these two major pits from our 1987 excavations had once been wells or not. In any case, they may have played some ritual function on the settlement, and the recovery of the bronze bird head in the one could relate to some such ritual activity. Future study of the form and contents of these features, and comparison with pits on other sites, will address these questions.

The Building Offering

In his investigations of the inner wall, Herrmann (1973, 141 and pl. 18, 1) came upon a human calotte in front (outside) of the wall, buried at a shallow depth in the Late Iron Age surface. It was 0.65 m from the later construction phase of the wall, 1.40 m from the earlier, and was positioned with the face toward the wall. The physical anthropological study indicated that it was from an individual over 50 years of age, probably over 60, and was probably a male. The person was killed by a sword blow on the left upper portion of the back of the head. The calotte was brought to this location already separated from the rest of the skull. Herrmann concludes that the calotte was certainly placed here intentionally. A possibly similar situation was found at Manching. There a burial of a child was discovered exactly in the middle of the southern portion of the entrance to the eastern gate (Gensen 1965, 56 and pl. 8,2). Gensen interpreted that find as a building offering. This practice is well attested in textual sources from the ancient world, especially in relation to the construction of fortifications (Hinz 1976).

Discussion

The principal need in the development of further understanding of this aspect of life at Kelheim is for comparative investigation at other settlements of the period, as well as those of earlier and later times. In the study of ritual and cult activity, especially, repetition of patterns observed at different sites is particularly important for establishing the character of the activity. After a substantial database is developed from the archaeological sites, then textual information from ancient authors and from relevant early medieval traditions (e.g. Davidson 1988, Green 1992) can be employed to aid in interpreting the ritual patterns and purposes.

As will be argued in the next chapter, we need to regard ritual activity not only as a component of everyday life of human communities, but also as a factor in cultural change. At Kelheim, the ritual activity in evidence is part of a system of behavior that was changing rapidly during phase La Tène D1 of the Late Iron Age. The *Viereckschanzen* appeared at about the same time as the oppida, according to our present understanding, and though some remained in use into the Roman period and even later, the principal use of the enclosures was contemporary with the oppida—that is, for around 75 years between about 130–120 and 50 B.C. Burial practice changed radically at the time that the oppida appeared. Representations of vultures proliferated, especially on the *Regenbogenschüsselchen* gold coins that were minted in Bavaria in large quantities. We need to view these changes in ritual and symbolic practice not just as responses to political and economic changes, but as significant components of the profound cultural changes that were taking place in all aspects of life in Late La Tène Europe.

Chapter 18
The Oppida and Cultural Change in Late Iron Age Europe

Introduction

The question of the causes behind the establishment of the oppida is complex and can be approached in several different ways. On the basis of the results to date from our investigations at Kelheim I wish to offer here some thoughts about these issues. I shall indicate how I view the situation at present, and at the same time suggest some avenues for further research.

The origins of the oppida need to be considered on several different levels. We need to view the issue both in terms of long-term cultural changes in Late Iron Age Europe, and as responses to specific political, military, and economic circumstances that developed in temperate Europe in the second half of the final century B.C. Furthermore, we must address the issue of origins both in relation to the whole class of sites designated as oppida, since they all share significant similarities and appeared at roughly the same time; but we must also examine the developmental process of each oppidum within the context of the settlement history of its particular cultural landscape. These are big goals, and in this report my aim is primarily to explore some of the principal issues, in order to suggest programs for future investigation, both in field research and in synthetic studies.

Long-Term Processual Change in the Late Iron Age

The third century B.C. is the starting point for my discussion (on relevant changes before this, see Pauli 1978, 1985; Collis 1984b; Wells 1984; 1990; Nash 1985). Throughout temperate Europe, this time is characterized by the flat-grave inhumation cemeteries of the La Tène C phase, with men frequently outfitted with iron weapons and women with bronze jewelry (Krämer 1985, Waldhauser 1987). Settlements were small, constituting hamlets or very small villages. Most of our evidence for community size derives from the hundreds of excavated cemeteries, but the few settlements of the period that have been excavated, such as Radovesice in Bohemia (Waldhauser 1977, 1984), confirm the size indicated by the cemeteries and provide detail on economy and character of households (discussion in Wells 1984, 133-137).

Historical accounts from Greek and Latin sources indicate that Celtic peoples were active in migration and invasion into southern and eastern parts of Europe, and into Asia Minor. The texts indicate a period of complex political and military machinations on the part of some Celtic groups at this time (recent discussion in Szabó 1991a). Celtic material culture, in the form of objects decorated with distinctive La Tène ornament and the characteristic burial practices, is well represented in many peripheral regions of temperate Europe, for example in the Balkans as far as Romania (Rusu 1969), as well as throughout Italy (Vitali 1991). To what extent this spread of La Tène ornament and burial practice was the result of actual movements of peoples, and to what extent of the transmission of styles and practices, is unclear. This subject requires further careful and thoughtful research.

Ancient historical sources inform us that substantial numbers of Celtic mercenaries were serving in armies in the Mediterranean world, especially in the service of Greek potentates, but sometimes as far afield as Asia Minor and Egypt (Griffith 1935; recent summary in Szabó 1991b). Coinage began in temperate Europe during this period, probably inspired by coins brought home from Greece by returning mercenaries (Mannsperger 1981, Polenz 1982).

Significant advances were made in iron production during the third century B.C. (Pleiner 1980, 1982). Larger quantities were being made, and the quality of iron tools was improving. Iron swords, spearheads, and shield parts were often deposited in men's graves. Among other crafts, the manufacture of glass bracelets began around the middle of the third century B.C. (Gebhard 1989, 128), and they became a principal component of the assemblages in women's graves.

In contrast to practices during the sixth and

fifth centuries B.C. before, and the second and final centuries B.C. after, during this period there were very few exceptionally richly outfitted burials, and luxury imports from the Mediterranean world were few in number. Some investigators have interpreted these configurations to indicate a period when there was little social differentiation, but as Bujna (1982) has demonstrated, the burial patterns among the flat inhumation graves in fact show subtle but significant status variation, even though many of the traditional emblems of elite display, such as imported bronze wine vessels, wheeled vehicles, and large gold ornaments, are rare. As Kossack (1974) and others have argued, exceptionally rich burials may be indicators not so much of the existence of status differences, but rather of periods of substantial cultural change, when competitive display of status signs was particularly important. The existence of many isolated examples of wealth display, such as the gold torcs from France (Eluère 1991), reinforce Bujna's argument that behind the material culture of the third century B.C., which at first glance appears egalitarian, major status differences were in fact being expressed.

In textual sources from the Mediterranean world, we are informed about changes that had a direct impact on the peoples of temperate Europe. One was the end of the period of most active mercenary service by Celts in Mediterranean armies, another the growing involvement of Rome in regions to the north and its expansion into lands occupied by Celtic peoples.

Early in the second century B.C., mercenary service of Celtic men fighting in armies of Mediterranean potentates declined. The end to this activity may have resulted in the return of many former mercenaries to their homelands in temperate Europe. This return may have had two important effects. Many of the returnees may have felt dissatisfied with the absence of various luxuries to which they had become accustomed in Mediterranean lands, such as plentiful wine and other southern consumables. More importantly, the return of large numbers, most likely thousands and perhaps tens of thousands, of professional fighting men is likely to have introduced a significant element of instability into temperate Europe. Many may not have found satisfactory outlets for their energies in the communities to which they returned, and they may have been eager to serve, as mercenaries, any local potentate willing to pay them.

During the second half of the third century B.C., Rome engaged in a number of important military encounters against Celtic groups in Italy. In 225 B.C. Celtic forces suffered a major defeat at Telamon on the Tyrrhenian coast of central Italy, and thereafter Celtic power in Italy was on the wane. By 180 B.C., Roman forces had conquered the lands as far north as the Po Plain. It is not clear whether substantial numbers of Celtic people emigrated from the Roman-conquered lands across the Alps into temperate Europe. Most likely, the majority stayed in Italy and lived on under the Roman political system.

At the same time, Rome became involved militarily in southern Gaul (Rivet 1988). By the beginning of second century B.C., Roman presence was established in the lands around Marseille, and the effects of this new political, military, and economic factor were felt throughout much of Gaul. Archaeologically, this development is reflected most clearly in the Roman trade goods that begin appearing in substantial quantities at sites north of the Alps from the start of the second century B.C. on, and especially after the middle of that century (Werner 1978, Will 1987).

Political and Military Crisis in the Late Second Century B.C., and the Appearance of the Oppida

Most of the oppida of southern Germany were established early in the phase La Tène D1, around 130–120 B.C. according to the current chronology (Krämer 1985, Miron 1986, Jockenhövel 1990). At Manching, where a sizable community had developed earlier (Gebhard 1991), a new settlement with a different orientation was established at this time, and the defensive walls were first constructed then. The massive and extensive walls of the oppida bespeak a need for defense on an unprecedented scale. At the same time that many oppida were established and walls constructed, many landscapes show evidence of the abandonment of smaller settlements (see Chapter 15), implying that people were leaving the countryside and moving into the protected environments of the newly fortified places.

This new need for defense that arose in the second half of the second century B.C. could be explained in terms of at least three developments that may have created a situation of increased danger to the communities of central Europe. One was the return of mercenaries from Greece and other Mediterranean lands, where the need for their services declined after the beginning of the second century B.C. (see above).

Another source of instability and danger was the movements of sizable groups of peoples from the north and east through the central regions of Europe. We know about these groups primarily from the textual sources. The Cimbri, believed to have originated in Jutland, are mentioned in the historical sources in 113 B.C. in central Europe, and we are told that subsequently they moved westward through what is now southern Germany and into Gaul (Ihm 1899, Todd 1992). During the final decade of the second century B.C. they offered stiff resistance to Roman armies in southern Gaul and in northern Italy, until they were finally defeated in 102 B.C. The Teutoni, also thought to have originated in northern Europe, are mentioned in the same kind of context. In succeeding decades, texts inform us of large-scale migrations by Boii, Suebi, Helvetii, and other groups. The texts imply that these were sizable bands of warriors often traveling with families and baggage.

It is likely that the particular groups mentioned in the historical sources were only parts of large-scale movements of peoples at this time (Seyer 1988, 49; Todd 1992, 2). Hedeager (1992, 245) views the emigration of the Cimbri and the Teutoni as the result of particular social and economic circumstances in their northern homelands, and similar conditions are likely to have applied to other peoples. The information that has been preserved in the surviving texts creates an impression of large and often violent bands of people threatening communities in central Europe during the second half of the final century B.C. The "great battle" at Manching that occurred at the La Tène C2–D1 transition (Sievers 1989), around 130–120 B.C., has been brought into connection with such marauding bands. Migrating populations would have surely fought to acquire food supplies to sustain themselves, and may well have plundered whatever else they could during their movement.

Third, the beginning of intensive Roman trade with communities in temperate Europe during the second half of the second century B.C. may have involved trade in slaves, among other goods. Archaeological evidence for slavery and slave trade is always sparse, even in instances when slavery is well attested by textual sources, but slave trade with the Roman world is probable in this period (Arnold 1988). If the pattern of development of slave trade in temperate Europe was like that documented in other contexts (Hopkins 1978, Harris 1980), then it is likely that different Celtic groups would have attacked their neighbors for the purpose of capturing slaves for trade. Caesar's portrayal of the Gallic tribes warring with one another at the time of his arrival could be understood in the context of such conflict.

Of these three potential elements causing a situation of military danger, the migrations by peoples on the move is the most likely. The other two potential causes are not well documented and must be regarded only as possibilities at this time. All three circumstances would have created unstable and potentially dangerous conditions in southern Germany and elsewhere in central and western Europe, and would have motivated people to band together for common defense and to establish fortified settlements in places where natural defensive advantages could be gained. The siting of the oppida (Dehn 1965) can be viewed in this light, as can the enormous efforts that went into the construction of the oppidum walls. As Murray's survey has shown, at Kelheim the evidence indicates that many small settlements were abandoned when the oppidum was established.

Commercial Intensification at the End of the Second Century B.C.

When the oppida were established, iron-working became especially active in these large centers, thought it was still carried out in the smaller outlying settlements as well. All oppida yield evidence of substantial iron-working, and for some, such as Kelheim, iron production seems to have been a major activity, perhaps a determining factor in the establishment of the oppidum on the site.

Commerce grew rapidly during the second half of the second century B.C., among the Celtic groups of temperate Europe, between them and the Roman world to the south, and between the Celtic peoples and their neighbors to the north. Trade growth within temperate Europe is clearest in the coinage. Silver and bronze coinage developed around the middle of the second century B.C., at about the same time that the oppida first appeared. With the growth of these coinages (as opposed to coins in gold only), a real money economy developed at the major centers (Steuer 1987, Kellner 1990). Most oppidum sites that have been investigated have yielded coins from different parts of Europe (Pič 1906, Allen 1980, Kellner 1990), indicating a substantial circulation of coins. But other materials circulated as well, including fine pottery, glass ornaments, and bronze jewelry.

Trade with the Roman world intensified from about the middle of the second century B.C. on. Will (1987) has shown that ceramic amphorae at

Manching began arriving early in the second century B.C., but the mass of Roman goods at the oppida and in graves north of the Alps date from after mid-century. These include amphorae, fine pottery, bronze vessels, medical tools, mirrors, and writing implements (Werner 1954, 1978; Christlein 1964; Stöckli 1979a; Svobodová 1985). Roman factories were mass producing goods specifically for the "barbarian" trade by this time (Dyson 1988), and the evidence north of the Alps suggests that commercial systems were changing to produce more goods for trade to the Roman world, to assure a continuing supply of desired Roman luxuries.

Commerce northward into central Germany and beyond is apparent in a number of different categories of materials that were produced in the Celtic oppidum region and that are recovered in lands to the north. These include characteristic elements of the everyday life at the oppida, such as graphite-clay pottery, coins, and glass bracelets (Kaufmann 1984, Berger 1985, Peschel 1989), but also more elaborate objects. Large numbers of bronze and bronze-and-iron caldrons manufactured in the Celtic areas were brought northward to the lower Elbe basin and Denmark (Eggers 1951, Redlich 1980, Hachmann 1990). Celtic-style swords are numerous in northern regions of Europe during this period (Frey 1986), though it is not always apparent whether they represent imports from the south or local versions of southern prototypes. Many objects of northern origin have been recovered in the Celtic regions (Meduna 1968), mostly items of jewelry that may reflect movements by individuals more than trade (Krämer 1961, Reim 1979).

The special role of the oppida with respect to commerce is apparent in the concentration on oppidum sites of industrial debris from the manufacture of goods, including many trade materials, and of imported objects. In the iron industry in particular, it is clear that manufacturing was carried out more intensively at some of the oppida, including Kelheim, than it had been on earlier settlements. The fast-turning potter's wheel was introduced in this period, and it provided a quicker means of making ceramic vessels using mass production techniques. The rotary quern was another application of more efficient technology to basic production processes (Waldhauser 1981).

The origins of the oppida need to be considered with respect to both of these issues—defense and commerce, because both aspects of the oppida are clearly apparent in the archaeological evidence. It should be noted, however, that defensive position and substantial walls around large settlements on the one hand, and long-distance trade and large-scale manufacturing on the other, are not always associated together at oppidum sites. Many oppida (defined in terms of the wall systems) have not yielded evidence of intensive occupation and may have served rather as *refugia* in times of danger; examples include Zarten, Heidengraben, and Finsterlohr in southern Germany (Fischer 1988; Weber 1989). And some large settlements that engaged in trade and industry were not situated defensively and did not have walls; examples include Breisach-Hochstetten in southwestern Germany and Basel-Gasfabrik in Switzerland (Fischer 1988).

The hoards of gold and silver which are so abundant during the La Tène D1 phase constitute another important change in economic life, while they were probably important ritually as well (Kellner 1990, 41). Numerous large hoards of gold coins can be dated to this phase (Overbeck 1987b), and the gold coin and ring hoards of Furger-Gunti's (1982) "Saint Louis" type also date to La Tène D1. Whatever the specific purpose of burying any particular hoard might have been, the deposition of such quantities of gold and silver had significant economic effects (Haselgrove 1988).

Political Changes in Celtic Europe

Roymans (1990) has recently reviewed the evidence available for understanding political systems in Gaul before the Roman conquest. While it is questionable whether circumstances in Gaul can be seen as representative of temperate Europe as a whole, particularly because of the very close contacts between Rome and Gaul since early in the second century B.C. (Rivet 1988), the historical sources that mention political and social patterns in pre-Roman Europe focus mostly on Gaul (e.g. Crumley 1974). In his summary of his research, Roymans (p. 261) characterizes the political systems of pre-Roman Gaul as hierarchical and segmentary, and he finds that kinship and clientship were particularly important mechanisms through which relations among people were structured. Even within Gaul, Roymans identifies considerable variation in specific kinds of structure. Investigation of the applicability of the models generated from the ancient written sources (Crumley 1974, 1987) to the lands east of Gaul, such as the region in which Kelheim is situated, is an important task for future research, but one that exceeds the bounds of this study.

From the archaeological evidence, it is apparent that at the same time as the establishment of oppida and the other changes we have been discussing, in the early part of La Tène D1, the practice of outfitting some burials with substantially greater wealth than most was reinstituted, after a hiatus of some three centuries. (There are indeed a small number of exceptionally rich graves from the fourth and third centuries B.C., such as Waldalgesheim, but they are fewer in number than those of preceding and succeeding times.) This new series of rich graves is characterized by many of the same categories of status signs that marked the earlier groups—bronze vessels, Mediterranean imports, wheeled vehicles, gold ornaments, and weapons (Haffner and Joachim 1984). We need to ask, of course, whether the reappearance of an exceptionally rich category of burials during La Tène D1 reflects a change in social structure, with the emergence of a new status group, or whether it instead represents only a new need to express status differences that already existed (Kossack 1974), perhaps in the context of this period of exceptional cultural stress and rapid change.

Crumley, Duval (1983), and Nash (1978) have argued that with the rapid growth in trade with Rome, in Gaul during this period social competition increased between persons and between groups for participation and leadership roles in the trade and in the larger interactions with the Roman world (see also Fitzpatrick 1989). This competition could have been expressed by lavish funerary display, such as we find in many burials at this time. Timpe (1985), in reviewing the textual evidence, has emphasized the role that elites played in Gaul in coordinating the growing commerce at the centers. The rich burials could be interpreted as the funerary monuments of such persons. A number of ancient authors note the practice among the Celts, and the Germans, of selecting special leaders in times of political and military need. The conditions that are likely to have obtained in temperate Europe during this period may well have given rise to such need, and stimulated the rise of persons to new positions of high status.

Changes in Ritual Practice

At about the same time that Kelheim and other oppida were established, changes took place in a number of different aspects of human behavior that we can associate with ritual practice and with the use of symbols. These changes were widespread throughout the broad band of temperate Europe where oppida occur (Figure 1.1). The dominant burial practice changed from inhumation with substantial burial goods (e.g. Waldhauser 1978, 1987; Krämer 1985), to cremation with few or no goods. For most of the oppida, including Kelheim and Manching, we know of very few burials that date to the principal period of settlement occupation. The reason may be that cremated remains often were interred in shallow pits that have been obliterated through agricultural activities (see Waldhauser 1979, 147), or perhaps other means of disposing of bodies were employed that might leave no trace in the archaeological record. Only in the regions along the Main River and between the Main and the English Channel do substantial cemeteries exist. In these, although cremation replaced inhumation, the old practice of outfitting graves with burial goods was maintained (Schönberger 1952, Polenz 1971, Haffner 1989).

The *Viereckschanzen* east of the Rhine seem to have been constructed first during La Tène D1, though precursors can be identified throughout the Iron Age (Rybová and Soudský 1962, Christlein and Stork 1980, Brunaux 1988). As Murray (Chapter 15) notes, prior to this period, many natural features of the landscape, such as caves, cliffs, and streams, were used as places in which rituals were carried out—evident archaeologically in the objects deposited. Distinctive of the *Viereckschanzen* is the fact that they were constructed intentionally and that the plan and internal character of these sites are highly standardized.

The time when the oppida were established and during which they flourished was also a period when the practice of depositing hoards of objects in the ground was exceptionally active. The hoards of gold coins, and those of rings and coins, can readily be interpreted in terms of ritual behavior (Furger-Gunti 1982; Haselgrove 1988; Kellner 1990, 41), and they seem to represent the dedication, or sacrifice, of substantial accumulated wealth. Another category of hoards—those containing iron tools and bronze implements—has also been interpreted in terms of ritual activity (Rybová and Motyková 1983). These were frequently deposited in wet places and, as Rybová and Motyková argue, the tools in them—many for tilling the soil and tending the hearth—can be understood to represent activities associated with fertility and nurturing.

Finally, during the time of the oppida, cast bronze figurines of animals are more abundant than during preceding periods (see references cited in Chapter 17). The animals represented include bulls, boars, horses, stags, and dogs, as well as the bird head noted above.

The systematic archaeological study of ritual activity in the Late Iron Age is still at a very early stage of development, but some suggestions can be made from these patterns. Most importantly, substantial change in a variety of ritual activities can be seen to have accompanied the changes in settlement, political organization, and economic patterns. This fact underscores the far-reaching aspects of the changes that took place in temperate Europe when the oppida were established. The construction of the *Viereckschanzen* and the hoarding of large amounts of gold, especially, indicate the devotion of substantial resources, in labor and in accumulated wealth, to the practice of ritual. If our interpretation of the enclosures and the hoards is correct—that they represent the offering of goods to deities in the hope of receiving favors or protection (Brunaux 1988, Davidson 1988), then the increase in the resources devoted to such activity can be interpreted as indicating exceptionally stressful and dangerous conditions.

A Hypothetical Scenario for the Establishment of the Oppidum at Kelheim

On the basis of the results of our excavations at Kelheim, those of the systematic salvage investigations and chance finds there, and information from other sites, I offer a hypothetical scenario for the establishment and growth of the Kelheim settlement. The main purpose of this exercise is to point up issues that most need further investigation if we are to obtain a more complete understanding of the origins, character, and demise of the oppida.

Sometime around 130–120 B.C., at the start of phase La Tène D1, people from the region around the modern city of Kelheim began to move onto the Mitterfeld below the Michelsberg. As they moved into the valley, they built houses and other structures, and dug cellar and storage pits. The reason for this shift in settlement pattern was primarily the perceived need to settle in larger groups and in places that offered natural defense against attack. The exact nature of the threat to the communities of the countryside is unclear, but it probably was connected to the movements of groups of peoples through much of temperate Europe during the final quarter of the second century B.C., described by Roman and Greek writers. The growth in trade with the Roman world, including perhaps trade in slaves, may have played a part as well. The Kelheim area had a substantial population long before the establishment of the oppidum settlement, and indeed the variety of settlement evidence and remains of apparent ritual activity from the Bronze and earlier Iron Age suggests that the place had regional importance well before the Late Iron Age. When the new settlement on the Mitterfeld began, the open settlement east of the later medieval city continued to be occupied, and the *Viereckschanze* there was constructed.

The new community that established itself on the Mitterfeld constructed the outer fortification wall over the Michelsberg first, and later renewed that wall and built the inner wall and the one along the south bank of the Altmühl (Engelhardt 1982, 28; Rind 1988, 50-51). The construction of the walls required a great effort on the part of the community. Kluge (1987, 56-61) estimates that about 500,000 cubic meters of earth, 100,000 cubic meters of cut limestone, and 11,500 tree trunks were procured, transported, and erected to form the wall system. She estimates that some 1,400,000 workdays were devoted to this task. On the basis of present information, it is not clear whether a large number of people built the wall in a relatively short period of time, or a smaller group over a longer period. If the principal motivating factor in the establishment of the oppida was military danger, it is likely that the wall was constructed in a relatively brief time. It is likely that labor was drawn from surrounding communities as well as from the residents of the oppidum settlement. The oppidum probably served as a refuge in times of danger for outlying communities, as well as for its resident population.

In the process of agglomeration of population from small communities to larger ones, changes in the leadership structure would have been required to manage the more complex decision-making processes, as Rathje (1975) has argued, for example, to direct the construction of the walls and to plan for the common defense. Bujna (1982) has shown that the burial patterns of the preceding centuries (La Tène B and C) do not reflect an egalitarian society as some have suggested, but one with considerable stratification already present, though not often expressed in lavish funerary display. A result of the changes that accompanied the establishment of the oppida was the reinstitution of the tradition of outfitting some graves with elaborate and lavish grave goods. The phase La Tène D1 is characterized by a reappearance of symbols of high status in graves, including bronze vessels, Roman imports, wheeled vehicles, and ornate weapons (Flouest and Stead 1977, Werner 1978, Haffner and Joachim 1984). At Kelheim, this new development is reflected in the Roman bronze jug and the oversized iron spearhead (Krämer 1985 pl. 70).

The new community was quick to exploit the rich iron resources available on the Michelsberg. It is likely that iron mining began before the oppidum settlement was established, but we do not yet have the evidence to show that. The eastern end of the Mitterfeld became the focus of occupation and of manufacturing activity in a variety of crafts, though production of iron—the main industry of the community—was carried out on different parts of the site, including on the Michelsberg (Behaghel 1940), on the Mitterfeld (this volume, Chapter 10), just outside the outer wall (Rind 1988, 51), and at nearby locations in the Altmühl Valley (Burger and Geisler 1983). Whereas the eastern half of the Mitterfeld was the focus of settlement activity, the other parts were settled much less densely. The western portions of the Mitterfeld that we explored in 1990 and 1991 give the impression of rural settlement. Further analysis of the settlement materials recovered through excavation will provide additional information on the contrasts between the eastern and western portions of the settlement.

The scale of iron production evident at Kelheim suggests that the community was producing that metal for export, and the trade was probably directed by local elites, if the evidence from Gaul can be a guide (Timpe 1985). According to available indications, iron was the only material produced at Kelheim in quantities greatly exceeding probable local needs. There is no indication that bronze casting, glass jewelry making, pottery manufacture, or textile production were carried out on a scale that would make export trade likely.

The End of the Oppidum Settlement at Kelheim

Since there is no evidence of materials dating to La Tène D2 at Kelheim, it is probable that the settlement was abandoned sometime around 70–50 B.C. (see Chapter 7). No indication of a violent end to the settlement has been identified (Vencl 1984; Kluge 1987, 193), such as swords or other weapons as found at Manching, nor a burned horizon on the settlement. As noted above, in comparison to Manching, which apparently suffered a catastrophic end to its early phase of occupation (Sievers 1989), the settlement deposits at Kelheim have yielded mainly small objects—fragmentary items and little things that may have been lost, in contrast to the substantial quantities of large tools, as well as the weapons, that were found at Manching (Jacobi 1974). This evidence supports the likelihood of a deliberate, unhurried departure from the site, not a rapid abandonment. The end of Kelheim, like that of most of the oppida of southern and central Germany, must be seen in the context of the historically-documented movements of peoples, of whom in this later phase the Suebi, Helvetii, and Boii are most commonly mentioned in the ancient sources (Kluge 1987, 193; Fischer 1988).

Materials which are characteristic of phase La Tène D2, as defined by Krämer (1962), have not been identified in the Kelheim Basin or in the lower Altmühl Valley (Kluge 1987, 193), though they are present elsewhere in southern Bavaria. Those types, which include the Beltz Type J and the *geschweifte* fibula, and the belt hooks known as the *Lochgürtelhaken* and the *Stabgürtelhaken* (see Krämer 1962, 306 fig. 1), indicate connections northward, in Saxony and on the North European Plain (Müller 1985). These finds have been interpreted as evidence for migration of "Germans" southward into Bavaria (Glüsing 1965), but others view them more as products of interaction with peoples to the north than as indications of migration (Ament 1984). Future studies at Kelheim and other sites will need to address these important questions of interaction, migration, and ethnic identity associated with the end of the central European oppida.

Chapter 19
Continuity of Religious Tradition at Kelheim and the Foundation of Weltenburg Abbey
by
Frederick Suppe

Kelheim, Weltenburg, and their environs are productive places in which to examine the question of continuity of religious activity during the period between 200 B.C. and 700 A.D., a period during which three different traditions successively held sway over the region. The Late La Tène Celtic tradition of the Iron Age was succeeded by the Roman Empire, for which the River Danube was a northern political boundary, and Rome was followed in turn by groups known as Germanic tribes, specifically the Bajuwari (Bavarians). Engelhardt (1989b) suggests that the oppidum overlooking Kelheim was the center of the Rucinates, a subgroup of the Celtic people called the Vindelici. According to tradition, Weltenburg, the earliest monastery in Bavaria, was founded under the aegis of the Irish monk Columbanus and his followers early in the seventh century A. D. on a site which had apparently been sacred during the Celtic and Roman periods.

The Kelheim area includes several extensive, contiguous sites. Geographically most prominent is the Michelsberg, the triangular natural promontory delineated by the confluence of the Danube and the River Altmühl. On two sides, natural steep or sheer drops offer great inherent defence to the site, and substantial earthen walls erected during the Late La Tène period along the west side defined the great Celtic oppidum. This was probably the site designated by the Greek geographer Ptolemy as *Alkimoennis* (see Reinecke 1924). Just north of the Michelsberg and on the flatlands lying along the River Altmühl about a kilometer outside modern Kelheim is the Mitterfeld site, where University of Minnesota teams conducted excavations during the summers of 1987, 1990, and 1991. A third site is Kelheim-Gmünd, an area which included both the left bank of the former course of the Altmühl directly across from medieval Kelheim and several islands in the Altmühl delta where it entered the Danube (see Engelhardt 1984, 60-61 fig. 20 and 63 fig. 21). Finally, the site of Weltenburg Abbey on the south bank of the Danube in a peninsula defined by a U-turn in the river, is across the river from the Michelsberg and has been associated with cultural developments occurring there for much of its history. This study focuses on the last two sites.

The Kelheim-Gmünd site was partially destroyed by construction of the new channel for the Rhein-Main-Donau Canal. Remains of a Celtic *Viereckschanze* were partially excavated at this site (Reinecke 1911; Burger 1981). Although much work remains to be done on *Viereckschanzen*, recent scholarship has shown that they had a religious or cultic role in the Late La Tène Celtic society of southern Germany and north-central France (Bittel 1978; Schwarz 1959). Most *Viereckschanzen* probably date from the late second or first century B. C. (Burger 1981). Although most *Viereckschanzen* were in relatively secluded areas, some, such as this one at Kelheim-Gmünd and another at Manching, were located close to oppida and had a special relationship with these population centers (Torbrügge, 1984a). After the Kelheim *Viereckschanze* had been partially leveled, seven unusual infant burials were placed on the site during the La Tène phase D (Torbrügge 1984b). This evidence suggests that the site continued to enjoy religious significance, although the physical forms on the place changed. Bittel (1978) argues for an analogous continuity for grave mounds and *Viereckschanzen*.

The Kelheim-Gmünd site was also the location for a Bavarian *Reihengräberfeld* with grave goods indicating usage from the early sixth century A. D. through the first half of the seventh. Several of the graves were on the exact site of the *Viereckschanze* (Koch 1968, 124-130, 154-155, 168-169). The earliest church on this spot is first mentioned sometime between 863 and 885 A.D., but it seems associated with the early Bavarian settlement and may well date from the later seventh or early eighth century (Codreanu-Windauer and Wanderwitz 1989). The apparent continuity of religious function at this site may be due in part to physical considerations. A now silted arm of the Altmühl made the site an island, and the *Viereckschanze*, cemetery, and early church were on high ground, at least two meters above the normal water level of the Danube and Altmühl, affording the area relative security from flooding (Burger 1984b, 72 fig. 27). However, the possibility of cultural continuity of religious function—that is, the religious use of the site by inhabitants of the district because of the awareness of a tradition of such use by earlier inhabitants—must also be considered.

The monastery of Weltenburg is located at the tip of a peninsula enclosed on three sides by a U bend in the Danube and delimited on the south by a series of three earthen walls. Known as the Frauenberg or Arzberg, this walled area was probably not an oppidum but did have religious significance well before the advent of Christianity on the site (Fehn 1970, 8). Discovery early in this century of several Early La Tène burials with bronze grave goods located directly under the crossing of the nave and transept of the abbey church strongly suggests that this site held religious significance at that time (Spindler 1981a, 75-77; Engelhardt 1989b, 91). The location certainly provokes the hypothesis of continuity at the site.

A bronze bull discovered near a former water hole in a field about one kilometer south-east of the outermost wall is stylistically comparable to a similar figure found at Manching and has been dated to the La Tène phase D (Krämer 1950; Bleibrunner 1964). Without further systematic excavation it is unclear whether the "Weltenburg Bull" was deposited deliberately as a votive offering at the water source or perhaps removed from its original location by chance in connection with later fortification of the monastery. However, although the bull's exact topographical context is unclear, the strong religious connotations of the bull in Celtic iconography (Green 1986, 176) reinforce the interpretation of the whole peninsula holding religious significance.

Weltenburg-Arzberg has been proposed as the location of the Artobriga mentioned by the second century A.D. Greek geographer Ptolemy (Dietz 1984, 228; Riess 1975, 2; Spindler 1969, plate 5d). Both elements in this name are Celtic, art meaning a bear and brig meaning a hill or high place (Pokorny 1959 I, 140, 875). The latter element aptly describes the elevation and steep cliffs of the Arzberg site, and it is possible that the area was associated with the bear gods attested at Berne and elsewhere in La Tène Celtic culture (Green 1986, 184).

According to a tradition reported in a late medieval inscription in the pilgrimage chapel of Mary located just above the monastery on the Frauenberg peninsula, that chapel was founded on the site of a Roman Minerva temple (Altmann and Thürmer 1981, 49; Riess 1975, 3). There may be a kernel of truth embodied in this tradition. After the Romans conquered the area south of the Danube that became the province of Raetia, they established a small military post at Frauenberg which was superceded circa 80 A.D. by a cohort fortress at Eining, some six km south-west of Weltenburg. During the reign of Valentinian I (364-375 A.D.) the Frauenberg site resumed an important military role when a new *castellum* was erected there (Spindler 1981a). From the mid second century A.D. until the eary fifth, the Roman garrison at Eining was Cohors III Brittanorum, a unit originally raised in Celtic Britain soon after the Roman invasion of that island in 43 A.D. (Fischer 1984, 130-131; Birley 1980). The name and form of Minerva occur frequently in Roman Britain in connection with worship of a Celtic goddess or goddesses under the *interpretatio Romana* (Ross 1967; Webster 1986, 54-55) and Roman troops originally from Britain stationed along the German *limes* brought some of their Celtic cults with them to Germany (Fleuriot 1982, 41). Discovery of awall fragment with the Roman herring-bone design (*opus spicatum*) close by the pilgrimage chapel indicates the presence there of a Roman civil settlement in addition to the Frauenberg *castellum* (Spindler 1981b). Since the Eining fortress was the closest large Roman post to Frauenberg and since the herring-bone pattern also occurs on many walls there, it seems likely that the garrison of the Frauenberg *castellum* was drawn from Cohors III Brittanorum. That this unit brought Celtic practices with it to Germany and worshipped Minerva at Frauenberg is thus a viable hypothesis which can explain the later medieval tradition and which merits testing by further excavation at the site and by comparisons with religious practices at other central European sites where Roman troops from Britain were stationed.

According to the traditional story about the foundation of Weltenburg preserved by its monks, the abbey was established early in the seventh century by Eustasius and Agilus, two monks who were followers of St. Columbanus, the much traveled Irish monk who established the monastery of Luxeuil in west central France (Prinz 1965, 356-358; Staber 1966, 4-5; Torbrügge 1984c; Werner n.d.). This tradition has occasioned much scholarly debate, with many dismissing it entirely (Torbrügge 1984c; Koller 1982), for, although contemporary written sources do discuss these monks' missionary activities, none of them mentions Weltenburg or any other specific locale in Bavaria. The saints' lives of Columbanus, Eustasius, and Agilus, all composed in the seventh century, report that Eustasius and Agilus left Luxeuil to convert the Varasci and then moved on to work among the Boii. They made many converts and left behind certain wise men (*sagaces viros*) to continue their work after they returned to Luxeuil. The first two lives add that another monk from Luxeuil, Agrestius, also undertook missionary work among the Boii but with scant success, apparently because of his unsuitable personality (Krusch 1905, 244-246; Carnandet 1868, 580; Bollandus 1865, 784; Laux 1919, 265).

Thus there is no primary source contemporary with the purported events of the Weltenburg foundation which reports them. Abbot Kammermeier, who wrote a history of the abbey in the mid eighteenth century before it was disestablished in 1803 with concomitant dispersal and loss of many muniments, found no such document (Kammermeier 1775). The earliest extant sources which relate to Weltenburg and its territorial possessions are some charters which may date from the latter ninth century at the earliest (Thiel 1958). Meyer (1931), however, points out both that the Magyar attacks of the late ninth and early tenth century seem to have destroyed many early documents relating to Bavaria and that full historical narrative accounts of the foundation of monasteries do not exist for this early portion of the Middle Ages. Lack of a such a document for Weltenburg is therefore not surprising.

There is, however, some documentary evidence which does lend some credence to the foundation legend. To supplement the written evidence of the saints' lives Paringer (1934, 1952) has adduced an illustration in a Weltenburg martyrology of 1045 which he interprets as depicting Eustasius and Agilus. And Brunhölzl (1981) has suggested that the distinctive "Luxeuil" uncial manuscript hand which characterizes a copy of the Carmenpaschale of Sedulius associated with Weltenburg supports the idea of books being brought from Luxeuil to the Bavarian monastery in the seventh century.

Several political and social factors also give credibility to the Weltenburg foundation tradition. There were strong political and genealogical links between the Franks and the dukes of Bavaria in the late sixth and early seventh centuries. As the Frankish empire expanded, its kings established Garibald (d. circa 590) as first in the family of Agilolfing dukes to rule Bavaria under their sway. Garibald had a daughter Theudelinde, who married two rulers of the Lombards in succession and was such a devout Christian that, when St. Columbanus was exiled from Luxeuil by Frankish court politics, she provided him with refuge and land for his final monastery at Bobbio in Lombard controlled northern Italy. The mission to the Boii had the strong support of Theudelinde and of the Frankish king Chlothar II and was probably part of a Frankish policy to increase Frankish influence and control in Bavaria (Staber 1966, 4-5; Prinz 1965, 356). The missionary monks also seem to have been carefully chosen for their family connections. Agilus bore a Latinized version of a *Leitname* of the Agilolfing Bavarian ducal family (Zöllner 1965), and Eustasius was a member of a Franco-Burgundian noble family with ties to the Frankish royal court (Prinz 1981, 78-79).

Physical and geographic factors also made Weltenburg a likely base for this early medieval missionary work. Irish missionary monks active on the Continent and their followers tended to settle on or near major travel routes including Roman roads. Such a road passed to the south of Weltenburg on its way from Eining to Regensburg (Staber 1966, 5; Spindler 1969, map 7). Many of the monasteries founded by the Irish missionaries were located within former Roman fortifications (Staber 1966, 5; Stokes 1895, 122; McNeill 1974, 159); Luxeuil itself is a typical example, being established within a defunct fortress and next to a cult site at a spring (Krusch 1905). Weltenburg, with its *castellum* and Roman reuse of the earthen wall fortifying the site, fits this pattern. One reason for this phenomenon is that Irish, Anglo-Saxon, and Merovingian monasteries always had some form of enclosure, more to delimit their sacred bounds from the profane world than for physical protection (James 1981, 40-41, 69-70; Riché 1981, 70). The walls of a defunct Roman fort could provide such an enclosure ready made. A second reason is that ownership of these former Roman military sites passed to local rulers in the early Middle Ages; a clear pattern of such continuity for the Roman forts along the Danube has been found to extend through the time of the Agilolfing dukes to the *Königsgut* of the eleventh century (Dachs 1965). Prinz (1981) has concluded that royal sponsorship and kindred-based organization were important reasons for the success of "Hiberno-Frankish" monasticism. Considering the royal Frankish and Agilolfing support for the mission of Eustasius and Agilus, Weltenburg seems to fit this pattern.

Konrad Spindler (1984b; 1985, 194-199) has argued that remains of an early church and a gold leaf cross found amidst a *Reihengräberfeld* at Staubing, some 1.5 km south-west of the Weltenburg monastery, suggest the presence of an early Christian community there which he feels was instrumental in establishing the monastery. The *-ing* place-name element clearly indicates that Staubing was among the earliest Bavarian settlements, perhaps dating from the late sixth century (Schwartz 1960, 55-56). That Staubing remains the parish church for the monastery suggests a long-standing connection between the two establishments (Engelhardt 1989b). Dannheimer (1973, 1984) dates the Staubing church to the later seventh century, considerably after the mission of Eustasius and Agilus. Whether early seventh century Christians at Staubing helped to found the Weltenburg monastery or whether the monastery came first and brought Christianity to Staubing, it seems clear that the district above the gorge of the Danube was an early Christian center in Bavaria.

The points discussed here lend support to the Weltenburg foundation tradition but do not conclusively prove it. The very fact that the tradition features Eustasius and Agilus, who had become quite obscure by the central Middle Ages, rather than figures more renowned at that time, suggests that it derives from the era of Hiberno-Frankish monasticism and should be seriously considered. Conclusive judgment about its veracity must await the opportunity for excavation at the monastery site.

The prehistory and early medieval history of southern Germany is a field both fascinating, because of the interactions between cultures, and frustrating, because of the paucity of data. This latter factor has impelled many scholars considering this region over this period to draw upon evidence generated by several disciplines, including history, archaeology, historical philology, and art history. But the problems of properly evaluating such diverse evidence and combining it to produce a synthetic chronological interpretation can trip up the unwary, especially when a scholar ventures outside his home discipline. Prinz (1974) and Renfrew (1987, especially chapters 6 and 11) have commented on these problems and Wainwright (1962) produced an excellent essay on the potential pit-falls and proper methodology for interdisciplinary scholarship. It seems appropriate to consider the underlying assumptions and epistemologies of these academic disciplines before proceeding to conclusions about cultural continuity at the Kelheim sites.

Historians, archaeologists, and linguistic scholars are all concerned with studying human societies over time. We may define a society as an organized group of people who act on the basis of certain shared beliefs and cultural values. Language is a central medium for this social organization. The raw material for historians—written documents—obviously directly reveals many of the actions and values of the social group under study, usually in their own language. Indeed, documents from this period, when most people were illiterate, usually reflect or record some form of oral social behavior such as ceremonies or dictation. However, this class of evidence has its limitations; such documents as exist from this period preponderantly concern the socially and economically dominant classes and are therefore biased towards reflecting political behavior. Thus, in positing historical periods—segments of time, each characterized by a homogeneous stage of social or political development—as the basis for chronological interpretation of a society over a long span of time, the historian will fasten upon political labels like the Celtic "Rucinates" or "Vindelici," the Roman empire and its province of Raetia, and the Germanic tribe of the Bavarians. Each of these labels will designate a period, with the underlying implicit assumption of sudden change, perhaps violent conquest or some natural disaster, occurring to delimit one period from another. Maps are then drawn which reinforce this view of the past by their very nature as separate sequential snapshots. This interpretation may very well reflect the political events of the time-segment under study, but it can ignore other important aspects of a society and thus distort and limit our understanding of that society.

The objects studied by archaeologists do not generally reveal language-related phenomena (unless the objects happen to have words on them), so the archaeologist must necessarily interpret these objects, often reasoning by analogy with better known societies, before making statements about the society which produced them. However, for a society which is largely preliterate, the archaeological raw data have the advantage that they can reflect both behavior by a wider range of the population than the politically dominant class and also types of behavior which did not generate writing. Hence such typical archaeological labels as *Reihengräberfeld* or "grave goods."

Some way of segmenting time is inherent in studying the past. Historians tend to favor politically based periods, as mentioned above. Archaeologists can use stratigraphy to develop relative chronology for a site or related sites and can use radiocarbon dating and similar techniques to approach an absolute chronology. Historical philologists can posit processes of linguistic development over time, but they are dependent upon documents with historically verifiable dates if they wish to attempt a genuine history of a language and its speakers or to suggest a specific chronological context for place-names. Lacking such a document base, philologists can describe linguistic development but cannot state how quickly or slowly such changes occurred at any particular time. It has been shown that cataclysmic political changes like the disintegration of the Roman Empire in the fifth century or the Norman conquest of England in 1066 unleashed rapid changes in languages, while a period of steady and secure government will tend to retard such changes (Jackson 1953). Folklore and similar oral phenomena, such as the apparently oral Weltenburg foundation tradition, require their own methodology. An oral story may preserve the basic facts and the relative chronology of events which are essential to the point of the story, but can be very cavalier about dates and the chronological spacing of events. A tradition reported by a non-contemporary written source may have begun its life as an oral story. While many of its facts may be accurate, at least in symbolic terms, its chronology should be checked by comparing those facts with known or plausible historical contexts.

Thus, those who contemplate "continuity" over the continuum of Celtic, Roman, and early Germanic Bavaria start with the assumption of separate, discrete periods with certain sorts of behavior overlapping from one period into another. However, Renfrew (1987) has suggested that gradualistic models can serve equally well to explain certain kinds of chronological developments, such as the apparent diffusion of Celtic languages and Celtic speakers from central Europe to Britain and Ireland. If one allows that Celtic tribes in Bavaria were indeed militarily conquered by the Roman Empire and that later Germanic tribes seized political control after the demise of the Empire, it does not necessarily follow that the whole existing population was eliminated by the conquerors in each case. Indeed, in many cases political conquerors wish merely to displace the existing political elite while retaining the economic system and the economically productive classes to sustain themselves.

Pescheck (1969), Widmann (1987), and Prinz (1985, 78) all believe that a Celtic element remained in the population of southern Germany well after the Roman conquest. Given the Roman toleration for a variety of religious practices, often through partial assimilation to Roman nomenclature, provided that these did not constitute a direct political threat, it seems quite possible that descendants of formerly free Celtic tribesmen could have continued some of their religious practices and beliefs. It is therefore conceivable that when the British Celts of Cohors III Brittanorum came to the Frauenberg area in the third century A. D., they may have encountered religious practices similar to their own. Or perhaps, even if the local practices were not similar, the local religious "ergonomics"—the relationship of topography to the idea of the sacred—were congenial. Thus, a sacred site which had seemed appropriate to the denizens of the Kelheim region because of its peninsular location, proximity to water, and religious history, may have seemed appropriate to the men of Cohors III for similar reasons. Likewise, perhaps monks trained in the Irish tradition by Saint Columbanus might have regarded the Frauenberg as an appropriate religious site, either because the local inhabitants regarded it this way or because the topography fitted Irish Celtic notions of sacred land. In the first case "cultural continuity" would mean the direct and conscious transfer of certain religious ideas and practices, especially those associated with a specific site, from one social group to another. In the latter, more tenuous case, "cultural continuity" would suggest that one group transformed a site according to its religious ideas and practices and that a subsequent group employed the same site for religious purposes because it, too, regarded that site as particularly suited to such purposes. The latter scenario may, of course, be due to coincidence, but if the same scenario recurs under similar conditions at numerous sites in the same region, the likelihood of coincidence diminishes.

Fehn (1970, especially p. 112), in a series of four maps, has shown that a pattern of what he terms *"zentralörtliche Funktionen"* shows chronological continuity during the Late La Tène, Roman, early medieval, and high medieval periods for a number of plotted sites in southern Germany. He posits four types of such "focal center" functions. Frauenberg/Weltenburg is a good example of his model for the "religious/cult" function. Like most of the other sites he considers, the Frauenberg site gained much of its topographic and geographic importance from its location astride the Danube riverine communications network.

Discussing appropriate methodology for interdisciplinary treatment of potential continuity, Prinz (1974) advocates that data and conclusions derived from different disciplines should not be mixed until the data from each discipline have been rigorously and critically analyzed according to the best standards of that discipline. Then it is possible to use interpretations from one discipline to supplement those from another. He also urges that detailed examination of specific sites is in order before it is appropriate or even possible to indulge in broader generalizations relevant to larger geographic regions.

Of the two sites considered in this article, the Frauenberg/Weltenburg peninsula most clearly shows religious continuity over several historical periods, for it had religious significance during the Celtic La Tène, Roman, and early medieval eras. Considered narrowly on the basis of historical criticism, the Weltenburg foundation tradition seems unprovable at best, but concatenation of factors and arguments from other disciplines suggest that it may well be true, at least in general outlines. The remarkable spatial coincidence of the La Tène burial site with the later central point of the abbey church is perhaps the most striking topographical argument in support of this view. While it is unlikely that new documentary evidence pertinent to the foundation of the abbey will appear, archaeology clearly has great potential to contribute new information on this matter.

The Kelheim-Gmünd site includes two episodes of Celtic religious usage, the Bavarian *Reihengräberfeld*, and the early medieval church, but nothing from the Roman period. Because Kelheim is just north of the Danube, which was the frontier of the Roman Empire in this area, this latter lack is not surprising. It seems possible that the Romans might have treated the tribes just beyond this frontier as *feoderati*, just as they did the tribes beyond Hadrian's Wall in northern Britain. In this instance artifacts found at Traprain Law and elsewhere confirm the pattern of Roman influence beyond their political boundary (Laing 1975, 22. 24). However, the possibility of finding such material at Kelheim-Gmünd has been much diminished by recent construction of the new canal, which has completely resited the course of the River Altmühl.

The evidence thus strongly supports the idea of continuity of religious function for Weltenburg. Such continuity is possible for Kelheim-Gmünd, but there are gaps in the relevant evidence. A factor common to both sites is their definition by clear physical boundaries—the bend in the Danube and the earthen wall in the former case, and the branches of the River Altmühl in the latter. The existence of such boundaries must have made these locations attractive candidates for religious functions to the Celtic, Roman, and Germanic cultures. Dachs' (1965) study of the Danube River forts and Fehn's (1970) work on cultural focal centers show that analogous continuities can persist over a millennium and can bridge major political changes.

Acknowledgments

I would like to thank both Ball State University and the Center for Ancient Studies at the University of Minnesota for financial support during the summers of 1987 and 1990 while I was conducting the research upon which this article is based. I am also grateful to the friendly and efficient staffs at the Bayerische Staatsbibliothek in Munich and the Kelheim Stadtsbücherei.

Chapter 20
Conclusion

The excavations at Kelheim that are reported here explored only a small portion of the settlement. But I think the results presented in this volume contribute usefully to oppidum studies and to our understanding of changes that took place in temperate Europe during the final two centuries before Christ. The trenches we were able to excavate in the time available were small, but they were distributed widely across the Mitterfeld and thus provide insight into the character of the cultural deposits on different parts of the settlement. The differences in density of settlement features and of portable objects, and in the character of some of the categories of materials, can be compared instructively with results from excavations at other oppida. Such information can help us to better understand what these settlements were actually like as places where people lived their lives. The analyses of plant remains, animal bones, ironworking debris, iron implements, pottery, and coins shed light on the character of the community's economy. Murray's survey enables us to view the Late La Tène oppidum in the context of its natural and cultural environment, both diachronically and synchronically. Suppe shows how prehistoric Kelheim relates to the historically-documented places of the early Middle Ages in the region.

This publication has two main goals. One is to present information from our investigations—including both the raw data of plans, profiles, and photographs and the analyses of some of those data—that may be of use to other researchers studying Late Iron Age temperate Europe. Thus I have included numerical information wherever possible and numerous photographs of cultural materials recovered, in order to make our data readily available to others. The second main goal of our publication is to suggest some new directions, or new emphases, for future investigation of late prehistoric settlements. I close with a few examples.

In our excavations we emphasized the collection of information about spatial patterning, not only of features but also of portable artifacts, and in the discussions above I have tried to show how analysis of the spatial patterns can help in the reconstruction of the community that lived on the site. In future studies, we shall attempt to derive more information about social groups and organization in the settlement from the spatial patterning of different kinds of objects, such as fine pottery, bronze ornaments, and coins. The observation, noted on pp. 142-143, that objects that characterize women's burials are common on the Kelheim settlement (as well as on other settlements of the period), but that objects that characterize men's burials are rare in settlement contexts, raises interesting questions about the ways in which material culture was used in defining gender identities. The sizable number of representations of animals recovered on or near the settlement is striking. Comparison of the contexts in which they occur with contexts of related objects at other sites would help to establish general patterns of use of animal representations for ritual and symbolic purposes. As Cunliffe (1992) has shown for Iron Age Britain and as I have indicated here for Kelheim (Chapter 17), close examination of contexts in which different categories of objects are recovered suggests that we can learn much more about ritual practice on settlements than we have done so far. A striking example is the ongoing discussion about the nature of the activities that account for the deposition of the large numbers of human bones on the Manching settlement (Lange 1983).

More attention to such questions as social patterning with respect to material culture, expression of identities in settlement deposits, and ritual practice in the everyday life of communities, will produce results that can help us to get closer to understanding what life was really like for people who lived in the rapidly changing world of Late Iron Age Europe.

References Cited

Adams, R.M. and H.J. Nissen. 1972. *The Uruk Countryside: The Natural Setting of Urban Societies*. Chicago: University of Chicago.

Allen, D.F. 1980. *The Coins of the Ancient Celts*. Edinburgh: Edinburgh University Press.

Altmann, L. and R. Thürmer. 1981. *Benediktinerabtei Weltenburg a. d. Donau gegründet um 600*. Munich: Schnell and Steiner.

Ament, H. 1984. "Der Rhein und die Ethnogenese der Germanen," *Praehistorische Zeitschrift* 59, pp. 37-47

Arnold, B. 1988. "Slavery in Late Prehistoric Europe," in D.B. Gibson and M.N. Geselowitz, editors, *Tribe and Polity in Late Prehistoric Europe*, pp. 179-192. New York: Plenum.

Arnold, D.E. 1985. *Ceramic Theory and Cultural Process*. Cambridge: Cambridge University Press.

Audouze, F. and O. Buchsenschutz. 1989. *Villes, villages et campagnes de l'Europe celtique*. Paris: Hachette.

Bachman, Hans. 1982. *The Identification of Slags from Archaeological Sites*. London: Institute of Archaeology.

Bahn, B.W. and H. Ullmann. 1986. "Eine Pferdchenfibel von der Steinsburg," *Alt-Thüringen* 21, pp. 209-227.

Bakels, C.C. 1978. *Four Linearbandkeramik Settlements and Their Environment: A Paleoecological Study of Sittard, Stein, Elsloo and Hienheim*. Leiden: Leiden University.

Barrett, J. 1988. "Fields of Discourse," *Critique of Anthropology* 7, 3, pp. 5-16.

Barrett, J., R. Bradley, and M. Green. 1991. *Landscape, Monuments and Society: The Prehistory of Cranborne Chase*. Cambridge: Cambridge University Press.

Bayerlein, M. 1985. *Die Gruppe Oberlauterbach in Niederbayern*. Kallmünz: Michael Lassleben.

Beck, H. 1981. "Brunnen - Religioses," in H. Beck, H. Jankuhn, K. Ranke, and R. Wenskus, editors, *Reallexikon der germanischen Altertumskunde* vol. 4, pp. 11-16. Berlin: Walter de Gruyter.

Behaghel, H. 1940. "Eine Eisenverhüttungsanlage der Latènezeit im Oppidum auf dem Michelsberg bei Kelheim-Donau," *Germania* 24, pp. 111-118.

Behaghel, H. 1952. "Eine Spätlatène-Grube mit Eisendepot vom Mitterfeld bei Kelheim," *Bayerische Vorgeschichtsblätter* 18-19, pp. 106-110.

Behm-Blancke, G. 1976. "Zur Funktion bronze- und eisenzeitlicher Kulthöhlen im Mittelgebirgsraum," *Ausgrabungen und Funde* 21, pp. 80-88.

Berger, F. 1985. "Keltische Fundmünzen aus Niedersachsen," *Die Kunde*, N.F. 36, pp. 207-215.

Binsteiner, A. 1987. "Geoelektrische Tiefensondierung in Baiersdorf, Lkr. Kelheim," in M.M. Rind, editor, *Feuerstein: Rohstoff der Steinzeit*, pp. 25-31. Buch am Erlbach: Marie Leidorf.

Binsteiner, A. and B. Engelhardt. 1987. "Das neolithische Silexbergwerk von Arnhofen, Gde. Abensberg, Lkr. Kelheim," in M.M. Rind, editor, *Feuerstein: Rohstoff der Steinzeit*, pp. 9-16. Buch am Erlbach: Marie Leidorf.

Birley, E. 1980. "Raetien, Britannien und das römische Heer," *Bayerische Vorgeschichtblätter* 45, pp. 77-89.

Bittel, K. 1978. "Viereckschanzen und Grabhügel," *Zeitschrift für Schweizerische Archäologie und Kunstgeschichte* 35, pp. 1-16.

Bittel, K. 1981. "Religion und Kult," in K. Bittel, W. Kimmig, and S. Schiek, editors, *Die Kelten in Baden-Württemberg*, pp. 85-117. Stuttgart: Konrad Theiss.

References Cited

Bittel, K., S. Schiek, and D. Müller. 1990. *Die keltischen Viereckschanzen*. Stuttgart: Konrad Theiss.

Blair, C. in press. "Smelt 1991: An Operational Overview," *Journal of Historic Metallurgy*.

Bleibrunner, H. 1964. *Der Landkreis Kelheim*. Kelheim: Landkreis Kelheim.

Bockisch, C. 1987. "Die Besiedlung des unteren Schwarzachtales in der Bronze- und Urnenfelderzeit," *Natur und Mensch* 1987, pp. 85-95.

Bökönyi, S. 1991. "Agriculture: Animal Husbandry," in S. Moscati, V. Kruta, O.-H. Frey, B. Raftery, and M. Szabó, editors, *The Celts*, pp. 429-435. New York: Rizzoli.

Boessneck, J., A. von den Driesch, U. Meyer-Lemppenau, and E. Wechsler-von Ohlen. 1971. *Die Tierknochenfunde aus dem Oppidum von Manching*. Wiesbaden: Steiner.

Bollandus, J. 1865. "Vita St. Eustasii," in *Acta Sanctorum*, Martii vol. 3, pp. 782-787. Paris: Victor Palme.

Bourdieu, P. 1977. *Outline of a Theory of Practice*. Cambridge: Cambridge University Press.

Bradley, R. 1991. "Ritual, Time and History," *World Archaeology* 23, pp. 209-219.

Břeň, J. 1971. "Das keltische Oppidum in Trisov," *Archeologické Rozhledy* 23, pp. 294-303.

Brunaux, J.L. 1988. *The Celtic Gauls: Gods, Rites and Sanctuaries*. Trans. by D. Nash. London: Seaby.

Brunhölzl, F. 1981. "Die lateinische Literatur," in M. Spindler, editor, *Handbuch der bayerischen Geschichte*, 2nd edition, vol. 1, pp. 582-606. Munich: C.H. Beck.

Buchsenschutz, O., G. Coulon, M. Gratier, A. Hesse, J. Holmgren, N. Mills, D. Orssaud, A. Querrien, Y. Rialland, C. Soyer, and A. Tabbagh. 1988. L'Evolution du canton de Levroux d'après les prospections et les sondages archéologiques. Levroux: *Revue Archéologique du Centre de la France*.

Bujna, J. 1982. "Spiegelung der Sozialstruktur auf latènezeitlichen Gräberfeldern im Karpatenbecken," *Památky Archeologické* 73, pp. 312-431.

Burger, I. 1981. *Die Viereckschanze von Kelheim*. Abensberg: Weltenburger Akademie.

Burger, I. 1984a. *Archäologisches Museum der Stadt Kelheim*. Kelheim: Stadt.

Burger, I. 1984b. "Der Michelsberg bei Kelheim," in S. Rieckhoff-Pauli and W. Torbrügge, editors, *Regensburg-Kelheim-Straubing II*. Führer zu archäologischen Denkmälern in Deutschland, vol. 6, pp. 68-75. Stuttgart: Konrad Theiss.

Burger, I. and H. Geisler. 1983. "Archäologisches zur Eisenverhüttung in und um Kelheim," in F. Bauer and A. Röhrl, editors, *Festschrift anlässlich des 60. Geburtstages von Prof. Dr. Erwin Rutte*, pp. 41-55. Abensberg: Weltenburger Akademie.

Campana, D.V. and P.J. Crabtree. 1987. "ANIMALS: A C Language Computer Program for the Analysis of Faunal Remains and its Use in the Study of Early Iron Age Fauna from Dun Ailinne," *Archaeozoologia* 1, pp. 57-68.

Carnandet, J., editor. 1868. "Vita S. Agili," in *Acta Sanctorum*, August, vol. 6. Paris: Victor Palme.

Castells, M. 1977. *The Urban Question*. London: Arnold.

Cech, B. 1988. "Eine latènezeitliche Eisenverhüttungsanlage in Loitzerdorf am Jaulerling," *Archaeologia Austriaca* 72, pp. 143-152.

Chapotat, G. 1970. *Vienne gauloise: le matériel de La Tène III*. Lyon: Audin.

Cherry, J.F., C.S. Gamble, and S.J. Shennan, editors. 1978. *Sampling in Contemporary British Archaeology*. Oxford: British Archaeological Reports.

Christlein, R. 1964. "Ein Bronzesiebfragment der Spätlatènezeit vom Zugmantel," *Saalburg Jahrbuch* 21, pp. 16-19.

Christlein, R. 1976. "Kelheim, Lkr. Kelheim," *Verhandlungen des Historischen Vereins für Niederbayern* 102, pp. 70-72.

Christlein, R. 1982. "Zu den jüngsten keltischen

Funden Südbayerns," *Bayerische Vorgeschichtsblätter* 47, pp. 275-292.

Christlein, R. and O. Braasch. 1982. *Das unterirdische Bayern*. Stuttgart: Konrad Theiss.

Christlein, R. and S. Stork. 1980. "Der hallstattzeitliche Tempelbezirk von Aiterhofen, Landkreis Straubing-Bogen, Niederbayern," *Jahresbericht der Bayerischen Bodendenkmalpflege* 21, pp. 56-61.

Čižmář, M. 1989a. "Erforschung des keltischen Oppidums Staré Hradisko in den Jahren 1983-1988 (Mähren, ČSSR)," *Archäologisches Korrespondenzblatt* 19, pp. 265-268.

Čižmář, M.1989b. "Pozdně laténské osídlení předhradí Závisti" ("Die spätlatènezeitliche Besiedlung der Vorburg von Závist"), *Památky Archeologické* 53, pp. 59-122.

Clarke, D.L. 1968. *Analytical Archaeology*. London: Methuen.

Codreanu-Windauer, S. and H. Wanderwitz. 1989. "Die frühe Kirche in der Diozese Regensburg: Betrachtungen zu den archäologischen und schriftlichen Quellen bis zum Ende des 8. Jahrhunderts," in *1250 Jahre Kunst und Kultur im Bistum Regensburg*. Munich: Schnell and Steiner.

Collis, J. 1975. "Excavations at Aulnat, Clermont Ferrand," *The Archaeological Journal* 132, pp. 1-15.

Collis, J. 1980. "Aulnat and Urbanisation in France," *The Archaeological Journal* 137, pp. 40-49.

Collis, J. 1984a. *Oppida: Earliest Towns North of the Alps*. Sheffield: University of Sheffield.

Collis, J. 1984b. *The European Iron Age*. New York: Schocken.

Conrad, G.W. and A. Demarest. 1984. *Religion and Empire*. Cambridge: Cambridge University Press.

Crew, P. 1986. "Bryn y Castell Hillfort: A Late Prehistoric Iron-Working Settlement in North-Western Wales," in B. Scott and H. Cleere, editors, *The Crafts of the Blacksmith*, pp. 91-100. Belfast: Belfast University Press.

Crew, P. 1990. "Excavations at Crawcwellt West Merionoth, 1986-1989," *Archaeology in Wales* 29, pp. 11-16.

Crew, P. 1991. "The Experimental Production of Prehistoric Bar Iron," *Historical Metallurgy* 25, 1.

Crumley, C.L. 1974. *Celtic Social Structures*. Ann Arbor: University of Michigan, Museum of Anthropology.

Crumley, C.L. 1987. "Celtic Settlement Before the Conquest: The Dialectics of Landscape and Power," in C.L. Crumley and W.H. Marquardt, editors, *Regional Dynamics: Burgundian Landscapes in Historical Perspective*, pp. 403-430. New York: Academic Press.

Cumberpatch, C.C. and M. Pawlikowski. 1988. "Preliminary Results of Mineralogical Analyses of Late La Tène Painted Pottery from Czechoslovakia," *Archeologické Rozhledy* 40, pp. 184-193.

Cunliffe, B. 1992. "Pits, Preconceptions and Propitiation in the British Iron Age," *Oxford Journal of Archaeology* 11, pp. 69-83.

Dachs, H. 1965. "Römerkastelle und frühmittelalterliches Herzogs- und Konigsgut an der Donau," in K. Bosl, editor, *Zur Geschichte der Bayern*. Darmstadt.

Dannheimer, H. 1973. "Neufunde eiserner Steckkreuzchen in Südbayern," *Archäologisches Korrespondenzblatt* 3, pp. 251-256.

Dannheimer, H. 1984. Führer durch die Ausstellung Frühe Holzkirchen aus Bayern. Munich: *Prähistorische Staatssammlung*.

Davidson, H.R. E. 1988. *Myths and Symbols in Pagan Europe*. Syracuse: Syracuse University Press.

Déchelette, J. 1914. *Manuel d'archéologie préhistorique, celtique et gallo-romaine*. II, 3. Paris: Picard.

Dehn, W. 1951. "Die gallischen 'Oppida' bei Cäsar," *Saalburg Jahrbuch* 10, pp. 36-49.

Dehn, W. 1965. "'Mediolanum': Lagetypen spätkeltischer Oppida," Beihefte der *Bonner Jahrbücher* 10, 2, pp. 117-128.

References Cited

De Navarro, J.M. 1959. "A Bronze Mount of the La Tène Period from Kelheim, Lower Bavaria," *Germania* 37, pp. 131-140.

Devore, J. and R. Peck. 1986. *Statistics*. St. Paul: West.

Dickinson, R.E. 1953. *Germany: A General and Regional Geography*. New York: Dutton.

Dietz, K. 1984. "Runicates," in S. Rieckhoff-Pauli and W. Torbrügge, editors, *Regensburg-Kelheim-Straubing I*, Führer zu archäologischen Denkmälern in Deutschland, vol. 5, pp. 224-236. Stuttgart: Konrad Theiss.

Douglas, M. and B. Isherwood. 1979. *The World of Goods*. New York: Norton.

von den Driesch, A. 1976. *A Guide to the Measurement of Animal Bones from Archaeological Sites*. Cambridge MA: Peabody Museum.

Duval, A. 1983. "Autour de Vercingetorix: de l'archéologie à histoire économique et sociale," in J. Collis, A. Duval, and R. Périchon, editors, *Le deuxième âge du fer en Auvergne et en Forez*, pp. 298-335. Sheffield: University of Sheffield.

Dyson, S.L. 1988. "Rise of Complex Societies in Italy: Historical Versus Archaeological Perspectives," in D.B. Gibson and M.N. Geselowitz, editors, *Tribe and Polity in Late Prehistoric Europe*, pp. 193-203. New York: Plenum.

Egger, M. 1984. "Keltische Münzfunde aus Manching III," *Jahrbuch für Numismatik und Geldgeschichte* 34, pp. 135-161.

Eggers, H.J. 1951. *Der römische Import im freien Germanien*. Hamburg: Museum für Völkerkunde und Vorgeschichte.

Ehrenreich, R.M. 1985. *Trade, Technology, and the Ironworking Community of Southern Britain in the Iron Age*. Oxford: British Archaeological Reports, British Series 144.

Elkins, T.H. 1968. *Germany*. London: Chatto & Windus.

Ellmers, D. 1969. "Keltischer Schiffbau," *Jahrbuch des Römisch-Germanischen Zentralmuseums* 16, pp. 73-122.

Eluère, C. 1991. "The Celts and Their Gold: Origins, Production and Social Role," in S. Moscati, O.-H. Frey, V. Kruta, B. Raftery, and M. Szabó, editors, *The Celts*, pp. 348-355. New York: Rizzoli.

van Endert, D. 1987. *Das Osttor des Oppidums von Manching*. Wiesbaden: Franz Steiner.

van Endert, D. 1991. *Die Bronzefunde aus dem Oppidum von Manching*. Stuttgart: Franz Steiner.

Engelhardt, B. 1980. "Archäologisches zur früh- und hochmittelalterlichen Geschichte Kelheims," in K. Spindler, editor, *Vorzeit zwischen Main und Donau*, pp. 273-298. Erlangen: Universitätsbund Erlangen-Nürnberg.

Engelhardt, B. 1982. "Führer zum archäologischen Wanderpfad 'Weltenburger Enge', 1. Von Kelheim nach Weltenburg," *Beilage zum Amtlichen Schul-Anzeiger für den Regierungsbezirk Niederbayern*. pp. 1-34.

Engelhardt, B. 1983. "Steinzeitlicher Silexabbau im Landkreis Kelheim," in F. Bauer and A. Röhrl, editors, *Festschrift anlässlich des 60. Geburtstages von Prof. Dr. Erwin Rutte*, pp. 65-77. Abensberg: Weltenburger Akademie.

Engelhardt, B. 1984. "Besiedlungsgeschichte einer ehemaligen Insel im Altmühlmündungsgebiet bei Kelheim-Gmünd," in S. Rieckhoff-Pauli and W. Torbrügge, editors, *Regensburg-Kelheim-Straubing II*, Führer zu archäologischen Denkmälern in Deutschland, vol. 6, pp. 59-68. Stuttgart: Konrad Theiss.

Engelhardt, B. 1987. *Ausgrabungen am Main-Donau-Kanal*. Buch am Erlbach: Maria Leidorf.

Engelhardt, B. 1989a. "Der Main-Donau-Kanal, ein Fenster in die heimische Vorgeschichte," in *Das Altmühltal und die Rhein-Main-Donau-Wasserstrasse, Natur und Technik* 8, pp. 61-71. Hamburg: Christians Verlag.

Engelhardt, B. 1989b. "Die Vorgeschichte des Landkreises Kelheim," in *Der Landkreis Kelheim*, pp. 49-110. Kelheim: Landkreis.

Engelhardt, B. and A. Binsteiner. 1988. "Vorbericht über die Ausgrabungen 1984-1986 im neolithischen Feuersteinabbaurevier von Arnhofen, Ldkr. Kelheim," *Germania* 66, pp. 1-28.

Engels, H.-J. 1976. *Die Viereckschanze: Grabung 1974/75. Der Donnersberg: Ausgrabungen, Forschungen, Geschichte.* Wiesbaden: Franz Steiner.

Ettelt, R. 1983. *Geschichte der Stadt Kelheim.* Kelheim: Stadt.

Etzel, C. 1990. *Die Grabungen 1987 und 1988 im keltischen Oppidum Alkimoennis bei Kelheim.* M.A. thesis, Universität Erlangen-Nürnberg.

Fehn, K. 1970. *Die zentralörtlichen Funktionen früher Zentren in Altbayern.* Wiesbaden: Franz Steiner.

Fischer, F. 1985. "Der Handel der Mittel- und Spät-Latène-Zeit in Mitteleuropa aufgrund archäologischer Zeugnisse," in K. Düwel, H. Jankuhn, H. Siems, and D. Timpe, editors, *Untersuchungen zu Handel und Verkehr der vor- und frühgeschichtlichen Zeit in Mittel- und Nordeuropa* part 1, pp. 285-298. Göttingen: Vandenhoeck and Ruprecht.

Fischer, F. 1988. "Südwestdeutschland im letzten Jahrhundert vor Christi Geburt," in D. Planck, editor, *Archäologie in Württemberg*, pp. 235-250. Stuttgart: Konrad Theiss.

Fischer, T. 1984. "Kastelle und Lagerdorf Eining-Abusina," in S. Rieckhoff-Pauli and W. Torbrügge, editors, *Regensburg-Kelheim-Straubing II*, Führer zu archäologischen Denkmälern in Deutschland, vol. 6, pp. 129-135. Stuttgart: Konrad Theiss.

Fischer, T., S. Rieckhoff-Pauli, and K. Spindler. 1984. "Grabungen in der spätkeltischen Siedlung im Sulztal bei Berching-Pollanten, Landkreis Heumarkt, Oberpfalz," *Germania* 62, pp. 311-372.

Fischer, T. and K. Spindler. 1984. *Das römische Grenzkastell Abusina-Eining.* Stuttgart: Konrad Theiss.

Fish, S.K. and S.A. Kowalewski, editors. 1990. *The Archaeology of Regions: A Case for Full-Coverage Survey.* Washington D.C.: Smithsonian.

Fitzpatrick, A.P. 1989. "The Uses of Roman Imperialism by the Celtic Barbarians in the Later Republic," in J.C. Barrett, A.P. Fitzpatrick, and L. Macinnes, editors, *Barbarians and Romans in North-West Europe*, pp. 27-54. Oxford: British Archaeological Reports, International Series, 471.

Fleuriot, L. 1982. *Les Origines de la Bretagne.* Paris: Payot.

Flouest, J.-L. and I.M. Stead. 1977. "Une tombe de La Tène III à Hannogne (Ardennes)," *Mémoires de la Société d'Agriculture, Commerce, Sciences et Arts du Département de la Marne* 92, pp. 55-72.

Ford, S., R. Bradley, J. Hawkes, and P. Fisher. 1984. "Flint-Working in the Metal Age," *Oxford Journal of Archaeology* 3, pp. 157-173.

Frey, O.-H. 1986. "Einige Überlegungen zu den Beziehungen zwischen Kelten und Germanen in der Spätlatènezeit," *Marburger Studien zur Vor- und Frühgeschichte* 7, pp. 45-79.

Fröhlich, J. and J. Waldhauser. 1989. "Příspěvky k Ekonomice Českých Keltů (Kamenictví a Distribuce Žernovů)" (Beiträge zur Keltenwirtschaft in Böhmen [Steinmetzerei und Distribution der Dreh-Handmühlen]"), *Archeologické Rozhledy* 41, pp. 16-58.

Furger-Gunti, A. 1975. "Oppidum Basel-Münsterhügel," *Jahrbuch der Schweizerische Gesellschaft für Urgeschichte* 58, pp. 106-109.

Furger-Gunti, A. 1979. *Die Ausgrabungen im Basler Münster I: Die spätkeltische und augusteische Zeit (1. Jahrhundert v. Chr.).* Derendingen-Solothurn: Habegger.

Furger-Gunti, A. 1980. "Der Murus Gallicus von Basel," *Jahrbuch der Schweizerischen Gesellschaft für Ur- und Frühgeschichte* 63, pp. 131-184.

Furger-Gunti, A. 1982. "Der 'Goldfund von Saint-Louis' bei Basel und ähnliche keltische Schatzfunde," *Zeitschrift für Schweizerische Archäologie und Kunstgeschichte* 39, pp. 1-47.

Furger-Gunti, A. and L. Berger. 1980. *Katalog und Tafeln der Funde aus der spätkeltischen Siedlung Basel-Gasfabrik.* Derendingen-Solothurn: Habegger.

Furger-Gunti, A. and H.M. von Kaenel. 1976. "Die keltischen Fundmünzen aus Basel," *Schweizerische numismatische Rundschau* 55, pp. 35-176.

References Cited

Gamble, C. 1978. "Optimising Information from Studies of Faunal Remains," in J. Cherry, C. Gamble, and S. Shennan, editors, *Sampling in Contemporary British Archaeology*, pp. 321-351. Oxford: British Archaeological Reports, British Series 50.

Gebhard, R. 1989. *Der Glasschmuck aus dem Oppidum von Manching*. Stuttgart: Franz Steiner.

Gebhard, R. 1991. *Die Fibeln aus dem Oppidum von Manching*. Wiesbaden: Franz Steiner.

Gensen, R. 1965. "Manching III: Die Ausgrabung des Osttores in den Jahren 1962 bis 1963," *Germania* 43, pp. 49-62.

Gerlach, S. 1990. "Eine spätkeltische Eberplastik aus Karlstadt am Main, Lkr. Main-Spessart, Unterfranken," *Archäologisches Korrespondenzblatt* 20, pp. 427-437.

Gerndt, S. 1976. *Unsere bayerische Landschaft*. Munich: Prestel.

Geselowitz, M.N. 1988. "The Role of Iron Production in the Formation of an 'Iron Age Economy' in Central Europe," *Research in Economic Anthropology* 10, pp. 225-255.

Geselowitz, M.N. 1991. "For Want of a Nail: Archaeometallurgy and Dating in Historical Archaeology," in R.M. Ehrenreich, editor, *Metals in Society II: Theory Beyond Analysis*, pp. 45-55. Philadelphia: University Museum.

Giddens, A. 1984. *The Constitution of Society: Outline of the Theory of Structuration*. Berkeley: University of California Press.

Gilles, J. 1958. "Versuchsschmeltze in einem vorgeschichtlichen Rennofen," *Stahl und Eisen* 78, pp. 1690-1695.

Glüsing, P. 1965. "Frühe Germanen südlich der Donau," *Offa* 21-22, pp. 7-20.

Goetze, B.-R. 1981. "Ausgrabungen im Vorgelände des Oppidums Alkimoennis bei Kelheim, Niederbayern," *Das archäologische Jahr in Bayern* 1980, pp. 104-105.

Goffer, Z. 1980 *Archaeological Chemistry*. New York: John Wiley.

Goudineau, C. and V. Kruta. 1980. "Y a-t-il une ville protohistorique?" in G. Duby, editor, *Histoire de la France urbaine*, pp. 139-231. Paris: Seuil.

Grant, A. 1982. "The Use of Tooth Wear as a Guide to the Age of Domestic Ungulates," in B. Wilson, C. Grigson, and S. Payne, editors, *Ageing and Sexing Animal Bones from Archaeological Sites*, pp. 91-108. Oxford: British Archaeological Reports, British Series 109.

Grayson, D.K. 1979. "On the Quantification of Vertebrate Archaeofaunas," in M.B. Schiffer, editor, *Advances in Archaeological Method and Theory*, vol. 2, pp. 200-237. New York: Academic Press.

Grayson, D.K. 1984. *Quantitative Zooarchaeology*. Orlando: Academic Press.

Green, M.J. 1986. *The Gods of the Celts*. Totowa, NJ: Barnes and Noble.

Green, M.J. 1989. *Symbol and Image in Celtic Religious Art*. London: Routledge.

Green, M.J. 1992. *Dictionary of Celtic Myth and Legend*. London: Thames and Hudson.

Griffith, G.T. 1935. *Mercenaries of the Hellenistic World*. Cambridge: Cambridge University Press.

Haarnagel, W. 1979. *Die Grabung Feddersen Wierde*. Wiesbaden: Franz Steiner.

Hachmann, R. 1990. "Gundestrup-Studien: Untersuchungen zu den spätkeltischen Grundlagen der frühgermanischen Kunst," *Bericht der Römisch-Germanischen Kommission* 71, pp. 565-903.

Haevernick, T.E. 1960. *Die Glasarmringe und Ringperlen der Mittel und Spätlatènezeit auf dem europäischen Festland*. Bonn: Rudolf Habelt.

Haffner, A. 1969. "Das Treverer-Gräberfeld mit Wagenbestattungen von Hoppstädten-Weiersbach, Kreis Birkenfeld," *Trierer Zeitschrift* 32, pp. 71-127.

Haffner, A. 1971. *Das keltisch-römische Gräberfeld von Wederath-Belginum, 1, Gräber 1-428*. Mainz: Philipp von Zabern.

Haffner, A. 1974a. *Das keltisch-römische Gräber-*

feld von Wederath-Belginum, 2, Gräber 429-883. Mainz: Philipp von Zabern.

Haffner, A. 1974b. "Zum Ende der Latènezeit im Mittelrhein," *Archäologisches Korrespondenzblatt* 4, pp. 59-72.

Haffner, A. 1978. *Das keltisch-römische Gräberfeld von Wederath-Belginum, 3, Gräber 885-1260*. Mainz: Philipp von Zabern.

Haffner, A. 1979. "Zur absoluten Chronologie der Mittellatènezeit," *Archäologisches Korrespondenzblatt* 9, pp. 405-409.

Haffner, A. 1989. *Gräber: Spiegel des Lebens - Zum Totenbrauchtum der Kelten und Römer am Beispiel des Treverer-Gräberfeldes Wederath-Belginum*. Mainz: Philipp von Zabern.

Haffner, A. and H.-E. Joachim. 1984. "Die keltischen Wagengräber der Mittelrheingruppe," in M. Guštin and L. Pauli, editors, *Keltski Voz*, pp. 71-88. Brežice: Posavski Muzej.

Hancock, M.L. 1983. "The Daub," in P.S. Wells, *Rural Economy in the Early Iron Age: Excavations at Hascherkeller, 1978-1981*, pp. 115-125. Cambridge MA: Peabody Museum.

Harris, W.V. 1980. "Towards a Study of the Roman Slave Trade," in J.H. D'Arms and E.C. Kopff, editors, *The Seaborne Commerce of Ancient Rome*, pp. 117-140. Rome: American Academy.

Haselgrove, C. 1988. "Coinage and Complexity: Archaeological Analysis of Socio-Political Change in Britain and non-Mediterranean Gaul during the Later Iron Age," in D.B. Gibson and M.N. Geselowitz, editors, *Tribe and Polity in Late Prehistoric Europe*, pp. 69-96. New York: Plenum.

Hedeager, L. 1992. *Iron-Age Societies*. Oxford: Blackwell.

Herrmann, F.-R. 1969. "Testgrabung im Oppidum von Kelheim 1964," *Germania* 47, pp. 91-96.

Herrmann, F.-R. 1973. "Die Grabung am inneren Wall im Oppidum von Kelheim im Jahre 1971," *Germania* 51, pp. 133-146.

Herrmann, F.-R. 1975. "Grabungen im Oppidum von Kelheim 1964 bis 1972," in *Ausgrabungen in Deutschland 1950-1975*, vol. 1, pp. 298-311. Mainz: Römisch-Germanisches Zentralmuseum.

Hinz, H. 1976. "Bauopfer," in H. Beck, H. Jankuhn, K. Ranke, and R. Wenskus, editors, *Reallexikon der germanischen Altertumskunde* vol. 2, pp. 111-112. Berlin: Walter de Gruyter.

Hochstetter, A. 1980. *Die Hügelgräberbronzezeit in Niederbayern*. Kallmünz: Michael Lassleben.

Hodder, I. 1986. *Reading the Past*. Cambridge: Cambridge University Press.

Hodder, I. 1990. *The Domestication of Europe*. Oxford: Blackwell.

Hollstein, E. 1980. *Mitteleuropäische Eichenchronologie*. Mainz: Philipp von Zabern.

Hope-Taylor, B. 1977. *Yeavering: An Anglo-British Centre of Early Northumbria*. London: Department of the Environment.

Hopkins, K. 1978. *Conquerors and Slaves*. Cambridge: Cambridge University Press.

Hvass, S. 1985. *Hodde*. Copenhagen: Akademisk Forlag.

Ihm, M. 1899. "Cimbri," in *Paulys Real-Encyclopädie der classischen Altertumswissenschaft*, vol. 3, cols. 2547-2553. Stuttgart: J.B. Metzler.

Jackson, K. 1953. *Language and History in Early Britain*. Edinburgh.

Jacobi, G. 1974. *Werkzeug und Gerät aus dem Oppidum von Manching*. Wiesbaden: Franz Steiner.

Jacomet, S., C. Brombacher, and M. Dick. 1989. *Archäobotanik am Zürichsee*. Zurich: Züricher Denkmalpflege.

James, E. 1981. "Archaeology and the Merovingian Monastery," in H.B. Clarke and M. Brennan, editors, *Columbanus and Merovingian Monasticism*, pp. 33-58. Oxford: British Archaeological Reports, International Series 113.

Jansová, L. 1960. "Die Brunnen in den befestigten Städten (Oppida) der La Tène-Zeit," *Památky Archeologické* 51, pp. 157-160.

References Cited

Jansová, L. 1986. *Hrazany: Das keltische Oppidum in Böhmen*. Vol. 1: *Die Befestigung und die anliegende Siedlungsbebauung*. Prague: Czechoslovak Academy of Sciences.

Joachim, H.-E. 1973. "Ein reich ausgestattetes Wagengrab der Spätlatènezeit aus Neuwied, Stadtteil Heimbach-Weis," *Bonner Jahrbücher* 173, pp. 1-44.

Joachim, H.-E. 1980. "Jüngerlatènezeitliche Siedlungen bei Eschweiler, Kr. Aachen," *Bonner Jahrbücher* 180, pp. 355-441.

Joby, G. 1966. "An Iron Age Homestead at West Brandon, Durham," *Archaeologia Aelinana* 40, pp. 1-34.

Jockenhövel, A. 1990. "Die Eisenzeit," in F.-R. Herrmann and A. Jockenhövel, editors, *Die Vorgeschichte Hessens*, pp. 244-294. Stuttgart: Konrad Theiss.

Kammermeier, M. 1775. "Coenobitae Weltenburgensis brevis Historia de Fundatione antiquissimi monasterii Weltenburgensis," in P. Finauer, editor, *Bibliothek zum Gebrauch der baierischen Staatskirchen- und Gelehrten-Geschichte*, part 3, pp. 235-239.

Kappel, I. 1969. *Die Graphittonkeramik von Manching*. Wiesbaden: Franz Steiner.

Kaufmann, H. 1984. "Einflüsse der Latènekultur im Gebiet nördlich des Erzgebirges," *Arbeits- und Forschungsberichte zur sächsischen Bodendenkmalpflege* 27-28, pp. 125-166.

Kellner, H.-J. 1990. *Die Münzfunde von Manching und die keltischen Fundmünzen aus Südbayern*. Stuttgart: Franz Steiner.

Kertzer, D.I. 1988. *Ritual, Politics, and Power*. New Haven: Yale University Press.

Klingender, F. 1971. *Animals in Art and Thought*. Cambridge MA: MIT Press.

Kluge, J. 1985. "Spätkeltische Gräber mit Säuglings- und Ferkelbestattungen aus Kelheim, Niederbayern," *Bayerische Vorgeschichtsblätter* 50, pp. 183-218.

Kluge, J. 1986. "Kelheim zwischen Altmühl und Donau," *Münstersche Beitrage zur antiken Handelsgeschichte* 5, pp. 37-58.

Kluge, J. 1987. *Die latènezeitliche Besiedlung des Kelheimer Beckens, Niederbayern*. Doctoral dissertation, Universität Münster.

Koch, H. 1991. *Die keltischen Siedlungen vom Frauenberg über Kloster Weltenburg, Stadt Kelheim, und von Harting (Neubaugebiet Süd), Stadt Regensburg*. Buch am Erlbach: Marie Leidorf.

Koch, U. 1968. *Die Grabfunde der Merowingerzeit aus dem Donautal um Regensburg*. Berlin: Walter de Gruyter.

Koller, H. 1982. "Die Iren und die Christianisierung der Baier," in H. Lowe, editor, *Die Iren und Europa im frühem Mittelalter*, pp. 342-374. Stuttgart: Klett-Cotta.

Kossack, G. 1959. *Südbayern während der Hallstattzeit*. Berlin: Walter de Gruyter.

Kossack, G. 1974. "Prunkgräber: Bemerkungen zu Eigenschaften und Aussagewert," in G. Kossack and G. Ulbert, editors, *Studien zur vor- und frühgeschichtlichen Archäologie*, vol. 1, pp. 3-33. Munich: C.H. Beck.

Krämer, W. 1950. "Der keltische Bronzestier von Weltenburg in Niederbayern," *Germania* 28, pp. 210-213.

Krämer, W. 1952. "Das Ende der Mittellatènefriedhöfe und die Grabfunde der Spätlatènezeit in Südbayern," *Germania* 30, pp. 330-337.

Krämer, W. 1957. "Zu den Ausgrabungen in dem keltischen Oppidum von Manching 1955," *Germania* 35, pp. 32-44.

Krämer, W. 1958. "Manching, ein vindelikisches Oppidum an der Donau," in W. Krämer, editor, *Neue Ausgrabungen in Deutschland*, pp. 175-202. Berlin: Gebr. Mann.

Krämer, W. 1961. "Fremder Frauenschmuck aus Manching," *Germania* 39, pp. 305-322.

Krämer, W. 1962. "Manching II: Zu den Ausgrabungen in den Jahren 1957 bis 1961," *Germania* 40, pp. 297-317.

Krämer, W. 1968. "Ein endlatènezeitlicher Stabgürtelhaken aus Eining in Niederbayern," *Bayerische Vorgeschichtsblätter* 33, pp. 81-91.

Krämer, W. 1985. *Die Grabfunde von Manching und die latènezeitlichen Flachgräber in Südbayern.* Wiesbaden: Franz Steiner.

Krämer, W. 1989. "Das eiserne Ross von Manching," *Germania* 67, pp. 519-539.

Krusch, B., editor. 1905. *Vita Sanctorum Columbani, Vedastis, Johannis.* Hannover.

Küster, H. 1986a. "Archäologisch-botanische Untersuchungen," in F. Maier, editor, "Vorbericht über die Ausgrabung 1985 in dem spätkeltischen Oppidum von Manching," *Germania* 64, pp. 41-43.

Küster, H. 1986b. "Werden und Wandel der Kulturlandschaft im Alpenvorland: Pollenanalytische Aussagen zur Siedlungsgeschichte am Auerberg in Südbayern," *Germania* 64, pp. 533-558.

Küster, H. 1988a. "Pflanzenreste der Späthallstatt-Frühlatènezeit aus Niedererlbach (Niederbayern)," *Bayerische Vorgeschichtsblätter* 53, pp. 77-82.

Küster, H. 1988b. "The History of the Landscape Around Auerberg, Southern Bavaria: A Pollen Analytical Study," in H.H. Birks, H.J.B. Birks, P.E. Kaland, and D. Moe, editors, *The Cultural Landscape: Past, Present, and Future*, pp. 301-310. Cambridge: Cambridge University Press.

Küster, H. 1988c. "Urnenfelderzeitliche Pflanzenreste aus Burkheim, Gemeinde Vogtsburg, Kreis Breisgau-Hochschwarzwald (Baden-Württemberg)," in H. Küster, editor, *Der prähistorische Mensch und seine Umwelt*, pp. 261-268. Stuttgart: Konrad Theiss.

Küster, H. 1991. *Postglaziale Vegetationsgeschichte Südbayerns: Geobotanische Studien zur prähistorischen Landschaftskunde.* Habilitationsschrift, Universität Munchen.

Küster, H. 1992. "Vegetationsgeschichtliche Untersuchungen," in F. Maier, U. Geilenbrügge, E. Hahn, H.-J. Köhler, and S. Sievers, *Ergebnisse der Ausgrabungen 1984-1987 in Manching*, pp. 433-476. Stuttgart: Franz Steiner.

Laing, L. 1975. *The Archaeology of Late Celtic Britain and Ireland.* London: Methuen.

Lange, G. 1983. *Die menschlichen Skelettreste aus dem Oppidum von Manching.* Wiesbaden: Franz Steiner.

Lappe, U. 1979. "Keltische Glasarmringe und Ringperlen aus Thüringen," *Alt-Thüringen* 16, pp. 84-111.

Laux, J. 1919. *Der heilige Kolumban.* Freiburg im Breisgau.

Lefebvre, H. 1976. "Reflections on the Politics of Space," *Antipode* 8, pp. 30-37.

Lehman, P.H. 1991. *The Iron Objects from the La Tène Oppidum at Kelheim, Bavaria, Germany.* M.A. thesis, University of Minnesota.

Leja, F. 1991. "Ungewöhnliche urnenfelderzeitliche Skelettfunde in der Höhle von Loch," *Das archäologische Jahr in Bayern* 1990, pp. 50-52.

Leppert, R. and B. Lincoln. 1989. "Introduction," *Cultural Critique* 12, pp. 5-23.

Lincoln, B. 1989. *Discourse and the Construction of Society.* New York: Oxford University Press.

Maier, F. 1970. *Die bemalte Spätlatène-Keramik von Manching.* Wiesbaden: Franz Steiner.

Maier, F. 1985. "Vorbericht über die Ausgrabung 1984 in dem spätkeltischen Oppidum von Manching," *Germania* 63, pp. 17-55.

Maier, F. 1986. "Vorbericht über die Ausgrabung 1985 in dem spätkeltischen Oppidum von Manching," *Germania* 64, pp. 1-43.

Maier, F. 1990. "Das Kultbäumchen von Manching: Ein Zeugnis hellenistischer und keltischer Goldschmiedekunst aus dem 3. Jahrhundert v. Chr.," *Germania* 68, pp. 129-165.

Maier, F. 1991. "The Celtic Oppida," in S. Moscati, O.-H. Frey, V. Kruta, B. Raftery, and M. Szabó, editors, *The Celts*, pp. 411-425. New York: Rizzoli.

Maier, R.A. 1965. "Eine vorgeschichtliche Felsspalten-Füllung im Fränkischen Jura mit Sach-, Tier- und Menschenresten," *Bayerische Vorgeschichtsblätter* 30, pp. 262-268.

Maier, R.A. 1984. "Schachthöhlen und Felstürme als urgeschichtliche Opferplätze," in S. Rieckhoff-

References Cited

Pauli and W. Torbrügge, editors, *Regensburg-Kelheim-Straubing I. Führer zu archäologischen Denkmälern in Deutschland*, vol. 5, pp. 204-211. Stuttgart: Konrad Theiss.

Mannsperger, D. 1981. "Münzen und Münzfunde," in K. Bittel, W. Kimmig, and S. Schiek, editors, *Die Kelten in Baden-Württemberg*, pp. 228-247. Stuttgart: Konrad Theiss.

Marquardt, W.H. and C.L. Crumley. 1987. "Theoretical Issues in the Analysis of Spatial Patterning," in C.L. Crumley and W.H. Marquardt, editors, *Regional Dynamics: Burgundian Landscapes in Historical Perspective*, pp. 1-18. New York: Academic Press.

Maute, M. 1991. "Das Fibelspektrum aus dem spätlatènezeitlichen Oppidum Altenburg, Kr. Waldshut," *Archäologisches Korrespondenzblatt* 21, pp. 393-397.

McIntosh, R.J. 1991. "Early Urban Clusters in China and Africa: The Arbitration of Social Ambiguity," *Journal of Field Archaeology*, 18, pp. 199-212.

McNeill, J. 1974. *The Celtic Churches: A History A.D. 200 to 1200*. Chicago: University of Chicago Press.

Meduna, J. 1968. "Příspěvek k Problematice pozdní doby laténske na Moravě" ("Ein Beitrag zur Problematik der späten Latènezeit in Mähren"), *Archeologické Rozhledy* 20, pp. 56-69.

Meduna, J. 1970a. "Das keltische Oppidum Staré Hradisko in Mähren," *Germania* 48, pp. 34-59.

Meduna, J. 1970b. *Staré Hradisko II*. Brno: Fontes Archaeologiae Moravicae, 5.

Meduna, J. 1980. *Die latènezeitlichen Siedlungen und Gräberfelder in Mähren*. Brno: Czechoslovak Academy of Sciences.

Megaw, J.V.S. 1970. *Art of the European Iron Age*. Bath: Adams and Dart.

Megaw, R. and V. Megaw. 1989. *Celtic Art*. London: Thames and Hudson.

van der Merwe, N.J. and D.H. Avery. 1988. "Science and Magic in African Technology: Traditional Iron Smelting in Malawi," in R. Maddin, editor, *The Beginning of the Use of Metals and Alloys*, pp. 245-260. Cambridge MA: MIT Press.

Meyer, O. 1931. "Die Klostergründung in Bayern und ihre Quellen vornehmlich im Hochmittelalter," *Zeitschrift der Savigny-Stiftung für Rechtsgeschichte*, Kanonistische Abteilung, 20, pp. 123-201.

Miron, A. 1986. "Das Gräberfeld von Horath: Untersuchungen zur Mittel- und Spätlatènezeit im Saar-Mosel-Raum," *Trierer Zeitschrift* 49, pp. 7-198.

Miron A. 1989. "Das Frauengrab 1242: Zur chronologischen Gliederung der Stufe Latène D2," in A. Haffner, *Gräber: Spiegel des Lebens*, pp. 215-228. Mainz: Philipp von Zabern.

Modderman, P.J.R. 1977. *Die neolithische Besiedlung bei Hienheim, Ldkr. Kelheim*. I. Kallmünz: Michael Lassleben.

Modderman, P.J.R. 1986. *Die neolithische Besiedlung bei Hienheim, Ldkr. Kelheim*. II. Kallmünz: Michael Lassleben.

Motyková-Sneiderová, K. 1962. "Osada pod Hradištěm u Stradonic" ("Die Ansiedlung unter dem Hradiste bei Stradonice"), *Památky Archeologické* 53, pp. 137-154.

Motyková, K., P. Drda, and A. Rybová. 1990. "Die Siedlungsstruktur des Oppidums Závist," *Archäologisches Korrespondenzblatt* 20, pp. 415-426.

Mueller, J., editor. 1975. *Sampling in Archaeology*. Tucson: University of Arizona Press.

Müller, R. 1985. *Die Grabfunde der Jastorf- und Latènezeit an unterer Saale und Mittelelbe*. Berlin: Deutscher Verlag der Wissenschaften.

Müller-Karpe, H. 1952. *Das Urnenfeld von Kelheim*. Kallmünz: Michael Lassleben.

Müller-Karpe, A. and M. Müller-Karpe. 1977. "Neue latènezeitliche Funde aus dem Heidetränk-Oppidum im Taunus," *Germania* 55, pp. 33-63.

Murray, M.L. 1992. "The Archaeology of Mystification: Ideology, Dominance, and the Urnfields of Southern Germany," in A.S. Goldsmith, S. Garvie,

D. Selin, and J. Smith, editors, *Ancient Images, Ancient Thought: The Archaeology of Ideology*, pp. 97-104. Calgary: University of Calgary.

Nadler, M. 1986. "Ausgrabungen in der Galeriehöhle II bei Kelheim 1983-1985," in B. Engelhardt and K. Schmotz, editors, *Vorträge des 4. Niederbayerischen Archäologentages*, pp. 65-72. Deggendorf: Marie Leidorf.

Narr, K.J. and G. Lass. 1985. "Gebrauch einfacher Steinwerkzeuge in der Bronze- und Eisenzeit," *Archäologisches Korrespondenzblatt* 15, pp. 459-461.

Nash, D. 1978. *Settlement and Coinage in Central Gaul c 200-50 B.C.* Oxford: British Archaeological Reports, Supplementary Series 39.

Nash, D. 1985. "Celtic Territorial Expansion and the Mediterranean World," in T.C. Champion and J.V.S. Megaw, editors, *Settlement and Society: Aspects of West European Prehistory in the First Millennium B.C.*, pp. 45-67. Leicester: Leicester University Press.

Nierhaus, R. 1981. "Zu den topographischen Angaben in der 'Geographie' des Klaudios Ptolemaios über das heutige Süddeutschland," *Fundberichte aus Baden-Württemberg* 6, pp. 475-500.

Nierhaus, R. 1983. "Zur literarischen Überlieferung des Oppidums Tarodunum," in K. Schmid, editor, *Kelten und Alemannen im Dreisamtal*, pp. 45-70. Bühl/Baden: Konkordia.

Nothdurfter, J. 1979. *Die Eisenfunde von Sanzeno im Nonsberg*. Mainz: Philipp von Zabern.

Osterhaus, U. 1988. "Eine spätlatènezeitliche Grosssiedlung in Köfering, Ortsflur Egglfing, Lkr. Regensburg, Opf.," in J. Prammer, editor, *Ausgrabungen und Funde in Altbayern 1987/88*, pp. 53-54. Straubing: Gäubodenmuseum.

Overbeck, B. 1980. "Die Münzen," in L. Pauli, editor, *Die Kelten in Mitteleuropa*, pp. 101-110. Salzburg: Landesregierung.

Overbeck, B. 1982. "Ein Schatzfund keltischer Münzen aus Neuses," *Das archäologische Jahr in Bayern 1981*, pp. 126-127. Stuttgart: Konrad Theiss.

Overbeck, B. 1986. "A Celtic Mint Recently Discovered in Kelheim-Mitterfeld," *Proceedings of the 10th International Congress of Numismatics*, pp. 107-111. London: International Association of Professional Numismatists.

Overbeck, B. 1987a. "Alkimoennis-Kelheim, eine neue keltische Münzstätte," *Bayerische Vorgeschichtsblätter* 52, pp. 245-248.

Overbeck, B. 1987b. "Celtic Chronology in South Germany," in A.M. Burnett and M.H. Crawford, editors, *The Coinage of the Roman World in the Late Republic*, pp. 1-12. Oxford: British Archaeological Reports, Supplementary Series 326.

Overbeck, B. and P.S. Wells, 1991. "Vier neue keltische Münzen vom Kelheimer Mitterfeld," *Bayerische Vorgeschichtsblätter* 56, pp. 163-168.

Pätzold, J. 1983. *Die vor- und frühgeschichtlichen Geländedenkmäler Niederbayerns*. Kallmünz: Michael Lassleben.

Paringer, B. 1934. "Das alte Weltenburger Martyrologium und seine Miniaturen: Ein Beitrag zur Frühgeschichte des Klosters Weltenburg," *Studien und Mitteilungen zur Geschichte des Benediktinerordens und seine Zweige* 52, pp. 146-165.

Paringer, B. 1952. "Wie die Bayern Christen wurden," *Der Zwiebelturm* 7, pp. 84-88.

Pauli, L. 1972. *Untersuchungen zur Späthallstattkultur in Nordwürttemberg*. Hamburg: Helmut Buske.

Pauli, L. 1978. *Der Dürrnberg bei Hallein III*. Munich: C.H. Beck.

Pauli, L. 1985. "Early Celtic Society: Two Centuries of Wealth and Turmoil in Central Europe," in T.C. Champion and J.V.S. Megaw, editors, *Settlement and Society: Aspects of West European Prehistory in the First Millennium B.C.*, pp. 23-43. Leicester: Leicester University Press.

Peddemors, A. 1975. "Latèneglasarmringe in den Niederlanden," *Analecta Praehistorica Leidensia* 8, pp. 93-145.

Pescheck, C. 1969. "Zum Bevölkerungswechsel von Kelten und Germanen in Unterfranken," *Bayerische Vorgeschichtsblätter* 25, pp. 75-99.

References Cited

Peschel, K. 1989. "Keltische Latènekultur und deren Randgruppen im Mittelgebirgsraum," in J. Herrmann, editor, *Archäologie in der Deutschen Demokratischen Republik*, vol. 1, pp. 130-139. Stuttgart: Konrad Theiss.

Pfauth, U. 1989. "Die urnenfelderzeitliche Nekropole von Herrnwahlthann, Gem. Hausen, Lkr. Kelheim," *Bericht der bayerischen Bodendenkmalpflege* 28-29, pp. 7-105.

Piaskowski, J. 1985. "Bemerkungen zu den Eisenverhüttungszentren auf polnischen Gebiet in ur- und frühgeschichtlicher Zeit," in J. Piaskowski, editor, *Produktionsverhältnisse in ur- und frühgeschichtlicher Zeit*, pp. 231-243. Berlin.

Pič, J.L. 1906. *Le Hradischt de Stradonice en Bohème*. Trans. by J. Déchelette. Leipzig: Karl Hiersemann.

Pingel, V. 1971. *Die glatte Drehscheiben-Keramik von Manching*. Wiesbaden: Franz Steiner.

Planck, D. 1982. "Eine neuentdeckte keltische Viereckschanze in Fellbach-Schmiden, Rems-Murr-Kreis," *Germania* 60, pp. 125-172.

Planck, D. 1985. "Die Viereckschanze von Fellbach-Schmiden," in D. Planck, editor, *Der Keltenfürst von Hochdorf: Methoden und Ergebnisse der Landesarchäologie*, pp. 340-353. Stuttgart: Konrad Theiss.

Pleiner, R. 1962. *Staré Evropské Kovářství (Alteuropäisches Schmiedehandwerk)*. Prague: Czechoslovak Academy of Sciences.

Pleiner, R. 1980. "Early Iron Metallurgy in Europe," in T.A. Wertime and J.D. Muhly, editors, *The Coming of the Age of Iron*, pp. 375-415. New Haven: Yale University Press.

Pleiner, R. 1981. "Die Wege des Eisens nach Europa," in R. Pleiner, editor, *Frühes Eisen in Europa*, pp. 115-128. Schaffhausen: Peter Meili.

Pleiner, R. 1982. "Untersuchungen zur Schmiedetechnik auf den keltischen Oppida," *Památky Archeologické* 73, pp. 86-173.

Pleiner, R. 1988. "Investigation into the Quality of the Earliest Iron in Europe," *PACT* 21, pp. 33-36.

Pleiner, R. 1989. "Introduction," in R. Pleiner, editor, *Archaeometallurgy of Iron 1967-1987*, pp. 1-10. Prague: Czechoslovak Academy of Sciences.

Plog, S. 1976. "Relative Efficiencies of Sampling Techniques for Archaeological Surveys," in K.V. Flannery, editor, *The Early Mesoamerican Village*, pp. 384-417. New York: Academic Press.

Pokorny, J. 1959. *Indogermanisches Etymologisches Wörterbuch*, vol. 1. Bern: Francke.

Polenz, H. 1971. *Mittel- und spätlatènezeitliche Brandgräber aus Dietzenbach, Landkreis Offenbach am Main*. Langen b. Ffm.: Kuhn.

Polenz, H. 1982. "Münzen in latènezeitlichen Gräbern Mitteleuropas aus der Zeit zwischen 300 und 50 vor Christi Geburt," *Bayerische Vorgeschichtsblätter* 47, pp. 27-222.

Pred, A. 1990. *Making Histories and Constructing Human Geographies: The Local Transformation of Practice, Power Relations, and Consciousness*. Boulder: Westview.

Prinz, F. 1965. *Frühes Mönchtum in Frankreich*. Munich.

Prinz, F. 1974. "Fragen der Kontinuität zwischen Antike und Mittelalter am Beispiel Bayerns," *Zeitschrift für bayerische Landesgeschichte* 37, pp. 699-727.

Prinz, F. 1981. "Columbanus, the Frankish Nobility, and the Territories East of the Rhine," in H.B. Clarke and M. Brennan, editors, *Columbanus and Merovingian Monasticism*, pp. 73-90. Oxford: British Archaeological Reports, International Series 113.

Prinz, F. 1985. *Grundlagen und Anfänge: Deutschland bis 1056*. Munich.

Rathje, W. L. 1975. "The Last Tango in Mayapan: A Tentative Trajectory of Production-Distribution Systems," in J.A. Sabloff and C.C. Lamberg-Karlovsky, editors, *Ancient Civilization and Trade*, pp. 409-448. Albuquerque: University of New Mexico Press.

Redlich, C. 1980. "Politische und wirtschaftliche Bedeutung der Bronzegefässe an Unterelbe und Saale zur Zeit der Römerkriege," *Studien zur Sachsenforschung* 2, pp. 329-374.

Redman, C.L. 1987. "Surface Collection, Sampling, and Research Design: A Retrospective," *American Antiquity* 52, pp. 249-265.

Reim, H. 1979. "Ein Versteckfund von Münzen und Fibeln aus der Spätlatènezeit bei Langenau, Alb-Donau-Kreis," *Archäologische Ausgrabungen* 1979, pp. 50-53.

Reinecke, P. 1911. "Kelheim (Niederbayern): Spätkeltische Viereckschanze," *Römisch-Germanisches Korrespondenzblatt* 4, pp. 19-21.

Reinecke, P. 1924. "Die örtliche Bestimmung der antiken geographischen Namen für das rechtsrheinische Bayern," *Bayerischer Vorgeschichtsfreund* 4, pp. 17-48.

Reinecke, P. 1935. "Bodendenkmale spätkeltischer Eisengewinnung an der untersten Altmühl," *Bericht der Römisch-Germanischen Kommission*, 24-25, pp. 166-228.

Reisch, L. 1974. *Der vorgeschichtliche Hornsteinabbau bei Lengfeld, Ldkr. Kelheim und die Interpretation "grobgerätiger" Silexindustrien in Bayern*. Kallmünz: Michael Lassleben.

Renfrew, C. 1985. *The Archaeology of Cult: The Sanctuary at Phylakopi*. Athens: British School of Archaeology.

Renfrew, C. 1987. *Archaeology and Language: The Puzzle of Indo-European Origins*. Cambridge: Cambridge University Press.

Renfrew, C. and P. Bahn. 1991. *Archaeology*. London: Thames and Hudson.

Richards, J.D. 1992. "Anglo-Saxon Symbolism," in M.O.H. Carver, editor, *The Age of Sutton Hoo*, pp. 131-148. Woodbridge: Boydell.

Riché, P. 1981. "Columbanus, His Followers, and the Merovingian Church," in H.B. Clarke and M. Brennan, editors, *Columbanus and Merovingian Monasticism*, pp. 59-72. Oxford: British Archaeological Reports, International Series 113.

Rieckhoff-Pauli, S. 1980. "Das Ende der keltischen Welt: Kelten-Römer-Germanen," in L. Pauli, editor, *Die Kelten in Mitteleuropa*, pp. 25-36. Salzburg: Landesregierung.

Riess, O. 1975. "Die Abtei Weltenburg zwischen dreissigjährigen Krieg und Sakularisation," *Beiträge zur Geschichte des Bistums Regensburg* 9, pp. 1-21.

Rind, M.M. 1988. *Kanalarchäologie im Altmühltal*. Buch am Erlbach: Marie Leidorf.

Rind, M.M. 1989. "Siedlungsarchäologie im unteren Altmühltal," in K. Schmotz, editor, *Vorträge des 7. Niederbayerischen Archäologentages*, pp. 49-84. Deggendorf.

Rind, M.M. 1991a. "Ausgrabung im Feuersteinbergwerk von Lengfeld, Gde. Bad Abbach," in M.M. Rind, editor, *80,000 Jahre Müll: Archäologische Forschungen im Landkreis Kelheim 1986 bis 1990*, pp. 26-31. Buch am Erlbach: Marie Leidorf.

Rind, M.M. 1991b. "Keramikfunde der Frühlatènezeit aus dem Donaudurchbruch bei Kelheim," in M.M. Rind, editor, *80,000 Jahre Müll: Archäologische Forschungen im Landkreis Kelheim 1986 bis 1990*, pp. 50-52. Buch am Erlbach: Marie Leidorf.

Rissman, P. 1988. "Public Displays and Private Values: A Guide to Buried Wealth in Harappan Archaeology," *World Archaeology* 20, pp. 209-228.

Rivet, A.L.F. 1988. *Gallia Narbonensis: Southern France in Roman Times*. London: Batsford.

Rochna, O. 1965. "Ein Gräberfeld der jüngeren Urnenfelderzeit (Ha B) von Altessing, Ldkr. Kelheim," *Bayerische Vorgeschichtsblätter* 30, pp. 105-134.

Röhrig, K.-H. 1986. "Spätlatènezeitliche Siedlungsbefunde aus Kelheim-Mitterfeld," *Das archäologische Jahr in Bayern 1985*, p. 94. Stuttgart: Konrad Theiss.

Ross, A. 1967. *Pagan Celtic Britain*. London: Routledge and Kegan Paul.

Rostoker, W. and B. Bronson. 1990. *Pre-Industrial Iron: Its Technology and Ethnology*. Philadelphia: Archaeomaterials, 1.

Roymans, N. 1990. *Tribal Societies in Northern Gaul: An Anthropological Perpsective*. Amsterdam: Cingula.

Ruoff, U. 1964. "Eine Spätlatènesiedlung bei Marthalen," *Jahrbuch der Schweizerischen Gesellschaft für Urgeschichte* 51, pp. 47-62.

Rusu, M. 1969. "Das keltische Fürstengrab von Ciumesti in Rumänien," *Bericht der Römisch-Germanischen Kommission* 50, pp. 267-300.

Rutte, E. 1981a. *Geologie im Landkreis Kelheim*. Kelheim: Landratsamt.

Rutte, E. 1981b. *Bayerns Erdgeschichte*. Munich: Ehrenwirth.

Rutte, E. 1990. "Geologie im Landkreis Kelheim," in H. Hauenstein, editor, *Der Landkreis Kelheim*, pp. 10-48. Kelheim: Landkreis Kelheim.

Rybová, A. and K. Motyková. 1983. "Der Eisendepotfund der Latènezeit von Kolín," *Památky Archeologické* 74, pp. 96-174.

Rybová, A. and B. Soudský. 1962. *Libenice: sanctuaire celtique en Bohème centrale*. Prague: Czechoslovak Academy of Sciences.

Sage, W. 1975. "Ausgrabungen an der Torlage des 'Römerwalles' auf dem Frauenberg oberhalb Weltenburg, Landkreis Kelheim," *Jahresbericht der Bayerischen Bodendenkmalpflege* 15-16, pp. 131-148.

Sanders, W.T., J.R. Parsons, and R.S. Santley. 1979. *The Basin of Mexico: Ecological Process in the Evolution of a Civilization*. New York: Academic Press.

Schaarf, W. 1988. *Untersuchungen zur vor- und frühgeschichtlichen Keramik aus dem unteren Altmühltal*. Doctoral dissertation, Universität Würzburg.

Schauer, P. 1981. "Urnenfelderzeitliche Opferplätze in Höhlen und Felsspalten," in H. Lorenz, editor, *Studien zur Bronzezeit: Festschrift W.A. von Brunn*, pp. 403-418. Mainz: Philipp von Zabern.

Schier, W. 1985. "Zur vorrömischen Besiedlung des Donautales südöstlich von Regensburg," *Bayerische Vorgeschichtsblätter* 50, pp. 9-80.

Schier, W. 1990. *Die vorgeschichtliche Besiedlung im südlichen Maindreiecke*. Kallmünz: Michael Lassleben.

Schmidt, U. 1986. "Zur Besiedlung des unteren Schwarzachtales in der Hallstatt- und Latènezeit," *Natur und Mensch* 1986, pp. 23-28.

Schmotz, K. 1989. *Die vorgeschichtliche Besiedlung im Isarmündungsgebiet*. Kallmünz: Michael Lassleben.

Schönberger, H. 1952. "Die Spätlatènezeit in der Wetterau," *Saalburg Jahrbuch* 11, pp. 21-130.

Schofield, A.J., editor, 1991. *Interpreting Artifact Scatters: Contributions to Ploughzone Archaeology*. Oxford: Oxbow Books.

Schubert, F. 1972. "Manching IV: Vorbericht über die Ausgrabung in den Jahren 1965 bis 1967," *Germania* 50, pp. 110-121.

Schwartz, E. 1960. *Sprache und Siedlung in Nordostbayern*. Nuremberg: Hans Carl.

Schwarz, K. 1959. *Atlas der spätkeltischen Viereckschanzen Bayerns*. Munich: Bayerisches Landesamt für Denkmalpflege.

Schwarz, K. 1975. "Die Geschichte eines keltischen Temenos im nördlichen Alpenvorland," in *Ausgrabungen in Deutschland*, vol. 1, pp. 324-358. Mainz: Römisch-Germanisches Zentralmuseum.

Schwarz, K., H. Tillmann, and W. Treibs. 1966. "Zur spätlatènezeitlichen und mittelalterlichen Eisenerzgewinnung auf der südlichen Frankenalb bei Kelheim," *Jahresbericht der Bayerischen Bodendenkmalpflege* 6-7, pp. 35-66.

Scott, B.G. 1990. *Early Irish Ironworking*. Belfast: Ulster Museum.

Scott, E. 1991. "Animal and Infant Burials in Romano-British Villas: A Revitalization Movement," in P. Garwood, D. Jennings, R. Skeates, and J. Toms, editors, *Sacred and Profane*, pp. 115-121. Oxford: Oxford University Committee for Archaeology.

Seyer, R. 1988. "Antike Nachrichten," in B. Krüger, editor, *Die Germanen*, vol. 1, pp. 37-63. Berlin: Akademie-Verlag.

Shennan, S. 1985. *Experiments in the Collection and Analysis of Archaeological Survey Data: The East Hampshire Survey*. Sheffield: University of Sheffield.

Sievers, S. 1989. "Die Waffen von Manching unter Berücksichtigung des Überganges von LTC zu LTD," *Germania* 67, pp. 97-120.

Silver, I.A. 1969. "The Ageing of Domestic Animals," in D. Brothwell and E. Higgs, editors, *Science in Archaeology*, revised edition, pp. 283-302. London: Thames and Hudson.

Simons, A. 1989. *Bronze- und eisenzeitliche Besiedlung in den rheinischen Lössbörden: Archäologische Siedlungsmuster im Braunkohlengebiet*. Oxford: British Archaeological Reports, International Series 467.

Soja, E.W. 1980. "The Socio-Spatial Dialectic," *Annals of the Association of American Geographers* 70, pp. 207-225.

Soja, E.W. 1989. *Postmodern Geographies: The Reassertion of Space in Critical Social Theory*. London: Verso.

Spehr, R. 1971. "Die Rolle der Eisenverarbeitung in der Wirtschaftsstruktur des Steinsburg-Oppidums," *Archeologické Rozhledy* 23, pp. 486-503.

Spindler, K. 1981a. *Die Archäologie des Frauenberges*. Regensburg: Friedrich Pustet.

Spindler, K. 1981b. *Die römischen Militärstationen auf dem Frauenberg über Kloster Weltenburg bei Kelheim an der Donau*. Abensberg: Weltenburger Akademie.

Spindler, K. 1984a. "Gewässerfunde," in S. Rieckhoff-Pauli and W. Torbrügge, editors, *Regensburg-Kelheim-Straubing I*, Führer zu archäologischen Denkmälern in Deutschland, vol. 5, pp. 212-223. Stuttgart: Konrad Theiss.

Spindler, K. 1984b. "Weltenburg-'Frauenberg' und Staubing," in S. Rieckhoff-Pauli and W. Torbrügge, editors, *Regensburg-Kelheim-Straubing II*, Führer zu archäologischen Denkmalerm in Deutschland, vol. 6, pp. 136-143. Stuttgart: Konrad Theiss.

Spindler, K. 1985. "Archäologische Aspekte zur Siedlungskontinuität und Kulturtradition von der Spätantike zum frühen Mittelalter im Umkreis des Klosters Weltenburg an der Donau," in B. Engelhardt, editor, *Archäologische Denkmalpflege in Niederbayern*, pp. 179-200. Munich: Bayerisches Landesamt für Denkmalpflege.

Spindler, M. 1969. *Bayerischer Geschichtsatlas*. Munich: Bayerischer Schulbuch-Verlag.

Staber, J. 1966. *Kirchengeschichte des Bistums Regensburg*. Regensburg.

Stein, F. 1976. *Bronzezeitliche Hortfunde in Süddeutschland*. Bonn: Rudolf Habelt.

Steuer, H. 1987. "Gewichtgeldwirtschaften im frühgeschichtlichen Europa," in K. Düwel, H. Jankuhn, H. Siems, and D. Timpe, editors, *Untersuchungen zu Handel und Verkehr der vor- und frühgeschichtlichen Zeit in Mittel- und Nordeuropa, part 4: Der Handel der Karolinger- und Wikingerzeit*, pp. 405-527. Göttingen: Vandenhoeck and Ruprecht.

Stöckli, W.E. 1974. "Bemerkungen zur räumlichen und zeitlichen Gruppierung der Funde im Oppidum von Manching," *Germania* 52, pp. 368-385.

Stöckli, W.E. 1979a. *Die Grob- und Importkeramik von Manching*. Wiesbaden: Franz Steiner.

Stöckli, W.E. 1979b. "Die Keltensiedlung von Altendorf (Landkreis Bamberg)," *Bayerische Vorgeschichtsblätter* 44, pp. 27-43.

Stokes, M. 1895. *Three Months in the Forests of France: A Pilgrimage in Search of Vestiges of the Irish Saints in France*. London.

Stork, S. 1983. *Die Hallstattzeit in Niederbayern*. Doctoral dissertation, Universität München.

Stroh, A. 1975. *Die vor- und frühgeschichtlichen Geländedenkmäler der Oberpfalz*. Kallmünz: Michael Lassleben.

Svobodová, H. 1985. "Antické importy z keltských oppid v Čechách a na Moravě" ("Antike Importe aus den keltischen Oppida in Böhmen und Mähren"), *Archeologické Rozhledy* 37, pp. 653-668.

Szabó, M. 1991a. "The Celts and Their Movements in the Third Century B.C.," in S. Moscati, O.-H. Frey, V. Kruta, B. Raftery, and M. Szabó, editors, *The Celts*, pp. 303-319. New York: Rizzoli.

Szabó, M. 1991b. "Mercenary Activity," in S. Moscati, O.-H. Frey, V. Kruta, B. Raftery, and M.

References Cited

Szabó, editors, *The Celts*, pp. 333-336. New York: Rizzoli.

Thiel, M., editor. 1958. *Die Traditionen, Urkunden und Urbare des Klosters Weltenburg*. Munich: C.H. Beck.

Timpe, D. 1985. "Der keltische Handel nach historischen Quellen," in K. Düwel, H. Jankuhn, H. Siems, and D. Timpe, editors, *Untersuchungen zu Handel und Verkehr der vor- und frühgeschichtlichen Zeit in Mittel- und Nordeuropa*, 1, pp. 258-284. Göttingen: Vandenhoeck and Ruprecht.

Todd, M. 1992. *The Early Germans*. Oxford: Blackwell.

Torbrügge, W. 1959. *Die Bronzezeit in der Oberpfalz*. Kallmünz: Michael Lassleben.

Torbrügge, W. 1971. "Vor- und frühgeschichtliche Flussfunde," *Berichte der Römisch-Germanischen Kommission* 51-52, pp. 1-146.

Torbrügge, W. 1979. *Die Hallstattzeit in der Oberpfalz*. Kallmünz: Michael Lassleben.

Torbrügge, W. 1984a. "Grabhügel, Viereckschanze und römischer Burgus bei Holzharlanden und Thaldorf," in S. Rieckhoff-Pauli and W. Torbrügge, editors, *Regensburg-Kelheim-Straubing II*, Führer zu archäologischen Denkmälern in Deutschland, vol. 6, pp. 149-151. Stuttgart: Konrad Theiss.

Torbrügge, W. 1984b. "Die Landschaften um Regensburg in vor- und frühgeschichtlicher Zeit," in S. Rieckhoff-Pauli and W. Torbrügge, editors, *Regensburg-Kelheim-Straubing I*, Führer zu archäologischen Denkmälern in Deutschland, vol. 5, pp. 28-117. Stuttgart: Konrad Theiss.

Torbrügge, W. 1984c. "Die Legende von der Weltburger Klostergründung," in S. Rieckhoff-Pauli and W. Torbrügge, editors, *Regensburg-Kelheim-Straubing II*, Führer zu archäologischen Denkmälern in Deutschland, vol. 6, pp. 143-149. Stuttgart: Konrad Theiss.

Turner, V. 1967. *The Forest of Symbols*. Ithaca NY: Cornell University Press.

Turner, V. 1969. *The Ritual Process*. Chicago: Aldine.

Tylecote, R. 1987. *The Early History of Metallurgy in Europe*. New York: Longman.

Urry, J. 1984. "Social Relations, Space and Time," in D. Gregory and J. Urry, editors, *Social Relations and Spatial Structure*, pp. 20-48. New York: St. Martin's Press.

Vencl, S. 1984. "War and Warfare in Archaeology," *Journal of Anthropological Archaeology* 3, pp. 116-132.

Venclová, N. 1990. *Prehistoric Glass*. Prague: Czechoslovak Academy of Sciences.

Vitali, D. 1991. "The Celts in Italy," in S. Moscati, O.-H. Frey, V. Kruta, B. Raftery, and M. Szabó, editors, *The Celts*, pp. 220-235. New York: Rizzoli.

Wainwright, F.T. 1962. *Archaeology and Place-Names and History: An Essay on Problems of Coordination*. London: Routledge and Kegan Paul.

Waldhauser, J. 1977. "Keltské sídliště u Radovesic v severozápadních Čechách" ("Die keltische Siedlung bei Radovesice, Bez. Teplice in Nordwest-Böhmen"), *Archeologické Rozhledy* 29, pp. 144-177.

Waldhauser, J., editor. 1978. *Das keltische Gräberfeld bei Jenišův Újezd in Böhmen*. Teplice: Krajské Muzeum.

Waldhauser, J. 1979. "Beitrag zum Studium der keltischen Siedlungen, Oppida und Gräberfelder in Böhmen," in P.-M. Duval and V. Kruta, editors, *Les mouvements celtiques du Ve au Ier siècle avant notre ère*, pp. 117-156. Paris: Centre National de la Recherche Scientifique.

Waldhauser, J. 1981. "Keltské Rotační Mlýny v Čechách" ("Keltische Drehmuhlen in Böhmen"), *Památky Archeologické* 72, pp. 153-221.

Waldhauser, J. 1984. "Mobilität und Stabilität der keltischen Besiedlung in Böhmen," in O.-H. Frey and H. Roth, editors, *Studien zu Siedlungsfragen der Latènezeit*, pp. 167-186. Marburg: Vorgeschichtliches Seminar.

Waldhauser, J. 1987. "Keltische Gräberfelder in Böhmen," *Berichte der Römisch-Germanischen Kommission* 68, pp. 25-179.

Waldhauser, J. 1992. "Keltische Distributionssysteme von Graphittonkeramik und die Ausbeutung der Graphitlagerstätten während der fortgeschrittenen Latènezeit," *Archäologisches Korrespondenzblatt* 22, pp. 377-392.

Wapnish, Paula and B. Hesse. 1988. "Urbanization and the Organization of Animal Production at Tell Jemmeh in the Middle Bronze Age Levant," *Journal of Near Eastern Studies* 47, pp. 81-94.

Weber, G. 1989. "Neues zur Befestigung des Oppidums Tarodunum, Gde. Kirchzarten, Kreis Breisgau-Hochschwarzwald," *Fundberichte aus Baden-Württemberg* 14, pp. 273-288.

Webster, G. 1986. *Celtic Religion in Roman Britain*, Totowa, NJ: Barnes and Noble.

Weissmüller, W. 1986. *Postmesolithische Funde aus Höhlen und Abris am Beispiel des südlichen Riesrandgebiets*. Oxford: British Archaeological Reports.

Wells, P.S. 1983. *Rural Economy in the Early Iron Age: Excavations at Hascherkeller, 1978-1981*. Cambridge MA: Peabody Museum.

Wells, P.S. 1984. *Farms, Villages, and Cities: Commerce and Urban Origins in Late Prehistoric Europe*. Ithaca NY: Cornell University Press.

Wells, P.S. 1987. "Industry, Commerce, and Temperate Europe's First Cities: Preliminary Report on 1987 Excavations at Kelheim, Bavaria," *Journal of Field Archaeology* 14, pp. 399-412.

Wells, P.S. 1988a. "Eine funddichte Fläche am Kelheimer Mitterfeld," *Das archäologische Jahr in Bayern 1987*, pp. 84-85. Stuttgart: Konrad Theiss.

Wells, P.S. 1988b. "Iron Age Kelheim: A Mill Town Blossoms on the Danube," *Archaeology* 41, 5, pp. 60-61.

Wells, P.S. 1989. "Ein spätlatènezeitlicher bronzener Vogelkopf vom Kelheimer Mitterfeld," *Archäologisches Korrespondenzblatt* 19, pp. 63-67.

Wells, P.S. 1990. "Iron Age Temperate Europe: Some Current Research Issues," *Journal of World Prehistory* 4, pp. 437-476.

Wells, P.S. 1991. "Zur Verbreitung der späteisenzeitlichen Siedlungsreste am Kelheimer Mitterfeld," *Archäologisches Korrespondenzblatt* 21, pp. 517-522.

Werner, B. n.d. "Geschichte des Klosters Weltenburg." Bayerische Staatsbibliothek, MS #Cgm 1844.

Werner, J. 1939. "Die Bedeutung des Städtewesens für die Kulturentwicklung des frühen Keltentums," *Die Welt als Geschichte*, 4, pp. 380-390.

Werner, J. 1954. "Die Bronzekanne von Kelheim," *Bayerische Vorgeschichtsblätter* 20, pp. 43-73.

Werner, J. 1978. "Zur Bronzekanne von Kelheim," *Bayerische Vorgeschichtsblätter* 43, pp. 1-18.

Widmann, W. 1987. "Von Eisenzeit bis keltische Städte," in H. Nöhbauer, editor, *Die Chronik Bayerns*, pp. 13-54. Dortmund.

Wiedemer, H.R. 1963. "Menschliche Skelettreste aus Spätlatène-Siedlungen im Alpenvorland: Zum Problem der römischen Landnahme in der Schweiz und Süddeutschland," *Germania* 41, pp. 269-280.

Wilkinson, T.J. 1988. "The Archaeological Component of Agricultural Soils in the Middle East: The Effects of Manuring in Antiquity," in W. Groenman-van Waateringe and M. Robinson, editors, *Man-Made Soils*, pp. 93-114. Oxford: British Archaeological Reports, International Series 410.

Will, E.L. 1987. "The Roman Amphoras from Manching," *Bayerische Vorgeschichtsblätter* 52, pp. 21-36.

Willets, A. 1987. *The Black County Nail Trade*. London: Dudley.

Withold, K. 1974. "Kelheim," in K. Bosl, editor, *Bayern*, 2nd edition, pp. 349-350. Stuttgart: Alfred Kröner.

Zeder, M.A. 1991. *Feeding Cities: Specialized Animal Economy in the Ancient Near East*. Washington: Smithsonian.

Zöllner, E. 1965. "Die Herkunft der Agilulfinger," in K. Bosl, editor, *Zur Geschichte der Bayern*, pp. 107-134. Darmstadt.

References Cited

Züchner, C. 1977. "Eisenzeitliche und mittelalterliche Funde aus dem Pulverloch bei Forchheim," *Jahresbericht der Bayerischen Bodendenkmalpflege* 17-18, pp. 9-33.

Zürn, H. 1971. "Die keltische Viereckschanze bei Tomerdingen, Kreis Ulm (Württemberg)," *Proceedings of the Prehistoric Society* 37, part 2, pp. 218-227.

The Authors

Carl Blair .... Interdisciplinary Archaeological Studies, 215 Ford Hall, University of Minnesota, Minneapolis, MN 55455, U.S.A.

Pam J. Crabtree .... Department of Anthropology, New York University, 100 Rufus D. Smith Hall, 25 Waverly Place, New York, NY 10003, U.S.A.

Michael N. Geselowitz .... Department of Anthropology, Yale University, P.O. Box 2114 Yale Station, New Haven, CT 06520, U.S.A.

Hansjörg Küster .... Arbeitsgruppe für Vegetationsgeschichte, Institut für Vor- und Frühgeschichte, Feldmochingerstrasse 7, 8000 München 50, Germany.

Susan Malin-Boyce .... Department of Anthropology, New York University, 100 Rufus D. Smith Hall, 25 Waverly Place, New York, NY 10003, U.S.A.

Matthew L. Murray .... Department of Anthropology, Harvard University. Mailing address: 314 Fulton Street, Mankato, MN 56001, U.S.A.

Bernhard Overbeck .... Staatliche Münzsammlung, Residenzstrasse 1, 8000 München 2, Germany.

Frederick Suppe .... Department of History, Ball State University, Muncie, IN 47306, U.S.A.

Peter S. Wells .... Department of Anthropology, 215 Ford Hall, University of Minnesota, Minneapolis, MN 55455, U.S.A.